The Enemy is Listening

Aileen Clayton

The Enemy is Listening

At last! Your story (or at least some of it).

John

Hutchinson

London Melbourne Sydney Auckland Johannesburg

Hutchinson & Co. (Publishers) Ltd
An imprint of the Hutchinson Publishing Group
3 Fitzroy Square, London W1P 6JD

Hutchinson Group (Australia) Pty Ltd
30–32 Cremorne Street, Richmond South, Victoria 3121
PO Box 151, Broadway, New South Wales 2007

Hutchinson Group (NZ) Ltd
32–34 View Road, PO Box 40–086, Glenfield, Auckland 10

Hutchinson Group (SA) (Pty) Ltd
PO Box 337, Bergvlei 2012, South Africa

First published 1980
© Aileen Clayton 1980

Set in Monotype Times

Printed in Great Britain by The Anchor Press Ltd
and bound by Wm Brendon & Son Ltd
both of Tiptree, Essex

British Library Cataloguing in Publication Data
Clayton, Aileen
    The enemy is listening.
    1. World War, 1939–1945 – Secret service – Great Britain
    2. World War, 1939–1945 – Personal narratives, British
    3. Great Britain. Royal Air Force, Y Service
    I. Title
    940.54′86′410924   D810–S7

ISBN 0 09 142340 6

To the Memory of
'Dearest', my Mother,
and to Geoffrey, my only brother,
who failed to return from Operations
with No. 221 Squadron, 8 March 1945,
aged 21 years

'Went the day well?
    We died and never knew.
But well or ill,
    England, we died for you.'

Contents

Illustrations

Foreword

by Air Chief Marshal Sir Frederick Rosier, GCB, CBE, DSO

Stories of the Second World War have poured from the pens of heroes and historians for well over thirty years. The great and the glamorous have presented their memoirs to the public. Campaigns and strategies have been analysed and exposed. Tales of courage and glory have passed down to stir the hearts of future generations. And yet it is only now, when most of the principal players have departed the stage, that the public is being made aware of others whose deeds are no less inspirational and without whom the course and the outcome of the war would have been vastly different.

It was only a few years ago, when the Ultra secrets were revealed, that the public was made aware of that extraordinary band of experts whose success in deciphering the enemy's high-level codes led to the production of intelligence which had an enormous impact on the Allied direction of the war. However, even with these revelations, the story of intelligence derived from the monitoring of enemy signals traffic was still incomplete. There were other men and women who not only produced the raw material for Ultra, but provided other intelligence without which our knowledge of the enemy's tactical dispositions and intentions would have been either incomplete or missing. They belonged to an organization known as the Y Service, and their story is told for the first time in this book.

As the war progressed, the Y Service became increasingly expert in decoding lower-grade messages, mostly of a tactical nature, and in making sense of plain language transmissions. Indeed, in their ceaseless task of monitoring and interpreting enemy radio transmissions the members of that Service provided information of inestimable value to commanders in the field.

The author of this book, Aileen Clayton – or 'Mike' as I have always known her – was a most important member of the Y Service.

She became totally immersed in it. She showed the same qualities of dedication, unselfishness and bearing as those engaged in the actual fighting. For her and her colleagues there was no publicity and no glamour, for they were engaged in a shadowy, secret war. They were sustained by the knowledge that what they were doing was saving lives and helping to win battles.

In May 1940, not long before Aileen Clayton was transferred to the Y Service, I escaped by parachute from a burning Hurricane fighter. I had been hit by one of a group of Me. 109s which had appeared in force and without warning as I, with my depleted force, was taking off from an airfield in northern France. For me, that was the end of two exciting, tiring and most frustrating days of operations. Whilst we had expected to be outnumbered in the air we were not prepared for the almost chaotic situation that prevailed on the ground and which came mostly from a lack of intelligence. As we received no reliable information on how, when, where and in what numbers the enemy would appear, it was not surprising that we were so often caught at a disadvantage.

Some two years later, when I first met Aileen Clayton in the Western Desert – a woman in a man's world – the situation was entirely different. No longer did we in the Tactical Air Force suffer from that feeling of isolation, even of helplessness, which comes from lack of information. Thanks to the Y Service and the developments in overland-looking radar, we were beginning to get what had been so lacking in France and earlier campaigns.

The Y Service was increasingly giving us warning of impending enemy raids and of the force he was likely to use. Sometimes we even heard what the target was going to be and who was going to lead the enemy force. Such information was invaluable, for not only did it enable decisions to be made on the type and strength of aircraft needed to counter the raids but it allowed our fighters to become airborne in good time. Radar then came into the act in that it gave the controllers the means of directing the intercepting fighters to make contact with the enemy raids.

However, this book is not only about the technical achievements of the Y Service and how these contributed to our success. It is also about the qualities of a certain band of men and women, and of those things that moulded our thinking and behaviour in those stirring wartime days and which added a special dimension to life. It is about the extraordinary resilience and adaptability of women who showed that they were supreme in what they were doing. It is also about the civilizing influence of humour in conditions of discomfort, stress and danger. But above all it is an affectionate tribute by a remarkable and courageous woman to a tenacious and gifted band of men and women, without whom the direction of events in the Second World War, and the ending, might have been very different.

I am proud to be associated with their story and with their memory.

Acknowledgements

Perhaps, someday, the whole story of the work of the Y Service during the Second World War will be written. I am well aware that this book recounts only a small part of it, and even that would not have been written by me but for the constant encouragement of many friends. My late mother, fearing that I would not survive the war, retained every one of the hundreds of letters that I wrote to her, and, though they contained no information about my work, they served as a reminder of the timing of events and formed a basis from which I could work.

I am particularly indebted to my old friend and severest critic, Mr Robert Wright, for his unfailing help and guidance and to Group Captain E. B. Haslam, who was formerly Head of Air Historical Branch (RAF) of the Ministry of Defence and whose constant support and advice on research has greatly helped me.

Much of this book is based on material held by the Public Records Office but I must stress that the views and opinions which are expressed herein are, unless otherwise stated, entirely mine, and that they are therefore personal and in no way a reflection of official opinion.

For confirming details, reminding me of events, or generally supporting my aim, I am most grateful to Philip T. W. Baker, RNVR, Miss Leni Baltazzi, E. A. Benjamin, Captain A. F. Bland, RN, Sir Arthur Bonsall, Professor G. E. R. Burroughs, Air Chief Marshal Sir Harry Broadhurst, Dame Jean Bromet, R. K. Budge, Air Commodore C. S. Cadell, James R. Carter, M. S. Clapham, Group Captain David Davies, Donald Foster, Group Captain T. P. Gleave, Cecil Gould, Brigadier T. E. H. Helby, F. C. Jones, Professor R. V. Jones, Asher Lee, Air Chief Marshal Sir Hugh Lloyd, Geoffrey Mason, James Mazdon, Mrs Vera Morley, Air Commodore E. J.

Morris, James Robertson, Air Chief Marshal Sir Frederick Rosier, Wing Commander D. H. S. Rusher, Mrs M. Ryan, the late Baroness Rudi de Sarigny, Keith Stainton, MP, Lady Sybil Stewart, the Hon. Mabel Strickland, Mrs Margaret Tabor, Lord Ventry, Group Captain F. W. Winterbotham, and many others.

I also wish to thank Air Commodore Henry Probert and his staff at the Air Historical Branch (RAF) of the Ministry of Defence, and the staff of the Public Record Office for all their help, and the Controller of Her Majesty's Stationery Office and the Director of the Imperial War Museum for permission to make use of Crown Copyright material. I acknowledge the assistance of the General Post Office and of the National Archives of Records and Services of the United States of America, and of the staffs of the Ipswich Public Library, the Eastbourne Borough Council and the North Yorkshire County Library, and I also thank the authors and publishers of those books from which I have quoted and which are listed in my Bibliography. I am grateful to Mrs M. A. Fitch for her close attention to the typing of my manuscript, and to Miss P. Stevens for her help with my papers.

And lastly, I wish to thank my husband for his tolerance and untiring support during five years of research.

Illustrations acknowledgements

Illustrations are reproduced by courtesy of the following:
P. T. W. Baker (Plates 9 and 10); E. A. Benjamin (Plate 8); R. K. Budge (Plate 3); Mrs Aileen Clayton (Plate 1); Imperial War Museum (Plates 5, 6, 11, 14, 15, 19, 21, 22, 24 and 26); F. C. Jones (Plate 2); G. F. Mason (Plates 7, 17 and 23); Mrs M. K. Ryan Plate 20); Sport and General Press Agency (Plate 27).

Introduction

During a war, from the earliest times, the actual interception by one side of the messages and instructions which were passed supposedly within the control of the forces of the other side has been one of the most valuable and reliable sources of positive information about what was going on in the enemy's camp. With the advent of wireless communications, a new dimension was brought into this aspect of what has come to be known generally as Intelligence, and the effect that that was to have on both tactics and strategy.

In the Second World War the distances over which the warring factions were operating, coupled with the need for speed, resulted in an ever-increasing use of radio communications, while the impetus of modern warfare accelerated the development of radio technology to deal with such problems as long-range navigation and the early detection of approaching forces.

Well before the outbreak of hostilities in 1939, radio signals from potentially enemy countries were being monitored by this country, and the information derived from them was carefully collated. The organization responsible for this task was to expand rapidly as the war progressed, and before long there could have been few enemy signals within radio range which were not intercepted by the many Allied listening stations located throughout the world.

Since 1974, when Group Captain F. W. Winterbotham published his book *The Ultra Secret*, much has been written about the invaluable source of intelligence which was culled from monitored signals enciphered by means of a machine known to the Germans by the Greek word for a puzzle – 'Enigma'. From the early 1920s, the Germans had been using this machine to encipher inter-formation communications between such of their organizations as the Army, the Navy, the Air Force and the SS. But just prior to the outbreak of war they had made certain modifications to the working of the Enigma machine, thereby increasing the problems of the cryptographers at the Government Code and Cypher School at Bletchley Park. However, in the spring of 1940, aided by the introduction of an early form of computer, the cryptographers had a major breakthrough and had begun to be able to read regularly the German Air Force Enigma cyphers. Later, they were able to decipher messages between German ground formations at all levels, covering every aspect of the progress of the war.

By careful cross-referencing and co-ordination with other sources, they were able to provide the Allied Commanders with intelligence on the strengths, movements, morale and frequently even the intentions of the enemy. Throughout the whole war, the German fondly, but erroneously, believed that their 'Enigma' cyphers were impregnable and the story of the 'Ultra' success became the greatest secret of the Second World War.

It had been said that Ultra was the crystal ball which the Allied Commanders kept in their knapsack. The value of this source of intelligence is certainly inestimable, and no one can question the debt that the free world owes to the dedicated and brilliant band of cryptographers and their staff at Bletchley.

But before the cryptographers could decipher the 'Enigma' messages, these messages had first to be intercepted by the listening service and sent back as quickly as possible for processing to Bletchley. Furthermore, much of the enemy's radio traffic, especially as far as the German Air Force – the Luftwaffe – was concerned, was sent in lower-grade cyphers. Breaking these helped to interpret 'Enigma' and vice versa.

The actual monitoring of all signals, whether in low-grade or high-grade cypher, radio telephony, or non-Morse transmissions, was the responsibility of the Y Service. To them there also fell the task of distributing to the Operational Commands the lower-grade signal intelligence. The story I am now telling covers a part of the work done by the Y Service.

Because of the unique position in which I found myself during the Second World War, a young woman in a man's world, I can sit back now and view with some objectivity the enormity of the task which was undertaken by the men and women working in the Y Service. It has been said that 'unsung, the noblest deed will die'. So proud am I of the contribution made by the wireless operators, the members of the Women's Auxiliary Air Force – known to everyone as the WAAF – who listened to enemy R/T and W/T transmissions, the intelligence personnel, the cypher staff and the aircrews who flew special investigational flights, and all the people who made their work possible, that my aim is to try to sing their praises a little, so that history may perhaps know more of their great efforts. So secret was the work that those who were engaged in it could never explain to their families and friends why their movements within the service were restricted and why their chances of promotion were minimal.

Even before my war service had ended, I was approached by Royal Air Force public relations to write about my experiences in signal intelligence. But the subject was then so secret that it was unthinkable that I should disclose the nature of the work in which my colleagues and I had been involved. So indoctrinated had I become in the need for secrecy that not even my father, who worked in the Air Ministry, knew what I was doing; and when, thirty years later, the Ultra cat was let out of the bag I was at first deeply shocked.

Following the relevation of Ultra, the suggestion was made to me that I might now write about the Y Service and I was given security clearance to do so, subject to certain provisos. The use that we had made of our radio eavesdropping now had little relevance in the light of modern technology. Sadly, the two men with whom I served who would have been better able to tell the story than I can – Group Captain G. R. Scott-Farnie and Wing Commander S. G. Morgan – are both dead, but I feel, particularly in view of the fact that there are so many gaps in the official records, that it is important to recall events whilst memory lasts. At first it had been my intention to write merely a factual record, but, since there have been so few books written by servicewomen about the Second World War, I have been persuaded to write in a more personal vein. For that reason, this story includes some of my own experiences, added to which is an account of part of the very valuable work undertaken by that secret and silent Y Service during the Second World War.

Aileen Clayton
IPSWICH, SUFFOLK

1

Prelude to a War

Life is very often a matter of what the Americans call 'happen-chance'. It so happened that, just prior to the outbreak of the Second World War in September 1939, I had been studying German; and it so happened that eight months later, I was in the right place at the right time for what, by sheer luck, was to develop over the next few years into perhaps the most interesting work undertaken by a woman on active service in the war.

The fact that I spoke German was, in itself, the outcome of yet another quirk of chance. When I left school and decided to study languages, my first choice after French, which I had spoken since I was a child, had been Spanish. But at the time Spain was in the throes of its civil war, and any ideas that I might have had about visiting that country were immediately quashed by my parents. So it was decided that I should concentrate, instead, on German. Since it is well known that one cannot get the true feeling of the language without living for some time with the people of the country, my mother further decided that I should live in Germany for a while, and so become sufficiently fluent to be able to attend a German University.

My first visit to Germany, in 1937, was to stay with a family in Duesseldorf, but that turned out to be singularly unproductive because they all spoke very much better English than I did German. Possibly because I was so young and shy, I returned home knowing little more than I did in the beginning. My mother, a clever and competent woman, then made a very sensible decision.

'Next time you go, you will stay with a family where they speak no English,' she decreed, 'then you'll just have to struggle.'

By the time that the British Prime Minister, Neville Chamberlain, was contemplating his visit to Hitler in the autumn of 1938, my parents' plans had led to my being safely installed with a family in Halle-an-der-Saale, the birth-place of Handel, near Leipzig (and now in East Germany). Young though I was, I had already come to understand the intrinsic evil of Nazi doctrines, especially in the persecution of the Jews, and in the denial of free expression. I had been horrified during a visit to Leipzig to witness the baiting of some unfortunate Jews, as they were led through the streets wearing large placards around their necks daubed with the word *Jude* – Jew – and to see with disgust the notices displayed in the windows of hotels and restaurants proclaiming *Eintritt für Juden verboten* – 'entry forbidden to Jews'. My Duesseldorf family had been virulently anti-Nazi: an uncle had even been imprisoned for daring to criticize the regime. So I was surprised, and not a little disgusted, when I discovered that the mother of the family in Halle was pro-Nazi. The father, a doctor of chemistry and the owner of a large printing-ink concern, was much too intelligent not to appreciate the inherent dangers of Hitler's lust for *Lebensraum* and his occupation of the German-speaking territories of Sudetenland and the Saar; but, equally, Doctor H—— was far too canny an industrialist to express any open criticism of the regime.

Through living with such a family, I came to meet prominent local Nazis among the guests at dinner parties, hunt balls and so on: during these gatherings, I overheard talk which left me in no doubt as to the seriousness of the situation. There could be no illusion about the attitude of a conquered Germany still smarting under the punitive terms of the Armistice which had been imposed upon the Germans after the Great War of 1914–18.

When the Munich crisis reached its height, in 1938, I was called home in a hurry by my parents. On arriving in Hamburg from Halle, I learnt that all German ships had been forbidden to leave port, pending the outcome of the talks between Hitler and Chamberlain. The office of the Hamburg–Amerika Line was thronged with people panicking to get out of Germany, and, along with the many others, I was not sure how I was going to get home. But eventually I managed to get a seat in a train leaving at midnight for the Hook of Holland. It was the train that was then believed would be the last out of Germany. We crossed into Holland, where I could see that each bridge was guarded by Dutch soldiers manning machine guns. The ferry from the Hook to Harwich was packed with bewildered Jews, understandably broken-hearted at leaving their homeland and possessions, terrified of what the future had in store for them, and even more terrified of what would befall their loved ones whom they had left behind in Germany.

But did not Neville Chamberlain return to England with his famous piece of paper held aloft, assuring us that there would be 'peace in our time'? As soon as the panic died down, I returned to Germany to stay again with the family in Halle and to study German further. By the following summer of 1939, however, it became obvious that for the sake of world peace, and for the well-being of the German people, Nazi domination would have to be brought to an end. I could understand how the Germans, who had been degraded to a point of desperation after the First World War and the subsequent financial collapse, had let the rise of the Nazi Party happen. Its ideals and principles were laudable enough in the beginning, but power had gone to the heads of the leaders – especially Hitler's – before the mass of the people had woken up to the realization that it was too late to stop the machine from engulfing the nation.

Although the college at which I was by now studying closed for the summer vacation, I stayed on with my Halle family for a few weeks and then went home for a short holiday, hoping that I could return to Leipzig University in the autumn. But friends of my father's in the Air Ministry warned him that they believed that war was imminent, and that I should on no account be allowed to return to Germany. They were right. Only a short time later the Second World War began.

A few weeks after my return to England, I joined the 9th County of London Detachment of the Women's Auxiliary Air Force. I had seen the evils of Hitler's regime and, if there was to be a war against the Nazis, I wanted to have a hand in it. I was somewhat dubious about telling 'Dearest', my mother, that I had joined up, as I did not wish to worry her. But on September an official letter arrived, addressed to 'Volunteer A. B. Morris, WAAF', instructing me to report the next day for duty.

'What is all this about?' my mother asked, handing me the letter. I had to confess, 'I'm afraid I've volunteered for service.'

Instead of being cross, as I had feared, my mother seemed to be very proud. 'That's just like you!' she exclaimed. 'I would have done the same had I been your age.'

My initial posting was to the Royal Air Force Record Office at Ruislip, in Middlesex, which was only a few stations down the railway line from my home at Gerrards Cross. My welcoming was typical of the times. 'You're in the Air Force now, Miss. It's twenty-four hours a day, seven days a week, and fifty-two weeks a year . . . and time off for meals is a privilege.' Such was the greeting from the unit Warrant Officer that I, as a 'Volunteer', the newly arrived 882602 Aircraftwoman Second Class Morris, A., received when I was allocated to the Casualties Section of the Record Office.

Until May 1940 my war was mainly clerical. The officer-in-charge of my section was a delightfully witty professor: a classical scholar named Squadron Leader Herbert Saunders. His letters and memoranda were a joy to read, his beautiful English being liberally sprinkled with Latin and Greek. I was ostensibly his secretary but, discovering that I was a linguist, he would send me occasionally to London to search through foreign newspapers for possible information about RAF crews shot down over enemy or neutral territory.

From the Casualties Office were sent the letters to parents and wives which contained the standard but nevertheless dreaded words: 'It is my painful duty to inform you that your son (or husband) No. ——, Sergeant X——has been reported Missing (or Missing, believed killed) as the result of operations. . . .' Each letter had to be typed meticulously without a trace of an error, for these were letters which a family might keep for ever. On too many evenings I stayed late in the office, typing these bitter words, tears streaming down my face at the thought of the sadness that they would bring to families in all parts of the United Kingdom.

Through this I had a harsh initiation into Service life. Within a couple of days of my reporting to Ruislip we had the awful task of advising families that their sons or husbands were missing or drowned when the aircraft carrier, HMS *Courageous* was sunk by a German U-boat in the Western Approaches. We sent off nearly 100 telegrams with follow-up letters to the next-of-kin. The help of all available typists had to be enlisted and we sat working away on ageing typewriters until the small hours of the morning, shocked into silence by the sadness that we knew it would mean for so many.

As I was so young and possibly over-sensitive, sending these letters caused in me feelings of very real distress. It broke my heart when elderly parents would haunt our office, either in person or on the telephone, with pleas for further information. One tiny, frail old lady kept coming down all the way from Northumberland. 'You see, Miss,' she would explain, 'he's my only son. We had him late, you know. He's all I've got.' Her face was pinched and ashen with grief. I remember hoping then that should anything ever happen to someone I loved, if they had to die, please, please God let it be quick and definite and *not* just the vague 'Missing' or 'Missing, believed killed'.

In these early days, we who came to be known as WAAFs had no proper uniform. We were issued with an 'Orphan Annie' outfit of raincoat, black stockings, lace-up shoes, and, if we were lucky, a beret on which we proudly wore the RAF badge. My unit Warrant Officer generously gave me his old cap badge, which had been worn smooth with years of polishing. It only needed breathing on to make it shine enough to satisfy the most hawk-eyed Sergeant. Later in the year our equipment was augmented, to use an appropriate word, by a couple of pairs of black stockingette bloomers, which if extended to their full length came up to one's armpits, with the legs down to one's knees. Inevitably, we called them 'anti-passion pants'. We were also issued with bright pink cotton sateen brassières. The difference between a size thirty-two inch and a size forty-inch bust was determined merely by the length of elastic at the back, and any attempt at uplift was purely illusory. Some of us were also lucky enough to acquire from the stores the odd blue shirt, but possibly without a collar, and a black tie. Bits and pieces of uniform kept coming in in dribs and drabs, and some of us even had uniform hats made in an attempt to smarten our appearance.

At the beginning of 1940 we, who had been among the earlier arrivals, heard that the new recruits at West Drayton were being issued on induction with proper and full uniform. We were furious, and we threatened to hold a parade wearing only those items of clothing with which we had been issued. The airmen in our unit were all for it. To mollify us, the Air Ministry granted us two shillings a week as recompense for having to wear our own clothes.

The men of the RAF with whom we were serving were both kind and tolerant in their attitude towards the motley assembly of young women which had been inflicted on their erstwhile all-male existence. In its history of our branch of the Service, the WAAF Directorate saw to it that this was placed on record with the statement: 'There can be few early members of the WAAF who do not recall with gratitude the kindly help, advice and forbearance received from some officer or NCO of the parent service. . . .'[1] While I thoroughly endorse this expression of a pleasant sentiment, I fully realize what thorns we must have been in their sides during those early days.

Bearing in mind the horrors of the First World War, the whole population of the country had been issued with gas masks, which we carried with us wherever we went. The civilian version was packed in neat little card-board boxes, but the Service variety was heavy and bulky, and it was packed into a khaki canvas satchel. In designing the WAAF uniform no thought had apparently been given to what women carried in their handbags, or what they would do when the carrying of handbags was not permitted, as was the ruling in the early days. Inevitably a heterogeneous assortment of feminine junk found its way into the inner pockets of the gas mask satchel. A spot check or a parade at which we were ordered to don our gas masks produced, to the astonishment of some and the amusement of others, an interesting conglomeration of girlish clobber, all the way from lipsticks and powder boxes to sanitary towels. I have known the odd WAAF fake a swoon on parade rather than expose what lurked in the inner corners of her satchel.

On our arrival at Ruislip it was our fate to have to spend the first nights sleeping uncomfortably on camp beds in a hangar. Since the doors of the hangar would not close properly, we began to wonder why we had ever joined up. But we were soon allocated billets in various private houses in and around Ruislip. If you were lucky, you found yourself in a pleasant billet, where the lady of the house mothered you, but some of the billets were quite dreadful. My first one was with a couple of nature-pathologists, who in deference to my more normal diet, did occasionally produce bacon, but for the most of my time with them, I lived on a surfeit of parsley soup. I remember I was always hungry.

But there was worse to come in my next billet. The young wife worked all day in a local factory, and her husband was on night shift work at a nearby railway junction She was never up before I left in the mornings, so I had to cope with my own breakfast of toast and tea, and she was rarely home in time for my evening meals. There would be scribbed notes left for me in the kitchen advising me 'sardines tonight' or 'tinned spaghetti' or merely 'B. and B.', indicating baked beans and bread. Each evening my meal was out of a can, and always on toast. Fortunately, with my parents living not too far away, I was able on my days off to have a decent meal at home.

The following months that I spent at the Record Office coincided with that period of masterly inactivity known as the 'Sitzkrieg', and there were comparatively few RAF battle casualties to report. But this respite had to come to an end, and by May 1940, with the advance of the German Army into France and the Low Countries, reports of casualties were beginning to come in thick and fast. On 8 June another British aircraft carrier, HMS *Glorious*, was sunk by a German warship off the Norwegian coast, with the serious loss of RAF men who were on board. But even while I was breaking my heart over each new report of an RAF casualty, with the accompanying torment of having to inform their next-of-kin, certain events were developing in the south-east corner of England which were soon to alter the whole course of my life.

During the years of the uneasy peace following the Great War, it became increasingly evident that this country was likely to become involved for a second time in this century in hostilities on the continent of Europe. The Japanese attack on Manchuria, the Italian invasion of Abyssinia, the German occupation of the Rhineland and the Saar, all these were ominous forewarnings of still greater ambitions on the part of what became known as the Axis. Appropriate steps were taken by the British Government to ensure that adequate signals intelligence resources were both available for, and experienced in, working against the wireless communications of these powers.

After the Munich crisis in September 1938, the intelligence agencies in every country in Europe were brought to an additional state of alert, and, understandably, the signals intelligence organizations of the British armed forces stepped up their watch on Germany's military radio communications. At the same time, General Wolfgang Martini, who was the Director of Luftwaffe Signals, was enlarging and improving the German signals intelligence service – called Abteilung 3 – as also were his counterparts in the German Navy and Army. We were entering the era of sophisticated electronic eavesdropping.

As early as May 1939, Martini had made a flight in the airship *Graf Zeppelin* along the eastern coast of England, the object of which was to intercept transmissions from our chain of RDF (radio direction-finding) stations, which later came to be called radar stations, in order to determine the wavelength on which they operated, the number and location of sites in operation, and, if possible, their efficiency. He was not successful, and somewhat inadvisably during the flight, which was watched throughout by our radar people, he reported his position back to Germany when near the Humber estuary. This message was picked up by British signals intelligence, who were sorely tempted to inform the Luftwaffe Command that the position of the *Graf Zeppelin* had been incorrectly calculated by those on board, but they wisely refrained from revealing their own hand. It was, of course, of considerable value to British Intelligence to know that the Germans were showing such a keen interest in our radar chain. At this time our early-warning facilities were in advance of those of the Germans, and they were, therefore, understandably curious to learn everything they could about our organization. We were to retain this superiority throughout the whole war.

By the end of May 1940 the Germans had virtually conquered Europe. Holland and Belgium had already fallen, and the Wehrmacht had smashed its way through the Ardennes into France. Our only hope of survival was to save as many of the British Expeditionary Force as possible, and to bring them back to England. On 9 June, the last of the brave armada of little ships left Dunkirk for England. In all nearly 350,000 Allied soldiers had escaped.

Since December 1939, there had been a marked increase in the branch of intelligence which was to be known as the Y Service: the service responsible for the interception of enemy communications. Every effort was being made to monitor Morse transmissions from the Luftwaffe and, for once, the powers-that-be had managed to put square pegs into square holes. Many of the officers posted to the signals intelligence units were 'Ham' operators – amateur radio enthusiasts – and listening in to interesting radio traffic and searching for weak and distant stations had been their peacetime hobby.

Initially, monitoring in the United Kingdom was confined to W/T (Morse) traffic, but early in 1940 the Air Ministry set up a unit at RAF Station Hawkinge, near Folkestone in Kent, in an attempt to monitor various non-Morse signals and radio-telephony traffic from the German Air Force. Until May the unit had had little success in monitoring voice transmissions but then, as the front line came nearer the Channel coast, the first messages were picked up on the 40-megacycle VHF (Very High Frequency) band.

It soon became apparent that these messages were from aircraft operating over the front line. There was great jubilation in the Y

Service unit, but the excitement of realizing that they were at long last monitoring radio-telephony messages from German pilots and their ground stations was somewhat marred by the realization that no one at the unit spoke German sufficiently well to understand what was being said. It may now seem to have been an incredible oversight but this was literally true. A hasty search was made of the RAF station to see if there were any linguists available and by chance, they found a young soldier named Corporal R. Mathieson, who had studied German and who was working on one of the gun sites guarding the airfield. He quickly found himself on indefinite attachment to the signals intelligence unit, writing down and translating the messages intercepted from the German aircraft and their controls. He later transferred to the Royal Air Force, but was killed on a special airborne investigational mission in July 1942.

From a study of the traffic it appeared that the messages were mainly between fighter or Stuka (Ju. 87) aircraft and their ground stations and that these aircraft were making ground attacks on the retreating armies. The potential of such intelligence was immediately appreciated, and the Air Ministry instructed that the Y Service unit should be increased with utmost speed in order to monitor as many German Air Force radio-telephony channels as possible.

A policy decision was made at top level that this was work which could well be done by the Women's Auxiliary Air Force, members of which were already successfully working in the radar stations around the coast and in the Fighter Operations Rooms and the Filter Room at the Headquarters of Fighter Command. An urgent call went out to the Record Office at Ruislip in Middlesex, asking them to locate German-speaking WAAF and on 13 June, a linguistic expert was sent there to interview a selection of likely candidates. Luckily, I was, as it were, on the doorstep.

A girl from Northern Ireland and I were selected to be sent immediately to the experimental unit at Hawkinge, though her security clearance took rather longer than mine since she was Irish. Two days later, on 15 June, I found myself heading for, as far as I was concerned, an unknown destination. I was given a sealed envelope – presumably so that I could not discuss my posting with my friends – which I opened at Ruislip Station. In it there was a railway warrant to Hastings on the south coast of Sussex. I did not know it, but by this time the R/T interception part of the Y Service unit had moved from Hawkinge to Fairlight, which stood on the cliffs above

Hastings. The new location had been selected in order to get the benefit of the longer range afforded by the additional height. My sealed orders were understandable in view of the need for acute security consciousness. England had become pathologically spy scared and a rash of posters by the cartoonist Fougasse had appeared in public places warning everyone that 'Hitler is listening'.[2]

Under normal peacetime circumstances, as a happy young daughter of middle-class parents, I would most probably have been thinking about the next tennis party or perhaps planning a weekend picnic by the sea. Now it was June 1940, and although on that fine summer's day I did indeed find myself going to the seaside, I was very apprehensive. I had been told the post was 'hush-hush', and I had a feeling that it must be some form of intelligence; but I had no idea of what would be involved, other than that it was obviously connected with my knowledge of German. My wily old Warrant Officer had once given me the old Service warning: 'Never volunteer for anything, girl.' But on this occasion, I had been asked, also in the Service fashion, to 'volunteer'. Had I been given the choice and if I had followed his advice, we would both have been wrong.

2

'Hellfire Corner'

Immediately after arriving at Fairlight, I learned the reason for the secrecy surrounding my posting. I discovered that my new duties were to monitor messages transmitted by the German Air Force. My knowledge of radio at that time was absolutely non-existent, and I doubt if I could have tuned in even a crystal set. However, along with the five other WAAF who had been posted to the unit from various RAF stations throughout the country, I was soon initiated into the gentle art of twiddling knobs on elaborate radio receivers and searching up and down the radio bands for messages transmitted by the Luftwaffe.

The unit was under the command of Flight Lieutenant E. J. Alway, and was installed in a signals office tender, which was a sort of caravan located close to the edge of the cliffs. At first our equipment was meagre, to say the least. We had two civilian receivers, which were the famous Hallicrafters, of the type beloved by pre-war amateur radio enthusiasts, an oscilloscope, and an aerial array. If I remember rightly there was also a sentry in a tent nearby whose duty it was to guard us from undesirable visits by inquisitive strangers.

We kept watch throughout the twenty-four hours, working six-hour shifts, earphones clamped to our heads and straining our ears to the unfamiliar task of listening to the often distorted messages passing between Luftwaffe pilots, and from German aircraft to their control stations. At first we listened to short-range (V H F) traffic on the 40-megacycle band, one WAAF operator searching the band until she picked up a likely sounding message. We soon got the hang of this, quickly spotting the words with which the Germans ended their spoken messages, 'Kommen' or 'Bitte Kommen': – 'Over to you – Over'. The operator would then enter the message or as much of it as she had heard in her log-book, recording the time of the message, the radio frequency on which it was heard, and the call-signs. In those days we wrote in the log-books on every other line, writing the translation underneath. These details were kept in order to collect as much data as possible for subsequent analysis by the Air Ministry and the cryptographers, for we had not yet sorted out which frequencies and callsigns had been allotted to which 'Geschwader' (Group) or 'Gruppe' (Wing). Any messages that were obviously of immediate tactical use were translated straight away and passed on to No. 11 Fighter Group, or to the Navy through the Air Ministry; but the remainder would be dealt with later, whenever there was a lull in the traffic. An experienced RAF Wireless Operator helped us search for stations, and the moment he picked up a German transmission, he would call out 'I've got one' and whichever WAAF was free would start to write down the messages. Our standard of monitoring in those early days was very amateurish and it was tiring work, especially as we were unaccustomed to listening in and searching for traffic. But it was all so fascinating that we just hated to go off watch. Looking back on it now, it is sobering to realize how very little we knew at that time of how the German Air Force operated.

A year before, when I was a student in Germany, I would never have believed that by the following summer I would be in such a secret way the opposite number of the young German Air Force officers with whom I had danced at the Air Wireless Training School at Halle-an-der-Saale. I had so often been invited to their Mess, and, by one of those coincidences in life, Halle was to become the centre for the training of their 'Horchdienst' – the German Y Service.

At first sight, these Hallicrafter receivers seemed to us to be very complicated affairs, all switches, knobs and dials, not at all the sort of radio sets that we were used to in our homes. However, we not only became proficient at reading the traffic but soon found ourselves breaking down the code-words which the German Air Force used for their air-to-air and air-to-ground messages, and the coded grids which they frequently gave to locate their own positions, and the positions of the ground forces which they were attacking or over which they were reconnoitring; until we could work out these grids, the messages were of little value. Breaking them was rather like doing crossword puzzles and, being young and enthusiastic, we felt we were playing a guessing game with the Luftwaffe, a deadly game, but nevertheless a game. Too soon, it was to become very, very serious.

Each day we sent our logs by the despatch rider up to Air Ministry Intelligence, where they would be quickly read and sent on immediately to 'Station X', the Government code-breaking centre at Bletchley in the Midlands. At the Government Code and Cypher School, to give it its official title, the crypto-analysts would study the monitored material and meticulously record salient details for combining with intelligence derived from the vast mass of intercepted material monitored by special units throughout the world, as well as with intelligence derived from many other sources, such as photographic reconnaissance and agents' reports.

Much of the traffic we were then listening to at Fairlight was from reconnaissance aircraft, and from the Ju. 87s which were 'strafing' the French roads where terrified refugees intermingled with retreating troops. We were told later that there were occasions when the messages we intercepted gave valuable information about the whereabouts of military detachments with which communications had been lost during the chaotic retreat from Abbeville to Cherbourg. Every day, sometimes several times a day, we girls would listen to messages from reconnaissance aircraft sending weather reports and reporting on the strength and position of the British convoys as they made their way up the Channel. These enemy sorties were known to the fighter pilots and to us as 'The Milk Train', because of their regularity, especially in the early morning.

Our ears were gradually becoming accustomed to hearing every sort of German accent, which we could usually 'read' – as we called it – despite the distortions caused by atmospherics and the impossible-sounding code-words. We soon deduced, for example, that 'Kirchturm' (church tower) meant height, 'Indianer' (Indians) meant enemy aircraft, and so on. We even came to recognize the voices of many of the German squadron commanders. At the same time, as we later learned, German Intelligence on the other side of the Channel was also conscientiously listening in to messages sent by the Royal Air Force. In fact, I think their Y Service may at that time have been rather more efficient than ours.

The Air Ministry realized immediately that the interception of enemy radio-telephony communications would indeed provide a valuable additional source of both tactical and strategic intelligence, especially in the event of an invasion, and that the initial experiment

B

had proved worthwhile. Already before the war, German Air Force W/T (Morse) traffic, most of which was enciphered, had been monitored at two RAF stations in the Midlands, Cheadle and Chicksands, and at several other Y units at home and overseas. The information derived from this traffic was proving of immense value in compiling, amongst other things, the German Air Force Order of Battle, its strength, its movements and sometimes its intentions. Soon there would be few messages transmitted by the Luftwaffe in the western theatre which the Y Service did not hear.

Whilst we were stationed at Fairlight, our billet was a nearby vegetarian guest-house. In retrospect, now that I am older and more tolerant, I have come to feel rather sorry for the proprietress and the guests there because we were quite beastly to them. They were entitled to their convictions as vegetarians, and it must have been very distressing for them that our rations, delivered each day by truck from RAF Hawkinge, included a considerable quantity of meat and fish, which had to be prepared in *their* kitchens and duly served in *their* dining room whilst they were eating. But with the callousness of youth, we flaunted our carnivorous diet and hooted with mirth when one guest, passing our table, sniffed distastefully and exclaimed: 'How revolting – carcass!'

Amongst the original six WAAF posted to the unit there was an older woman, the Hon. Mrs Geoffrey Pearson, who was regrettably rather deaf and was therefore quite unsuitable as a Y operator, although she spoke good German.

'I want this or that done, Mrs Peacock,' she would command.

'Pocock, Mrs Pearson,' the tired little woman would insist. 'My name is Pocock.'

'Pee or Po, it's really all the same to me,' Mrs Pearson would counter pompously, and we would collapse with mirth.

Also amongst the first 'Secret Six of Y', as we were called, there was one Non-Commissioned Officer, a Corporal S. L. Phillips, who had been posted to us from RAF Halton. I suppose she was only in her thirties, but to me, then, she seemed quite middle-aged. She was a wonderful, motherly woman, who proved to be a sheet anchor throughout the whole war for officers and other ranks alike on our side of the Y Service. Unfortunately, like Mrs Pearson, she was not suited to interception duties, so the brunt of the work fell on the four of us.

I usually shared a watch with Barbara Pemberton, who was later to be awarded the MBE for her work in the Y Service. Barbara was a happy, attractive girl, with a lovely smile. She had spent most of her childhood in Hamburg. Whenever we were off duty during the day we would lie on rugs in the garden of the guest-house, reading and watching the vapour trails of the aircraft flying overhead in the blue sky, for the weather had now remembered that it was summer-time. Despite the horrors of Dunkirk, there was amongst the civilian population that summer a surprising lack of any mood of urgency. It was as though the fact that the Wehrmacht was already goose-stepping down the Champs-Élysées was something that was happening to foreigners across the Channel, which did not really affect the more important problems of the cricket scores. To me, it was a completely unreal existence, like a dream, and I expected to wake up at any minute.

It soon became obvious that the working accommodation in our cliff-top van was completely inadequate. It could only house two receivers, and there were obviously many more radio-telephony channels to be covered. Furthermore, we needed better telephone links to pass on the information we were gleaning direct to the recipients without the inevitable delay caused by passing the messages through the Air Ministry. I think, also, that the threat of possible enemy landings was so very real that the Air Staff was somewhat worried about having a handful of young women working more or less on their own on top of a vulnerable stretch of coastline. There was admittedly a radar station further along the cliffs, but it was quite separate from our unit, which overlooked the Romney Marshes, a flat stretch of coastline known for centuries as a smugglers' paradise. At night when the mists spread out across the marshes and the wide dykes, curling up the side of the cliffs, it was easy to realize that here was the perfect place for an enemy landing. It was eerie to be on watch when the sounds of the day were silenced and the mist swirled around the van, obliterating all other sense of habitation.

The Air Ministry decided that we should return to Hawkinge, a forward aerodrome on the Downs behind Folkestone, where in a small house called 'Maypole Cottage', just outside the perimeter of the station, the original R/T interceptions had been heard. This was to be our new home, now augmented by a further six German-speaking WAAF and several RAF wireless operators and mechanics. We were transferred there at the beginning of July. Shortly after this, our Commanding Officer, Flight Lieutenant Alway, was killed flying from Boscombe Down whilst carrying out flying trials on special signals equipment, and Flight Lieutenant R. K. Budge became our unit commander.

The traffic we were monitoring was now falling into patterns, and each day we were learning more about the Luftwaffe. There were air-to-air instructions between the German fighters and fighter-bombers during attacks on airfields and convoys in the south-eastern corner of England; there were orders from the squadrons' home bases about landing; and at least twice a day German reconnaissance aircraft would search up and down the shipping lanes in the Channel reporting any movements. Any messages about the convoys were vital. As soon as we heard that ships had been spotted by the enemy we would warn the Navy at Dover, and also 11 Group at Uxbridge. This was the Group controlling fighter operations in the south-east of England, which would immediately despatch fighter cover to protect the convoy, since an imminent attack was almost inevitable.

There were times when we would hear a German pilot reporting a British airman 'in the drink' – the RAF expression for a forced landing in the sea. This we would report at once, and our air–sea rescue launches would try to beat the Germans in getting to him. Unfortunately, in the early days of the Battle of Britain the German air–sea rescue service was rather better than ours; they had very fast launches and they frequently used Heinkel 59 seaplanes to rescue aircrews down in the Channel. At that time, too, our monitoring unit had no direction-finding (D/F) equipment, and unless the message was in plain language, or we could tell from the coded grid the position given by the German pilot, we would be uncertain of the exact location of the drowning man.

Gradually Air Intelligence was building up a complete Order of Battle of the German Air Force units – their strength, their equipment and their locations – and it was becoming possible for the listening service to identify many of them from their callsigns.[1] Information was gleaned from every source: from monitored traffic, from prisoners-of-war, from crashed aircraft, and from 'special sources'. By now we knew that facing us across the Channel there were two German Air Force Commands: Luftflotte 2 in the Low Countries, and Luftflotte 3 in France, and we had a fairly clear picture of their activities.

When we moved from Fairlight to Hawkinge, we WAAF lived in the RAF Married Quarters and worked in 'Maypole Cottage'. Our vegetarian guest-house with its large garden had been pleasantly restful whenever we were off watch, but now there was to be no peace. Constant air traffic swept in to, out of, or over the airfield, giving us little chance of sleep. Nearby, Dover and Folkestone harbours were subjected to constant attack. Aircraft zoomed and twirled overhead like some ghastly aerial ballet dancing to the fiendish rhythm of machine-gun and anti-aircraft fire. Our corner of Kent soon became known as 'Hellfire Corner', and no matter how old I live to be I shall never forget the screaming whine of an aircraft crashing to earth out of control, followed by the dull crump as it hit the ground. I was to hear that sound many, many more times during the coming months, and each time that I heard it I felt physically sick.

The balloon barrage flying high over Dover deflected many attacks, but those large fat balloons, glistening silver in the summer sun, were favourite targets for the Me. 109s. Occasionally, in a high wind, a balloon would break loose from its moorings, trailing wires dangerously behind it. Then the RAF fighters would have to give chase, bringing it down in a sad writhing mass of silver. I regret to admit that we always cheered when this happened; I suppose it relieved the tension under which we were living.

We soon came to form a close liaison with the Royal Navy at Dover, and when on 18 July 1940 they told us that the Goodwin lightship had been attacked and sunk we were deeply shocked. Our watch on those frequencies which by now we knew were used by the reconnaissance aircraft was stepped up as was our monitoring of the radio traffic from the German E-boats – the fast torpedo gun and mine-laying boats – which transmitted on shortwave frequencies. It was imperative that the convoys steaming up the Channel should get through with their vital supplies of food and fuel, and every single message which might help to frustrate the enemy attack was of value.

On one terrible day, Friday 19 July, we witnessed the massacre of six out of nine Defiants of No. 141 Squadron which had only just arrived for flying from Hawkinge. Every day we heard of more losses either from Hawkinge or from neighbouring airfields. Goering had rightly appreciated that one of the prerequisites for Hitler's planned invasion of Britain was the annihilation of the opposing RAF, and now he was working up to a massive air onslaught on Britain which would clear the way for invasion by German seaborne forces. It was the start of what was to become the Battle of Britain.

Before long the enemy bombers were active almost every night, droning across the sky. The bright fingers of the searchlights probed the clouds and the dull crump of the anti-aircraft batteries seemed ceaseless. To add to our discomfort, the heavy batteries on the cliffs at Cap Gris Nez started shelling our corner of England. Day after day, night after night, we popped in and out of the air-raid shelters, though we never left our sets when we were on watch.

It was the same in the Operations Rooms at airfields nearby at Biggin Hill, Manston, West Malling, and the many others. The WAAF stayed at their posts, giving invaluable service as they plotted the incoming raids. When the Luftwaffe turned its attention to the coastal radar chain, in an attempt to obliterate the early-warning system, there was the same pattern of devotion to duty. No one would dispute the fact that during the Battle of Britain the Operations Rooms were largely dependent on the WAAF, and any doubts that there might have been about women's reactions under battle conditions were dispelled for ever. I was to observe throughout the war that, on the whole, women are initially much braver under bombardment than men but their morale has a tendency to decline, whereas though many men are somewhat panicky at first they seem to pull themselves together and become gradually braver, so that in the end, there is little to choose between men and women.

One day, when the bombing and shelling had been rather noisier than usual, one of the men in the unit cracked under the strain. I was senior WAAF on duty, having been recently promoted to Corporal, and I could see that one or two of the girls were already on the verge of tears. Lack of sleep and the constant bombing were beginning to tell, and I could feel that hysteria was not far off. I had to act quickly, and so for the first time in my life I slapped a man across the face hard, and several times. It had the desired effect. Unfortunately the hysterical man was my senior in rank, and as our Commanding Officer, Flight Lieutenant Budge, was away looking for suitable sites for other units which were to be set up along the south and east coasts of England, I was unable to contact him to ask his advice. Instead I telephoned Squadron Leader (later Group Captain) G. R. 'Rowley' Scott-Farnie who was in the Y section of Air Intelligence in the Air Ministry, telling him of the situation and saying that I feared I might be court-martialled for my actions. I need not have worried as I heard nothing more about the affair.

Towards the end of July we started to intercept messages which clearly indicated that the Germans were using civil aircraft with Red Cross markings for reconnaissance flights over the Channel convoys. As this was flagrantly contrary to international agreement we notified the Air Ministry. A solemn warning was issued to the German High Command that any such aircraft would be granted no immunity. But by this time the pilot of one of the aircraft engaged on 'The Milk Train', which was perfectly legitimate reconnaissance, had become quite a friend of ours, and we quite frankly looked forward to him 'coming on the air' to give his reports. His callsign, I remember, was 'Amsel Eins'. He assumed that we were listening, and he would chatter away at us in English.

'I know, you English listening station, can you hear me?' he would cheerfully declare. 'Would you like me to drop a bomb on you? Listen – whee! – boomp!' and he would chuckle into his microphone.

I would have liked to have met him for he was quite a character. But war makes the most savage demands, and the day had to come when we were instructed to let No. 11 Fighter Group know each time we heard him operating. This led, one day, to a flight of Spitfires jumping him, and he was shot down in flames. He was unable to get out and we listened to him as he screamed and screamed for his mother and cursed the Fuehrer. I found myself praying: 'Get out, bale out – oh, please dear God, get him out.' But it was no use, he could not make it. We heard him the whole way down until he fell below reception range. I went outside and was sick.

Only then did I realize that I was in part his executioner; only then did I realize what I had done to that young pilot. I thought of the sad letters I had written when I was in the Casualties Section in Record Office, and I knew that tomorrow a German mother's heart would break. It was then I made a vow that I would do my utmost to end this carnage as soon as possible. 'Amsel Eins' was just as brave as our pilots, for the demands of duty spell the same meaning in any language. We missed him sadly, for we had known him as such a happy young man.

On 23 July 1940, my promotion to officer rank in the Women's Auxiliary Air Force was approved and I was shortly to be posted to Reading for the Officers' Training Course. But I was so exhausted from too much work and lack of sleep that I remember very little about the course, other than that it was held in a boys' boarding school. My parents, naturally, were very proud of me, especially as I had the honour of being the first WAAF to be commissioned for intelligence duties. I was glad then that I had earlier refused a commission as a Code and Cypher officer, and that I had waited for a more interesting appointment. At the end of the course, when the postings lists were put up on the Notice Board, the other cadets were very intrigued to read – '1246 Assistant Section Officer A. B. Morris – (Admin. – For Intelligence duties)'. They tried very hard to find out what I was doing but I was well aware that I could not tell them.

3

The Battle for Britain

During that month of August 1940, the onslaught on 'Hellfire Corner' continued with ever-increasing ferocity. We WAAF at the Hawkinge unit were well up in the front line, and from 8 August we were to become involved in a new and serious intensification of enemy action. On the advice of Abteilung 5 of the Luftwaffe Intelligence, the German High Command had issued orders that all ports and harbours of any importance around England were to be destroyed, and that all British convoys in the Channel must be attacked and prevented from reaching their destinations.

As a result, our neighbouring harbours of Dover and Folkestone were subjected to an almost incessant barrage of shelling and bombing raids, and so intense did the pressure become that the Admiralty were forced to abandon Dover as an advanced base for anti-invasion destroyers. The Luftwaffe was also attacking other ports on the south coast, and constant bombing raids were inflicted on Portsmouth, Southampton, and the more westerly ports of Plymouth and Bristol. Nearly every night German aircraft flew mine-laying sorties along the shipping lanes, dropping their deadly cargoes in strategic positions.

Over the southern counties of England, throughout those long summer days, fierce dog-fights between the opposing air forces rent the air. Blazing machines would hurtle to earth followed by snow-flakes of parachutes, whilst the anti-aircraft guns continually stained the skies with shell bursts. Sometimes one of the silver barrage balloons guarding the harbours would be hit and we would watch it squirm in flames to earth, writhing in agony like some tortured aerial slug.

Our neighbouring airfields were attacked almost daily and there was no landing ground left unscathed in our corner of England:

Hawkinge, Lympne, Manston, West Malling, Biggin Hill, Tangmere, and many others – all of them were bombed and shot up by the Luftwaffe. Every day one heard of more damage and more casualties, and only when the weather closed in was there any respite for the weary fighter pilots and the anti-aircraft gun crews. Nowadays instant news flashes with extensive war coverage on television have accustomed the public to the sights and sounds of war; but in those pre-television days, before we had become hardened or inured, violence of this dimension was new and very terrible.

After the attacks on the forward airfields, it was the turn of the radar stations, which were very much in the front line, and which formed a chain around the east and south coasts of Britain. The German High Command rightly considered it vital to destroy this essential early-warning system, but, for all their efforts, they were never successful. Even though the Luftwaffe managed to score hits on some radar stations they were soon back again in operation.

Hawkinge continued to be one of the Luftwaffe's targets, and on 12 August a squadron of Ju. 88s dropped a murderous deluge of bombs on the airfield. Hangars were smashed, aircraft were damaged, and the airfield was pitted with craters. Inevitably there were several casualties, but luckily none of the WAAF was hurt.

The 'Luftkrieg gegen England' (the air war against England) of the German song was really well under way, and now it was our lot to stand alone. The Wehrmacht was already the undisputed master of Europe, and Hitler had convinced himself that Britain would surrender without much opposition. Hermann Goering had estimated, somewhat ambitiously, that it would take only four days to eliminate the Royal Air Force. He had planned 13 August as his 'Adlertag' – his 'Eagle Day' – the day chosen for the commencement of the major offensive against England. But once again the weather was kind to the people of Britain, and his main attack had to be postponed until the afternoon, when formation after formation of fifty or more aircraft swept across the English coast, with waves of Dorniers, escorted by Me. 109s, and squadrons of Ju. 88s swarming across southern England.

We WAAF operators monitoring the traffic at Hawkinge became exhausted from recording page after page in our log-books and listening to every kind of German accent. Our hands were cramped from writing, and our heads ached; and we could well have used another dozen linguists. All day long we telephoned messages to No.

11 Group at Uxbridge, and to the Navy at Dover for there was not yet a naval intercept station at North Foreland. And on the next day, and on the days after that, successive waves of bomber attacks went on being mounted against 'Hellfire Corner', all with strong fighter cover. The air was never still. The records show that during the twenty-four hours of 15 August, the Luftwaffe flew more than 1700 sorties against the Royal Air Force, and for the first time the enemy bombers were able to penetrate as far as London.

As we listened in, it was disconcerting to say the least, to hear – 'Bomben zum Abwurf klarmachen!' (Ready for bombing) – when one realized the speaker was rather too close for comfort. But the cry 'Achtung Jaeger!' (Look out, fighters!) was more reassuring.

Above all else it was the cheerful 'Tally-ho' called out by the RAF fighter pilots when they had sighted and were about to attack an enemy formation that was the most comforting. To me, the expression epitomized the high spirits of those who were to become known as 'The Few'.

The War Cabinet was all too well aware that the odds were seriously against the Royal Air Force. Facing them in France and the Low Countries were the two largest German air commands; Luftflotten 2 and 3 commanded by Generals Albert Kesselring and Hugo Sperrle. Between them, we believed, they had a combined force of over 1000 bombers and 900 fighters. Further to the north, in Norway, General Hans-Juergen Stumpff commanded the much lesser force of Luftflotte 5, with 100 bombers and about 30 long-range fighters. Against this formidable array of German aircraft, the RAF's Fighter Command, which had the task of aerial defence of the United Kingdom, could rarely muster more than 600 fighters.

The close attention that we were receiving from the Luftwaffe was becoming altogether too disruptive for our signals intelligence unit and the Air Ministry sensibly decided to move the main body further inland, leaving a small party of RAF wireless operators behind at Hawkinge to listen to non-Morse transmissions. Apart from everything else, there was at that time a very real danger of an imminent invasion by the Germans. It was Hitler's intention to mount 'Seeloewe' (Sealion) – the invasion of England – within the next few weeks, and an armada of barges was already being assembled at ports in France and the Low Countries ready for that purpose.

Flight Lieutenant R. K. Budge, our new Commanding Officer, had managed to find a more suitable site for the unit at West Kingsdown on the North Kentish Downs. The Air Ministry agreed that we should move there immediately. The position was selected mainly because it was the highest point in Kent, and we needed the height in order to increase our reception range as much as possible. The German Air Force radio-telephony traffic which we were at that time monitoring was transmitted mainly on VHF and, generally speaking, the higher the frequency, the shorter the range.

A small house, named 'Mizpah', was requisitioned with an adjacent disused toy factory which could be used as an operations room; and to increase the reception range still further, a seventy foot mast for the aerials was erected in the garden. When we first moved there, all personnel, both RAF and WAAF, were billeted out amongst the neighbouring houses – and the villagers of West Kingsdown were infinitely kind to us.

In the middle of August, whilst we were still at Hawkinge, Assistant Section Officer Jean Conan-Doyle had been posted to our unit as WAAF Administrative Officer. She was the daughter of the author Sir Arthur Conan-Doyle and was later to become Director of the WRAF in post-war years. She is now Dame Jean Bromet. 'Billy', as she was then nicknamed, was an enthusiastic young woman who sported an eyeglass. She laughed readily, but in laughing she had the disconcerting habit of throwing her head back, thereby dropping her eyeglass, which would crash against the buckle of her uniform belt. I cannot think how many eyeglasses she must have wrecked before we finally persuaded her to shorten the cord. During the move from Hawkinge to Kingsdown she had been away looking for suitable billets for the new Y listening stations which were to be set up at Beachy Head and at Strete, near Kingsbridge in Devon, and when she returned to Hawkinge she found the birds had flown. We teased her about mislaying her unit.

The Battle of Britain was now reaching a crescendo, with the full force of the German Air Force being hurled against us. The armies and the navies of Britain and Germany were facing each other across the Channel awaiting the outcome of the conflict being fought in the skies above them. Had that small, indomitable band of young airmen lost the battle, the invasion of Britain would have been inevitable, with consequences that are too appalling to contemplate.

This then was the battle that we were monitoring – a handful of young women listening in to Goering's 'Eagles', as they liked to think of themselves, as they tried to wrest freedom from the British people.

But we were too busy at that time to realize the implications of what was at stake. Monitoring or, as we more usually called it, intercepting the traffic during raids, though exhilarating, became more and more nerve-racking. Many of us had aircrew friends or relatives, and a cold chill would go down our spines each time we heard a German pilot gleefully shouting that he had shot down one of our fighters: 'Indianer abgeschossen' (Indian shot down).

Early in the operations against England the Luftwaffe made use of 'Stukas' – the Ju. 87s – in their offensive, especially when attacking convoys and airfields, for during their conquest of Poland, Denmark, France and the Low Countries, the German Air Force had encountered almost negligible opposition, and these 'Jericho's Trumpeters', the screeching dive-bombers, had had considerable success. They would scream down on their target, drop their bombs and return quickly to the safety of their base. But when they met our Spitfires and Hurricanes it was a different story. As we listened to a 'Stuka' raid we would often hear one of their pilots yell: 'Achtung, Spitfeuer!' – followed by an urgent command by their leader: 'Lucie Anton! Lucie Anton!' – 'Return and land!' and they would scuttle for home. They were easy prey for the Spitfires and Hurricanes, which would swoop down on them out of the sun, guns firing, and their losses became so great that even before the end of August the German High Command was obliged to withdraw them from the battle against England.

As soon as we moved to Kingsdown and had more room, we were again able to increase the number of receivers and the scope of our listening watches. Several more WAAF linguists were now posted to the unit, but of the original Fairlight operators there remained only Barbara Pemberton, Liz Strang, who was later to be mentioned in despatches, the lovely Joan Davis, whose long hair, to the constant disapproval of the WAAF administrative officers, was forever falling down, and myself. We had been joined at Hawkinge by Enid Vaughan (Bertrand), recommended later by the Royal Navy for the BEM for her excellent work on the east coast, Rosemary Horstmann and Veronica More, who were later to join me in the Middle East, Doreen King, an enchanting but delightfully vague Dresden china doll brought up in Vienna, Mardi Campbell, Rosemary Hargreaves, and several others. There are few of the early Y WAAF whose names I cannot remember after all these years.

We worked as a team with a dedication quite exceptional considering our youth, and we were becoming better organized in passing on useful intelligence derived from the messages we intercepted. With the experience we had acquired, we had grown up, and we were much more professional in our approach. Direct telephone links were installed so that there would be the minimum of delay in passing information to No. 11 Group at Uxbridge, to the main W/T monitoring station at Cheadle in the Midlands with which we had a close liaison, and to the Air Ministry. Occasionally, if we could spare a receiver, we would listen in to the frequencies used by our own fighters. This helped us in our reading of the logs of the German traffic as we could then compare both sides of the battle.

It did not take Fighter Command long to realize that in the Kingsdown Y Service they had a most useful additional source of information. Amongst other things, our intercepts were a means of cross-checking reports of enemy casualties, since in the heat of battle it was not unusual for two pilots to claim to have shot down the same aircraft. There has always been controversy about this; the daily claims made showing that, on both sides, they did not tally with the actual losses.

From our monitoring we soon realized that the enemy was working with an aircraft control system quite different from that which was in use by the Royal Air Force. Our fighters were controlled direct from Sector Operations Rooms. Instructions regarding height and direction to fly in order to engage the enemy formations were fed constantly to the flight leader by the Fighter Controllers, who based their instructions on what they saw on their Operations Room tables: the combined information which had been derived from filtered radar plots, the Observer Corps, and other sources. The Fighter Controller might order:

'Bachelor to Tumbler White – Angels Two, Vector one eight zero Bandits attacking shipping off Dover. Buster.'

Unlike the British system of light and instant control, the Luftwaffe pilots appeared, from the messages that we heard, to fly on carefully pre-arranged plans, having been given heights and other directions to fly at their flight briefings before setting off on their raids. To a certain extent this was understandable, since they were on the offensive and they knew where they were intending to go, whereas the defending force had to meet the opposition wherever it was attacking. The Germans were well aware that we had radar, but they underestimated the use that we were making of it. It must have been infuriating for them to realize, from the messages intercepted by their own Y Service, that our fighters were somehow controlled direct from the ground by some new procedure unknown to them. There were always Royal Air Force fighters waiting for them after they crossed the Channel. During a raid, the German fighters escorting the heavy bombers worked to a set routine of defence as the formation flew towards its target. The fighter leader would only take control of the aircraft under his immediate command during actual 'wing to wing' fighting. By September, listening in at Kingsdown, it became patently obvious to us that there was a growing tension amongst the German fighter pilots. They would lose their tempers, get irritable with each other and at times sound downright panicky; and our knowledge of German swear words increased considerably.

With the odds overwhelmingly against the Royal Air Force, the need to conserve our fighter strength was paramount. The advance warning of incoming raids provided by the radar chain round the coasts of Britain, which was so greatly superior to the German radar coverage at that time, and by signals intelligence made sure that every enemy formation had an enthusiastic reception committee waiting for it. But each scrap of additional intelligence was vital, and the more details we could give about the attacking formations, the more it helped Fighter Command to see the whole picture.

By this time, the cryptographers at Station X at Bletchley were reading into the Luftwaffe's high-grade machine-enciphered Enigma traffic, and were producing what came to be classified as Ultra intelligence.* This traffic included messages from the German Air Ministry to the Commands, as well as between lower formations, and they provided invaluable information regarding the enemy's strength and movements, and even their intentions. But this source was so secret and so precious that, throughout the whole war, it was known only to a stringently restricted list of officers. We at Kingsdown were not then amongst the privileged few.

Amongst the very few at that time 'in the picture' was the Air Officer Commanding, Fighter Command, Air Chief Marshal Sir Hugh Dowding. His was the task of deciding how best to use our meagre defence forces against the onslaught of the Luftwaffe. Somehow he had to spread very little butter over a large slice of bread. With the prior knowledge gained from the few Ultra messages which

*See p. 343.

were at that time available, combined with other intelligence information, and with the invaluable assistance of the early-warning system,
he managed to accomplish the impossible.[1]

During the Battle of Britain, communications between the signals
intelligence units along the south and east coasts and Kingsdown and
with the Fighter Groups were so inadequate that the operational
value of many of the messages that we picked up was limited, and
even wasted. There were occasions when we would intercept a
message from a German formation approaching RAF fighters, well
above them and out of the sun, and having spotted our aircraft before
they themselves were observed. We were then likely to hear: 'Indianer
unten fuenf Uhr, Kirchturm 4, Aufpassen' (Bandits below at five
o'clock, height 4000 metres, look out).

In those days we were unable to get this information through in
time for it to be of tactical use, and would get hopping mad that we
had no means of warning our fighters that they were about to be
jumped.

Then 'Angreifen!' (attack) the formation leader would yell, and we
would know that the German fighters were diving on their
target.

I would often hear one of the WAAF operators murmuring: 'Oh
God, . . . oh God, . . . please, . . . *please* look up . . .', and I knew how
helpless she felt. I could see her willing the RAF leader to notice the
approaching enemy. He would already have known from the Controller that the German aircraft were closing in, but that split second
of prior knowledge might make all the difference between life and
death.

Later, when an extensive network of telephone lines was installed
with the Y Headquarters at West Kingsdown at the centre and with
our outstations feeding in to us, we could quickly pass on information
derived from intercepted messages, and immediate operational use
could be made of it. Eventually, we were able to bring the time-lag
down to one minute.

The RAF system of watching the enemy formations on radar was
established before the outbreak of war. At the closely linked radar
stations forming an over-lapping chain round the south and east
coasts of Britain, operators would scan their cathode ray tubes
watching for the blips that were responses from aircraft, and as soon
as they appeared on the tubes, calibrated information about them
was passed over the constantly manned telephone lines to the Filter

Room at the Headquarters of Fighter Command. Until further information became available, such as by the electronic recognition device known as IFF (Identification Friend or Foe) which was installed in our aircraft, the plot was recorded as a 'Bogey' – an unidentified aircraft – and plots from the stations were placed on the huge table in the Filter Room indicating the location and height of the aircraft being watched. As the various plots went down on the table they were filtered by highly skilled Filter Officers, and a track was established. If there were no known friendly aircraft in the vicinity, the identification would immediately be labelled as 'Hostile'. From tracks in the Filter Room, the information was passed by further land-lines linked simultaneously to the Operations Room next door at the Headquarters of Fighter Command, and to Group and Sector Operations Rooms where the established tracks were on display. From that our fighters were ordered into the air and directed towards the incoming raids. As soon as these raids crossed the coast the Observer Corps would possibly add to the general knowledge being made available by identifying the types of aircraft and confirming the number, their height, and course. But in times of poor visibility this would be difficult for them, and Y intelligence then became an additional source of valuable information.

By the end of the summer of 1940, the Air Ministry Intelligence had an almost complete picture of the Luftwaffe's Order of Battle, particularly in Western Europe. With all this knowledge added to the information that we were amassing at Kingsdown about the callsigns and frequencies used by the various German squadrons to which we were listening, we were able, for instance, to advise No. 11 Group that the enemy raid that was approaching Beachy Head was probably made up of Me. 109s of II/JG 51 based at St Omer. This would be most helpful for the Controllers, who would then be able to anticipate the probable return route of the enemy aircraft. Later, when we had direction-finding (D/F) facilities, we could pinpoint the transmissions and thus knew the exact position of the enemy formation whose messages we were hearing. But even in those early days of the summer of 1940, we could almost certainly confirm the height at which the formations were approaching, and we might also be able to give some indication, from what we were hearing, of their intended action.

Obviously a message like 'fly at five thousand metres and rendezvous with bombers over Dover' had useful tactical value, but our ability to interpret fully the traffic we heard did not come all at once. Gradually we were getting to understand the other side, piecing together bits of intelligence from various sources. Regular reports were received from the Air Ministry, from the W/T monitoring headquarters at Cheadle in the Midlands, and from the cryptographers at Station X at Bletchley, all helping us to sort out the jigsaw puzzle. Every message we heard was meticulously recorded and later analysed, both by us and by Bletchley, so that the information became of ever-increasing value. Many were the sessions we had late into the night browsing over the day's logs, whilst drinking copious mugs of cocoa. Over and over again we would read some new coded expression heard during the day, puzzling out the probable meaning, working out the grid code. Everyone available would join in, offering their suggestions, arguing and discussing with the fervour of university students.

Some of the code-words had been easy to determine – 'Moebelwagen' (furniture van) – was logically bomber aircraft; 'Lucie Anton' obviously meant 'zurueck und landen' (return and land); 'Indianer' (Indians) were British fighters. But other code-words were more obscure, and these took time to break. Sometimes we would actually recognize the voice of a pilot, or a callsign, or an expression peculiar to a particular Gruppe or Geschwader that was in the habit of using it.

'Hey, listen to this,' one of the girls would call out. 'There's old Taube Drei [Dove Three: a callsign]. What's he doing on that frequency?'

This might give us a clue that one of the enemy squadrons had moved to another base, and we would watch the frequency carefully to see if our deductions were correct. Conversely, we might have been asked by the Air Ministry to listen for confirmation of the move of a unit to a specific airfield, and this was just the evidence they needed. The Air Ministry's information could have been derived from Ultra sources or it could have been gathered during the interrogation of a prisoner-of-war, or it could have come from agents. The move of a unit might, perhaps, indicate that there had been heavy aircraft losses from some particular base or in certain squadrons or that reinforcements were being transferred and made ready for a concentrated effort against a certain target. Every scrap of information helped to build up the complete picture of the Luftwaffe's activities and intentions.

A year later, Rowley Scott-Farnie, who was then at the Air Ministry was to write: 'Intelligence is rarely dramatic – the best results are obtained from the continuous study of details, which although singly of little value are collectively of great importance.' But he stressed, 'it is incorrect to draw conclusions through wishful thinking, sincere but faulty observations, ambiguous or inaccurate recording.'[2] These were to be valuable guidelines for me during the whole of the war.

Until the spring of 1941 I was the only Intelligence Officer in the Kingsdown network. At first I would alternate as Duty Officer with my Commanding Officer, R. K. Budge, who was now a Squadron Leader, and with Flying Officer F. C. (Jonah) Jones. 'RKB', as he was known to us all, was a small, wiry son of Devon, with the bright intelligent eyes of his sailor forefathers. He had enormous energy, and a great capacity to instil enthusiasm into our team. Whenever we scored some radio victory over the Luftwaffe on a technical level his glee was infectious. Jonah Jones, on the other hand, was tall with the figure of a rugger full-back. He was steady and not easily ruffled, and he stood as a good complement to Reggie Budge. Having spent many years as a teaplanter in India, Jonah had learned to handle crises and men with good-humoured equanimity.

Our masters at the Air Ministry were the section then known as AI 1(e) with the Deputy Director of Signals Y at its head. It was later to be renamed AI4, under the Deputy Director of Intelligence 4 (DDI 4). They were the people who laid down the outline policy for our work, setting out the requirements of the various RAF Commands and of the Navy, and acting as intermediary between us and Bletchley. It was my responsibility to brief the WAAF operators of the Kingsdown network on what particular type of traffic to concentrate upon that day, and to decide which messages should be passed through.

As neither RKB nor Jonah Jones spoke any German, the co-ordination and compilation of immediate intelligence from the traffic was basically my headache. Until Barbara Pemberton and Liz Strang were commissioned in the spring of 1941, this meant that whenever either of the two technical officers, Budge and Jones, was away, and they were very rarely both at the station together, I would be on duty for thirty-six hours out of every forty-eight. During that long and busy winter of the Blitz, I became so weary that the time eventually came when I had to ask my doctor to prescribe Benzedrine

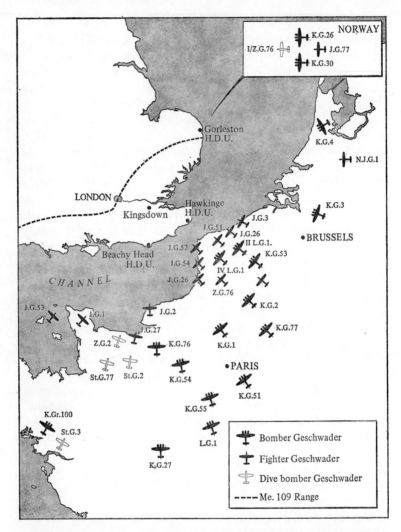

The Battle of Britain, 1940. Distribution of Luftwaffe forces aligned for the onslaught against England, showing the maximum range of the Me. 109 fighters. The strategic position of the monitoring units of Kingsdown, Beachy Head, Gorleston and Hawkinge is clearly indicated. A further HDU was located at Strete in Devon.

to keep me awake whilst on watch and sleeping pills to knock me out if and when I did get a chance to rest. Living, as I did, mainly on a diet of black coffee and cocoa, the dark circles under my eyes made me look like a Panda bear, and yet I hated to go to my billet in case I missed any of the action: something vital might come up and I felt responsible.

'Now then, AB,' Jonah would chide me in his big-brotherly fashion, 'Home. If you haven't gone within ten minutes, I'll wallop you.'

In the early days we passed any operational messages of immediate value only to No. 11 Group at Uxbridge in Middlesex, for it was the squadrons under the control of this Group which were responsible for the defence of south-eastern England, and which bore the brunt of the onslaught during the Battle of Britain. But it was not long before the other Fighter Groups came to appreciate the value of our information, and they then demanded that Kingsdown Y should also be made available to them. The Air Ministry immediately approved the creation of a number of coastal intercept stations, which were to be known by the camouflage title of Home Defence Units (HDUs). This was to ensure a complete coverage of all German Air Force R/T transmissions from Denmark to Brittany and to make full use of all operational information gained by the interception of this traffic.

RKB and Jonah Jones searched the south and east coasts of England for suitable sites for these new stations. By the end of 1940 units were located at Strete, in Devon, to deal with the requirements of No. 10 Group, whose Headquarters were based at Box in Wiltshire and which operated in the south and west of England, and at Gorleston, on the Norfolk coast, which was to feed No. 12 Group Headquarters at Watnall, in Nottinghamshire, which defended the area north of a line through Bedford and below a line through York. A third unit was located close to the castle overlooking Scarborough. This was to deal with No. 13 Group, based at Newcastle-on-Tyne, whose area was northern England and Scotland. A further station was installed near the radar site on the top of Beachy Head on the Sussex coast, to act as a back-up for Kingsdown, and to concentrate on attacks on convoys, and raids on the southern ports and south coast airfields. All these Home Defence Units were in constant communication by telephone with the Headquarters at Kingsdown, which steered the interception programmes. In addition, the HDUs also kept their neighbouring Naval Headquarters fed with Y information, though by now the Royal Navy had several R/T monitoring stations of its own in operation, mainly for the interception of E-boat traffic.

It was imperative that the WAAF operators should not only be good linguists but should also be intelligent, with a high sense of initiative and responsibility. The work was very exacting, needing sustained concentration, and it was obviously very secret. It was iniquitous, therefore, that these WAAF should continue as airwomen in the lowest ranks in the Service. Budge, Jonah and I were determined that we would get for the girls the rank, and consequently the remuneration, that the work merited. Since the beginning of the war, personnel of the WAAF engaged on encoding and decoding the normal RAF signals traffic had been given commissioned rank as WAAF Code and Cypher Officers. This was partly on the grounds of security, though I was never able to comprehend why making anyone an officer made them any more secure than when they were non-commissioned. Our Y WAAF who dealt with secret and often encoded material in a foreign language should be at least, we felt, non-commissioned officers.

There had been many rules and regulations laid down by the WAAF Directorate regarding the conditions under which WAAF might or might not be employed, so it was significant that already by October 1940, the Deputy Director of Signals Y, realizing the very special nature of our duties, had issued an edict –

that the recent order regarding employment of W.A.A.F. personnel at R.A.F. Stations does not in any way affect the conditions of service of those members at present serving with the Home Defence Units (Y Units),

adding that –

It may be regarded that the overriding necessities of the Service permit this depature from the rule.[3]

This instruction was issued to cover the exceptional circumstances under which the women worked, often under extremely uncomfortable conditions, at Beachy Head, Strete, Gorleston, Scarborough, and other places. Later this ruling was to be of great help to me when I was overseas and it became necessary for me to go into forward areas. It precluded any protestations from WAAF Administration that some place or other in the firing line was not suitable for a WAAF to visit.

Many of the linguists arriving at Kingsdown were raw recruits straight from the Recruitment Centres and they held the lowest possible rank of the Service: that of Aircraftwoman Second Class. There was a considerable opposition from the WAAF Administration to any idea of meteoric promotion. But eventually, much to the disapproval of many of the 'Queen Bees', as we called the senior officers of the WAAF hierarchy, the Air Ministry authorized that my WAAF should be given the rank of Sergeant. When the promotions were finally approved we had a great celebration, and it was to their credit that I did not hear of a single airman in our set-up grizzling about this decision.

Every couple of months I would have to attend special Selection Boards at the WAAF Directorate in Kingsway in London to which possible Y operators were called for interview. The Board was usually headed by the Director of the WAAF herself, Air Commandant (later Dame) Jane Trefusis-Forbes. She was constantly asking me, 'You *are* English, aren't you, Morris? You have quite an accent yourself.' I was not aware of this but I suppose that through being a bit of a mimic this was inevitable, particularly as I was steeped in German all day long. Indignantly I would reply – 'Of course I am, Ma'am – utterly and completely.' I always got the impression that she was somewhat suspicious of all of us. I may have been wrong, but I do not think that the Director approved of having 'foreigners' in the WAAF. I found these Selection Boards an ordeal. As a very junior officer I was overawed by so much 'top brass', many of whom were old enough to be my mother. Indeed, I am sure I was just as terrified as the women I interviewed.

My task at these Boards was to test the airwoman's knowledge of the German language and to give my recommendation whether, from my experience, they would be suitable for our arduous work. It did not follow that because a woman had a good knowledge of German grammar and literature she would be a successful Y operator. For one thing, as we had already discovered, she had to have exceptional hearing and it was very important that she should not 'flap'. She needed to be sufficiently fluent so that she could quickly grasp the slang and chatter of the German airmen. This meant, essentially, that she must have lived for some considerable time in a German-speaking country, since it is impossible to learn slang from a textbook. For that reason a number of the women selected for our work were not of British origin. They came from Poland, Austria, Germany, Greece, Czechoslovakia, France, Belgium; from almost every country in Western Europe. The original Y operators were all English middle-class girls – 'The Boarding School Girls' they were often called rather derisively by the others – but as we were unable to find enough of these to fill our ever-increasing requirements we needed to enlist recruits of foreign birth.

Selection of non-English personnel inevitably meant a delay in their arrival at Kingsdown because they had to be most carefully screened for security. But it was worth the delay; I cannot praise too highly their enthusiasm and conscientiousness. It was always one of my deepest regrets that those who were not British were precluded from being commissioned in the Y Service merely because of their foreign birth, even though some of them were by far the most useful and the most intelligent members of our team. There were officers of many different foreign nationalities serving in the Royal Air Force, and I felt that it was unfair that there should be discrimination against these women. If they were not secure enough to do this most secret work they should not have been employed in the Y Service in any capacity. The security of Ultra was not in jeopardy, for there were surprisingly few personnel employed in the Y Service who ever saw Enigma traffic in its decoded state or knew of its value to intelligence.

The need at Station X at Bletchley, and at the Air Ministry, for intelligence officers of British birth with a fluent knowledge of German was a constant drain on our operators. It would have been grossly unfair to withhold from these intelligent young women the possibility of a commission merely because they were exceptionally good at monitoring. Most of the earlier girls were, in any case, what was pompously referred to as 'officer material', but, understandably, it was with mixed feelings that we let them go. We needed them so badly ourselves.

No sooner had we settled into our toy factory at Kingsdown than the Luftwaffe commenced large formation raids on London. Ju. 88, Dornier and Heinkel bombers droned relentlessly over the English countryside, surrounded during daylight by squadrons of Messerschmitt fighters. Above us, we watched the steady white vapour trails writing their clear lines of warning across the sky, as the enemy formations headed towards the airfields of the Home Counties and then to London. Anti-aircraft fire would crack around the bombers, which, seemingly undeterred, would fly on along their pre-arranged route, as though disdainful of the attempts of the guns to blast them out of the skies. I marvelled at the stolid courage of the German pilots, even though they were flying at between 18,000 and 20,000 feet, frequently well above the range of the guns.

When our fighters entered the fray, the anti-aircraft barrage would cease, and the Me. 109s would zoom around their charges like angry wasps. As we listened in on our radio receivers the staccato sounds of machine-gun fire replaced the crack of the anti-aircraft guns, punctuating the constant stream of transmissions as the flight commanders gave instructions to the aircraft under their command. Occasionally we would hear a scream as an airman was hit, or a German pilot would break radio security silence in the distress of seeing a friend shot down in flames, and by so doing he might give us a clue to some code-word or phrase which had been puzzling us for days.

By this time we were becoming more clinical, and much less emotional in our approach to our work. We had even heard on the intercepted R/T reference to British airmen being shot at as they hung helplessly from their parachutes, and this had hardened our hearts. Yet somehow, to most of us, the Germans whose messages we were monitoring bore no resemblance to the German friends we had known in peacetime. It was better so; we were all young and vulnerable and it would have hurt us too much to have thought otherwise. But even amongst the Jewish girls there was little hate.

Still, menacingly, on droned the bombers. The guns would continue to shake the air, and then, in the distance, we would hear the dull crump, crump as bombs straddled a nearby airfield, or reduced to rubble another part of London. From our vantage point high on the Kentish Downs we could see the columns of smoke rising in the distance. There can be few people who lived in the south-eastern corner of England during August and September of 1940 who do not recall with horror the vast formations of German bombers throbbing their way across the countryside. It seemed incredible that the Spitfires and Hurricanes, grossly outnumbered as they were, could manage to ensure that so few of these massive raids penetrated to the heart of London.

As the Battle of Britain progressed, and as the score against the enemy rose, there was no mistaking the signs of tension and strain in the voices of the fighter pilots whose transmissions we were monitoring. They were finding that it was not going to be as easy to eliminate the RAF as Goering had promised them. The German losses were high – much higher even than ours – and 30 September saw the last of the great daylight raids on the capital. The Battle of Britain had been won.

Nowadays it is considered somewhat trite to repeat Churchill's famous words, but how very true they were. So very much was owed by so many to those few brave young airmen of the RAF. We, who, as onlookers on the ground, watched those aerial battles, are perhaps more fully appreciative of their great courage.

By the middle of September, Bomber Command was adding rail centres to the havoc it was wreaking on the invasion barges that were lined up at ports in France and Belgium and by 12 October, it was deduced from Enigma traffic that Hitler had indefinitely postponed the invasion of Britain. His reaction to the first raid on Berlin had been hysterical, and in the end his threat to rub the cities of Britain off the map was frustrated. Despite the fact that the powerful Luftwaffe was launching attacks from bases on the Continent stretching opposite two thirds of the coast of Britain, his air force had not managed to defeat the RAF.

This then was the end of the chapter of the daylight fighting; but it was to be followed only too soon by the heavier all-night Blitz, which had started even while the day bombing was still at its worst.

4

Bombers and Beams

By now, the Luftwaffe was fully realizing that the Spitfire was proving to be a formidable match for their Me. 109. Also the range of the Me. 109 was at times severely restricted through high fuel consumption in action. Fighter escort could only be provided for a bomber attack as far as London from airfields in the Calais area, and for just past Portsmouth from bases in the Cherbourg Peninsula but lasting only a few minutes over the targets. So the limits for the Luftwaffe's daylight bombing raids with adequate fighter escorts were seriously curtailed. Appreciating this weakness, the Air Officer Commander-in-Chief of Fighter Command, the redoubtable Air Chief Marshal Sir Hugh (later Lord) Dowding, used his squadrons wisely, not only meeting the opposition over the Channel but also in areas beyond the effective reach of their fighter escort. When the Germans found that the opposition from the forward airfields of the R A F continued, despite the bombing, to be vigorous, and was hurting them severely, the problem of attacking the more distant targets had to be tackled in a different way. It was inevitable, therefore, that they had to think about changing their tactics, and the Luftwaffe turned to night bombing attacks which would not require fighter cover.

Unlike the fighters, the German bomber formations made an effort to keep radio silence when flying towards and over England, restricting their transmissions to sending only essential messages. There was none of the chatter between the bomber pilots that there was with the fighter pilots. Generally, it was only during their return flights that we would hear the bombers as they asked for D/F fixes in order to ascertain their position, or when they were being guided back to their home bases. These messages were usually sent in Morse (W/T), normally using a three-letter code on medium or high frequencies.

With the night bombing there came more work for the unit which was mainly responsible for monitoring operational W/T traffic, as opposed to inter-ground formation traffic. This was No. 61 Wireless Unit, at Cheadle, near Stafford in the Midlands. It was under the command of Wing Commander W. G. Swanborough, and with its satellite D/F stations it was a much larger organization than ours. With its dozens of monitors it was able to man many more receivers than we could, covering all the messages from and to bomber, long-range shipping and weather reconnaissance and transport aircraft. As the twin-engined aircraft of the Luftwaffe at that time were mostly using medium and high frequencies for communicating with their ground stations, and since, under normal conditions, such frequencies have a much greater range than the very high frequencies, such as those then used by the fighters, No. 61 W U could well afford to be sited further back from the coast.

Since nearly all traffic from the 'heavies' was sent in three-letter code in W/T, there was no need for Cheadle's monitors to be familiar with the German language. The decoding and collation of the traffic that had to be done was handled by a group of German-speaking intelligence personnel working under Squadron Leader Garrett. As with ours, all their logs were sent to Station X at Bletchley, where they were subjected to minute scrutiny, and the information that they contained was analysed and co-ordinated with other material and then carefully cross-indexed.

Already by the autumn of 1940, Cheadle was intercepting vast quantities of operational W/T. There would have been few messages from within possible range that they missed and by using their D/F network they could pinpoint the source of the transmissions. They listened to bombers on raids against British targets, and to aircraft laying mines in the shipping lanes; they listened to the huge Focke-Wulf aircraft, the 'Big Bad Wolves' as they were nicknamed, as they flew way out into the Atlantic searching for Allied convoys and submarines and they listened to the weather reconnaissance patrols and transport flights. They even monitored training flights. All the messages were carefully recorded, and, although much of the traffic monitored at Cheadle was of longer-term value, many of the messages heard during a raid or a reconnaissance flight were of immediate operational value and use. Inevitably, the decoding required slowed up the handling of this traffic.

When the night bombing offensive started in earnest, particularly when the Germans began to use beams for navigation, we observed that they had a habit of changing frequencies from H/F or M/F to VHF during the course of a raid, and often breaking into plain language. Since very few of the wireless operators at Cheadle could read German, and as we were better geared to intercept VHF traffic, we evolved a system whereby as soon as their operators picked up a transmission from a bomber, or had an indication that a raid was imminent, they would contact us, giving details of the callsigns heard, the probable units involved, and the relevant frequencies. Duly warned, we would listen on those VHF frequencies which we now knew were used by the bombers and their home or controlling stations. We were then ready to take over monitoring from Cheadle, or, should we pick up a raid first, we would let Cheadle know. The interchange monitoring was made easier because the bombers would use phonetically the last letter or letters of their H/F or M/F callsigns. As these were also the unit code frequently painted on the fuselage of the aircraft, the Luftwaffe was unwittingly helping us still further to build up details of its Order of Battle. Later, however, the bomber units changed their system, and they then used instead coded call-signs such as girls' names, or the names of birds, in place of letter callsigns for their R/T transmissions, thus making it rather more difficult to identify immediately the various units.

No. 61 WU had by now set up a highly efficient D/F network – ours was to come later – which enabled them to pinpoint quickly an enemy ground station, and also to locate the exact position of an individual aircraft, assuming that it transmitted long enough for the D/F operators to get a good fix. Since we now knew where most of the units were based, if we were to hear Vannes control, for instance, communicating with aircraft, we could be fairly certain which units were operating even if the aircraft callsign was not given.

The aircraft markings of the Luftwaffe were composed of four symbols – such as 6N + DH – with each flight allocated identification letters in a regular pattern which was standard throughout the whole force. As the war progressed we were to learn that the Germans' devotion to systematic routine was one of their greatest weaknesses, and a blessing for us. Identification of these markings was determined from various sources, including crashed aircraft and interrogation of prisoners, as well as from Y, and by the end of 1941 the markings of all the more important units of the German Air Force were known to British Air Intelligence.

The organization of the Luftwaffe was quite different from that of the RAF and it is difficult to compare exactly the German structure with that of the British. Broadly speaking, however, a Luftflotte was more or less equivalent to an RAF Command, but there were under it subsidiary commands called Fliegerkorps or more usually Fliegerdivisionen. Below this were the Geschwader comprising two to four Gruppen, each with their various Staffeln. A Geschwader usually comprised about ninety aircraft in three Gruppen plus a Staff Flight. If there were a fourth Gruppe, it would be a training unit. Within a Geschwader the aircraft were normally confined to specific tasks, such as night-fighting or long-range reconnaissance duties. In many respects the Luftflotten were self-contained commands able to wage independently every aspect of war in the air.

Since it was not unusual for a German radio operator who was having difficulty contacting his ground control in R/T to break into W/T and repeat the message, we always had to be ready for this. Hence Budge decreed that we should all learn the Morse code, even though the bulk of the W/T traffic monitored at Kingsdown was received by a small, hard-working band of RAF wireless operators. Being more experienced at Morse than we were, they could read messages at far greater speeds.

I was admittedly never very fast at Morse, because after a certain speed or time the words blurred. I would be thinking of the intelligence implications of what I was receiving and that was disastrous. Taking down Morse has to be an automatic process similar to shorthand: you must not think and so let the sender get ahead of you, for if you do you have lost part of the message. To the despair of our tutor, Corporal Joseph Binnings, he could never get me, try as he would, beyond eighteen words per minute. Fortunately the German operators were not much better than I was and they rarely transmitted faster than eighteen words per minute.

Since the beginning of 1940 German bomber aircraft had been making sporadic long-range bombing sorties to various parts of England. By the end of August, the Germans were stepping up their bombing offensive to include almost nightly raids ranged over the British Isles from the borders of Scotland to Kent, and covering the Midlands, Merseyside and South Wales. The south-west ports suffered a foretaste of things to come, and by early September the Blitz on London had commenced in earnest. From then on until the middle of November the Luftwaffe bombed the capital almost every night with an average force of 130 bombers, coming over singly in a steady stream with the aircraft about four minutes apart. Little had we realized when we moved back for safety's sake from Hawkinge to Kingsdown that we would be on the Berlin/London 'bus route.

Each evening the air-raid sirens would start to wail, and soon the sky was full of the clustering beams of the searchlights. The criss-cross patterns etched by their bright fingers probed the clouds, swooping about until a silver moth of an aircraft was caught in a beam. Then the other searchlights would swing on to the intruder, coning the aircraft and illuminating it as a target. The anti-aircraft guns would bark and we could see little red points where the shells exploded in the air. Still the bombers flew on, keeping high above the barrage balloons encircling London. From where we watched on the ground, the gunfire so often seemed to be firing behind or below the enemy bombers, but we knew from our intercepts that, not surprisingly, it seriously worried the pilots and the crews of these bombers.

Returning to my billet along the blacked-out country lanes of Kent was a hazardous operation, and not even my tin hat afforded me much courage as I listened to the plopping sound of shrapnel falling through the trees. Strangely enough I was never afraid of the bombs. If they hit you, they hit you, and that was that; but a piece of shrapnel could have been nasty. I hated walking home alone, and I would sing to myself to keep up my spirits.

Analysing the earlier long-range night bombing attacks on various parts of England, Air Ministry Intelligence and the cryptographers at Bletchley were convinced that these raids were a form of operational training prior to the main bombing offensive. Evidence suggested that some of the aircraft involved were using a type of radio beam to home on to their target. At first, many of the experts were somewhat sceptical of this theory, but young Dr R. V. Jones – the brilliant pupil of the famous Professor Lindemann, Churchill's closest adviser on scientific matters – who was in charge of Scientific Intelligence at the Air Ministry, firmly believed that the Germans were testing a new bombing aid. There was evidence from documents captured from a Heinkel aircraft of KG 26 shot down earlier in the year that for some operational purpose a beam that they called Knickebein (Crooked Leg) had been brought into use.

By the middle of June an organization had already been set up under the direction of Dr Jones to investigate these German beam-type transmissions, especially those heard on the 30-megacycle wavelength. It was not long before there was ample evidence to establish that these transmissions were indeed radio beams being used for navigational purposes. Documents retrieved from a wrecked Heinkel 111 shot down in that month indicated that a Knickebein transmitter at Cleve, on the Dutch-German border, had been operating on 31.5 megacycles and Cheadle was able to confirm that they had heard a beam on that frequency on the night concerned which seemed to tie up with a bombing raid.

About the same time as this development, prisoner-of-war interrogation revealed that Knickebein was a beam similar to the X-Geraet, of which Intelligence had already heard rumours. The X-Geraet (X-Apparatus) was believed to be Lorenz-type beam of the sort used for assisted landings, modified for use in blind bombing. Other prisoners confirmed that on long-distance sorties the bombers had to fly very high if they were to pick up the beam. This was necessary in order to make provision for the curvature of the earth.

The pieces of the jigsaw puzzle were fitting together, but how was further information to be acquired quickly enough about these beams? We needed to know on exactly what radio frequencies they were transmitted, their characteristics, and their efficiency. Although the personnel at the prisoner-of-war interrogation unit were carefully briefed about the sort of technical and operational information that was required it was by no means certain that they would be able to produce the answers in time, nor could we be certain of discovering them from crashed aircraft or from Enigma traffic. As soon as the Germans mounted a concentrated night bombing offensive, instead of the present sporadic sorties involving only a few aircraft, the likelihood was that the problem would become even more acute. Time was not on our side. With navigational beams directed on to strategic targets, the lack of visibility during night operations would be of little handicap to the intruders, but being unable to see in the dark would still be a problem for the RAF night-fighter pilots.

This then was the new menace. During daylight raids Fighter Command was able to deal successfully with the attacking bomber formations. Our own radar coverage enabled us to direct our defending fighter defences to within close range of the raiders, leaving the final approach to direct attack to the visual contact by the pilots. But at night, especially in cloudy weather or when there was no moon, this method of defence was still hopelessly inadequate. The scientists had not yet sufficiently developed A I, the radar set installed in twin-engined two-seater aircraft which enabled the pilot, through the observer or radar operator, to home on to his target. The night-fighter pilots were still largely operating on the 'cat's eye' principle of trying to see in the dark in their efforts to track down their quarry.

If countermeasures were to be taken against them, every possible detail about the beams had to be obtained as a matter of urgency, and it was this which led the Air Ministry to agree that a search should be made for the beams using aircraft fitted with a Hallicrafter 30-megacycle receiver. A special flight – the Wireless Intelligence Development Unit (WIDU) – stationed at Wyton, in Huntingdon-shire, was set the task. Under the command of Squadron Leader R. S. Blucke, three Ansons were equipped with these receivers and skilled wireless operators were assigned to operate them, with the scientific research being co-ordinated by Flight Lieutenant Alway, who had been our first CO at Hawkinge. It took only three sorties for one of the pilots, Flight Lieutenant H. E. Bufton, and his wireless operator to locate a Lorenz-type beam which was passing over the English coast near Spalding and a second beam passing through a point near Beeston. The date was 21 June 1940. The wireless opera-tor/observer, Corporal Mackie, was able to determine that the first beam had Morse 'dots' to the south and 'dashes' to the north side of the beam and that it emanated from the Cleve area near the Dutch frontier, while the second beam had similar characteristics but with the 'dots' to the north and 'dashes' to the south, and that both beams were synchronized. When Bufton submitted his excellent and com-prehensive report on the beam's characteristics, his findings proved to be exactly what the experts needed.[1]

Meanwhile, further clues that had been gleaned from documents which had been retrieved from another wrecked aircraft confirmed that beam transmitters were indeed located at Stollberg in Schleswig-Holstein and near Cleve. Now we had most of the information to complete the picture and it was imperative that steps should be taken as quickly as possible to devise countermeasures in order to frustrate the enemy's new navigational aid.

What were the options? To try to bomb the beam stations – if we could pin-point them by photographic reconnaissance? That would be difficult, because they were comparatively small targets. Attempt a Commando-type attack on them? That would be risky because it

C

would give the game away. And, in any case, there were now believed to be several Knickebein stations, and eliminating just one would not be of very great help. The third alternative was to render the beams ineffective through some means of radio countermeasures – by jamming the beam. This was the obvious answer. To this end Dr Jones assigned to Dr (now Sir) Robert Cockburn, who was a young and brilliant scientist working at the Telecommunications Research Establishment (TRE) at Worth Matravers, near Swanage, Dorset, the task of co-ordinating the development of radio-jamming equipment, which would be capable of nullifying the beam as a navigational aid.

At Cabinet level it was decided that an organization should be set up without delay specifically to frustrate the enemy's electronic devices. Wing Commander E. B. Addison was given the responsibility of forming a section under Air Commodore O. G. W. G. Lywood, who was Deputy Director of Signals Y at the Air Ministry; and on 18 June a radio countermeasures headquarters was established at the Mildmay Institute at Garston, near Watford.[2] This was to be the nucleus of No. 80 Wing, which eventually became No. 100 Group in Bomber Command, and their radio countermeasures were to prove invaluable in both defence and attack throughout the war.

At Kingsdown, and later also at our out-stations, the so-called Home Defence Units (HDUs) along the south and east coasts, it was our task, apart from intercepting and interpreting radio-telephony transmissions, to identify and to monitor enemy navigational signals. We had already started to hear certain German Air Force messages during the day, obviously from ground stations, which referred frequently to Knickebein, and we had picked up pulse transmissions on the 30- and 70-megacycle bands, which had all the characteristics of navigational beams. The messages were usually transmitted during the morning or early afternoon, and they gave every indication that some sort of radio apparatus was being tested or calibrated. Mention was made of what appeared to be radio frequencies and coded grid positions, and these, when deciphered, indicated that they referred to various places on the mainland of Europe, and also to certain towns in England. On one occasion these grid positions indicated, when decoded, that the reference was to Derby, in the Midlands, where the Rolls-Royce factory was working at high pressure to replace aero-engines faster than the Luftwaffe was shooting our aircraft out of the skies.

The way in which Knickebein was used was as a beam directed at the target along which the bombers would fly. When the pilot switched on his Knickebein receiver he would hear a continuous note, if he was on course. If, however, he deviated from this course – either to the left or to the right – he would hear 'dots' or 'dashes' and he would then change course until he was again flying along the continuous note zone. So long as he heard the continuous note, he knew that he was flying straight towards the target. An intersecting beam, which gave a different note in the pilot's earphones, would be laid to cross the main beam either at a point where he must release his bombs or at a given distance from the target, from which point he would make a short run-up to the target along a pre-arranged course.

It was all very simple, needing very little training of the crews and no special equipment in the aircraft beyond the standard Lorenz blind approach receivers which we already knew, from wrecked aircraft, were carried by all German bombers. Any Lorenz equipment so far salvaged appeared to be calibrated for 30, 31.5 or 33.3 megacycles, so it was reasonable for us to assume these were the three frequencies in use for Knickebein.

Towards the end of August the enemy started to mount massive night bombing attacks, with Liverpool and the Midlands as their favourite targets until, early in September, the Blitz against London started in earnest. It was now becoming obvious from our monitoring at Kingsdown and No. 61 W U, at Cheadle, that the intruders were using beams on most nights to guide them to their targets. By now, fortunately, the cryptographers at Bletchley had broken the codes that were being used by the bombers and their ground-stations – the so-called 'L M' codes, of which at that time there were six in use – sufficiently for us to read most of their messages. Even though the accuracy of Knickebein-controlled bombing was no greater than to within a square mile, this method of attack was causing considerable damage to vital installations, and was devastating towns; and if the whole stream of bombers had managed to get through to the target zones, the effects would have been catastrophic. But through compromising their beam navigation on those early practice raids, the Luftwaffe had done itself a great disservice, and had given No. 80 Wing a head start. The Wing was ready with countermeasures.

There was at the time a great deal of coming and going between the Air Ministry, TRE, 80 Wing, 61 WU, and Kingsdown. We had a steady stream of visitors, including 'RV' – as Dr Jones was known, Wing Commander Addison, from 80 Wing, Wing Commander Swanborough from the Cheadle Y unit, Squadron Leader Scott-Farnie, from signals intelligence at Air Ministry, and Mr T. L. Eckersley, the scientific consultant to the Y Service from Marconi, and many others, all of whom would discuss at length the characteristics of the beam signals.

Not being particularly knowledgeable about radio, I found it very difficult to understand the technicalities of the various navigational systems, but I could at least see, when the various transmissions were fed through an oscilloscope, that there was a marked difference in their appearance. RKB was very kind and helpful in explaining to the WAAF how the beam signals worked. He and the other signals officers at Kingsdown, Jonah Jones and, later in 1941, Pilot Officers J. F. 'Jimmy' Mazdon and Joe Payne, were all deeply involved in unravelling the way the beams operated.

As soon as we picked up a transmission which indicated that a beam was being tested, they would examine the beam signal on the oscilloscope to check its exact frequency and characteristics. They would then confirm the findings that they had made to No. 80 Wing, the Headquarters of which had been moved to Radlett, in Hertfordshire,[3] and which was controlling a network of listening and jamming stations engaged exclusively on beam and beacon transmissions. Our task at Kingsdown and the out-stations was to log every message remotely connected with the setting up or operation of the beams and it was the responsibility of the Duty Officer to keep both the Air Ministry and No. 80 Wing fully informed of any developments.

By August a programme had been started by No. 80 Wing which, it was hoped, would nullify the operational value of Knickebein. In the beginning, diathermy apparatus borrowed from hospitals was set up in vans and various police stations around the coast[4] and by the use of this apparatus a mush of sound was transmitted with the object of obliterating the beam signals. This meant the German pilots would be unable to determine whether or not they were on course. The jamming units were appropriately named 'Headache' units – a name that I always imagined was thought up by either Dr Jones or Dr Cockburn with their boyish sense of humour for the beams were certainly a headache to us.

But the diathermy jammers had only a limited range and it was obvious that something more efficient was needed. By the first major night raid on London on 7 September, Dr Cockburn had found the necessary antidote to Knickebein in 'Aspirin' – the code name in keeping with the hospital theme given to the new high-powered jammers. Cockburn had modified some Lorenz transmitters to radiate a beam signal similar to Knickebein but transmitting 'dashes'. This meant that on hearing a 'dash' on his receiver the German bomber pilot would assume he was off course to the right, and would naturally attempt to make a correction. But instead of reaching a continuous note zone, which would indicate he was back on course, he would still hear 'dashes', and so would over-correct. If, however, he were flying to the left, in a zone of 'dots', he would hear 'dashes' as well as the 'dots', and so would become utterly confused.

This operation was popularly referred to as 'bending the beam', an expression that we did not try to correct, despite its technical inaccuracy. In fact, Intelligence was delighted to learn from agents that rumours of 'beam-bending' were wide-spread amongst the Luftwaffe pilots and at Kingsdown we chortled with glee when we were told that a captured airman had recounted tales of pilots going hopelessly astray. Sometimes a decoy cross-beam would be transmitted by No. 80 Wing to intersect the main Knickebein beam short of the enemy's planned point of intersection. Misjudging his position, the pilot would release his bombs either wide or short of the target.

In *Their Finest Hour* Winston Churchill wrote:[5] 'An officer in my Defence Office sent his wife and two young children to the country during the London raids. Ten miles away from any town they were much astonished to see a series of enormous explosions occurring three fields away. They counted over a hundred heavy bombs. They wondered what the Germans could be aiming at, and thanked God they were spared. The officer mentioned the incident the next day, but so closely was the secret kept, so narrow the circle, so highly specialized the information, that no satisfactory explanation could be given him, even in his intimate position. The very few who knew exchanged celestial grins.'

It was understandable that No. 80 Wing's jamming was especially effective when the intruder was on a distant raid far from home. The German signals would then be weaker than ours, and easier to swamp by interference. The general public has never appreciated, I feel, how much of this highly technical achievement depended on the scientists working at TRE and under Jones and Cockburn. The fact that so many of the bombs which fell on London during the later raids of the Blitz were dispersed and not concentrated is much more to their credit than to the night fighters and the anti-aircraft guns.

No. 80 Wing's countermeasures were eroding the confidence of the German bomber pilots. So doubtful was the Luftwaffe becoming of the efficiency of their Knickebein beams that, despite Goering's assurance to the Fuehrer of their accuracy, by the end of November we at Kingsdown were constantly hearing complaints from the pilots. On one occasion, a pilot of Kampfgruppe 100 (KGr 100) – the Pathfinder unit – was heard checking on the accuracy of both Knickebein III transmitting from Dieppe and Knickebein IV from Cherbourg. Both these beams were ostensibly lined up on Birmingham, but he reported that the point of intersection was east of the city, though we knew that No. 80 Wing had, in fact, so jammed the beams that the actual point of intersection was twelve miles to the south-west of the city. It was understandable that his bombing was pretty inaccurate.

In their effort to overcome the jamming, the Luftwaffe would constantly change the frequencies on which the beams were operating, but the listening stations were ready for this, and when it happened No. 80 Wing would soon switch its jammers over to the new frequency. On one raid we heard Knickebein beam transmissions on seven different frequencies, and the jammers were switched over to counter the changes. They also began to transmit 'spoof' messages in the hope of deceiving us.

To add further to the navigational confusion of the German pilots, No. 80 Wing was 'masking' or 'meaconing' the enemy's beacons which radiated on long and medium wavelengths. These beacons had been set up by the German Air Force along the North Sea and Channel coasts, rather like lighthouses for ships, to assist their aircraft back to their bases. The exact positions and frequencies of these beacons were known, of course, to the Luftwaffe pilots, who would take periodic bearings on them to check that they were on course. No. 80 Wing would pick up the German beacon signals, and then, in conjunction with a Post Office transmitter, would re-transmit them. This led to the German pilots being unable to get true bearings on the beacons, and through that, being unable to determine their exact positions. There were nine 'meacons' operating by the middle of August 1940, and by a month later the 'meaconing' had become

so effective that the Germans took to altering the callsigns and frequencies of their M/F beacons at irregular intervals in the hope of
beating No. 80 Wing's game. An extension of the 'meaconing'
scheme was to pick up the aircraft's request for a check bearing and
re-radiate his message, leaving the ground control unable to calculate
where the aircraft was flying.

On watch at Kingsdown and at the H D Us we would hear intruder
pilots protesting to their ground stations that their D/F (direction-
finding) apparatus was not functioning properly, or that they could
not hear a certain beacon. Sometimes they would become really
angry. One prisoner-of-war reported ruefully that he had even heard
a case where a pilot flew around in a circle trying in vain to get a
correct fix.

By November 1940, the Germans had erected five Knickebein
stations – at Bredstedt, Cleve, Dieppe, Cherbourg and Morlaix – and
it *should* have been possible for them, operating with combinations
of these beams, to make a deadly approach to their chosen target.
But No. 80 Wing had improved their jamming techniques so much
that they were by this time interfering severely with all the Luftwaffe's navigational aids.

If all had gone well for the enemy bombers, there would have been
little or no need for them to deviate from their fairly high standard
of radio security. But all was not going well. All too frequently the
Germans found themselves very unsure of their position, and there
were the times when we would hear one of their pilots in a state of
near panic. On finding himself lost over what was to him enemy
territory a pilot's immediate reaction would be to ask his base for a
fix on his position or to make complaints about the efficiency of his
beam receiver. By taking a D/F bearing on him when we picked up
his transmission we could often have told him exactly where he was.
Indeed, such messages were just what we wanted to hear as they
added greatly to our own information.

These pleas for assistance were usually sent in Morse in one of the
six three-letter codes, which by now, thanks to the cryptographers at
Bletchley, we were largely able to read. But sometimes the pilot or
wireless operator would break into plain language, either on W/T or
R/T. As they usually prefixed their messages with their callsign, we
would be able, with our ever-increasing knowledge of the Luftwaffe
Order of Battle, to determine which unit was operating, and from
that the location of his home base. This was important and

useful information for both Bomber and Fighter Command.

There was an incident on the night of 5/6 November when a raiding Heinkel of KG 26 attempted to locate his position. Using radio bearings on the St Malo beacon, he turned for home but because of 'meaconing', he flew right over the beacon until he calculated he was over southern Brittany. When he broke cloud, he found that he was still over the sea. Imagining this must be the Bay of Biscay, he turned back to what he thought was the beacon. By now he was running short of petrol. 'Ich habe Durst' (I am thirsty), he signalled his control station. Seeing a coastline ahead, he decided that he had better put his aircraft down on the beach. In the crash landing, unfortunately, some of his crew were either killed or injured. To his dismay he found, when he was captured, that instead of landing on what he had assumed was the coast of Brittany he had come down on the coast of Dorset.

On another evening about this time a raider wandered erratically all over southern England until he finally ditched in the North Sea off the East Anglian coast, still under the fond, but mistaken impression that he was somewhere near Normandy. But we had little sympathy for the Luftwaffe pilots. It was one of their weaknesses that they and their crews relied too much on electronic aids. They seemed singularly untrained in astro-navigation and dead-reckoning, unlike our pilots. When their electronic aids failed or were interfered with, they were bewildered.

Luckily for us, it would have been impossible for the German crews to remember accurately all the details about callsigns, frequencies and locations of beacons, so they carried lists of these, which, of course, they were supposed to destroy in an emergency. Some of the lists were short, giving only those beacons which the pilot expected to use on a particular mission; but, no matter how conscientious a German airman intended to be, it was inevitable that from time to time these lists were retrieved from captured aircraft. Such windfalls helped us enormously to narrow down our search but an indication of the success of 'meaconing' was to be found in the number of times the Germans were obliged to alter the frequencies and the callsigns of the various beacons. From our monitoring and from prisoner-of-war interrogation, it became obvious that the German bomber crews were increasingly distrustful not only of the Knickebein beams but also of their beacon-assisted navigational aids.

'If the British know where the beams are laid, patently they must be ready to attack us anywhere along the beams,' was the pilots' reasoning.

In fact, although some of our night-fighters did search along the route over which the beams were laid, they had few encounters, but the mere psychological deterrent to the enemy was valuable. It was important, therefore, that we should record every message which gave any indication at all of the success or otherwise of No. 80 Wing countermeasures or of the decreasing morale of the German crews. I recall this period as one of unholy glee at the alarm and despondency of the Luftwaffe crews.

Across all the tables used by the Luftwaffe for encoding messages there was a notice printed in red, which reminded everybody that 'DER FEIND HOERT MIT'. This warning that 'the enemy is listening' was reasonable enough. We were indeed listening, all day and every day, and night after night. During the hours of daylight, perhaps in the afternoon, we would hear German traffic associated with the aligning of the Knickebein beams in readiness for the night's bombing operations. 'It looks as though it may be hot to-night,' RKB would comment. 'Who's on duty, Mike? and how many have we got on watch? See they're properly briefed.'

When the evening watch came on they would be warned that bomber activity was likely, and some of the operators would be detailed to search the bands on which we knew by now the various bomber aircraft transmitted. It might be Cheadle, with its dozens of wireless operators, or perhaps it might be one of our out-stations which would pick up the first message. Immediately this became known the whole listening network would be alerted, and, if possible, the approximate position of the aircraft ascertained by D/F; and from then on Fighter Command and the appropriate fighter Group would be kept constantly advised.

It might take two or three messages before we could be certain which of the six codes the bombers were using that night, but from the moment we knew which code was to be used, it was more or less plain sailing. Almost everything that we intercepted in the 'LM' codes we could read without any great difficulty.

Fighter Command at Bentley Priory, Stanmore, would tie up our information with their own about hostile plots on the table in the Filter Room, and then the chases were on. Meanwhile No. 80 Wing would also have been alerted, and they would start up their appropriate jammers, if these were not already operating.

In the stuffiness of the blacked-out Operations Room at Kingsdown, and in the vans and huts of the out-stations, the Y girls and the RAF operators would hunch over their radio sets, earphones glued to their heads, listening to the game of life and death. It became a matter of honour with us not to miss a single message transmitted by the Luftwaffe, however noisy the interference might be from atmospherics. On occasions, such as a raid that was known to be an important operation, we would, if possible, assign two listeners to some particular frequency, and so, by double-banking, ensure an absolute coverage.

The experience of that time has led many of us to agree, all these years later, that we are still hyper-sensitive to noise. We learned to detect faint messages through the most awful crackling of atmospherics as we strained our hearing to the limit to make sense out of them. But, inevitably, there were times when we heard only part of a message, and then the Duty Officer would try to puzzle out the whole message or its meaning. Any WAAF monitor who was not actually intercepting would offer her suggestions. It was essentially a team effort.

5

X-Geraet and the Coventry Tragedy

Beating the Knickebein was only the beginning of the radio war. Although by November the Germans had almost completely abandoned using this type of beam as a blind bombing aid, they had been perfecting the use of an even more accurate beam, the 'X-Geraet', which we initially code-named 'Rivers' and later 'Ruffian'. This was a much more complicated affair, needing special apparatus in the aircraft and highly-trained crews.

Much of the early intelligence regarding the setting up and use of beams was gleaned from messages that were sent between ground formations in high-grade cyphers encoded by a machine known to the Germans by the ancient Greek word 'Enigma', a puzzle, and the intelligence derived from which we came to call Ultra. Some time before the war information had filtered through to British Intelligence that the Germans were using this highly sophisticated enciphering machine for encoding secret messages between ground formations from the High Command down to Division and Corps level, and to their equivalents in the Navy, the Air Force, the SS and other state organizations. With the help of the courageous Polish Intelligence, whose cryptographers had been working since 1932 on a means of unravelling Enigma, the British Secret Service had obtained an example of a complete Enigma machine. With this, and after months of painstaking study of intercepted messages, the cryptographers at the Government Code and Cypher School – Station X at Bletchley – had evolved an electro-mechanical means of breaking some of the Enigma cyphers. Others, like the naval cypher, which remained unbroken until 1941, were to prove more difficult.

The way the machine worked was roughly like this. The operator would type his message on a keyboard similar to a typewriter or a teleprinter, but instead of the letters being struck on a piece of paper, each time the operator hit a key, a letter showed up in light in a little box. This letter was copied down by a second operator. Inside the machine was a series of drums or wheels on which were fixed the letters of the alphabet. The electrically-powered drums would revolve according to a pre-arranged setting and could be further complicated by the use of plugs to vary the connection between the drums and the lights. When the operator typed an 'a', according to the setting, perhaps a 'p' would light up in the little box, but the next time an 'a' was struck, it might appear as an 'x', and so on. When the first operator had finished typing his message, the second operator had a recorded message which was exactly the same length as the original but with all the letters changed. This now encoded message was transmitted by W/T which the recipient was able to unscramble by putting the encoded letters through the same process in reverse. The setting of the drums and the plugs was the key to the secret and it was only by using early computer technology that the brilliant mathematicians at Bletchley were able to work out which setting was being used at any one time.*

A very special kind of intelligence is needed to tackle the breaking of high-grade cyphers, particularly when it is known that they are constantly changing. I cannot pretend to understand the intricacies of how the Enigma machine worked, or how it was possible to break the system even with the aid of a computer, since a computer has first of all to be programmed. The Germans were convinced that their Enigma cyphers were unbreakable, and as they were oblivious of the fact that, from as early as May 1940, our cryptographers at Bletchley had started to find a means of deciphering some of this traffic, they went on sending signals between formations giving precise details of their activities and intentions.

During the early days of the war many of the secret messages sent between units of the German forces operating within the Reich were passed by landline – by teleprinter or telephone – but as the RAF achieved more and more success in disrupting communications a greater proportion of this traffic was, of necessity, sent over the air. Since speed was so vital to the progress of the war, where distances were great or the front line was fluid, such as in the occupied countries, the Mediterranean, the Balkans, the Russian Front and in Africa, radio was the obvious method of communication. Needless

*Ralph Bennett gives a full explanation of the working of the Enigma machine in his *Ultra in the West*, pp. 21–33.

to say, the more messages the cryptographers and intelligence staff at Bletchley had to work on, the quicker they became at decoding and evaluating them.

But, of course, before the traffic – which we in the Y Service called 'E' traffic – could be deciphered, it had to be intercepted, and to this end, the monitoring network with listening channels and D/F facilities for pinpointing the enemy stations had to be expanded quickly both at home and abroad. The Headquarters of this side of the Y Service was in a minor stately home called Chicksands Priory, in the Midlands, surrounded by a veritable cobweb of aerials capable of receiving the most distant signals. Working in this complex were dozens of wireless operators, both men and women, keeping a twenty-four hour watch on Axis ground communications. By the middle of 1942 Chicksands alone had increased its cover to 100 receivers listening to German traffic, with a further 10 sets monitoring their Italian allies. As the Germans constructed some 100,000 Enigma machines during the war, the enormity of the task can be appreciated.

One of the first of the innumerable successes that Ultra was eventually to present, and an illustration of the dramatic part this special intelligence played in the conduct of the war, came on 17 September 1940. From various intelligence sources the British Chiefs of Staff were well aware that Hitler was amassing an armada of naval and air forces ready for 'Operation Sealion', the invasion of Britain. But on that day Bletchley was able to decode a message ordering the dismantling of air-loading equipment on Dutch airfields. This, the Chiefs of Staff deduced, marked the end of the threat of invasion, and confirmation was soon forthcoming that Hitler had been forced to abandon his plans, at least for that winter.

So efficient did Bletchley become in handling this material that there were even cases where, during poor conditions for reception, the German recipient of a signal was obliged to ask the sender for the message to be repeated, whereas our listening stations had recorded it fully the first time. This placed British Intelligence in the position of knowing the contents of a signal before the intended recipient. One of the better examples of this in the early days of the Mediterranean war was when the British Chiefs of Staff knew at the same time as most of Rommel's troops, and possibly even before them, that they were to form the 'Afrika Korps' to bolster up their Italian allies in Libya.

There is little doubt that Enigma traffic was the greatest single source of high-level intelligence to be made available throughout the war. Marshal of the Royal Air Force, Sir John Slessor, in referring to the character and methods of some great leaders – Churchill, Montgomery, Patton and Dowding – wrote in 1974: 'It may detract a bit from the glamour surrounding some of them to know that they might not have done so well, had they not so often held in their hands pretty full details of the enemy's strength and dispositions, logistic situation and operational plans, before and throughout the battles.'[1] As the records become available all too slowly in the Public Record Office, it will be interesting to see if he is proved to be correct.

In order to preserve the security of this highly confidential source, information derived from Ultra was frequently prefixed, for the benefit of those who were not initiated into the secret, by the camouflage expression: 'The following recovered from a wastepaper-basket. . . .' or, more simply 'from a special (or reliable) source.' At Kingsdown, not then knowing what Station X was reading into this high-grade traffic, we would marvel at the carelessness of the German High Command for leaving secret litter in their wastepaper-baskets. Later, of course, some of us were to know the truth but throughout the whole war, the number of those 'in the picture', even in the Y Service itself, was kept to an absolute minimum, and any information that was so obtained was treated with the utmost secrecy and discretion. It was imperative that the Germans should never know that we had broken Enigma. If they had discovered that we had done so they might well have evolved another encoding machine even more sophisticated which we might have had even greater difficulty in breaking.

For several months there had been indications that the Germans were using a more sophisticated aid to navigation than the Knickebein beams. As early as August we had heard a group of four beam-type transmissions in the 70-megacycle band, which was a higher frequency than those on which the Knickebein beams operated. Air Ministry Intelligence believed that the special Luftwaffe bomber unit, KGr 100, which was highly trained in the use of V H F beams, was to be used as what we later called 'pathfinders' for raids on this country. It was apparently planned that they should arrive over the target ahead of the main bomber stream, and, by dropping loads of incendiaries on the target, would light up the bombing area for the main task force.

The apparatus to be used for this new technique was the 'X-

Geraet'. It was believed to have been used for the first time against Warsaw. The beams, which we called the Rivers Group because they were referred to in Enigma signals by the names of German rivers, had probably first been used by KGr 100 in a raid against England during their attempted attack on a Birmingham aircraft factory on the night of 13/14 August. By the end of September it was known that this specialist unit had made forty raids on targets within the British Isles. KGr 100 was unquestionably the most highly skilled precision bombing unit, and it must have been infuriating for them to have to limit their bombing potential by reducing their effort to fire-raising. But their experience and navigational training had to be put to the most effective use, and this meant helping the main bomber task force to reach its target. The German aircraft, which were being increasingly deprived of the Knickebein beams by No. 80 Wing's jamming, were liable to go seriously astray without someone metaphorically holding their hand. Just such a fire-raising operation was to be carried out in the middle of November, and it was to become an operation which for years has been the cause of acrimonious controversy between historians. It was the heavy raid on the city of Coventry.

On 11 November Squadron Leader Denys Felkin reported that a prisoner-of-war, a pilot of KG 1, who had been shot down on 9 November, had been overheard discussing with a fellow prisoner a colossal raid which was scheduled to be launched against targets in the United Kingdom during the period of the full moon between 15 and 20 November. The targets would be Birmingham and Coventry, and every bomber in the Luftwaffe would take part. The prisoner thought that every Knickebein route would be used, and the intention, it was believed, was to attack workmen's dwellings with the object of demoralizing the working classes, who were believed by the Germans to be near revolt.[2] On that same day Ultra sources revealed that the Germans were planning a gigantic raid under the code-name 'Moonlight Sonata'.

By the following day Air Intelligence was able to amplify this information sufficiently to confirm that an air operation of very considerable dimensions was probable at the time of the full moon, and that Knickebein and X-Geraet beams would be employed. They were also aware that the Second and Third Luftflotten, including KGr 100, would be participating; that, furthermore, the operation would be in three phases and that there were three target areas, which were alternatives. The operation was to be co-ordinated by the Commander-in-Chief of the Luftwaffe, Reichsmarschall Hermann Goering.

It happened that at this time my Commanding Officer, Budge, was making one of his periodic visits to the Air Ministry in King Charles Street, Westminster, to discuss policy and developments. On this occasion he was sent for by Air Commodore L. F. P. Blandy, the Deputy Director of Signals Y. Blandy handed him a teleprinter message from Bletchley which began with the then usual euphemism for Ultra information: 'Following recovered from a wastepaper-basket'. Budge did not at that time know of the existence of this source. The message gave details of Operation 'Moonlight Sonata' which was to take place on the first night that the appropriate weather conditions prevailed. The message also stated that radio signals would be sent at 1355 hours each day on a stated frequency in W/T consisting of groups of four letters. On the day selected for the operation the group 'Mond' ('moon' in German) would appear in the early groups of the message.

Long afterwards Budge recalled:[3] 'While I read the message Air Commodore Blandy made a telephone call and asked someone to come into his office. This turned out to be a Group Captain from one of the operational branches who, after introductions, said that it was quite clear that this was to be a sizeable attack on a Midlands town, which one he did not know, but for which a counter-operation 'Cold Water' was to be carried out. The intention behind this was that, as almost all German bomber bases in Holland, Belgium and France were known, it was proposed to bomb these bases at last light on the day of their proposed attack with all our available bombers. The essential thing was that they – R A F Operations – must know the day on which the attack was intended.

'I pointed out that a most efficient organization existed for the interception of W/T traffic at Cheadle which would, no doubt, be instructed to keep a special watch on the frequency given at the time stated. Our job at Kingsdown was the interception and interpretation of radio-telephony and navigational signals and I had already learned that incursions into another unit's field required protocol to be observed. Air Commodore Blandy readily agreed that it was Cheadle's job and they would, of course, be instructed to cover the situation as a matter of priority, but asked if I would not also cover it to make sure it was not missed. It was a matter of great importance.

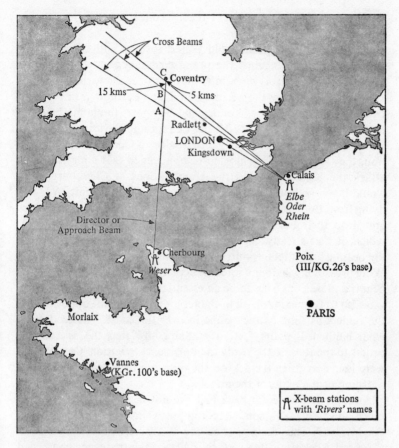

The Coventry Raid, 14 November 1940, showing the alignment of the approach or director beam and the cross-beams – the X-beams or 'Rivers' beams – laid on to the target. Aircraft of K Gr 100 took off from Vannes in Brittany, flying along the director or approach beam. At point A, the bomb-aimer heard an advance signal indicating the commencement of his run-up to the target. At point B, as he heard the fore signal, 20 kilometres from the target, he started a mechanical computer involving a stop clock. At point C, he heard the main signal and stopped the bombing clock, after feeding into the computer the correct height information from his altimeter. The mechanism then automatically calculated when the bombs should be released.

Naturally, as he was the boss, I readily concurred and the meeting ended.'

The plans for Operation 'Cold Water' covered both offensive and defensive measures against the proposed attack, and they were to include security patrols by bomber aircraft over the various airfields known to be used by the Second and Third Luftflotten in the Low Countries and in France. Vannes and St Leger, the home bases of KGr 100, were to receive particular attention in the attack. A heavy raid was also to be mounted against a selected German city. In addition, the Director of Signals had recommended that aircraft should attack the Knickebein and X-Geraet stations at Cherbourg. This would be carried out by aircraft of the special signals unit, WIDU, flying from Boscombe Down. They were to navigate along the beams and drop their bombs over what was known as 'the silent zone' which, it had already been determined, existed immediately above the beam transmitters. Radio countermeasures in the form of No. 80 Wing providing maximum interference with the enemy's navigational beams and beacons were to be an essential part of the defence. There was also to be maximum night-fighter and anti-aircraft opposition to the raiders as soon as they came in over the coast. The records of what happened in the Coventry affair show that the operational orders to the RAF to be ready to implement Operation 'Cold Water' were issued at three o'clock on the morning of 14 November – the morning of the night of the attack.

As soon as Budge got back to Kingsdown, he called me into his office and told me in some detail about what had happened at the Air Ministry. Then he instructed one of our best wireless operators, Corporal Allen, to watch very carefully on the frequency concerned at the scheduled time each afternoon. The moment he heard the group 'Mond', he was to inform the Duty Officer. Allen was a most conscientious operator, and he recorded meticulously the four-letter groups which the ground station transmitted on the stated frequency at the precise time each day. At 1355 hours on the afternoon of 14 November, Allen heard the group 'Mond' sent twice during the course of a message. Earlier in the morning of that day we had heard preliminary activity on the beam frequencies.

There could be little doubt about this being the day for the attack. RKB immediately telephoned to Cheadle to check whether they had also heard the message, and to ask if they had advised the Air Ministry about it. To Budge's surprise, they told him that they had not heard the signal, so he immediately telephoned the Air Ministry and gave them the information. In view of all the arguments and discussions about whether there was a warning, it should be noted that a post mortem report compiled by the Air Ministry on 17 November,[4] two days after the raid, clearly reveals that by three o'clock on the afternoon of the raid, No. 80 Wing was able to report that the X-Geraet beams were intersecting over Coventry. All RAF Commands were informed, as were Home Security and Home Forces.

During that night of the Coventry raid, I was the Duty Officer at Kingsdown and I can remember vividly all that happened. Soon after the evening watch came on duty, we, along with those at Cheadle, started hearing messages from the pilots of the aircraft of K Gr 100. They flew from their base at Vannes and came in over the south coast of England, and in accordance with their normal procedure, they transmitted very few messages on the way to their target. But we did hear them querying with their control whether the beams were laid on that target. The control assured them that this was so. I had a discussion over the telephone with the Air Ministry, who asked me to verify whether the German controller's reply had been that the beams 'were laid on target' or 'were not laid on target'. I had confidence in our WAAF monitor and after checking with her, I confirmed that the message had read 'were laid on target'. From subsequent messages which we heard it was obvious that No. 80 Wing's jamming was causing little interference in the reception by the aircraft of the X-Geraet beams. We were to learn later that our jamming had been ineffective as it was transmitted on the wrong audio frequency.

There was a brilliant moon that night, and the evening had been crisp and clear with excellent visibility. K Gr 100 had little difficulty in locating their targets. Shortly after eight o'clock we heard the German aircraft advising their base that the target was well ablaze, and that they were returning home. The city of Coventry had been showered with incendiaries. By this time the main attacking force of enemy bombers was streaming in across the south and east coasts and converging on their target, the flames of which they must have been able to see from miles away.

All that we and those at Cheadle could do was to continue monitoring the vast amount of traffic from the raiders, realizing miserably, from the number of callsigns that we heard, the enormity of the raid.

News came through to us by telephone from Fighter Command reporting the destruction being wreaked on the stricken city. Not until dawn was breaking did the last of Goering's bombers return home. Over 500 aircraft had taken part in the raid, most of them reaching the target where they dropped vast quantities of incendiaries, high explosive bombs and parachute mines and leaving Coventry to mourn its 554 dead and almost a 1000 injured.

Only one German bomber was destroyed over England that night. So clear was the sky that the single searchlight beams were ineffective; the raiders had no difficulty in spotting any approaching night fighter and were easily able to take evasive action. But whilst the Luftwaffe was creating havoc with Coventry, the Royal Air Force was retaliating with the 'Cold Water' plan. Coastal Command aircraft attacked the airfields of Vannes, St Leger, Rosendael, Gravelenes, and the jetty at Calais; and Bomber Command raided military objectives in Berlin as well as several major airfields in France and the Low Countries. In all a total of twenty-seven airfields were attacked, and ten of our bombers were lost during the night's operations.

Meanwhile, two aircraft from the special signals unit based at Boscombe Down attacked the beam transmitting stations on the Cherbourg peninsula, and they were successful in straddling the Knickebein IV beam station with bombs. It was apparently put out of action, as it ceased to operate that night. An instruction was intercepted ordering the X-Geraet beam station at Cherbourg to switch to another target. The reply came that the apparatus was unserviceable, so it was presumed that our special bombing attacks had succeeded in putting two beam transmitters out of action during the night.

There has been a great deal of speculation over recent years in an attempt to apportion the blame for what has been thought of as the inadequate defence of the city of Coventry. There has also been what can only be described as confusion over the facts relating to that raid. I have already mentioned some of the facts, but they are so important that they bear examination. First of all it was known from combined prisoner-of-war and Ultra sources that there was to be a major raid on one of three targets. It was to be carried out at the first opportunity permitted by the weather during the period of the full moon. We also had advance warning that a message would be sent to the Luftwaffe units that were to take part in the operation on the afternoon of the proposed raid, indicating that Operation 'Moonlight Sonata' would proceed that night. But which was to be the actual target? Information from Ultra sources had suggested various alternative targets.

Although we heard the German beams being tested earlier in the day, we did not know until two o'clock on the afternoon of the night of the raid that it was to be mounted that night and until three o'clock that the beams were intersecting over Coventry. Even with the speed at which this information could be handled, it must have been at least four o'clock before any decisions could possibly have been reached about alerting the essential services. Coventry could never have been evacuated in time; and in any case, what was to be done with Birmingham and the other towns which had been named as possible alternatives? It will be recalled that we had heard a message later, during the operation, ordering the beam to change targets, and had the station not been unserviceable it might well have done so. It is an inescapable fact that any evacuation plan would not have been practicable.

And then, as early as eight o'clock, the first incendiaries showered down on Coventry. It would certainly have been a physical impossibility to get all the guns and searchlights needed for defence, as well as the fire engines and other equipment, moved from other places to the target zone. There's no denying that Coventry suffered, and suffered grievously, but it is an equally hard fact that, with the information that was available to us, there was no way in which the city and its people could have been saved from that suffering.

The Germans' success in their onslaught on Coventry had been due partly to the use by KGr 100 of the X-Geraet beams and it was said at the time that 'possibly gaining inspiration from the name of the Commanding Officer, Aschenbrenner, the German High Command decided to let KGr 100 blaze a trail for the de-Knickebeined Luftwaffe'. Whatever the reason, for the rest of the period of the Blitz, the group's main duty was to act as fire-raisers.

The X-Geraet beam system was more complex than the Crooked Leg, which we had now fairly satisfactorily pulled. Instead of the one major beam and an intersecting beam, as in Knickebein, the X system employed several beams, and the use of the system required much longer and more careful training of the bomber crews. The Germans had not expected to be deprived of Knickebein quite so soon, and they had insufficient apparatus and trained crews for the X-Geraet to be installed in every bomber aircraft. It was because of this that they had been forced to extemporize by using the highly skilled KGr 100 to lead the main bomber force to the target.

If the scientists, Dr R. V. Jones, Dr R. Cockburn, Dr F. C. Frank, Mr T. L. Eckersley, and their teams – who were always referred to by us as 'The Boffins' – were to evolve a successful countermeasure to this new bombing aid, it was essential that they should have a complete understanding of how the beams operated and their probable efficiency. This was where the monitoring service could help. Every signal that it was possible to hear which might be relevant to the setting up of the beams, to their use by operational units, and even to details about the units themselves had to be recorded. A word here, or an expression there, anything might provide an important clue.

Messages were intercepted referring to 'Left and Right Oskars', and to operational frequencies which always seemed to be given as so many 'Anna' degrees. We heard words like 'Leitstrahl' (main beam), 'Muehle 1 and Muehle 2' (Mill 1 and Mill 2). A mention was made of a 'Kontrollwagen' and various other code words. Every message that we monitored was carefully logged, and then sent forward for detailed analysis by both Station X and the scientists, who compared our logs with information obtained from prisoners, from crashed aircraft, from Ultra and from the results of the special signals investigation flights. Agents sent back details of apparatus seen in France and the Low Countries; and the reports made by the aircrews of Bomber, Coastal and Fighter Commands after they had returned from operations were all examined for further clues.

The experts were soon able to deduce that this latest system incorporated a principal pair of beams transmitted from a given station. These were the 'Right and Left Oskars', spaced about two degrees apart, with 'dashes' between the pair and 'dots' on either side. Only one beam of the pair could be pointed at the target, usually the right beam. The pilot would fly along this beam, which had dots to the right and dashes to the left. If, however, he veered too far off course to the left, he would then cross over the left hand beam and would again hear dots. Thus if he was hearing dots, he could not necessarily tell which way to turn to correct his course, so to assist him a coarse director beam was superimposed. By use of the coarse beam, the pilot was able to keep to the right of the main pair of beams. A number of cross-beams were so aligned that they intersected the main beam – the 'Leitstrahl' – at right angles. These cross-beams were adjusted according to the target selected for attack.

Each enemy aircraft carried two receivers: one for the pilot, and the other for the observer. The pilot would fly along the main approach beam, and as each cross-beam was heard the observer would press a lever. A special clock mechanism in the aircraft would then automatically calculate the precise moment for the release of the bombs, even actually tripping off the bomb release mechanism. So meticulously directed on to the target were the beams that bombing with this sophisticated radio navigational aid was much more accurate than with the Knickebein beams, provided always that the beams were not subjected to interference from us.

But our scientists were not to be caught napping. As soon as the X-Geraet signals were first heard, and with the prior experience of the Knickebein system to help them, they were immediately at work on countermeasures. The jammers that they evolved were code-names 'Bromides', to keep to the hospital theme. They were a refinement of the 'Aspirin' jammers which had caused such havoc with the Knickebeins.

Each day, after the high command of the Luftwaffe had selected the target for the night, the beam stations would be advised by Vannes, and given the details of timings and bearings. The German bombers would take off about dusk, and the pilots would soon be heard reporting the efficiency of the beams. That was just what we needed. We knew a raid had started, and from then on we and Cheadle would be intensely busy logging every message that was transmitted, and we would be able to warn all those who might be concerned.

As soon as the Luftwaffe realized that we were interfering with their X-beams, they naturally made attempts to fox us by changing the frequency on which the beams were transmitted. Unfortunately for them this entailed quite considerable radio activity, all of which we carefully recorded. Despite their efforts, however, they never did succeed for long in frustrating No. 80 Wing's jamming efforts; and the intercepted messages enabled Station X to keep an almost complete diary of the raids on which KGr 100 used this type of beam.

Once again the German love of order let them down. The regularity of the distance between the various cross-beams helped our scientists to establish their source. Subsequent photo-reconnaissance confirmed the positions of the beam stations, and also provided scientific details of the actual apparatus that was being used. Gradually, but surely, the jigsaw puzzle was being completed.

There was now no doubt that the talents of the specialist unit, KGr 100, were being used to lead the main bomber force to the target by flying ahead and marking it by setting it alight. Our next move was obviously to mislead the main swarm and to fool them into bombing the wrong target. This was done by starting up decoy fires, but these had to be lit sufficiently close to the real target to deceive the enemy. Starting decoy fires miles away from the target would have been useless. Although, especially in clear weather, some of the more experienced pilots were not fooled by these decoy fires, which were code-named 'Starfish', we at Kingsdown were delighted when we heard a pilot reporting 'Target attacked . . . several fires blazing,' when we knew that his bombs had fallen inoffensively on a Yorkshire moor rather than on the factories of Derby. The fires that he thought that he had started at the target were, in fact, decoys lit by Colonel (later Sir John) Turner and his 'Starfish' team.

But, to be fully effective, countermeasures had to be used with subtlety. Crude methods would have led the enemy to discard completely a system which they felt was a total failure and they would then have been forced to seek something better, perhaps even more complicated, which might prove much more difficult to frustrate. As we listened, we could get the feel of the reaction of the bomber crews, and we could tell from what we were hearing that they were becoming very disillusioned with the beams.

As it was inevitable that it could not be long before the Germans would introduce new methods of navigation and blind bombing, it was one of the prime aims of signals intelligence and the scientists to anticipate the introduction by the enemy of a new aid, and also to anticipate its probable type and use. For that reason all information that could possibly be made available had to be fed quickly to the scientists. This required, amongst other things, that the Y Service should be adequately equipped with good receivers to cover all wave bands, with ancillary equipment able to take accurate measurements. In turn, the scientists would have to be capable of rapid appreciation of any new type of transmission, and be ready with suitable counter-measures.

The electronic war was accelerating, and we in the Y Service were very much a part of it.

6

'Little Screw'

During that long winter of the Blitz, when enemy bombers swarmed over the British Isles dropping their murderous loads, we in the Kingsdown network, along with our colleagues at Cheadle, listened to every message that was exchanged between the bomber aircraft and their ground controls that it was possible to hear. At the same time we were eavesdropping on every aspect of Luftwaffe traffic in Western Europe, including the day and night fighters, the transport aircraft, the shipping reconnaissance patrols and the weather patrols, even training flights. Meanwhile it was the task of the Chicksands set-up to keep a constant watch on the high-grade Enigma traffic between the ground formations.

It was imperative that we should be constantly on our guard for new types of traffic, new callsigns and new frequencies. We never knew what we might hear next. There was always the possibility that we might pick up some early clues to a new method of attack or defence which was being introduced by the Germans.

The start of one such discovery was made one evening at the beginning of October 1940. The night watch at Kingsdown had just settled down in front of their sets with their headphones hugging their ears, and their fingers twiddling knobs as they searched for a station. As always, there was that somewhat restless period when we waited for the nightly raiders to come on the air. Suddenly one of the girls bent her head and began to write furiously in her log-book, pressing her earphones even more tightly to her head in order to catch every word of the message.

I went over to her bench and read over her shoulder what she was writing down. It was a most peculiar collection of words, which were obviously code-words. They seemed to me to be sheer gobbledygook.

'He keeps talking about a little screw, or something like that,' she said to me, 'and closing a parlour. I can't make head or tail of it. Can you get it?'

Grabbing a pair of headphones, I quickly tuned in on an adjacent receiver. It was certainly new traffic. I was not even sure that it was the Luftwaffe. It could well have been traffic between military ground stations.

The next morning, having been duly warned to keep their wits about them, one of the operators suddenly called out: 'There he is again. I've got him loud and clear. He's playing around with his little screw again.' There was a loud and understandable guffaw of mirth from the RAF operators sharing our Operations Room. 'What's so funny about that?' exclaimed the WAAF in all innocence, looking hurt.

The traffic was being transmitted on a couple of adjacent frequencies in the 3- to 6-megacycle band and it was almost entirely in code. The messages appeared to refer to some form of training, and as luck would have it, they seemed to be experiencing trouble; some problem that we could not quite grasp but it apparently had to do with the equipment that they were operating. As usually happened when a German airman ran into radio troubles he broke into plain language instead of speaking in code. This was the lead we needed. It was now obvious he was the pilot of an aircraft, and that he was being directed by a control station.

But what was the pilot up to? Was he a fighter under special control? And what exactly were those new code-words? And what did they mean? I rang up the Air Ministry and asked for their advice, but they were unable to enlighten me. We arranged to double-bank the watch to ensure that every word was recorded. As we listened to further transmissions, there was constant reference to 'Kleine Schraube' (Little Screw), to 'Stube' (Parlour), and to 'Laterne' (Lantern). The aircraft seemed to be orbiting a given point and he received a steady stream of instructions from the ground control.

It seemed at first as though the traffic was related to some form of blind flying practice, or perhaps night interception by mechanical means. At this time we were still not certain about the extent to which the Germans were making operational use of radar. As always when new code-words were heard, or a different type of traffic, I asked the girls to listen most carefully in an attempt to determine exactly what code-words were used and in what context, as this would help Station X and the scientists to break down the way the system worked with a view to possible countermeasures.

But what *were* the words they were using? Was it really 'Kleine Schraube' or were we mishearing? Finally, a few nights later, a German pilot enunciated the words mostly clearly in a sonorous voice – 'Klei . . . ne Schrau . . . be.' Now there was no mistake. But what did a screw do? It turned, or was turned, but why? Some of the other code-words we had already fathomed, as they were used by the day-fighters. 'Kirchturm' (church-tower) was 'own height'; 'Gartenzaun' (Garden-fence) would be 'airfield', but what was 'Stube abschliessen' (Close the parlour)? And was the 'Laterne' (Lantern) to which they constantly referred a beacon, a searchlight, or what? Did it mean cloud illumination? 'Antreten' followed by a figure between 0 and 360 seemed logically to indicate an approach course.

Each morning a despatch rider rushed a copy of the 'Little Screw' logs to Dr Charles Frank, a young scientist who was one of Dr Jones' team in the Air Ministry. Another copy went straight to Station X at Bletchley for their analysis and each day I telephoned Rowley Scott-Farnie at the Air Ministry. 'They were at it again last night,' I would report. 'Doesn't anyone yet have a clue what the traffic is all about?'

'Mike and her "Little Screw"' became a source of ribald remarks but I went on pestering everyone about it. The traffic was disturbing, not only because it was so completely different from anything that we had yet heard but also because Reggie Budge, Jonah Jones and I had a very worrying suspicion that it sounded like a system of radar-controlled fighter defence. The Germans might even be using airborne radar. In actual fact, German airborne radar was not fully operational until the spring of 1942, though we may well have heard practice flights several months before this. But so far there had been no indication that the Luftwaffe was using any system of ground controlled interception similar to that used by the RAF. The unit we were listening to was obviously still in a state of training, but if our suspicions were correct then the sooner we sorted out the way the patrol worked the better. We realized only too well that it would prove an additional menace to the RAF bombers attacking targets in Germany and German-occupied Europe.

I made copious lists of every context in which we heard the various code-words, trying to determine from the messages how the patrol worked. Every possible source of additional information was examined by us, by the Air Ministry, by Bletchley and by the scientists at

TRE. Information derived from prisoner-of-war interrogation reports, Bomber Command de-briefings, photographic reconnaissance surveys and 'other sources', including Ultra, was scrutinized for clues. I also managed to persuade one of the local night-fighter stations, under some pretext or other, to let me sit in on a controlled night-fighter operation to see if it would give me any clues to help in decoding the traffic.

Up to October 1940, Bomber Command's night raids over the Reich had encountered comparatively ineffective opposition from German fighters. The OKL (Oberkommando der Luftwaffe) had refused even to contemplate the possibility of heavy scale bombing attacks at night. 'Night-fighting,' they had said, 'it'll never come to that.'

But they had begun to realize that the boasts of Goering and his ilk were very suspect, and that now they had a lot of leeway to make up in the sphere of radar and radar-controlled fighters. This was a typical example of the German High Command's marked disinclination from time to time to face up to unpalatable facts, a characteristic which persisted throughout the war. If, however, the Germans were now beginning to operate a system of radar-controlling night-fighters, Bomber Command was faced with a new and serious hazard. In view of that it was imperative that the fullest possible information should be gathered with the utmost speed. We faced some tough questions. How did the system work? What were its limitations and its likelihood of success? How many aircraft were involved, and what sort of aircraft were in use, and over which areas? And, most important, what steps could be taken to reduce the potential danger?

At the time when the Luftwaffe started to bomb England with the aid of their beams, our search for information about the systems that they used had been simplified by the availability, from time to time, of prisoners-of-war and of aircraft shot down over the British Isles. Captured airmen would sometimes divulge information about equipment and tactics; crashed aircraft supplied equipment for examination – even if slightly 'bent' when salvaged. But no similar source of information would be available regarding the German night-fighters operating over Europe. If and when they crashed, they crashed on their own territory and we would be denied access to both airmen and equipment. So it was obvious that monitored traffic would be virtually the sole source of intelligence regarding the enemy's method of controlling their night-fighters.

There was evidence even early on in the war that the Germans had developed a form of radar – their 'DT' (Dezimeter Telegraphie) – and a watch had been instituted at Hawkinge to monitor the pulse signals which were associated with the radar techniques being employed. Now, from various sources, we had confirmation that they were using an improved version of this apparatus, which they called 'Freya'.

Y intercepts in both Enigma (Ultra) and lower-grade enciphered traffic began to indicate that the enemy's night-fighter force was on the increase and also that a new radar apparatus – the 'Wuerzburg', as it was called, whose primary concern had been gun-laying, was being used in connection with the control of the night-fighters. Whereas the Freyas with their rectangular mesh aerials could pick up an approaching aircraft from sixty or more miles away, and were able to determine range and bearing, they could not estimate the height. As was always the case, the height of an approaching enemy aircraft was of vital importance. The Wuerzburg, however, was able to calculate altitude but it was deficient in range, which was restricted to about twenty-five miles. Later, in the winter of 1941, the Luftwaffe introduced an improved version – the 'Giant Wuerzburg' – the paraboloid aerial of which looked rather like an immense electric 'bowl fire' twenty-four feet across, and had a much greater range and accuracy.

On 17 July 1940, Goering had instructed Colonel (later General) Josef Kammhuber to set up a night-fighter organization. At that time, his resources were very meagre, with only thirty-five aircraft at his disposal. Eventually he was to have under his control six Geschwader comprising about 700 specially equipped aircraft. These operated with six searchlight regiments, and about 1500 radar stations, which were spread across Western Europe all the way from Norway right down through to Sicily – and on over into Africa.

General Kammhuber's original system of night-fighting was his so-called 'Helle Nachtjagd' (illuminated night-fighting). This relied on searchlights, which had been previously warned by the long-range radar, to pick out the intruder so that the night-fighter could close in for the kill. But this system had proved expensive in both men and machines, as the anti-aircraft guns that worked with the searchlights had a disconcerting tendency to hit the wrong aircraft.

It was obvious that Kammhuber would have to separate the night-fighters from the guns. So whilst leaving some searchlights to work with the anti-aircraft batteries that guarded the towns and cities, he set up a belt of searchlights which ran parallel to the coast, and away from the artillery. This searchlight belt was divided into a series of 'boxes', or zones, in which individual night-fighters patrolled. With the assistance of waving vertical searchlights and visual beacons, the ground controller guided the aircraft towards the raider as soon as it came within radar range. Hopefully the searchlights would catch and hold the bomber in their beams until the night-fighter could attack.

The main snag about this system was that it depended for success largely on the weather. A low cloud bank would render the search-lights almost useless, despite the assistance of radar-controlled 'Master' searchlights, from whose allegedly bluish-tinged light the RAF bombers found difficulty in escaping no matter how much they resorted to evasive action. When trapped in the merciless cone of these searchlights the bomber was like a moth trying unsuccessfully to escape from the pursuing lights.

Usually the German's first intimation of a forthcoming raid was from their Y Service – the 'Horchdienst' – which was under the control of Hauptmann Kuhlmann. At that time our radio security in the RAF was not all it should have been. In fact, it was at times definitely weak. There was, for one thing, far too much chatter and general testing of radio sets and other electronic equipment in the bombers before they even set out on a raid. Whenever Bomber Command mounted an offensive operation, just as we would listen in to the Luftwaffe, so also would Kuhlmann's people conscientiously monitor our bombers right from the time they became airborne and set course for their target. From the 'Kuhlmannmeldungen' – as the Luftwaffe called the monitored traffic – their Y Service frequently knew as early as three o'clock in the afternoon how many British bombers would be operating that night.

The advance 'Kuhlmann' warnings were also passed to the controllers of the 'Little Screw' patrols, and as soon as the route through which the raid might pass could be calculated, the enemy night-fighters from nearby airfields would be ordered into the air. Apart from alerting the waiting night-fighter patrols, this valuable information was used to good advantage by 1/NJG 2, the only long-range intruder Gruppe. With great audacity they would attempt to swoop down on the bombers as they took off for the raid or catch them on

their return as the landing lights were switched on, scattering frag-
mentation bombs amongst the taxi-ing bombers.

Eventually we came to learn that the 'Little Screw' system of night-
fighter interception was nicknamed 'Himmelbett' (four-poster bed)
by the Germans. It is indicative of the conscientious listening of the
WAAF linguists of the Kingsdown organization that when the
night-fighters started their 'Himmelbett' operations in earnest on the
Dutch-German border in October 1940, we heard the associated
traffic almost immediately. By early November sufficient messages
had been recorded from this 'Little Screw' traffic for it to become the
subject of serious, urgent research by the Air Ministry, by Bletchley
and by the TRE scientists at Worth Matravers, who thought at first
the intercepts indicated a use of airborne radar. By 3 January 1941,
Dr Jones and Dr Cockburn were able to issue a preliminary report
outlining how it was believed the system worked; yet even as late as
May 1941 the Deputy Director of Intelligence 4 (DDI4) in the Air
Ministry had to admit that 'It is impossible yet to elucidate full technical details of the system employed but it is believed to be similar to
our GCI.'[1]

Pending the arrival of a British bomber into his 'box', the German
night-fighter pilot would be ordered to orbit a radio beacon (the
Little Screw) conveniently situated as a waiting point. This, we soon
realized, was the meaning of 'Stube abschliessen' (Close the parlour).
The longer-range Freya radar would first pick up the incoming
bomber but as it was unable to determine height the controller had
to wait until the raider came within range of one of the Wuerzburgs
before he could finalize his plans for the attack.

Whilst the night-fighter's movements were being followed by one
Wuerzburg, another station would be carefully tracking the approaching bomber. We were to learn subsequently that the positions
of both aircraft were displayed by means of red and green lights on a
special plotting board made of ground glass, called a 'Seeburg' table,
over which the controller sat directing operations. Also filtered into
him were messages from the German Observer Corps – the 'Flugmeldedienst' – many of whose plots were passed in a clockface code.
Meanwhile their Y stations were also monitoring the progress of the
raid.

As soon as our bomber approached his 'patrol zone', the German
controller would warn the pilot of the night-fighter in the relevant
waiting area ('Stube') and direct him towards the intruder in the

interception area ('Raum'). Listening in we would hear the encoded instructions:

'Mauerblume. Antreten 180' (Wallflower, (i.e. enemy activity) – Fly course 180).

With the help of the vertical master searchlight, the twin-engined night-fighter would stalk his quarry, constantly receiving a stream of instructions from his controller as to what course, height and distance to fly.

'Kurier Hanny sechs. Lisa, Lisa, dreimal Lisa' (Enemy bomber flying at height 18,000 feet. Turn left, 30 degrees to the left).

Further orders would follow until:

'Otto Otto' (Enemy in searchlight beam), the controller would advise the night-fighter.

'Ich suche' (I am searching for the enemy), the pilot would reply. More instructions would then be given to bring him close to his prey.

'Immer noch Otto, Otto' (Enemy still in searchlight beam). Until, finally, the night-fighter would be within visual range of the bomber and would inform his control:

'Ich beruhre' (I am touching, meaning 'I can see the target'). The pilot might then ask for the searchlight to be dowsed, and as he closed in on his target –

'Angreifen!' (Attack!)

and we would sit there, helpless, as we monitored the traffic, hoping against hope that we would not hear a jubilant 'Sieg Heil' from the pilot, which signified a kill.

One could almost feel the relaxation of tension if instead we again heard the pilot announcing:

'Ich suche,' (indicating that he had lost the enemy and was still searching).

Sometimes we would hear an anxious 'Kreuzung, Kreuzung.' Then we knew that this time the RAF had won the round. The enemy night-fighter had been hit, and was heading for home.

I always found it in my heart to commiserate with the Luftwaffe pilots who had to learn such long lists of complicated code-words and expressions. But inevitably in the heat of combat, or during a daytime training session, the occasional pilot would forget signals security and break into plain language. This helped us enormously to unravel the meanings of the various messages, but such occasions were all too few. Cracking the codes entailed sheer mental slogging over the monitored traffic, puzzling out how the patrol system worked. Hours and hours would be spent in conjecture about the meaning of what we were hearing. Sometimes our guesses were correct, other times they did not fit. We had to be watchful lest we should convince ourselves that such-and-such an expression meant a certain action, for we could all too easily find ourselves heading along a blind alley. It became a race between the Air Ministry, Station X, TRE and us to be the first to break the meaning of a code-phrase.

We were not always able to hear all the transmissions during a patrol. Sometimes the signals would fade. But we were not the only ones to suffer from this. Poor communications were in the early days one of the weaknesses of the German night-fighter system. We would frequently hear a pilot asking his controller to repeat instructions, particularly during the day practice flights, when one aircraft would play the part of the 'British bomber' and another would try to intercept him. Kingsdown could often have been of help to him – and indeed later we were, except that we deliberately misled the German pilots. This was a form of countermeasure which commenced in October 1943, and which was to be known to us under the code-name 'Corona'.[2]

Sometimes we would hear, especially during practice flights, a rattled controller having considerable trouble working out his plots on the Seeburg table – this would result in more chat than usual, which delighted us.

'Leopard von Jaguar,' we would hear. 'Antreten 50, Kann nicht stimmen. Nochmal antreten' (I am uncertain of your position. Alter course again).

'Warten Sie,' the controller would order. 'Jetzt antreten 270. Ah, das kann eben stimmen' (Wait. Now fly course 270. Ah, that's more like it).

Then there might follow another instruction: 'Antreten 310 eine Minute' (Fly 310 for 1 minute).

'Ist gut. Nun langsam wiederholen' (Fine, now overtake slowly).

This was typical of the traffic that we heard during training sessions.

In the spring of 1941 it was decided by DDI4 Air Ministry, that it would be helpful for me if I were to go to Bletchley to discuss the 'Little Screw' traffic – and at the same time to learn a little of how the cryptographic centre worked. I could by now get away occasionally from Kingsdown as both Barbara Pemberton and Liz Strang had been commissioned and they could help with the intelligence duties.

D

Station X was centred on a secluded Victorian country house surrounded by a number of wooden huts outside the then small Midlands town of Bletchley. It was under the control of Commander Alastair Denniston, a quiet, middle-aged man, who seemed more like a professor than a naval officer. It was to him I had to report and I was immediately impressed by his kindness and by the courtesy with which he greeted me. I was a very junior officer and abysmally ignorant of things cryptographic.

I was handed straight over to the Air Section, where I was soon to meet Professor 'Josh' Cooper. He was one of the most unforgettable people I have ever met. A brilliant mathematician, and much younger than he appeared to be at first sight, he was the archetypal absent-minded academic – slightly deaf, incredibly unkempt in his dress, dark hair flopping over his face, hair which he constantly brushed back with a vaguely irritated gesture, often thereby dislodging his thick spectacles. Yet one was aware of an inner brilliance, of an intelligence far beyond the realms of the normal human being.

When I first entered Josh Cooper's office, which was in one of the huts, he was working on high-grade Italian cypher traffic.

'It's double transposition,' he informed me, 'and they're changing it pretty frequently.' He waved me to a chair – 'Sit down, sit down.'

I sat quietly for a while, waiting for him to speak.

'We'll break it, you know. We'll break it,' he assured me seriously and brushed aside the errant lock of hair. Then with a rather impatient gesture, he pushed aside the papers on which he had been working, and took up a large buff envelope, out of which he shook a motley collection of bits and pieces. Not having then been initiated into the secrets of Enigma (Ultra), I wondered vaguely if this was one of the 'contents of a wastepaper-basket'.

But no. 'These came from the pockets of the observer of a bomber shot down over East Anglia,' Josh explained. 'He baled out and his aircraft crashed in the sea.'

Picking up an odd scrap of paper, he continued – 'Now, let me see what I've got.'

As though suddenly remembering I was there, the Professor peered at me through his spectacles.

'You're from Kingsdown, I believe,' he said. 'Do you know about these things?' He waved at the scraps. Then he continued kindly: 'I'll show you how we glean information from these oddments.'

Picking up a small piece of paper, Cooper explained: 'Here's a

ticket for a performance in Rotterdam. Foolish fellow – he should
have thrown that away. Careless, very careless.' He shook his head
disapprovingly. 'This tells me he was in Rotterdam on 24 March.
Now he would not have been there on leave. He would go home to
Germany for his leave. So that means he was on a pass, weekend or
evening. That suggests he was stationed somewhere not far from
Rotterdam that night.'

Shaking out the remains of a squashed packet, he commented:
'These cigarettes are of a kind sold in Belgium and Holland. Definitely not German. Good, good, further confirmation. So he probably
flew from an airfield near the Dutch-German border.'

And so he continued, meticulously examining and considering each
scrap from every angle. Nowadays we are blasé about detective
stories, seeing them so often on the television – but to me, then, it
was quite fascinating to see how, from such little things, so much
information could be gleaned.

Eventually Josh started his summing up: 'Now who do we have
based in that area? He was shot down on the 26 March and we know
from intercepts the units operating from that area on that night.' He
checked a list that he had on his desk, and then he finally announced
that he was quite confident that the aircraft had belonged to a unit,
that he named, which was based at a certain airfield in Holland.

The captured documents had already been examined by the
prisoner-of-war interrogation centre, which had sent them on to
Station X to see if the cryptographers could discover any further information which would add to their knowledge of the prisoner and
his unit before confronting him again. Armed with such further intimate details, a skilled interrogator might persuade a young airman
to divulge more, and possibly valuable information about his unit
and his aircraft.

'But you came about "Little Screw".' The Professor suddenly
brought the conversation round to my main reason for being at
Bletchley. 'I have been reading the logs. I have some here. You've
managed to pick up some good traffic. Very interesting. There's no
doubt there is a definite connection with GCI. But let me have your
views.'

Somewhat diffidently in the presence of such a brilliant man I
explained that I was convinced that the traffic was a form of controlled night-fighting on the lines of our own GCI but making
considerable use of a beacon or beacons, and of searchlights.

Cooper already knew that we had taken D/F (direction-finding) bearings on the traffic, and he believed that the activity originated in the Venlo area on the Dutch-German border. He agreed the aircraft were probably Me. 110s or Ju. 88s of NJG 1, which was the first Luftwaffe night-fighter Geschwader.

Together we went carefully through the batch of logs that I had brought with me, and he confirmed that our findings at Kingsdown were in agreement with those which had been arrived at by the experts at Bletchley and TRE. He commented: 'Bomber Command tells me pilots flying over the Zuyder Zee have reported seeing clusters of searchlights on their return flight from raids at the same time as night-fighters have attempted to intercept them.' This seemed to be a confirmation of our decoding of 'Stangen' (poles) as 'searchlights'.

As the war developed there was cause for British Intelligence to be grateful for the orderliness of the German mind. With them everything followed a set pattern; there was little room for individuality in the Luftwaffe. This made it much easier for us to read into monitored traffic. There was a regularity which made repetition inevitable, and repetition is a God-send to the code-breaker.

An interesting sidelight to this occurred early on in the war. Station X – always known affectionately to us as 'BP' for Bletchley Park – had broken one of the lists of callsigns used by the German Air Force, which the cryptographers nicknamed 'The Bird Book', but they were uncertain whether one of the groups included the letter 'i' or 'j'. There seemed to be an inexplicable variation. This somewhat irritated the precise, mathematical minds of the cryptographers. Many months later, when a copy of the lists was captured, it was noted with great satisfaction that, owing to a printer's error, there was a faulty-shaped letter in one of the groups. Some Luftwaffe signals officers and radio operators had read the letter as an 'i' and others as a 'j'. The honour of the code-breakers was satisfied.

There were various snags in the 'Himmelbett' (Little Screw) system. In view of the limitations of the various forms of radar used by the enemy and the width of the front over which the British bombers were likely to enter or depart on raids, the coastal belt had to be divided into a series of 'boxes', with three or more 'boxes' being worked by one controller. It did not take us long to deduce, from the monitored traffic, that although the German controller could handle four or five aircraft at one time, he could only deal with one bomber and one night-fighter in a single 'box' at any one time and that each night-fighter's patrol area was defined by lights on the ground. Also each night-fighter communicated with his control on a different frequency from the one in the next 'box'. This was the source of a very serious defect in the system.

Sometimes we would hear a pilot who was on the trail of a British bomber become quite furious when he was ordered to hand over the pursuit of his quarry to another night-fighter. But his frustration was to no avail, and back he was vectored to his own 'Little Screw' beacon to await the arrival of another bomber.

'Sansibar Nord (Sud, West, Ost)', we would hear the controller order. This meant: 'Leave the interception area at once and fly north (south, west, east) and stooge around outside the interception area'.

The whole performance would begin all over again when the next bomber came within the pilot's area, and it would go on until his patrol time came to an end. This might be because he had run short of fuel or perhaps had engine trouble – 'Pferd lahmt links' – (Horse lame on left, meaning 'trouble with port engine'). Whatever reason, perhaps merely the end of his flying time, he would be heard asking for permission to land.

The obvious defect of this system was that if the RAF were to fly during the course of a raid both in and out in a stream over a narrow front at close intervals of about twelve miles distance, the whole German night-fighter system would be saturated. When we cross-checked with Bomber Command de-briefing reports we found that there was clear confirmation of this theory. If the bomber force strayed over a wide front the losses were higher than if they flew in a narrow stream, and woe betide any stragglers. Anyone who allowed himself to straggle behind was liable to be picked off by one of the German night-fighters. Timing and concentration both on the inward and the outward journeys over the night-fighter belt were imperative. When later the British bombers flew on the so-called 'saturation' raids, the Luftwaffe had to review its night-fighter tactics.

By the summer of 1941 Kingsdown and the HDUs on the East Coast at Gorleston, Ingoldmells and Scarborough must have been monitoring 95 per cent of the Little Screw traffic, which meant that we were listening to anything up to thirty patrols a night. One of our chief headaches came in sorting out as quickly as possible which patrol was operating because the Germans would be constantly changing callsigns and frequencies; and our own direction-finding facilities were still inadequate. At first we were helped by slight variations in the code-words used by the different patrols, but by the following winter the code was more or less standardized throughout the whole of the night-fighter force, and since no map grids or place names were given we had problems of identification.

Fortunately for us, it was not long before Bletchley observed, by analysis of the logs from the various monitoring stations, that when a night-fighter ended his patrol he changed over from the high frequency on which he had been operating to medium frequency, and he then asked for landing instructions in W/T. This was an exciting lead for us because we were then able to identify the units involved from their M/F callsigns. And when, in the spring of 1942, we heard the night-fighters asking on their operational frequency in R/T for landing instructions, we knew that this was confirmation that the night-fighter force had been augmented by the use of single-engined fighters. Since these were single-seater aircraft, they were never to be heard operating on medium frequency or using W/T; they were obliged to ask for their homing instructions on their operational frequency in R/T.

On a few occasions we did hear R/T traffic on 553 kc/s using Little Screw code-words, but it was obvious from the traffic that it was either from anti-aircraft or searchlight batteries, and this was further confirmation that the night-fighter patrols were linked with these batteries.

When we made further examination of our logs, we also realized that there was no mention of any other German aircraft, except for an occasional reference to the relieving night-fighter or to the aircraft in the next box having shot down a bomber. This posed the question of why there was no mention of German bombers. The Luftwaffe was busy 'blitzing' the British Isles. How did they get out and get back in again across their coast without being challenged by their own night-fighters? Did they fly on a special route, at a specified height, or had they some means of identification? The monitored M/F homing traffic provided one answer. When the German bombers returned from raids over England they crossed the Dutch coast between the Hook of Holland and Brouwerdoven, and they usually flew below a certain height, leaving the night-fighters to tackle the RAF bombers which would be flying much higher.

It was vital that Bomber Command, which had recently intensified its night bombing activity, should know as much as possible about how the German night-fighter patrol system worked. The success of their raids and the lives of the crews of the bombers depended on such information, and although monitored traffic was providing much of it, there remained a great many questions about the extent and the efficiency of the enemy's defences.

In July 1941, at the suggestion of Mr S. J. Grose, a signals expert who was working on Air Vice-Marshal Lywood's staff at the Air Ministry, it was decided that the signals investigation flights of No. 109 Squadron should be extended to include a systematic survey along the known night-fighter belt, listening in to the pulse transmissions that were known to be associated with Freya and Wuerzburg radar.[3] The plan was for specially equipped Wellingtons to fly with a wave of bombers so as to allay suspicion, and when they were over the night-fighter belt they should be manoeuvred, deliberately, in such a way as to provoke reactions from both search-lights and night-fighters. These reactions would be carefully recorded. Arrangements were made for Kingsdown to pass to the special air-craft the frequencies used by the enemy's night-fighters in the area in which the investigational flight was being carried out, as soon as the relevant patrols and frequencies could be identified. We were warned in advance which route the bombers would take.

Some of Bomber Command's aircrews, who were operating at the time, were convinced that if they switched on their IFF (Identification Friend or Foe) the German searchlights would be dowsed. For various technical reasons TRE doubted the feasibility of this, but nevertheless No. 109 Squadron was asked to investigate this during their flights. The outcome was that there was no conclusive proof that this happened but, since there was just a possibility that the use of IFF over enemy territory might have some beneficial effect, the sets were slightly modified so that the bombers could use them in this way. Despite careful analysis over several months, Bomber Command's research team could still find no justification for the theory, but for psychological reasons the aircrews were allowed to continue using their IFF during raids.

In the Y Service we knew all too well that the best signals security was absolute silence in the matter of transmissions – of any sort. 'The enemy is listening . . .', 'Der Feind hoert mit. . . .' It was inevitable that the Germans should find a way to make use of these IFF transmissions for tracking our aircraft as they proceeded on their raids, and the Y Service's fears about this practice were to be confirmed later when, in the autumn of 1943, we intercepted traffic between units of a German Air Force Signals Regiment, that showed that the enemy had found a means of triggering off the IFF device carried by the RAF bombers, and were thus able to track the bomber formations as they flew over occupied territory.[4]

Each of the Wellingtons of No. 109 Squadron engaged in these investigations carried special radio personnel. Among these were men such as the young scientist, Eric Ackermann, who had already made several flights to monitor transmissions from radar stations, and who had been given an honorary commission in the RAF in case he had the misfortune to be shot down. Trained artillery and searchlight observers were also carried on some sorties, mainly to enable them to give expert opinions as to whether or not the enemy searchlights were radar-controlled.

As these special aircraft flew back and forth over the danger areas, despite being coned in searchlights, with anti-aircraft barking around them and with the very real possibility of being attacked at any moment by radar-controlled night-fighters, the operators calmly and meticulously noted the reactions of the enemy opposition, recording all the details of the signals associated with the actual enemy radar. With special equipment and these specialist operators on board, the aircrews were warned that if they were to be shot down, they should make every effort to 'ditch' in the sea.

It was bound to happen that several of this squadron's aircraft failed to return from operations. Unfortunately, amongst the special operators who were lost was Sergeant Mathieson, the young soldier who had been the first monitor of Luftwaffe R/T during the Dunkirk evacuation in the early Hawkinge days, and who had subsequently transferred to the RAF.

After their return, the special Wellingtons' logs would be carefully compared with ours in order to marry up the instructions we had heard being given to the night-fighters with the reactions noted by the No. 109 Squadron aircrews. I have often wondered whether the other Bomber Command aircrews realized how much they owed to the investigational squadron.

As soon as the approximate position of a radar site could be determined from analysis of the No. 109 Squadron logs and Y information, including Ultra, photographic reconnaissance aircraft would try to pinpoint the station, the pilots flying in as low as they dared in order to get detailed photographs of the installations. By the autumn we knew that the German radar coverage extended from north Norway to Bordeaux in the south. But from monitored traffic we realized that the performance of the Wuerzburg was poor at low levels, and that if an aircraft was sufficiently nimble in its manoeuvres, the Wuerzburg had difficulty in holding it because of the narrowness of the beam over which it could 'see'. This had been verified by No. 109 Squadron. So this pointed to the desirability of evasive action by the bombers at speed, especially in making changes in height. Soon Group Captain Blandy, as DDI4 at the Air Ministry, was able to issue a report, along with a map, which was of great operational value to all RAF Commands. It showed the ranges and heights at which aircraft were liable to be detected by German radar.

Our D/F facilities, especially at Gorleston and Sutton Valence, had been steadily improving, and we now had a rough idea of the area in which the Little Screw patrols operated. But H/F D/F is notoriously unreliable at night. We knew that control stations with callsigns such as 'Kiebitz', 'Jaguar' and 'Tiger' operated in the northern belt below the German-Danish border and 'Seeadler' and 'Zander' worked in the southern sector over Holland, and that the coastal patrol areas were about forty miles apart. Twice already the patrol areas had been extended to cope with the increase in British bombing offensive. From the callsigns of aircraft which we heard asking for homing instructions we knew to which units they belonged and where they were based. But we needed to be more precise about the exact location of the various Himmelbett stations so that we could warn Bomber Command as quickly as possible when and where the night-fighter patrols were operating.

Already the whole picture was crystallizing to the point where the routing of a raid was considerably influenced by information derived from Y sources. The one thing of which we were certain was that it was imperative that the Horchdienst should be deprived of early warning. We knew from other monitored traffic and from prisoners-of-war that German Y was covering areas well across England. With the knowledge of how much we of the Y Service could learn from intercepted signals – both wireless transmissions and navigational aids – we stressed to Bomber Command the need to keep radio silence before setting course for the target, especially if flying high, since the higher an aircraft flew, the greater the range at which signals could be monitored and the aircraft detected by radar. Every indication pointed to the value of early saturation of the enemy fighter defences.

It soon became evident from various sources that the inner chain of the German radar was not switched on until warning had been given by the long-range Freya station. This meant that if our bombers flew in low enough to escape detection by the outer chain they might also escape detection by the inner chain. But what was most important was that there should be no regular pattern of approach to any target, either in height or route. Above 15,000 feet the bombers might avoid the worst of the 'Flak' but, against that, they would be spotted earlier; and, in any case, a night-fighter could fly higher than a loaded bomber. There must have been many a bomber pilot who, not realizing the reason, thought that his briefing indicated a suicidal level at which to fly: but evidence of the effectiveness of these tactics was confirmed by the 'Knapsack' raid on Antwerp, when low-flying Blenheims slipped in and were on their way back home before the German fighters were even airborne.

That summer, we at Kingsdown became a little unpopular in some quarters of the RAF. So worried were we over the lack of signals security by some of the RAF aircrews and controllers – we would occasionally tune into their frequencies and listen to what they were saying on the air – that it was decided that we should log some of their traffic so as to be able to show them just how, to use a popular warning at the time, 'Careless talk cost lives'. In due course, we produced our logs and we made our point.

The Luftwaffe was constantly introducing new code-words, and about the beginning of August 1941, we heard some new phrases and what appeared to be a variation in procedure by some of the Little Screw patrols. As soon as the night-fighter had taken up his position in the 'waiting room' ('Stube' – parlour) and a British aircraft was reported in the vicinity, instead of the usual course directions being given by the ground station the fighter would be asked whether the 'star shines' ('Stern leuchtet'). The 'star' was apparently some sort of visual indicator in the aircraft. But despite its 'shining', the ground station still had to give instructions regarding course and height. We did not hear this new technique often – it was probably still in the experimental stage – but whatever it was that was involved, it certainly did not appear to result in more successful attacks on British bombers. Was this perhaps what we had been dreading? Had the Germans now developed AI (airborne radar)?

We were wrong in this surmise. We had noted previously that the ground station always needed confirmation from the aircraft whenever the fighter contacted Little Screw and was circling round in the waiting area. Whenever he strayed outside his Stube, he would be ordered back and told to circle over the visual beacon 'Karussel fahren' (ride the roundabout), presumably as a means of identification by the radar. This had indicated to us that the German aircraft were not yet fitted, as ours were, with an efficient IFF apparatus. In the new technique, there seemed to be no need to ride any roundabouts. We were to learn that the 'Stern' was, in fact, the newly developed FuGe 25, the German equivalent to IFF, which was to be installed in some aircraft. The instrument came into operation when the Wuerzburg radar 'illuminated' the aircraft, triggering off a transmitter in the machine which sent an identifying code signal. This was received by the Wuerzburg on a loud-speaker, and the controller could then differentiate between the plot which was the raider and that which was his own fighter aircraft. Airborne radar was to come later.

The Little Screw patrol belt had been restricted to an area roughly from Ostend to the Island of Sylt, and from Hamburg inland as far as Cologne, in three main areas of control, guarding the approaches to the Ruhr; one between Eindhoven and Cologne, another between Leeuwarden, Schipol and Deelen, and the third in the Rheine-Delmenhorst area. But the 'Kammhuber Line', as it became known, was extending all the time. Already the HDUs at Strete, Shaftesbury, and Beachy Head were picking up traffic over north-western France. The line was soon to stretch from Norway in a wide sickle-shape to the Swiss Frontier, with further patrol areas in Italy, Sicily and Africa; and the time was approaching when there would be little hope of routing a bomber offensive round the controlled areas.

By that autumn of 1941 a new code-word had crept into the R/T messages sent by the Little Screw patrols. The word was 'Emil'. We would hear a controller asking if 'Emil, Emil' is functioning – 'Ist Emil Emil klar?' The fighter would often reply that it was not. Sometimes they would use instead of the word 'klar', the word 'activ' (active). As far as we could make out, the 'Emil Emil' apparatus was

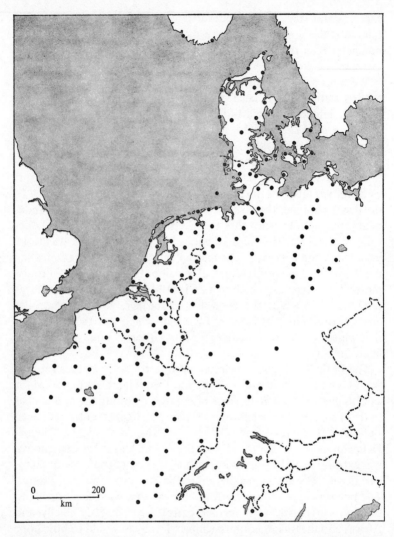

The Kammhuber Line. The map shows the locations of the radar control
stations throughout Western Europe by the spring of 1943 before Allied
use of 'Window' led to the introduction of the 'Wilde Sau' technique of
night-fighting.

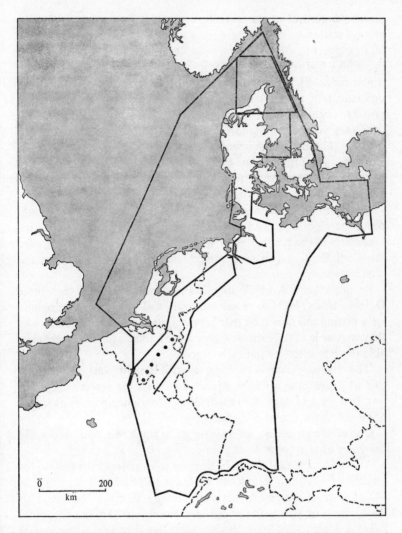

Kleine Schraube, September 1942. Only the six night-fighter control stations in Belgium had been pinpointed in the corridor known as the Kammhuber Line. The larger area from Scandinavia to the Swiss border was known to be a general air-defence region.

under the control of the aircraft, and the only part played by the ground station was to ask whether it was functioning, or, occasionally, to suggest that it should be used. It was clear to us that the Germans now had some form of airborne detection apparatus. Whether it was radar AI, as we knew it, or infra-red was not yet clear, and, unfortunately, the Germans' level of signals security was too high to give us conclusive evidence either way.

'Kurier verreist,' the pilot of the night-fighter would tell his controller – (The British bomber has made off).

'Achtung! Aufpassen auf Emil. Marie 2,' the ground station might then warn – (Look out! Watch your Emil Emil. British bomber 2 kilometres away).

Listening to these messages, we realized that the controller could bring the night-fighter to within between half a kilometre and two kilometres of the bomber, after which the pilot or the navigator used his 'Emil Emil', which we assumed was a special device for actual interception.

By now the WAAF Y linguists at Kingsdown and the Home Defence Units (HDUs) round the south and east coasts of England were getting to know the Little Screw pilots quite well. This was why they were able to spot any new procedure immediately. We were even able to recognize some of their voices.

'The Viennese chap is on Tiger control tonight,' one of the monitors at Scarborough might inform me down the special telephone link that we had with our out-stations. 'Poor chap sounds as if he's got a cold,' she would add cheerfully.

One of the girls even went so far as to think she could recognize the voice of a pre-war boy-friend.

A Little Screw pilot would be ordered to patrol over his beacon for anything from a few minutes to well over half an hour, according to the number of customers that were coming his way. The Me. 110s could stay on patrol for about two hours but the Ju. 88s could manage longer. Realizing this we were not surprised when a pilot would announce 'Ich habe Durst' (I am thirsty). We knew when he would be running short of petrol. The control would then order him back home, unless the RAF had bombed his base, in which case he would be sent to an alternative airfield. Then we would hear another aircraft ordered to take over the patrol. The British bombers were never pursued beyond a forty-mile limit from the enemy coast by the night-fighter patrols: but they still had to contend with 1/NJG 2 'intruding' over their homes bases, just as the RAF did over the enemy airfields.

Whenever an attack was successful, the Wuerzburg (or Giant Wuerzburg) would follow the crippled British bomber down until it crashed, leaving the fighter to be sent back to his beacon ready for the next pursuit.

It would be wrong to give the impression that all the coded expressions were quickly and easily broken by us, for in some cases it took weeks and weeks of concerted effort by the Air Ministry, Station X, the scientific experts at TRE, and by us, before we could sort them out. But in the end we had a pretty good picture of exactly how the patrol system worked and the meaning of the various instructions which were passed to the night-fighters by the controller.

Eventually, a copy of the 'Signaltafel fuer Tag und Nachtjagd' (Code table for Day and Night fighters)[5] was captured and it was interesting to see how accurate our interpretations had been of the various messages intercepted by us.

As the success of any bombing operation that might be mounted by the RAF depended largely on getting through the Little Screw belt to the target, consideration had to be given by our planners to jamming the patrol system. The Royal Navy had been jamming for some time the gun-laying radar on the coast of northern France with the object of interfering with shelling attacks on convoys passing through the Dover Strait. So in September 1941 the possibility of jamming the radar associated with the searchlights and guns as well as the R/T transmissions of the actual Little Screw patrols was discussed by the Radio Countermeasures Committee. But they were worried lest jamming should give premature disclosure of our knowledge of the patrols. There was also the possibility that such jamming might incite the enemy to take corresponding action against our night-fighters.

The Chief of Air Staff, Air Chief Marshal Sir Charles Portal, felt very strongly 'that we should never refrain from using a device to assist our bombers merely because the capture of such a device would help the German bombers to beat our defences. On the other hand, we should never risk giving the Germans any idea which, though it improves our own defences at home, would improve his as well.'[6] Portal made this statement in November 1941, and experimental jamming flights were made by No. 109 Squadron aircraft soon afterwards. But it was not until early in the following year, when the increased use of 'Emil Emil' caused the patrols to become such a danger, that steps were finally taken to interfere by various means with the German signals.

Although monitored traffic and the investigational flights were providing a great deal of valuable information about the extent of the enemy radar chain and the way their patrols actually operated, they had not yielded, by the end of 1941, much about the technical side of the radar equipment on the ground. It was becoming urgent that we should capture an enemy radar set.

Out in North Africa, the Eighth Army was having considerable success in the Western Desert. They were asked as a matter of the greatest urgency and importance to make every effort to capture some of the enemy radar apparatus, preferably intact, and to ship it home so that the experts could make a detailed examination.

It was decided, at the highest level, that another, and possibly quicker, way to obtain some of the German scientific and technical data that was needed by the scientists was to lay on a surface raid across the Channel, to seize the essential parts of a working radar station.

The story of the daring Commando raid that resulted in the capture of equipment and German personnel from the Wuerzburg station perched high on the cliffs at Bruneval, in Normandy, on 28 February 1942, is already one of the legends of the Second World War. Brilliantly planned and executed, this successful raid produced much of the information that was needed by Dr Jones and the scientists at TRE. They were then able to make a thorough examination of the pieces of equipment brought back from Bruneval. Even many of the Germans admired the sheer audacity of the operation and one German paratroop leader stated after the war 'that the Bruneval operation was outstandingly the best, both in conception and execution, of all the British commando raids'.

Right: 'Mike', 1942

Below: The first operations
room at A M W/T Station,
Kingsdown, with W A A F
monitors intercepting on
Hallicrafter sets

3 *Above:* Wing Cdr R. K.
Budge, O B E, Officer
Commanding, Kingsdown
network

4 *Above right:* Baroness
Rudi de Sarigny (*née*
Eisenklam)

5 *Opposite:* Do. 17s over
Woolwich Arsenal,
7 September 1940

6 *Above:* German radar
station in northern France
under attack showing close
proximity of Freya and
Wuerzburg radar sites for
controlling night-fighters

7 *Top right:* Armoured car
used to control jamming
aircraft on 'Jostle' operations
in Western Desert at L G 75,
1941. *Left to right:* P/O
D. Fenton, Lieut. Col. R. P. G.
Denman, F/O G. F. Mason,
Squadron Ldr W. B. S.
Simpson

8 *Bottom right:* 'The Museum'
headquarters, No. 276 Wing,
Heliopolis, Cairo

9 *Left:* Gun-mounted yogi aerial used for pinpointing Wuerzburg radar stations by No. 162 Squadron

10 *Below:* No. 162 Squadron Wellington showing gun-mounted yogi aerial. *Left to right:* Sgt Dreever, L/R/O T. O. Taylor, RN, Lieut. P. T. W. Baker, DSC, RNVR, unidentified, Sgt A. Levy, F/O M. Knowles and C. O. V. Willis, DFC, RNZAF. Note the naval hammock which was slung in the aircraft for comfort!

11 *Top right:* Underground coastal defence operations room at War Headquarters, Valletta, Malta

12 *Bottom right:* At Headquarters, Western Desert, Air Force, 1942. *Left to right:* Group Capt. Guy Carter, A/V/M 'Mary' Coningham, Wing Cdr Fred Rosier, Wing Cdr Barney Beresford, Wing Cdr Clive Mayers

13 *Left:* Wing Cdr D. H. S. Rusher, DSO, OC, No. 162 Squadron, with Wing Cdr G. R. Scott-Farnie at Bilbeis, 1942

14 *Below:* Barrage of fire meeting Axis raiders silhouetting No. 4 Field Unit in Western Desert, 1942

7

Luftwaffe Pressure

Even before the Luftwaffe realized that we were interfering with their X-Geraet beams, Dr R. V. Jones had his suspicions that the enemy had developed another system of beam navigation which was much more sophisticated than X-Geraet or Knickebein, and that the system involved the use of a ranging device together with a directional beam. He believed that there might be some connection with the information that had been received very early in the war from a secret source through the British Embassy in Oslo. This information had referred to the development of a device that was capable of measuring the ranges of distant aircraft.

In October 1940 an Enigma-enciphered message addressed to a 'Wotan II' station in the Cherbourg peninsula was intercepted by Chicksands. The message gave the 'Y co-ordinates' of a specific target, and on examination these proved to be the co-ordinates of the Armoured Corps Depot at Bovington Camp, in Dorset. A few nights later this camp was attacked by enemy aircraft.

Shortly afterwards, we noticed for the first time in our work at Kingsdown a beam-type signal during our monitoring of VHF traffic on the 40- to 50-megacycle band. But the characteristics of this new signal were quite different from those that we associated with either the Knickebein or the X-Geraet beams. At the same time we also heard messages transmitted on the same frequency band which appeared to be traffic between aircraft of III/KG 26 and their ground control. This unit, which we knew was involved, like its rival KGr 100, in fire-raising at target areas, was based at Poix, in Normandy. There seemed to us to be some connection between the new signal and the intercepted traffic.

Our routine at Kingsdown was such that if anything new, or even slightly different, was heard, the Duty Officer was to be informed immediately. The operator would hold the frequency and take down everything that he or she could hear, whilst another operator, who did not happen to be monitoring traffic at the time, would search the wave-band to see if similar traffic could be heard on a neighbouring frequency. It was not long before we were able to determine that the new beam-type signal and the aircraft traffic were indeed related, with the ground station transmitting on 42.7 megacycles per second and the aircraft using the higher frequency of 46.9 megacycles per second. The early messages that we heard of this type of traffic originated almost certainly during practice flights. This was fortunate because, inevitably, the occasional difficulty arose which resulted in signals security being broken by either the aircraft or the ground station. As Dr Jones has written: 'Luckily for us the Germans made the classic mistake, which we were later to repeat, of trying out devices on a small scale before depending on them for major efforts.'[1] We probably learned as much at Kingsdown about the various Luftwaffe systems from slip-ups made by the Germans during practice as in actual operations, possibly even more.

We immediately reported our findings to the Air Ministry, and once again we had an influx of scientists at Kingsdown. But it was not until both the aircraft and the ground station signals were viewed on an oscilloscope, and their characteristics compared, that the experts were convinced that they were the same. A radio signal is rather like a fingerprint: it has identifiable characteristics. Arrangements were made for these beam-type signals to be analysed and photographed at our outstation at Hawkinge, so that, by knowing more about them, the scientists could develop efficient countermeasures.

Was the new signal that we were hearing emanating from the 'Wotan II' referred to in the Enigma message that had been intercepted a few weeks earlier? And were 'Wotan' and the range-finder mentioned in the Oslo Report one and the same? We were to learn later that there were two types of 'Wotan' stations: 'Wotan I' was the code-name given by the Germans to the X-Geraet beam stations, whilst 'Wotan II' was the control station of the new navigational aid which the enemy called 'Y-Geraet'. Only one beam appeared to be involved in this new system, and Dr Jones soon gave it the code-name 'Benito'. His explanation for this was 'because we reckoned that Mussolini was the one-eyed end of the Axis'.

Most of the operational messages that we heard in this new traffic were sent in one of the three-letter codes used by the bomber units, but sometimes the international 'Q' code would be used. For instance, 'QTE 340' might be sent, which meant 'correct course to 340 degrees'. There were also lapses into plain language R/T, and a certain strange sequence of messages was sent during each raid that greatly puzzled us. What did EEE TT EEE 777 FFF mean? It seemed to be connected in some way with the actual bombing. What did 'Auf' signify? We believed it meant opening something, or turning something on. A message sent by the aircraft with 'Bra' followed by a number seemed logically to indicate the number of fires ('Braende') started in the target zone. What could be '90 more'? Probably the number of degrees to be added to the course. And where were 'Loge', 'Bruder', 'Schmalstigel', and other code-words which were obviously code-names for targets?

We noticed that although course corrections were constantly sent by the controller to the pilot on his way out, it was not until he was on his return journey that the pilot would be given his actual position – usually in coded grid – and his course back to his base at Poix. He might also be warned of enemy activity near his base, or that night-fighters were patrolling in the Channel, or we might hear a pilot asking his control if there were any air-raid alarms at his base.

The Air Ministry arranged for No. 11 Group to send us radar tracings of raids to help us co-ordinate the monitored traffic with the radar tracks, and then, with the now improved direction finding facilities of the Y Service, we were soon able to fix the locations of the Benito stations. We had learned from Ultra that there were now two stations: one at Cassel, and the other at Beaumont, near Cherbourg.

Having been forewarned of the existence of a range-finding device and certain details of its method of operation, Dr Jones and Dr Cockburn, and their colleagues, did not take long to unravel the very complicated beam system, or to find a means of interfering with the transmissions. They deduced that the bomber flew along a complex, highly directional and audible beam, which was laid on a distant target. Inside the aircraft there was a special electronic analyser which could determine the position of the aircraft in relation to the beam. In order to find out how far down the beam it was flying the ground station would transmit a second signal superimposed on the main beam signal. This would be re-radiated by equipment within the aircraft. As the speed of radio waves is a known factor, the ground station could calculate, from the time that it took for the re-radiated signal to be received back at the Benito station, exactly where the aircraft was at the time.

Once the control could calculate that the aircraft was over the target it would send out a bomb release signal. This was the meaning of the EEE TT EEE signal that we had been hearing. We had realized by now that the aircraft of III/KG 26 could use either the Cassel or the Beaumont beam, and that once they had navigated on to the beam they normally kept radio silence until after they had left the target area. We could see from the No. 11 Group radar tracings the reason for needing fixes on the way home. They no longer flew on the beam.

We soon discovered that such a ground control could handle four or more aircraft during the same raid, each aircraft working on a slightly different frequency from the next, which meant that the control could differentiate between the various aircraft. The control also took the precaution of giving the aircraft's callsign when sending a message. This, in itself, was helpful information. But there were still many more questions to be answered, and again, No. 109 Squadron, under the command of Wing Commander W. S. Hebden, was asked to investigate the signals. Flying with experienced investigational pilots such as Flight Lieutenant C. O. V. Willis, the young scientist, Flying Officer E. J. Ackermann, and other special operators, including civilian personnel from TRE, made long and dangerous sorties listening in to the beam transmissions.

It was inevitable that one of III/KG 26s aircraft would be shot down. The aircraft was a Heinkel 111, number 1H + RT, which crashed at Eastleigh on 19 January 1941. The crew were killed, but amongst the documents that were salvaged from the wreckage there was a table from which it could be calculated that the code-word 'Loge' that we had been hearing was London, 'Bruder' was Bristol, and 'Schmalstigel' was Sheffield. We also learned the code-names for other towns, and it was further revealed that the pilot had approached his target from the direction of Cassel, where one Benito station was sited, and that he had intended to return direct to his base at Poix. The captured list also included magnetic variations at the various English towns, and a second table gave approach bearings for different targets.

It may be wondered why the aircraft was carrying such secret information on operations. But this was not a breach of security: it was because the radio operators of each aircraft needed to know this type of vital information while in flight, and as they could not be expected to remember so many details in the heat of action they had to have lists. From the examination of the captured documents it was also revealed that this Heinkel had been involved in a raid on Avon-mouth on 16 January and another one on Swansea on the following night. As we knew that KGr 100 had used X beams to bomb these same targets on those nights, this was confirmation that both X-Geraet and Y-Geraet beams could be directed onto the same target.

The countermeasures that the scientists of TRE had evolved for the Knickebein and X-Geraet beams would have no effect, of course, on this new system, which worked on the different band of 40 to 50 megacycles. Fortunately for us the early traffic that we heard in November had been during training flights, so that by the time that the Y-Geraet was in full operational use, and with the help of the prior Oslo information, Dr Cockburn had been able to produce a fairly effective jammer that he code-named 'Domino'. A receiver at Highgate, in North London, was used to pick up the ranging signal 'echoed' from the German bomber's transmitter; the signal would be passed through to the BBC's television transmitter at Alexandra Palace, and this transmitter would re-radiate the 'echo' on the frequency used by the German control. Thus, instead of the German control hearing the signal coming straight back from the aircraft it was completely swamped by the Alexandra Palace transmission. This made impossible any range measurement, and it resulted in the Y-Geraet becoming virtually useless as a bombing aid before it had even had a chance to show its potential.

We would hear at times the German control telling the pilot of a Heinkel as he approached the target: 'Measuring impossible, carry on on your own.'[2] It was essential, of course, for the purpose of satisfactory interference that No. 80 Wing's jamming transmissions should be on exactly the correct modulation frequency, otherwise the enemy controller would detect the difference. He would then be able to read through the jamming on his visual presentation screen. It was also necessary for the signal to be strong enough to confuse the controller into believing that it was indeed the aircraft under his control. To make sure of bringing into use really effective counter-measures a second Domino was set up on Beacon Hill, near Salisbury. Later, a third Domino operated from near Honiton, in Devon, to interfere with the Benito beams when they were directed against western targets. This was necessary because by now the Luftwaffe had turned its attention to Bristol, Avonmouth, Swansea, Merseyside, Belfast and Clydeside in an attempt to blockade the country by preventing imports from reaching Britain.

Meanwhile, combined Y Service monitoring revealed that once the target for the night had been decided upon, at some time during the day the co-ordinates for the target were given to the beam stations. Each of them would then calculate the necessary technical details for setting up the beam ready for the night's raid. Later in the day, transmissions from the crew of an aircraft would usually be heard as they made a trial flight to see that the beam was correctly calibrated.

We naturally kept a very sharp look out for this practice traffic, and we would advise No. 80 Wing immediately we heard either the traffic or the beams so that they could make preparations to jam the appropriate frequencies effectively and with the minimum of delay. During the actual raids, we listened not only for the first indication of an aircraft likely to use a beam, but also for the signals associated with the bombing procedure, and for any comments that the pilot might make regarding the effectiveness of his bombing attack, or difficulties with the beam.

The bombing accuracy of the Y beam system was in the region of 200 to 300 metres, as was proved in the early offensive flights before complete swamping of the beam had been effected, so the nation was indebted to the scientists and No. 80 Wing, who, for example, in March 1941 alone, managed to frustrate all but eighteen out of ninety bombing raids using this beam technique. Their jamming was so effective that the ground control was quite unable to order bombs to be dropped with any degree of accuracy. If, as the result of jamming, the fire-raisers were not successful in setting the target alight before the arrival of the main bomber attack, the whole operation would go off badly. 'No fires visible,' the monitors might hear a pilot of another squadron report. 'Will bomb alternative target.'

On one occasion, shortly after No. 80 Wing had started playing Dominoes with III/KG 26, they had a most successful jamming session. It was the night of 28 February/1 March and the squadron's target was London. The ground controller had not yet realized what was going on, and we heard him telling the pilot of one aircraft:

'You're doing nothing up there. You've probably switched on to telephony. Switch on (your Y-Geraet) now.'

Immediately after the bombing signal had been heard, the pilot was again reprimanded:

'You're making a . . . mistake. Have you understood?' The aircraft then despondently turned for home, reported when he crossed the coast, and admitted that 'no fires' had been started.

The control was equally vague about the whereabouts of another aircraft on that raid and suggested to the pilot that he should take 'an alternative target – go farther out – course about 100 degrees.' Again this led to some part of London having a lucky escape; the German raider dropped its load of bombs harmlessly at Ford End, near Dunmow, in Essex. Yet another pilot was heard to ask: 'Was ist mit uns los?' (What's the matter with us?) He, too, was given an alternative target, and eventually off-loaded his bombs outside Southend. One late-comer even went astray in mid-Channel, No. 80 Wing's jamming being effective to a distance of about twenty miles south of the Isle of Wight. He overshot London, and went on flying north-east towards King's Lynn. Then he was ordered to break off his task, and given an alternative target. He finally jettisoned his load near Broxted. No significant damage was done during this whole raid, and no bombs fell that night on any vital areas. No. 80 Wing had definitely won that round, and we, at Kingsdown, hugged ourselves with glee.

The Luftwaffe could not help but realize that there was something amiss, and a few days later we heard them testing the Benito apparatus over enemy-occupied territory, trying to reproduce the effects which they had experienced on their recent frustrated raids. Some of the interceptions we heard were statements such as:

'The notes we are receiving are very cut up and the receiver is faint and not functioning properly.'

'Press on the key.'

'Does reception resemble last evening?'

'Yes, but not one hundred per cent – there is a resemblance.'

'Switch on.'

'Now switch on again.'

'Everything is in order like this.'

'O.K. We can end transmission now.'

And back he flew to base – with the German 'Boffins' puzzling out what was happening to their new beam system. It cannot have taken them long because on 11 March a determined attempt was made to bomb the Beacon Hill jammer. Fortunately the damage caused was not enough to prevent it from operating the next night.

In an effort to counter our countermeasures, the Luftwaffe tried to overcome the jamming by changing their beam frequencies during the night. On 3 May, we heard some new code-words during a practice flight of III/KG 26. The name of a tree was given – 'Ulme' (Elm) or 'Ahorn' (Maple) – after which the pilot of the aircraft was asked to give the height at which he was flying. Then we heard the name of a continent or country, followed by the 'bombing signal', the message ending with the name of a bird, such as 'Adler', or 'Habicht' (Eagle or Hawk). We telephoned to the Air Ministry to tell them about this new development and informing them that, as far as we could gather, it appeared to be a new bombing routine involving the changing of the beam frequency. After examination of the logs of the traffic, the Air Ministry agreed with us, and we were instructed that as soon as we heard the 'tree' named during an operation, we should inform No. 80 Wing to stand by for a probable change in beam frequency. On average it took them less than ten minutes to change the jammers over to the new frequency, and once again we were able to frustrate the efforts of the 'fire-raisers'.

A few nights after this the unfortunate III/KG 26 had a bad night when they lost three of their Heinkel 111s. From the wreckage of each of the aircraft Y-Geraet equipment was salvaged. There was now nothing to hold back our experts. From their examination of the equipment it was obvious that the Germans had made the whole bombing procedure automatic; perhaps they did not trust the accuracy of their aircrews. Within a month, we had available a new countermeasure called 'Benjamin' and it was put into operation, with No. 109 Squadron flying investigational flights to test its efficiency. The countermeasure was, of course, more effective when the aircraft was nearer to the jammer than to his own beam station.

By June, there was a further development in that we began to hear at Kingsdown a quaint 'cuckoo' sound superimposed on the Benito beam which was transmitted from St Valerie-en-Caux during what was obviously a practice flight.[3] We could not then puzzle out the reason for its use, though we assumed that it was probably some new procedure to make jamming more difficult. The German scientists would, no doubt, soon have worked out a means of counteracting Benjamin but they had little opportunity at that time to experiment during raids over Britain. The invasion of Russia was imminent, and Goering was by now transferring many of the bomber units to the Russian Front. But this was by no means the last we would hear of Benito.

Since the time of their success during the bombing of Oslo KGr 100 had been regarded as the top-dogs of the bombing league, and they were generally considered to be the crack precision bombing unit. But their obvious lack of success with the X-Geraet had incurred them considerable displeasure with their master, the dreaded Goering, who was known throughout the Luftwaffe as 'The Iron One'. They were now under a cloud, and they had become superseded by III/KG 26, the unit that was chiefly involved with the early Benito beams. But KGr 100 were nevertheless still trying. The X-Geraet beams – which we had by now code-named 'The Ruffians', because we identified each individual beam by the name of one of the Axis villains, such as 'Himmler', 'Heydrich', or 'Goering' – still tried to help 'The Blacks', as KGr 100 called themselves, to get to their proper targets, but the Luftwaffe was having to work hard to overcome the effects of No. 80 Wing's jamming. One method they tried was to use the maximum number of beam frequencies at any one time, changing them constantly; and on one occasion ten different frequencies were recorded within the space of less than four hours. The changes meant, of course, that No. 80 Wing had to alter the frequencies on which their Bromides operated. The enemy's hope was obviously that the operators in their aircraft would get a chance to take a reading before our transmitters could be moved over to the new frequency.

Their next game was to lay 'spoof' beams in the direction of false targets, and another ploy was for KGr 100 to try to keep complete W/T silence on the raids until after the first wave of bombers had delivered their attack. When this did not work, they started to super-impose an identification letter on the beam signal, so that the opera-tor in the aircraft might differentiate between the proper signal and No. 80 Wing's jammer. But the standard of the German Morse-sending was often deplorable. We decided that even the squadron's signals officers must have agreed with us because the identification letter was soon sent by automatic tape. Yet even then, on one occa-sion, some idiot managed to reverse the tape. Whatever devices the Luftwaffe thought up at this stage of the war to thwart our counter-measures, they were swiftly followed by further action by No. 80 Wing, guided by Dr Jones and the specialists at TRE. It was a cat-

and-mouse game, with the Kingsdown network as audience listening to the enemy's efforts to shake off No. 80 Wing's countermeasures.

In order to worry the Luftwaffe still further, the Wellingtons of No. 109 Squadron would, from time to time, whilst on their investigational flights, make bombing attacks on the beam transmitters. This special squadron kept a regular watch on the activities of the beam stations, sometimes using captured German receivers, and it was inevitable that in the course of this hazardous work, some of their crews should fail to return from their exacting tasks.

By now No. 80 Wing were expanding rapidly in order to keep abreast with the enemy's increasing use of radio navigational systems; but there were times, of course, when they were not successful, especially when their jammers were poorly sited to interfere with the beams for that particular night. Such was the case on the night of 26 March 1941, when aircraft of KGr 100 led an attack on Plymouth. Their bombing devastated the city.

But it was not only the two fire-raising units that were experiencing difficulties in navigation. Although these squadrons certainly had problems enough in getting to the target, the rest of the German bomber force had their own difficulties. The British night-fighter system was now in operation, with improved airborne radar, and was becoming much more skilled in locating and attacking the intruders.[4] No. 80 Wing had become so large an organization that they had divided the country into six areas and they were having increased success 'meaconing' the M/F navigational beacons, which the enemy needed to find their way back to their bases, especially now that they could no longer rely on their Knickebein beams. It did not seem to matter how often the frequencies of the beacons were changed, 'meaconing' was soon effective.

Already by April 1941, we had been aware from Y intercepts that only a quarter of all the bearings given by the German ground stations to their aircraft were accurate, and quite frequently the controller was at a loss, quite unable to give a pilot an accurate indication of his position. Listening in to the resultant confusion gave us enormous satisfaction. Some pilots would panic, while others would lose their tempers and a slanging match would ensue. 'You stupid idiots, can't you even get a proper fix?' an irate pilot would snarl. The radio operator would blame his 'blank-blank' equipment, and the controller would grumble about the inefficiency of all aircrews. While these were rare intercepts, they nevertheless added spice to our lives. It must be said that most of the German pilots remembered the need for signals security, and bore their trials in stoic silence. Yet we knew from the radar tracings of their erratic courses how disorientated they could become in their flying.

The Y monitors throughout Britain would sit recording the traffic as the bombers – sixty, seventy, eighty or more aircraft a night – tried to home on their various bases: II/KG 53 back to Lille Sud, I/KG 3 to Le Coulot, the KG 4s back to Soesterberg – whichever units had operated that night. Just as their 'Horchdienst' was counting our returning bombers, so were we counting theirs.

From the prisoner-of-war reports compiled at the interrogation centre, there was little doubt that the German bomber units were increasingly disillusioned about the effectiveness of their radio navigational aids and captured crews of III/KG 26 were depressed that the British appeared to be definitely ahead of the Germans in radio development. There was also an added bonus for No. 80 Wing's 'meaconing' activity. This was the frustrating of the enemy mine-laying aircraft which relied heavily on the chain of M/F beacons to check their position before dropping their mines in the shipping lanes of the North Sea.

A good example of the problems that were faced by the enemy bombers was the occasion on the night of 27/28 September 1941, when an aircraft of II/KG 40 was monitored as it wandered around the skies over Britain between Scarborough and London. We knew that the pilot was getting little, if not useless, help from his control. Finally he was ordered to continue on a course of 100 degrees for as long as possible, and then to bale out if overland, or to land on the sea, take to his dinghy, and try and make his way to the south. Each time his ground station tried to give him a fix there was a variation from between south of Portsmouth to east of Colchester; and, as far as we could tell, at no time did it agree with where he was actually flying.

Perhaps one of the better examples of the confusion that would set in on board an enemy aircraft occurred on 12 October 1941, when a Do. 217 forced landed at Lydd aerodrome, in Kent. The pilot had been pottering about over southern England for hours trying hopefully to get correct instructions from his ground station, or a decent fix from various M/F beacons. Somehow the coastline below him did not seem to marry up with where he thought he was. Meanwhile, his erratic course was being meticulously plotted by

British radar, whilst we were eavesdropping on his repeated requests for fixes. Finally, announcing that his fuel was spent, the pilot came in to land. He was convinced that the airfield that he saw beneath him must be Evreux, in Normandy, and he was sadly disillusioned when, on landing at Lydd, he was promptly arrested by a British soldier. For us, it was a matter of being handed on a plate a fine, undamaged Do. 217. About this time, two other German aircraft also landed on British airfields as a result of 'meaconing' but they, realizing in time the error that they had made, managed to get away.

Incidents such as these did much to compensate us for the long, exhausting hours spent in the blacked-out Operations Room at Kingsdown, or sitting in great discomfort in the listening huts around the coast. On the other hand, however, we at least had some idea of what was going on in the skies above us from the traffic that we were monitoring and through being in constant contact with air and naval operations. But this was not so for the wireless operators and teleprinter operators at Chicksands, where the bulk of the Enigma traffic was being intercepted. For them the encoded messages were a meaningless jumble of letter groups, and they were never to know the content of what they were logging. It speaks well for the conscientiousness of these young men and women that they carried on hour after hour, day after day, meticulously recording the enemy's seemingly unintelligible communications, hindered only by atmospherics and fading signals. The work was tedious, and undertaken at such great pressure that psychiatric advice was sought to devise means of relieving the boredom and, if possible, the stress. It was during a visit to Chicksands that I first heard of industrial psychology.

So important was the question of speed in handling this traffic, particularly on the more important channels, that every minute of delay mattered. The old Priory had never been built to cope with an operational headquarters in war-time, and the layout of the rooms was far from ideal. It was discovered, on examination of the movement of messages from one part of the house to another, that there seemed to be an unnecessary time-lag in one stage of the proceedings. The industrial psychologist, who was a time and motion expert, realized that messengers taking signals from the interception room to the Duty Officers had to walk the length of a long, narrow corridor which, following the customary procedure of the Royal Air Force, was considered a perfect display area for the myriads of notices which form the background to service life. There would be, understandably enough, some notice about a forthcoming football match, the latest edition of Daily Routine Orders, and similar ephemera, all of it catching the eye of the messenger, who would slow down to read them. By removing all the notices, and by ingeniously painting a line four feet up the corridor wall, the effect of the converging lines speeded the messengers on their way, thus saving precious minutes in the handling of the traffic. As the war progressed, the unit was considerably enlarged and more modern accommodation built.

Apart from the immediate operational value of specific messages, the cumulative intelligence derived from Enigma helped considerably with reading the traffic sent in lower-grade cyphers and provided us with many a lead-in for our own work. We would have, for instance, the prior knowledge of where units were based, when new equipment was to be allocated to them, routes that were to be taken by convoys, even the cargoes of the ships, and other information which would often make all the difference between a message being obscure, taking several hours to read, or being of immediate tactical use.

It would be wrong, however, to underrate the value of the great mass of traffic that was intercepted in lower-grade codes. Each arm of the forces had its own monitoring services – Air was under AI4, the Army under MI8, and the Navy under NID9 – and they were all closely linked right from the start of the war. One of the earliest examples of this co-operation was during the Dunkirk period, when the vast quantity of traffic intercepted by RAF Y supplied information that greatly assisted the evacuation of the troops from the Dunkirk beaches and also gave warnings of attacks on convoys. Later, before the fall of France, raids on French cities were forecast, and the messages between the Bordeaux Government and the German High Command prior to the armistice were heard. Out of this there came the co-operation between the Army, the Royal Navy and the Royal Air Force monitoring services which was to continue throughout the campaigns in Africa and Italy, culminating in their combined efforts in Western Europe following the Normandy landings.

Our relationship with the Royal Navy was particularly close. During the early days of the war, the enemy inflicted enormous losses on shipping. Not only were German surface craft attacking our convoys and U-boats hunting in packs to waylay the ships as they brought to Britain much needed food and supplies, but the Luftwaffe was lending its weight. The 'Lion Geschwader' – KG 26 – were particularly skilled in attacking the freighters sailing between east coast ports. Night after night, Y listened to the aircraft flying mine-laying sorties, locating whenever possible their areas of operation, which were of vital importance when the aircraft were flying out of range of the radar screen. During the early days at Hawkinge, before the Navy had its own R/T interception units, our WAAF linguists had heard traffic from the fast mine-laying motor-launches as they attacked shipping in the Channel, and the coastal HDUs were to continue to help the Navy with monitoring messages from these E-boats.

Perhaps the most valuable contribution to the Navy, especially during the desperate months of the Battle of the Atlantic, was the watch kept on the activities of the 'Zenit' flights. Each day, when weather permitted, enemy aircraft were active over the shipping lanes in the North Sea, the Western Approaches, the Bay of Biscay, and the Mediterranean, sending back to their controls reconnaissance and meteorological reports. We had named these patrols the 'Zenit' patrols because of the word they had used pre-war to prefix their messages. By January 1941 there was evidence that the great four-engined Focke-Wulf 200 – the Condors – of the unit KG 40, which was based at Bordeaux-Merignac airfield, were not only attacking convoys but also co-operating with the U-boats shadowing allied shipping far out into the Atlantic. On one occasion, the crew of one of the Focke-Wulfs was heard reporting the position of a convoy, and asking his control to inform neighbouring submarines that they would make bearing transmission to enable the U-boats to home on to the convoy. Later analysis of messages sent by the U-boats and their control produced confirmation of this. In the same way, the sighting made by the U-boat would be relayed by the KG 40 base at Bordeaux to the patrolling aircraft, which would then locate and attack the convoy. Such was the case when, on 9 February 1941, a convoy which had set out from Gibraltar was attacked between Portugal and the Azores, with the loss of half of the ships.

But the installation of better direction-finding facilities by our people, which enabled a more exact pinpointing of the transmissions from these aircraft, was soon instrumental in helping aircraft of Coastal Command to attack both the Condors and the submarines. In addition, traffic monitored from German fighter patrols would often give tell-tale information relating to the presence of German and Italian convoys or battleships. An example of this was when the German heavy cruiser *Prinz Eugen* escaped from the shelter of Brest dockyard.[5] The HDU at Strete intercepted traffic from the fighter cover which was guarding the ship.

In the beginning the various air and naval operations rooms were somewhat sceptical of Y intelligence. Furthermore, they were uncertain how best to make use of it. But as the amount of information passed to them increased they became more accustomed to handling it and marrying it up with other intelligence. Then Y came to be in great demand, and the controllers would not hesitate to ring us up. 'Have you got anything on Y about our raid on. . . .?' they would ask, or they would tell us: 'There's a convoy entering the Channel tomorrow evening just before dusk. Let us know the moment you get any reaction from our friends.'

From this we knew that, at last, we had been accepted.

8

The Sphere of Listening Widens

By the middle of 1941 I had come, by experience, to agree with my old Warrant Officer of the early days at the Record Office when he stated: 'Time off for meals is a privilege.' Although several other signals officers had been posted to the Kingsdown organization, and Liz Strang and Barbara Pemberton could now take turns as intelligence officers and help with the Duty Officer roster, I rarely seemed to have any time to relax. There was a great deal of work we had to do in checking the translations and decodes of the operational traffic intercepted by Kingsdown and the HDUs, and we also had to ensure that the right co-ordinated intelligence was being passed quickly to operational Commands. This meant that we had to keep constantly up-to-date with all aspects of enemy radio signals heard by the other Y units in the United Kingdom: the W/T traffic on medium frequency associated with landing instructions for enemy bomber and reconnaissance aircraft, beam and radar developments, and the navigational beacons. All of this might give leads at any moment into some new development associated with intercepted W/T or R/T traffic. There were always logs to read, reports to write, and information from intelligence sources other than Y to absorb. It was not until after I had left that an RAF Intelligence officer was posted to Kingsdown. This was Flying Officer H. Law Robertson, who was one of the best German scholars in the Y Service.

Our Commanding Officer and Jonah Jones would have to make frequent visits to the outstations, as also did the other signals officers such as Jimmy Mazdon and Joe Payne. This meant that they would be away from the Headquarters for several days, thus adding to the load of work for the rest of us. One night I was so weary that when I went into Budge's office to talk over the day's traffic I had to sit down, exhausted, on a little sea-chest in which he kept his most secret papers. Jonah came in, and we had a mug of coffee together. It was then that I realized that even if you had paid me, I just could not have got up to walk back through the lanes to my billet. 'You're whacked, kid,' Jonah said in his usual big-brotherly way. 'Come on, let's get you home.' He picked me up in his arms, carried me out to his car, and drove me back to my billet. I think it was only the kindness of the Gratwicks, with whom he and Budge were billeted, that kept me sane during those long, arduous months of the Blitz.

As at the other Y stations throughout Britain and in the Mediterranean and the Middle East, the level of traffic we were monitoring was steadily increasing and we were hard-pressed to cover all the channels likely to produce material of interest to Operations and Intelligence. More and more personnel were recruited: radio technicians, wireless operators and linguists. Station X was also expanding rapidly and was regrettably, together with the Air Ministry Intelligence, creaming off some of our best linguists. We at No. 63 Wireless Unit, Kingsdown, had long since outgrown our toy-factory and were now housed in a Victorian mansion named Hollywood Manor, on the highest point on the Kentish Downs. We could look down from the roof in springtime and see a snowfield of apple and cherry blossom stretching across the orchards of Kent.

As our station grew larger, it was inevitable that our rather casual approach towards what might be called 'military discipline' had to come to an end. The main house became the WAAF hostel, and 'Billy' Conan-Doyle, our WAAF Administrative Officer, laid down various rules that promptly caused resentment on the part of the Sergeant linguists. She issued instructions that all other ranks of the WAAF, irrespective of rank, should be in quarters at night by ten o'clock. Billy and I were the best of friends, she had the welfare of the girls very much at heart, and I believe that she had a higher sense of integrity than probably any woman I have ever met, but in those early days I do not think she fully appreciated the strain under which 'my' WAAF were working. It was a strain that was caused both by the work itself and, for several of them, who were displaced Europeans, by the added worry of great personal problems. But Billy's sympathetic understanding of the problems of young women, and her success in administration, were to lead eventually to her appointment, after the war, as Director of the WRAF.

Throughout the war there was a constant undercurrent of friction between the administrative, and the technical, or what was termed

E

'RAF substitution' personnel of the WAAF. This was heightened, especially amongst the officers, by the rapid promotion of those who were in administration, which was known as the WAAF 'G'. Promotion in the substitution branches, on the other hand, was seriously restricted and

This lack of promotion was keenly felt by many of the officers concerned for not only did it cause them financial hardship but they suffered from invidious comparison with 'G' officers. Relations and friends and the general public would hardly be expected to understand that promotion could only be granted to establishment vacancies. Many of the officers themselves never understood why their promotion was so slow, and their subconscious antagonism to the 'G' branch was thereby increased.[1]

In my experience the antagonism was often very conscious indeed, particularly as many of the 'substitution' officers, being technical personnel, were *de facto* of a higher educational and intelligence level than some of the WAAF 'G' officers. The Air Ministry has even conceded that some of the early WAAF Administrative officers 'were indifferent; while some few did distinct harm to the service before they were asked to resign'.[2]

I know of one occasion when, shortly after the cessation of hostilities, a WAAF technical officer, who had been engaged on arduous work, was 'torn off a strip' for some minor offence by a WAAF 'G' officer who, though she had been commissioned a year or so after the offender, was by then her senior in rank. The offender's view of it was the justified comment: 'The bloody woman, she hasn't even been near enough to the war to hear a shot fired in anger and she has the nerve to criticize me!'

There was the added irritation that any recommendation for a commission always had to be channelled through the WAAF Administrative officer in charge of the section or unit, and I knew of cases where excellent potential technical officers had their applications for commissions turned down as being 'unsuitable' merely because, for instance, the applicant might wear her hair touching her collar or had been seen outside her quarters a few times with the buttons of her greatcoat undone!

Such faulty, and even trivial, reasoning was often due to the fact that the WAAF 'G' officer concerned had never worked or lived in the outside world and did not realize that the non-conformist can sometimes be a most valuable member of a team, particularly in time of war. I always believed in and appreciated the value of discipline, especially in a uniformed force, but in technical work such as that of the Y Service, radar, meteorology, and photographic interpretation, to name some of the tasks which required special qualifications and demanded work at high pressure, frequently under very uncomfortable conditions, there had to be a leeway. Administrative personnel usually worked what might be described as a normal working day, and in comparative comfort. It was easy for them to remain neat and tidy with their hair in their own approved fashion. It was not so easy if you had to struggle across a ploughed field, and then sit hunched up in a van, your feet and hands blue with cold. And much depended on a contented team of monitors. The conscientious and accurate recording of messages was paramount, and a resentful atmosphere let loose in our group of young women would have been disastrous. The success of the Kingsdown network was largely due to the excellence of our team spirit. There were naturally disagreements from time to time but, compared with other units, we were an exceptionally happy organization.

With the increase in German bomber R/T traffic on VHF, and the activities of their night- and day-fighters, better direction-finding facilities were essential. Line bearings were not good enough: we needed two or three cross-bearings to get a definite 'fix' on an aircraft or ground station. And as the transmissions would probably be very brief, it was imperative that Kingsdown should be able to contact the HDUs immediately. We needed, too, to be in constant communication with No. 80 Wing, and to keep them informed during raids of the operational information obtained from the monitored traffic. The Commands, the Fighter Groups, and the Navy were all anxious to get relevant information as soon as possible, and, of course, we needed to keep in touch with the Air Ministry, the cryptographers at Bletchley, and our Y counterparts at Cheadle. This all pointed to the need for a network of direct telephone links centred on Kingsdown, with secure lines to our various customers and to our HDUs at Strete, Beachy Head, Sutton Valence, Gorleston, Hawkinge, Ingoldmells and Scarborough, and, as we grew, to the other coastal units.

Apart from our responsibility for monitoring Luftwaffe R/T, we also had the task of investigating what we called 'Noises'. These included beam and pulse transmissions from enemy radar, and such signals as high-speed Morse transmissions. In this Reggie Budge

and Jonah Jones, who were particularly interested in signals developments in the higher frequencies, worked in close collaboration with
No. 80 Wing, TRE and the naval signals specialists. As these higher
frequency transmissions have a strictly limited range, we opened up
a new HDU at Capel, near Dover, and an attempt was even made
in July 1941 to set up a listening watch in a man-carrying balloon
to cover decimetre band transmissions which we thought might be
connected with the setting up of the beams.[3] The balloon which was
used was an R-type Cacquot of the kind used during the First World
War for observation purposes. The ascents were made at night
under the expert guidance of Squadron Leader Lord Ventry and
Flight Lieutenant John Evason. The principal radio operators involved in this hazardous venture, who spent many airsick hours in a
gondola slung beneath the swaying balloon 3000 or 4000 feet above
Dover, with air-raids in progress beneath them, were the then Flying
Officer Jimmy Mazdon and Pilot Officer Basil Sadler. By coincidence,
Sadler was the great grandson of the early English balloonist of the
same name. (He was to be killed later during an investigational flight
over Western Europe.) The venture was short-lived, as the Air
Ministry considered it was too expensive in manpower and they had
found a way to operate the receivers in the gondolas by remote
control.

We had become convinced that there must be more Luftwaffe
R/T traffic which we were not hearing merely because we were out
of range. Budge therefore erected a ninety-foot tower at Kingsdown
and we installed a new HDU at Shaftesbury, in Dorset, with the
object of filling in any possible gaps in coverage along the south
coast between Beachy Head and Strete. The inland site of Shaftesbury was chosen as it was the official opinion that there was still the
possibility of a German invasion.

As if we did not have enough to do with the bombers and the
Little Screw patrols, the day-fighters were also keeping us busy.
Dependent on where RAF sweeps were concentrating, or where a
convoy was sailing, so, inevitably, there was more traffic from that
area. At first these patrols operated in six main areas: the Friesian
Islands, the Alkmaar, the Flushing, the Channel, the Dieppe, and
the Havre-Cherbourg areas. As a result of our better direction-
finding facilities, in addition to the occasional grid references mentioned in a message, the callsigns, and the unwitting idiosyncracies
of the different patrols, we could usually identify them without too

much trouble, and by April 1941 we had got them all pretty well under surveillance. We knew, for instance, that the Friesian patrol was centred on Jever, operating from the airfields at Nordeney, Langerooge and Borkum, whilst the Alkmaar aircraft patrolled over shipping as far as the mouth of the Scheldt, mainly between Den Helder and The Hague, with the addition of a second control near Rotterdam.

The RAF kept the Flushing patrol busy with its onslaughts on Axis shipping, and, in retaliation, the Channel patrol, which later split into two sectors covering the Ostend–Berck area, made a nuisance of themselves attacking British convoys passing through the Straits of Dover. They were a menace, and they obviously received a lot of help from our rivals, the German Y Service. We knew from the messages intercepted from their control at St Omer-Mardyck that they were constantly supplied with information from Y sources about the movements of British fighter aircraft, especially when they were on an offensive sweep across the Channel. The German Observer Corps, on the other hand, was pretty hopeless, constantly reporting, for example, an 'unidentified formation approaching Cap Gris Nez', which the leader of the formation would rather cuttingly advise them was his own aircraft. The Dieppe patrol were engaged much of the time on protective duties, as were the Le Havre-Cherbourg units, but it was the practice for all patrols if they had half a chance to attack any British convoys reported in their area.

The keenest interest was always shown by Fighter Command in what the German Y Service were reporting about British fighters preparing to attack a German formation. This was very much a case of fore-warned being fore-armed. We became so concerned about the amount of information the Horchdienst was obviously getting that in July 1941 we set up a watch at Kingsdown on British fighter R/T in the 100- to 120-megacycle band, and from that we were able to give Fighter Command a few home truths, including issuing to them a comparison between British and German fighter security.

We knew that we were able to monitor Luftwaffe R/T up to 500 miles on the 2- to 6-megacycle band, and by this time we were covering the whole of the western European coastline from Jutland to La Rochelle. There was little reason why the Germans should not also have as extensive a cover; indeed, we knew that they had. When it came to a general comparison of the signals security of the British and German fighters, we came to the conclusion that the Germans revealed more information by trusting to the inviolability of their code-words and map systems than by careless and unnecessary chatter, whilst exactly the reverse applied to the British pilots and their controllers. The very nature of the tight system of control employed by the RAF required more communication between aircraft and controller than was the case with the German day-fighters. Yet even with the Little Screw traffic, whose close control system was similar to our own, the Germans seemed to be more aware of the need to limit the number and the length of the air-to-ground messages. On the whole they were much more 'cagey' than our pilots. It is no good having a code language if some idiot compromises it. One might just as well talk in plain language. I often wondered how long it took the German Y Service to 'de-code' our 'Gate' and 'Buster' ('slow down' and 'step on it')? What was the sense of a controller saying: 'Understand you are popeye, increase angels and see if you come to quilt,' since patently, 'Angels' (height) had been well and truly compromised very early on in the war. And how kind of one controller to advise the German Y station of the limit of his control zone by warning a pilot: 'You'd better come back or you'll be getting out of my control,' or 'Bandit (enemy aircraft) has turned north and is going off our table.'

For a while, German Y may have puzzled (as we did over 'Stern') over what 'Pip Squeak' meant, but some controllers had a tendency to transmit such messages as – 'Your Pip Squeak shows you south of X for X-Ray.' And a pilot, chatting to a friend, must also have proved helpful to the enemy when he divulged: 'A good way to find base is to fly up river.' We knew only too well how helpful this type of information was to one's enemy. We even heard a controller telling a pilot: 'You are now crossing the river east of Gravesend. If you fly west, you will find the airfield ten miles ahead,' and a pilot who, somewhat relieved, informed his ground controller that he 'nearly flew into the balloon barrage slightly north of base'. It would have been even more helpful to the Germans had he also given the height of the barrage.

The Golden Rule, as we were always stressing to the operational Commands, was 'Stick to the Code' and nothing but the code. To say something in code and then to elaborate upon it in plain language was ridiculous. Apart from giving away something about the present operation, the offending pilot or controller had ensured that no future operation using the compromised code expression would ever be safe.

Whenever a British convoy was expected to run the gauntlet of the enemy air force and the shore gun-batteries on the French coast, we would be warned in advance. The HDUs along the south coast would then be on the alert for the slightest indication of any enemy fighter activity. When this happened the Duty Officer for the day at Kingsdown would telephone the Flight Sergeants in charge of the WAAF linguists at Strete, Beachy Head, and, when it was later sited, at Shaftesbury, and discuss with them which frequencies were to be their special watch. They would also be given, as far as we could, some idea of when the convoy would be likely to approach within striking distance of the enemy fighter patrols which they were monitoring.

On one occasion, on 11 May 1941, we had been warned the night before that a convoy was expected in the Channel early in the morning. The WAAF monitors were on the alert at Beachy Head, and the Flight Sergeant WAAF in charge had come up early from her billet in Eastbourne. I was on duty, at Kingsdown, as I had realized how essential it was that the convoy should get through unmolested and every possible operational message be passed through with the minimum of delay.

At first light the German fighters were airborne, and they were followed by their bombers. There was a steady stream of intercepted messages telephoned through first from Strete and then from Beachy Head, and all the interested operational headquarters were kept informed of the reactions of the Luftwaffe.

Eventually, we were told by Coastal Command to relax. The convoy was safe. I went off for a quick meal before returning to cope with the nightly Little Screw patrols and the bombers. When I got back the next message I received from Beachy Head was again passed by the Flight Sergeant, and once more, I told her that she could now relax and go home.

'It's all right, Ma'am,' she said cheerfully. 'The others have gone for their tea and I'm holding the fort.'

A little later, I realized the same WAAF was still passing messages. Somewhat crossly, I suggested that she should hand over to one of her Sergeants. There was something in the way she answered that worried me.

'Is anything wrong, Flight?' I asked. 'Has there been an accident?'

'No. Really, Ma'am. I'm all right,' she replied. 'Don't worry, I'll be off soon.'

But I was not satisfied, and since we could not telephone the WAAFs billet, we got on to the police at Eastbourne. They told us that a departing Ju. 88 had off-loaded its cargo just before leaving the coast, and had straddled Beachy Head with unexploded bombs one of which they thought might be a delayed action bomb. Despite their advice, the Flight Sergeant, realizing how important the intercepted traffic would be, had taken it on herself to stay on duty.

Two Post Office workmen were commended by the King for their bravery in repairing the vital telephone line to the adjacent radar station.[4] A few days later, I had to go up to the Air Ministry for a selection board for German-speaking WAAF. While I was there I told Air Commandant Trefusis-Forbes, the Director, WAAF about the Flight Sergeant's conduct, and I suggested that we should try to get a commendation for her.

'Morris,' she said pompously, 'I expect my WAAF to show devotion to duty.'

I wondered how often she had sat for hours beside an unexploded bomb?

There were other occasions when devotion to duty was displayed by the WAAF employed in the Y Service. One of them was on 18 March 1941, when swarms of German bombers attacked the Yorkshire town of Scarborough in what was its most severe raid of the war. Only a few nights previously, the town had been showered with incendiaries, and on that morning, No. 80 Wing had calculated that the beams were lined up on Scarborough. The Y unit on the top of Castle Hill were instructed to pass on as quickly as possible every single message that they intercepted.

Night fell, and the German bomber traffic began to mount up. The messages from Castle Hill were passed to me by Sergeant Doreen King, who had lived most of her young life in Vienna. She was a gay, irresponsible girl with a mass of fair hair piled on top of her head, and large blue eyes. She looked rather like a doll dressed up in uniform.

Several times I telephoned the unit, but there was no reply. When I finally got through I declared: 'For Heaven's sake, King, concentrate. I want you at the end of the line constantly.'

'Yes, Ma'am,' replied Sergeant King cheerfully. 'Sorry.'

A little later the same thing happened, and then again a third time. I admit now, to my shame, that I became thoroughly angry. When I did manage to get King again on the 'phone I warned her: 'If you don't stay put on the end of this line, I'll have you up on a charge. Do *not* leave the 'phone!'

'Sorry, Ma'am, I really am,' Doreen King answered, 'but, you see, the others are busy intercepting, and I have to keep going outside and swatting incendiaries.'

In their report of the raid the *Scarborough Evening News* recorded:

On this night (March 18th), there was a great deal of enemy activity apparent in the neighbourhood for nearly an hour before the local warning was given. Enemy planes which had crossed the coast and passed in a southerly direction showered incendiary bombs on a prodigious scale in an arc extending from Filey and skirting Flixton and Folkton and the Carrs. The attack gradually closed in on Scarborough. There were showers of bombs over the sea, and at one period, coast observers saw them bouncing down the face of Castle Hill [where the HDU was sited] on to the Marine Drive like a cascade of fire. . . . Enemy planes cruised over the town at no great height, leisurely picking their targets and letting go heavy bombs. The attack was intensive for about two hours and was followed by desultory bombing during the next three or four hours. Three parachute mines were dropped . . . and some heavy bombs were reported to have fallen in the sea, where thousands of incendiaries also fell, and somehow or other, burned for a few seconds.

No. 80 Wing's countermeasures had apparently been partly successful.

The Lords of the Admiralty came to think so highly of the Y WAAF at Gorleston for the valuable work that they did in intercepting E-boat traffic off the East Coast that they arranged for a wherry and a couple of dinghies to be placed at their disposal for their off-duty enjoyment on Wroxham Broad. It was a kind expression of their gratitude which the Navy would not have lightly given to the junior service.

Many of the Y WAAF were multi-lingual, and this was frequently to prove most valuable. The fall of France led the Italians to believe that the Germans must be on a winning streak, and they eagerly decided to throw in their lot with the Nazis. The Y Service, in the United Kingdom and overseas, had been assiduously monitoring

Italian wireless traffic for some considerable time. Much of this material was sent straight to Station X for decoding and after collation it was signalled back to Cairo or Malta or East Africa for use by Intelligence in those theatres of operations.

In the autumn of 1940 the OKL (Oberkommando der Luftwaffe – the High Command of the German Air Force) decided to let their newly-acquired allies participate in the action on the Western European front. We were not unduly surprised in the Kingsdown organization when we started to intercept Italian Air Force R/T which apparently came from fighter aircraft based in Belgium. And then after a short period of training, there came the initiation of the Italian Air Force in offensive operations against the United Kingdom. Their efforts could hardly be described as a roaring success. Nobody could have told them about a band of young women who were listening in to the enemy R/T, and whose conscientious monitoring would be largely responsible for British fighters being so well placed that they were able to effect a crushing defeat on the first Italian sortie of note made on 11 November. Their stay on the Western Front was short-lived and they soon returned for operations in the Mediterranean and Africa.

One of our minor amusements at Kingsdown was to listen to the Italian Observer Corps reporting on British raids on northern Italian targets. Reception of this traffic was undoubtedly due to what is called 'skip', which is a phenomenon which causes radio waves to come on a second 'bounce' back to earth from the ionosphere. One could not help feeling sorry for the Italians because they really did get distressed about the raids, particularly if they happened to be near the epicentre. We would hear them using the clock-code:

'Case ventuno a Casa ventidue. Rumore di velivoli. Otto. Otto. Cappa. Cappa.' (Casa 21 to Casa 22. Noise of aircraft at 8 o'clock – Over to you, over), and on one occasion we heard a terrified man reporting bombing raids immediately overhead:

'Rosa dieci a Rosa una. Rumore di velivoli. Rumore di velivoli. O Mama mia – zero, zero. Rumore di velivoli zero.' (Rosa 10 to Rosa 1. Noise of aircraft. O Holy Virgin – zero, zero.)

Once one of the WAAF monitors swore she actually heard bombing but this may have been wishful thinking.

The 'Rosas' and the 'Casas' were our source of light relief. One Italian operator who had a typically Neapolitan sing-song voice was our greatest joy, and we would wander round the Operations Room gently crooning to ourselves: 'Casa ventiquattro a Casa ventidue. Cappa. Cappa. Cappa.'

The weather for June in Kent that year of 1941 was glorious. Whenever the girls had any time off during the day they played tennis or sunbathed in the gardens of Hollywood Manor. Then it would be time again to return to the night watch, and to listening in to the tactics of the Little Screw patrols and the German bombers as they droned across Britain. And then came Hitler's colossal mistake: his invasion of Russia.

Because of the atmospheric conditions over Europe, we were again able to hear distant R/T traffic and unexpectedly became involved in that invasion. Amongst our WAAF linguists was a young Polish Baroness, Rudi Eisenklam (de Sarigny), who happened to have been studying English in Cambridge when the war broke out, and had been unable to return to her homeland. As Rudi was so intimately involved with the incident, I asked her to record in her own way our Y side of the story of the beginning of 'Operation Barbarossa' – the German invasion of Russia. She has written:

June 22nd had been a typical night spent monitoring the progress of our bomber raids as they were attacked by German night fighters. Between four and five in the morning, when the last of the bombers were making their way home, we, on watch, had to bring our log-books up to date, assess the situation and pass the report to the Duty Officer before the arrival of the morning watch at eight o'clock. We had taken over at midnight from the evening watch and we had been immediately thrown into hours of work. The Duty Officer was Flight Lieutenant Jones. As usual when things got quieter and the summer morning approached, we removed the wooden black-out boards from the small windows of our hut, opened the windows wide to let in the fresh air and let out the hours of cigarette smoke. I, as became a junior, was sent to the cookhouse in the main house for coffee and sandwiches. I remember how much I enjoyed the short walk through the woods inhaling the fragrant Kentish air. On returning to the watchroom with the food, I found an atmosphere of feverish activity. Liz Larter, my watch leader, Vera Elkan and Jo Henstridge, who, incidentally, could write longhand quicker than anybody else, were listening in and writing quickly and at the same time calling out to Olly Simpson to get the Duty Officer. I immediately put down the tray and picked up my own earphones attached to a small EK set. The band from 2.9 to 40 megacycles was alive with German traffic, different in pattern from the bomber and fighter jargon we normally heard. The whole thing felt strange. Once we got the first place name spelled in clear, I realized that the traffic was coming from south-east Poland, an area of which I had a fair knowledge since I was born and brought up there. The name of the town, Przemysl, confirmed our belief that the transmissions were coming from spotter aircraft, and by the location could only mean that the Germans were invading the Russian-held part of Eastern Poland.

The only gridded and detailed maps in the watchroom were the ones of the Continent including France, Belgium, Holland and Germany, and even Italy but certainly not Eastern Poland. The Duty Officer somehow magically obtained a small school atlas. Przemysl was not marked but I knew where it was and was able to pinpoint it with reference to the town of Lwow, marked on the map. By 8 o'clock when the morning watch took over, both the watchroom and the control section were full of people. I was asked to stay on and work as a 'map' with the morning watch. Only at 9 o'clock did somebody come in to tell us that they had heard an official announcement of the German invasion of Russia. According to our civilian scientists, the traffic we were receiving was entirely due to a freak weather condition which allowed us to listen in and to take part in the greatest gamble undertaken by Hitler.

We were asked to make our log-books with an extra copy which was then passed on to the Army. As a matter of fact, during the following days we had an Army intelligence officer working at Kingsdown. The Army was anxious to determine where the Germans were fighting, and the Kingsdown intercepts were an unexpected windfall, giving them details of the front line.

The offensive was swift and the opposition almost non-existent. The Germans worked efficiently and quickly. The aircraft spotted a small town or village and gave its name in plain language to the artillery. Then came figures and clock code, indicating standard artillery zeroing in. After some thirty minutes of intense shelling, the aircraft spoke again, in plain language, to the 'Panzer' leader, describing the road ahead and giving such details as 'a small bridge' ('eine kleine Bruecke'). There were two occasions when the advancing Germans were so much ahead that they were cut off from their field kitchen ('Feldkueche') and their ambulance ('Sanitaetswagen'). The obliging aircraft went back to advise that food and medical attention were urgently needed. After the tanks, came the 'Jagdtruppen', advancing infantry, with their full equipment. Since Przemsyl lay to the west of the town of Lwow, they followed the straight road into the town, which seemed to fall with very little opposition. They kept advancing eastwards. A small town of Kolomyja was mentioned, too. I remember it particularly well, since I had an aunt living there. When the Germans reached Tarnopol, which took them some five days, the signals started fading and we could only hear occasional instructions given to the artillery but no more chat with the Panzer Division or the 'Jagdtruppen'. They were then obviously out of range. They seemed to have covered

120 miles in five days. When I had my '33' hours off, I went to Cambridge where I used to find peace and tranquillity. Walking along the Backs, little did I know that the previous week would change the life of Hitler and would also change my whole life. Hitler's gamble did not come off and because of his Russian invasion, he lost the war, whilst I lost my family and my country.

For all the sadness which came into her life, Rudi Eisenklam was one of the most conscientious of our monitors. Almost without exception, I could rely on the WAAF from European countries to give of their best; their integrity was exceptional.

9

The War Moves East

From the time of the outbreak of the war, the signals intelligence organization of the Services working in the Middle East had been concentrating mainly on the interception of Italian traffic, which had reached a peak during the campaign in Eritrea and Somaliland with German monitoring taking a poor second place. By the spring of 1941 the situation had altered radically as there came about the crumbling of Mussolini's hopes of an African empire. His troops had been defeated in East Africa and in the Western Desert, where the British Army under General Sir Archibald Wavell, had sent Marshal Graziani's forces packing, pushing them back across Libya and Cyrenaica as far as El Agheila. But our hopes of obliterating the Axis presence in North Africa were ruined when, on 12 February 1941, General Erwin Rommel arrived in Tripoli.[1] He was soon leading his Afrika Korps eastwards towards Egypt, with the towns of Benghazi, Derna, Bardia and Sollum falling in quick succession. Only the dogged determination of the troops in Tobruk had withstood the advance, and they were now besieged in their garrison, miles behind the front line, surrounded by Germans and the remnants of the Italian Army, and all the time being subjected to constant shelling and bombardment.

In southern Europe the situation was also deteriorating. In April 1941 the Germans added their weight to an Italian offensive against Greece, over-running Yugoslavia and Albania en route and the British Government had immediately gone to the aid of her traditional ally, Greece. The German High Command had realized that they must safeguard the sorely-needed fuel supplies from the Rumanian oilfields and were tempted by the prize of the Middle East oilfields. They had therefore launched their 'Drang nach Osten', pushing forward across southern Russia towards the Caucasus.

The British Army could ill afford to spare troops for Greece for the pressure in the Western Desert was intensifying. The Air Force was short of aircraft and equipment and the Germans now had an overwhelming numerical superiority in the air in both Greece and Libya. To add to our troubles, pro-Axis forces were causing trouble in Syria and Iraq. With the protection of the Middle East oil installations a major commitment, in view of their vital importance to the British war effort, aircraft badly needed to destroy German-held air fields in Greece and Libya had to be deployed against the Iraqi rebels.

There was little chance of stemming the tide of the Axis advance through the Balkans and when the Greek Government declared its intention of capitulating there was no alternative for the Allied forces but to withdraw to Crete, and there to make an attempt to hold the island in view of its key position in the eastern Mediterranean for stemming any advance made towards the Middle East oilfields.

Back in England intercepted Enigma traffic indicated from the movements of German units that an airborne assault on Crete was imminent. I recall Flight Lieutenants Freddie Maggs and Asher Lee, who worked in the section of Air Intelligence in the Air Ministry largely responsible for compiling the Luftwaffe Order of Battle[2] from signals intelligence sources, being alarmed over the vast and rapid build-up of transport aircraft, gliders, fighters, and bombers in and around Greece. But when they submitted estimates of the available German air strength, they were accused of exaggerating, and their estimates were not accepted.

On 20 May an intensive bombardment of Crete by Do. 17s of KG2 and He. 111s of II/KG 26 was followed by an onslaught by Stukas shrieking down on the anti-aircraft batteries and the infantry positions. Then out of the skies came an armada of some 500 transport aircraft and gliders laden with paratroops. Their initial target was to secure Malemes airfield in the western end of the island for the arrival of further airborne troops but they met with strong opposition. Yet, despite the great efforts of the New Zealanders under Major-General Sir Bernard Freyberg, the airfield was captured by the Germans after two days of strenuous fighting.

With the Army unable to defend adequately the airfields on the island, it became impossible to provide sufficient air cover, and so to prevent further airborne landings. Middle East and Egyptian airfields were too far away to permit the fighter patrols which were needed over the battle area. What is so regrettable is that neither the Army nor the Navy fully appreciated the air situation. They were sceptical of the Enigma warnings, and blamed the RAF for letting them down, which led, not for the first time, to ill-feeling between the Services.[3]

Amongst the WAAF operators with us at Kingsdown we had a Greek girl, Leni Baltazzi. Though her heart must have been breaking over what was happening in Greece she never once failed in her work of interception of the Luftwaffe in its operations against England. There was little news coming through about the fate of the Greeks and we were not much better informed than the average citizen about what was happening in the Mediterranean. We learned of the terrible sea battles that were waged off the coast of Crete, with the British fleet trying to prevent seaborne landings from the mainland. We learned, too, of the appalling losses by both sides of men, equipment and ships. For the fighting men, Crete was a particular hell.

Winston Churchill decided that, despite the value of Crete to the Navy and Air Force in the eastern Mediterranean, it was more important to halt Rommel's advance in the Desert, with its menace to Egypt and the oilfields of Iraq and Persia, than to sustain the island. Soon news came through of a 'second Dunkirk', and of the enormous efforts that were having to be made to evacuate as many of our troops as possible from the island. But there was one gain. In his reference to it Marshal of the Royal Air Force Lord Tedder has recorded: 'We could not then know that the British and Commonwealth defenders of Crete had inflicted on their invaders losses so severe that the enemy would never attempt again in the Second World War a major airborne landing. It has been well said that "Freyberg and his troops, though they lost the battle of Crete, may have won the more important battle of Malta".'[4]

The whole focus of the fighting of the war had now veered away from the Western European theatre to the fronts in the Mediterranean and in Russia. Experience in the United Kingdom had proved beyond doubt the operational value of signals intelligence and with Bletchley reading more and more into the Enigma traffic it became important to give the valuable channels which produced this material complete coverage. In addition there was a vast amount of Luftwaffe traffic in lower-grade cyphers, which would certainly prove productive. Already No. 61 WU at Cheadle managed to monitor enough to indicate the potential value of the communications to and from aircraft based in southern Italy and Greece, and even from those operating as far away as the Balkan 'Zenit' reconnaissance. It was therefore obvious that the nearer the monitoring station could be located to the source of the messages the better it would be with results.

By February 1941 the Air Ministry had taken steps to increase considerably the coverage in the Middle East. With the emphasis turning from the Italian Air Force to the Luftwaffe, there had been despatched to Cairo a German scholar, Pilot Officer Hugh Waters, who was to be followed soon after by four signals officers and further German-speaking intelligence officers, all sent out with the specific task of dealing with the Luftwaffe and Italian Air Force traffic that was now audible in the Middle East. Units that were no longer needed for the interception of East African Italian traffic were brought back to the Nile Delta to join up with the wireless operators sent out from England. A Y unit intended to assist the hard-pressed forces in Greece could be of little use even in Crete, and its stay there was short.

Just as there was a branch of Air Ministry Intelligence that was the co-ordinating and policy-making authority for every aspect of signals intelligence in England, and was responsible for ensuring that the Chiefs of Staff and the operational Commands were constantly informed of developments,[5] so there was a need for a similar authority in the Middle East. It was decided that Rowley Scott-Farnie, who was by now a Wing Commander, was the best man to become the head of such a branch at the Headquarters of the RAF in the Middle East. He was an experienced signals officer with good administrative abilities, and he had shown during a mission to Russia soon after the start of the German invasion that he was able to handle difficult situations tactfully. Arrangements were made for Rowley to fly out to Cairo in the early autumn of 1941. He was to work on the staff of the Air Officer Commanding-in-Chief, Air Marshal Sir Arthur Tedder, working directly under the latter's Chief Intelligence Staff Officer. The task set Scott-Farnie was to co-ordinate and control all RAF Y throughout the Middle East, including Malta and Iraq, to interpret policy decisions laid down by the Air Ministry, and the requirements of Station X at Bletchley, and to ensure signals intelligence was available in suitably evaluated form for the various operational Commands in the theatre.

With the opening of the Russian Front, and the developing campaigns in the Desert, many of the Luftwaffe units, which had been fully occupied 'blitzing' Britain during the previous year, had now moved south and east, and the amount of traffic being intercepted by the Middle East unit was increasing rapidly. So far, however, no attempt had been made to intercept Luftwaffe R/T, the monitoring having been restricted to Morse transmissions. Aware of the already proven value of this source, the Air Ministry realized that this gap in coverage must be filled. German fighter pilots operating in the Western Desert could provide us with as much information as their fellow airmen in the western theatre. But it was here that there was a problem.

So far the interception of enemy R/T had been undertaken exclusively by women, and the WAAF Directorate had only just approved that a very limited number of Code and Cypher officers should be sent to the Middle East Command.[6] It was understandable that women should not be allowed to work in the front line, where there was possible risk of capture. But fighter R/T had only a limited range, so those who were to do the monitoring could not be based back in Cairo. Even if airmen were used, there was a further problem. Most of the signals and intelligence officers already out in Cairo had come from the W/T monitoring centres in the United Kingdom and none of them had any experience of German fighter traffic. The suggestion was made by Rowley that I should be approached about going out to the Middle East to help organize the interception of R/T. No WAAF could be posted overseas against her will, but he hoped that I would agree to join him in Cairo as his deputy with special responsibility for R/T interception.

My first reaction was to reject an overseas posting. Not only did I enjoy working at Kingsdown but with the slackening of Luftwaffe bomber activity over Britain, subsequent to the Russian invasion, I had at long last been able to relax a little and was more than a little in love with an RAF officer at a neighbouring station.

But reading a Wireless Intelligence Summary, I realized that two of the German fighter units whose activities I had been closely watching during the last months, had already been transferred to the Mediterranean. I knew then that I had to go to the Middle East. The situation there was serious and I knew that it would be helpful to have someone out there who understood fighter traffic. So I told R K B, my Commanding Officer, that he could let Air Ministry know my decision, and that they could fly me out to the Middle East as soon as possible.

On 1 December 1941 I had one of my rare days off and, since I was not on duty until the evening, I took the opportunity to go shopping in London. A thick fog was descending when I got back to my billet in Kent only to learn that there had been a panic with everyone looking for me. Air Ministry had ordered me to report in civilian clothes at 9 o'clock the next morning, as I was to fly immediately to the Middle East.

There were last minute arrangements to make for various intelligence papers to be sent out to me in Cairo by the special diplomatic bag which was flown out to the Middle East each week with secret documents and the drums for the Typex encoding machines.

By now I had butterflies in my tummy. Kingsdown had been my home through all the trials of the Battle of Britain and the Blitz. I was going to miss all the people with whom I had become so closely associated, sitting up at night drinking copious mugs of cocoa whilst waiting for the Little Screw patrols to start their antics, listening to the frustrations of German bomber pilots whose beams were being jammed, or hearing the last desperate moments of a stricken pilot.

Ahead of me was a drive through a 'peasouper' of a fog across London to my home in Gerrards Cross to collect my civilian clothes, as I would be flying through neutral territory. After packing, with my mind a turmoil about what lay ahead of me, it was time to say good-bye to my mother. I hated leaving her; she looked so brave standing there, determined not to cry. I suppose that when you are a mother, you just do not expect your daughter to go off to the wars; a son, perhaps, but not a daughter. It was doubly hard for her generation, for they were now experiencing the second of two great wars. As a young woman, newly wed, her husband had been called to the front. Now in her middle years, she was to watch her children go to war. For myself, I could not help wonder if she and I would ever see each other again, and if so, when?

After reporting to the Air Ministry to get my instructions and rushing off to be inoculated, I took a train across fog-bound England to Bristol, where I was sent to a depressingly squalid hotel. To add to my loneliness, the sirens started to wail, and then the searchlights swept the skies and the guns began to shake the air. It seemed as if the Luftwaffe had decided to stage a reception committee for me. I hoped that No. 80 Wing would manage to jam any beams that were intended for the city, but from what I experienced, it was regrettably not one of their more successful efforts. That night Bristol was well and truly blitzed. It was an unnerving experience to be alone in a drab hotel, in a strange city, in the blackout, with bombs falling all round me.

The next day I joined my fellow-travellers to the Middle East, who included Lord Rennell of Rodd, later to become Chief of the Allied Military Government in Sicily, and various senior Army, Navy and Foreign Office personnel, all of whom were disguised as 'civilians' for the journey. From bomb-scarred Bristol we flew to Dublin, and then drove across Ireland at breakneck speed to Shannon, where about midnight we embarked on a huge Boeing Clipper seaplane en route for Lisbon. As we became airborne I had a moment of panic that we might encounter the Western Zenit – the great German reconnaissance Focke-Wulf bristling with guns. I knew all about their patrols over the Atlantic shipping lanes over which we would be flying, and tried hard to remember the current schedule of their flights.

Our brief stay in Lisbon was enhanced by the sheer joy of being in a neutral territory far from rationing, the black-out and bombing, and we revelled in the freedom and the winter sunshine. By now, I had learned that I was the only woman on the flight to the Middle East and I was grateful to my very senior companions for their kindness in looking after 'our young WAAF'.

Whilst we were in Portugal, the startling news came through about the bombing of the United States Navy in Pearl Harbour. The whole hotel was agog. Throwing discretion to the winds, many of our party gathered in small groups to discuss the implications of America's entry into the war. At tables just across the lobby, a party of Germans was doing the same. It was a grotesque situation. And when I went upstairs to change later, I was met in the corridor by one of my fellow-passengers, Mr Carmel Offy, a political adviser to President Roosevelt, who held out his hand with the greeting 'Say, Miss Morris, I'm your ally now.'

From Lisbon we flew south towards The Gambia, and for the sake of safety we had to fly far out into the Atlantic, not returning to the African coast until we were somewhere opposite Dakar. As we neared the Senegal coast the Vichy French gun-batteries took exception to our proximity and showed their displeasure by sending up a barrage of 'ack-ack' fire.[7]

That night, we again flew south to Lagos, where those of us who were urgently needed in the Middle East were told we would be flying overland via Kano, Maiduguri, Fort Lamy, El Geneina and El Fasher to Khartoum, whilst the others went on by flying boat via the longer Congo route. Half an hour out from Lagos our Lockheed Loadstar developed engine trouble and our pilot, Captain Bowes-Lyon, a cousin of the Queen, had to return to make an undignified landing in a mangrove swamp on the edge of the airfield. We finally reached Khartoum a few days later, where I had the awe-inspiring honour of being asked to dine with the Governor at the splendid Government House. The following day we joined a flying-boat coming up from South Africa, and after a brief stop for lunch at Wadi Halfa, flew on to Egypt, skimming down just as dusk was falling on the Nile at Rod-el-Farag, where I was met by Rowley Scott-Farnie and Kenneth Jowers, the Commanding Officer of the Y set-up at Suez Road, Heliopolis. It had been a fascinating ten days' journey.

10

Y in the Middle East

By the time that I arrived in Cairo there had been a signals intelligence organization in existence in the Middle East for some considerable time; and soon after the beginning of the war the RAF element of the Y Service had started operating from a base near to Heliopolis airfield just outside Cairo. By the end of 1940 there was a need to expand considerably the facilities for intercepting and collating German and Italian communications and this had prompted a move into larger quarters.

Our new Y headquarters was a partly finished building which had been intended originally for use as a Desert Museum, or Institute, but the war had overtaken the completion of the project and the building had been lying unoccupied. The site, though far from perfect, was large enough to accommodate both the RAF and the Army signals intelligence headquarters. The Navy did not join them, preferring to maintain their own Y establishment at a site on the coast near Alexandria. The Museum was built on the edge of the desert, on the Suez Road, which ran through the outskirts of Heliopolis. So exposed was the site, and so badly constructed was the building, that when the wind blew we had difficulty in keeping out the sand. Despite various later improvements, the building was always a miserable place to work in during the dust-laden wind or storms that came from the desert, and which all who served in the Egyptian desert will remember as the 'Hamsin'.

The Museum was spacious enough, with the ground and first floors constructed round a marble-floored atrium. There was also a large basement which consisted of four corridors with rooms that opened off them. The unit, which was known as AM W/T Station, Suez Road, was at first under the command of Squadron Leader J. R. Jeudwine.[1]

By early 1941 the volume of enemy communications both in East Africa and in the Mediterranean had increased to such proportions that the personnel available at the unit at Suez Road were unable to monitor and handle all the channels it was technically possible to intercept. The cryptographers of Station X at Bletchley were by now reading well into Enigma traffic, and they were anxious to receive as much monitored material as possible. The more messages that they had to work on, the better their chances became of quickly decoding them, and the greater the accumulation of intelligence derived from the traffic. It was the same with the messages intercepted in lower-grade codes, which in turn correlated to the Enigma traffic. In order to keep pace with this increase, more and more wireless operators, signals, and intelligence personnel were sent out from the United Kingdom. But, it must be admitted, the whole Y organization in the Middle East was a pretty hybrid set-up. To start with, the Museum headquarters housed not only AM W/T Station, Suez Road, which was technically an RAF station incorporating Nos 50 and 53 Wireless Units, but also an Army establishment comprising some fourteen officers and about three dozen other ranks, that was previously known as GSI(S)B, and which had been moved out to Heliopolis from GHQ in Cairo. The Army contingent worked on the first floor of the building. It included No. 5 SIS covering German Army communications, and No. 7 SIS dealing with their Italian counterparts. Both these units had their own log and compilation rooms, and a combined cypher section for handling military traffic. The senior Army Officer at the Museum was Lieutenant-Colonel 'Freddie' Jacobs, who was a very experienced intelligence officer. He was also in charge of what was called Combined Bureau Middle East (CBME), which was virtually a satellite of Bletchley. There was also an office on the first floor occupied from time to time by the Naval liaison officer, who was on the staff of Naval Intelligence 9 of the Headquarters of the Commander-in-Chief of the Royal Navy in the Middle East, which was at Alexandria. The whole of the ground floor of Suez Road was used by the RAF signals intelligence element, again with separate sections covering German and Italian monitoring. Each had its own departments for decoding and collating traffic, and for disseminating the information that was derived from it to the various recipients of Y intelligence.

The rapid increase in the organization and the very secret nature of the work had their inherent problems. The structure had evolved from a quasi-civilian organization, but by 1941 it had developed into a heterogeneous assortment of civilians[2] and civilians disguised in uniform, several of whom had little or no sense of military discipline, and even less desire to understand it. They all worked with or under career and conscripted Army and RAF personnel, and this inevitably led to some frictions and misunderstandings. But through the sheer enthusiasm of the staff, and their desire to pit their wits against the enemy, somehow the system worked, even if it did leave the officer commanding the station with problems of his own which called for the exercise of considerable tact.

To add to the complications, the Y Service was beholden to several masters. Firstly, there was Station X at Bletchley, which was responsible for the steering of all interception relevant to Enigma traffic. Bletchley was also the nerve centre from which guidance on all codes, callsigns, orders of battle and other similar information was sent to the signals intelligence units both at home and overseas. Secondly, in the case of the RAF, there was the Deputy Director of Intelligence 4 – DDI4 – at the Air Ministry, who laid down the overall Y policy in the light of the requirements specified by the Chiefs of Staff and by Bletchley. These requirements were interpreted in the Middle East through Scott-Farnie, who as AI4 was on the staff of the Air Officer Commanding RAF Middle East, in Cairo; in principle, Suez Road did not communicate direct with the Air Ministry. Thirdly, and of equal importance, were our direct 'customers' in the Mediterranean theatre – the Air Staff of the Headquarters RAF Middle East, the operational formations within the Command, the Navy, and, to a lesser extent, the Army. All these, as recipients of Y information, made their demands for day-to-day tactical information as well as for longer term strategic intelligence. In addition, we were also closely involved in the monitoring of enemy radar and non-Morse transmissions, and with radio countermeasures, and as these came within the portfolio of the Director of Signals at the Air Ministry, we were also deeply involved with the Chief Signals Officer at Air Headquarters, Middle East, who at that time was Air Commodore W. E. G. 'Pedro' Mann.

It was inevitable, therefore, that there were conflicting demands from time to time. This was only to be expected, and it was particularly so as the value of signals intelligence came to be better appreciated by the operational commands. It was for this reason that the Air Ministry had sent out Rowley Scott-Farnie to act as coordinator and arbiter. His brief was specific: firstly, the production of the maximum possible amount of intelligence for use within the theatre of operations, taking care to relate the number of personnel engaged on monitoring commitments to the actual value of the intelligence that they yielded; and secondly, the production of the maximum possible amount of material for consumption in the United Kingdom, namely by Bletchley and by the Air Ministry, in order to ensure a comprehensive study of the enemy's communications and navigational aids.

One of our major problems was with communications, the basic essentials of which were speed and accuracy. It was these factors which determined the efficiency and hence the value of the Y Service as a whole, all the way from the initial monitoring of enemy traffic down through decoding to the passing of information to the interested operational units. In England it was a simple matter of picking up a telephone, or sending a teleprinter message. This was quick and, above all, it was comparatively secure. By the end of 1941 a complex network of telephone and teleprinter lines had been laid across Britain for the passing of information and traffic between the formtions and units both directly and indirectly involved in Y. In cases where there was a need to pass highly secret information, a telephone message could be 'scrambled' by means of a special attachment to the telephone. This ensured that the speech could be so distorted as to be unintelligible to an eavesdropper. Teleprinter messages could, when necessary, be encoded.

But in an overseas operational command such as the Middle East, with the great distances involved, and security so vital, it was an entirely different problem. Highly secret messages had to be sent to and from the United Kingdom, between Suez Road and the customers, and between Suez Road and its ever-increasing number of outstations or Field Units. The telephone could be used over short distances, between Cairo and Alexandria, for instance, and this could be made more secure by the use of scramblers, and, similarly, teleprinter links could be installed between larger static formations, but the only possible method of communicating over long distances was by wireless or, in the case of the Malta-Alexandria link, sometimes by cable. We were the people who knew, better than anyone, what information could be derived from intercepted traffic, if it could be decoded. It was imperative, therefore, that Y messages should be sent in an unbreakable code, and since speed was so important, there had to be ample cypher personnel available at both ends to encode and decode the messages with the minimum of delay. It must be stressed here that the cypher personnel were not responsible for decoding any of the enemy traffic.

As an example of what could happen: if the pilot of a German reconnaissance aircraft operating from, say, Heraklion in Crete, was heard sending a message back to his ground control, the message that was intercepted by us would have to be decoded as quickly as possible. If, after decoding by the intelligence staff, it transpired that the message included the sighting of a British convoy, giving its position, strength, speed, and direction, the Navy would have to be informed immediately so that they could warn the convoy to be on its guard for the inevitable, and imminent, attack. We would also have to advise the relevant RAF naval co-operation units, giving them, if possible, further information about the unit, and hence the probable type of aircraft involved if this could be determined from the aircraft's callsign. But one could be certain that the availability of this sort of information would not have continued for long if the Germans had become aware of the speed and accuracy with which the Y Service was able to read the messages. Speed, therefore, had to be tempered with security.

All this is an indication of the great need that had developed for a large and efficient cypher section at the Headquarters of Suez Road, along with ready access to transmitting and receiving equipment to handle the distribution of the Y communications. There were two basic types of cypher used: one, a machine cypher for messages between larger formations, and with the United Kingdom; the other, the rather slow and tedious one-time pad, which was the usual method of enciphering messages to and from the smaller units whose size and need for mobility would not justify the use of full-time cypher personnel. The one-time pad method involved the use of a master code and a pad of tear-off sheets, on each sheet of which were columns of four digit groups printed absolutely at random. As a page of the note pad was used up, it was torn out of the pad and never used again. The advantage of this system, especially in small forward units, was that it was simple to use and was virtually a secure cypher.

At Suez Road, our cypher room was manned largely by WAAF officers, with whom, at first, we were to have our problems. Most of them had had little intensive experience of cyphers at home, and they knew virtually nothing about signals security or the enemy intercept services. We had to make them realize that they had a personal enemy in the German cryptographers, who would take advantage of any slips that they might make. But they soon settled down to form, in co-operation with RAF cypher personnel, a sound and conscientious team, who 'drudged away at re-encoding wholly unintelligible messages back to Bletchley'.[3] Their praiseworthy efforts during the Mediterranean campaigns were to reach a peak in June 1943 when, in a period of twenty-four hours on 22 June, they attained an all-time high for the RAF by enciphering 104,764 groups to England alone, quite apart from the thousands of groups sent out to the Field Units and our various customers round the Mediterranean.

Whilst I had been on my way out from the United Kingdom, Operation 'Crusader' had been in progress, and was going well. This was the plan to retake Cyrenaica from the enemy as a preliminary to invading Tripolitania. It was envisaged that once the African coastline was secured we could pay attention to the northern side of the Mediterranean, and through that frustrate any ideas that the Axis might have of a drive through the Caucasus, to the tempting prey of the oilfields of Iraq and Persia. A few days before I arrived in Cairo the beleaguered troops in Tobruk had been relieved but our elation was soon tempered by the realization that Rommel had managed to escape with much of his armour from an encirclement at Gazala. The Eighth Army was, nevertheless, pressing on with the avowed intention, despite the ever-lengthening lines of communication, of reaching Benghazi by Christmas.

To provide adequate signals intelligence cover for the whole of the Middle East, Suez Road was controlling, by the beginning of 1942, several monitoring units in the field. In the early days these had been known as Wireless Intelligence Units but for security reasons they were renamed merely 'Field Units' (FUs). One of these units was working closely with the Navy and the Air Force in Malta; another was located near Alexandria to feed material to the Navy and No. 201 Group of the RAF, which was the group mainly co-operating with the naval forces in the eastern Mediterranean; a third was at Sidi Barrani supplying information to the newly formed Air Headquarters, Western Desert. To monitor traffic from further north – from the Balkans and over the Russian Front – a unit had been sent to Palestine. This unit was also serving Air Headquarters, Levant, and yet another Field Unit was to be set up close to the RAF station at Habbaniyah, near Baghdad, with the object of covering traffic emanating from even farther into the areas of conflict in Russia. The sheer volume of the traffic being handled was enormous. Signals, intelligence and cipher personnel were working under pressure around the clock. There seemed never to be enough people to cope with all the requirements.

The intelligence staff at the headquarters at Suez Road were responsible for keeping the units in the field constantly up-to-date with current data about frequencies, callsigns, and codes used by the various German and Italian units, the movements of these units, their strengths and their equipment: everything that would help the Field Units in their task of monitoring, and which would enable them, where applicable, to give their local operational Headquarters high quality intelligence that would be of tactical and strategic value. Every day we would receive from the cryptographers at Bletchley information derived from decoded Enigma traffic, and from less sensitive sources, including lower-grade enciphered traffic. The information would be married up by us with locally-produced data, so that a comprehensive picture could be produced for distribution to our ever-lengthening list of customers.

This then was the structure of the Y organization when I arrived in Egypt in December 1941. Although I did not particularly relish the idea of being a staff officer I was, nevertheless, excited over the prospect of becoming involved in the interception of all aspects of enemy transmissions, and not merely the monitoring of R/T and non-Morse transmissions that had been my task at Kingsdown. The complexities of the organization were explained to me by Rowley Scott-Farnie and Kenneth Jowers. They were both very kind and helpful in seeing that I met all the people with whom I would be working, both in the Y Service and in the many other offices of the RAF, the Army and the Navy.

In selecting Rowley Scott-Farnie for the post of AI4, Middle East, Group Captain Blandy at the Air Ministry had made a good choice. He got on well with all his officers, senior and junior. Although he was directly responsible to the Chief Intelligence Staff Officer, Air Commodore N. S. Paynter, it was vital that he should and could have direct access at a high level to both the Army and the Navy. 'SF', as he was frequently called, was a tall, sturdily-built man with the figure of a Rugby football full-back, which, in fact, he had been until an injury to his knee in a motor-cycle accident had ruined his chances of a Welsh cap and had left him with a stiff leg. He was of an open, extrovert nature, but once he decided on a plan of action, Rowley could be as tenacious as a bulldog. There were times in the years that lay ahead when I would get furious with him but I respected his competence both as an administrator and as a signals officer and I was later to admire him greatly for his personal courage.

As co-ordinators of signals intelligence, our main responsibility was to work closely with the Operations and Signals Branches, and with the various other intelligence sections, such as those dealing with prisoner-of-war interrogations (CSDIC), and with captured equipment. Each day Suez Road would send in a report of the enemy activity that had been monitored by the various units the previous day. It was for us to ensure that any points of interest were drawn to the attention of the relevant section of the Air Staff, and that the reports should be married up with the summaries of any operations carried out within the theatre. This was necessary in order to check on the German air reaction to offensive sorties by the RAF. Although Y reports were circulated to a considerable number of relevant senior and intelligence officers, we learned that we needed to 'interpret' for them the trends and developments. Suez Road also produced monthly and periodic co-ordinated reports and returns and both they and we often had to stress the implications of, for example, the moves of certain German Air Force units.

Alongside the information produced directly by Suez Road and its satellites there was always the vital Ultra intelligence. Much of this material pertaining to the Middle East theatre of operations had been intercepted in its original state by the Headquarters at Suez Road or its outstations, and it had been enciphered and sent straight back to Bletchley for decoding before re-transmission to the Command in its decoded and evaluated form. The offices responsible for distributing this most secret information were known as the Special Liaison Units, abbreviated to 'SLUs'. One of the first things Rowley arranged was for me to be 'indoctrinated' by Lieutenant-Colonel Robert Gore-Brown, who was the officer commanding the SLU units in the Middle East, so that I might be permitted to handle certain Ultra material. As Scott-Farnie would obviously have to be away from time to time it was essential I should be 'in the picture', as we referred to those who were privy to the Ultra secret. Having handled this very high grade of intelligence at Kingsdown, I was very aware of its existence and the level of secrecy involved.

The Headquarters of Middle East Command RAF were in Cairo, in a building that was named 'Grey Pillars'. It was a large, converted block of flats, surrounded by a wire fence, in the district known as 'The Garden City'. Office hours at Headquarters started at eight o'clock and continued until eight at night or even later with a break in the heat of the day during which we rested, played games or, when work piled up, caught up with a back-log of files.

Officers of all the Services who worked on the Headquarters staffs lived out in private accommodation – in flats, pensions, and hotels around the city. Until I was able to find my feet, Rowley Scott-Farnie had booked me in at Shepheard's Hotel, which in those days before the great post-war revolution, was sheer Edwardian opulence. There seemed to be myriads of Egyptian and Sudanese suffragis flip-flopping around the hotel in their heel-less slippers, clad in white galabiyahs, and red cummerbunds and fezes. The food, after the deprivations of England, was good and plentiful, and the service was so impeccable that it was not difficult to understand why the troops roughing it in the comfortless wastes of the Western Desert referred to the 'fleshpots of Cairo', and were scurrilous in their criticism of the 'Short Range Desert Group' or the 'Gaberdine Swine', as the Delta-based Service people were scathingly nicknamed. The plentifully stocked shops, and the gay night clubs, were all a far cry from the battles that were raging in the desert.

My first assignment outside Cairo took me to Alexandria. Rowley Scott-Farnie was not entirely happy about the way information was being passed from the nearby Field Unit to the local Operations Headquarters, or how No. 201 Group, the reconnaissance Group, and No. 252 Wing, the Fighter Wing responsible for the defence of the Delta, were using the Y material that was being supplied to them. With the need to ensure the flow of supplies by sea to the forces fighting in the desert, it was vital that convoys should be provided with adequate protection. Any information about enemy recon-naissance aircraft that gave indications of the almost inevitable sub-sequent attack had to be sent through to the Operations Room with the least possible delay. After a session with the Senior Intelligence Officer of Air Headquarters Egypt – Squadron Leader Basil Reay – I was sent to 'Alex' with the injunction 'to sort it out'. Discussions there with the Field Unit, Reay, and with Squadron Leader H. L.

Tudor, who was the Senior Intelligence Officer of No. 201 Group, revealed that the main problem was one of uncertainty about how best to use Y information compatible with security. This was to be the first of many visits to No. 201 Group Operations Room, which was deep inside a small hill outside Alexandria. Throughout the war there was always a particularly close liaison between this formation and the Y Service, as there was with our opposite number, SO Y at Naval Headquarters.

One of the main reasons for my being out in the Middle East was the need to organize the coverage of R/T traffic in forward areas. Since WAAF were obviously precluded from working in the front line Field Units, and as there were insufficient German-speaking other ranks available in the Command, a policy decision was reached that, as in England, non-British personnel could be employed on monitoring duties. In Palestine, which was still a British Protectorate, there was a plentiful supply of German-speaking European Jews who had been forced to flee from the countries of their birth. There were many who were only too anxious to lend their support in bringing about the defeat of the Nazis.

With the object of recruiting some of these Palestinians, as they were referred to at that time, we started a series of selection boards at Air Headquarters Levant, which was in Jerusalem. After stringent security vetting suitable airmen were posted down to Suez Road. They went through a short indoctrination and were then sent to work with the forward R/T Field Units. Eventually they were to move up with these units across the Western Desert to North Africa and beyond. I cannot speak too highly of their loyalty and the conscientious effort that they put into their work throughout the Mediterranean campaigns. There were many who doubted the wisdom of employing Palestinians on intelligence duties, but they repaid our trust, and they were to become special friends of mine.

One day in January 1942, I was surprised to receive a cable from my parents congratulating me on my having been awarded a decoration. During the war there was a system of sending cables to the Forces overseas using a simple figure code, which translated into a list of stereotyped phrases, such as 'have received your letter', which was transmitted merely as '24'. '143' meant 'the Lord bless and sustain you in your loss'; and '89' stood for 'so glad to hear you are better'. There was a whole range of such numbers, so I dismissed the cable as an error in decoding, thinking that it should have read something about letters being received, and sending their love. Then a week later I received another cable 'en clair' via cable and wireless. To settle the matter, we sent a signal to the Air Ministry, who confirmed that I had been awarded the MBE. The authorities had forgotten to let me know about it.

During February, Group Captain Blandy of the Air Ministry came out on an inspectional visit to the Middle East. This was to be his swansong before he handed over to his Deputy, Group Captain C. S. Cadell, who had joined the staff of DDI4 after having been with the radio countermeasures wing at Radlett. Colin Cadell was a much younger man, and he provided just the right impetus that was needed by the Y Service. With him holding the reins, Y in the United Kingdom and overseas was to forge ahead. Rowley and I took Group Captain Blandy up to the Field Unit at Sidi Barrani. This was my first visit to the Western Desert, and the unit, which was entirely mobile, was operating in vans and tents huddled together behind a barricade of earth and sandbags. I had never imagined that the desert could be so bitterly cold at night. We were gratified to learn that the unit, which was monitoring mainly enemy W/T transmissions, was providing valuable intelligence to Rear Air Headquarters Western Desert; but, once again, we were worried that the time-lag in handling the traffic was frequently too great. Speed was to be our constant enemy.

Our Eighth Army had vowed that they would be in Benghazi for Christmas 1941, and now they were pushing the Italian and German armour back across the 90,000 square miles of desolate country known as the Western Desert. Since the beginning of the war Cyrenaica had seen the advance and retreat of four armies – Graziani had led Il Duce's troops on as far as Sidi Barrani – but then it had been Wavell's turn to advance, only to be sent back by Erwin Rommel's Afrika Korps; and now General Sir Claud Auchinleck's men were pushing forward again along the broad front towards Benghazi. What was it Vichy France derisively called it? 'La Promenade des Anglais'.

For nearly a year the Royal Air Force had blasted the city of Benghazi, pounding its harbour and buildings and then, at last, the day before Christmas 1941, the city had fallen. The Eighth Army had kept its promise, and the news that reached Cairo was that the Afrika Korps was retreating yet further into Tripolitania as far south as Agedabia. But the elation of the British troops was short-lived, and was dissipated by cold, drenching rain. The Army was exhausted, and a long way from civilization. Tempers flared as lorries got stuck in the thick, red mud – mud which cloyed round the wheels of the aircraft at Benina airfield, outside Benghazi, making it difficult for the aircraft to take off on the sorties that were so desperately needed in the effort to keep up the impetus of the advance.

The Nile Delta was almost 700 miles away, and lines of communication were stretched to the limit. Reinforcement overland was tedious and inadequate, especially in the appalling weather, and the sea route from Alexandria and Port Said was perilous. Since the fall of Crete during the previous June, in addition to having to face the enemy reconnaissance and bomber aircraft from bases in Sicily and Italy, the Royal Navy had had to run the gauntlet of the élite 'Lehrgeschwader' – I/LG 1 – which was based at Heraklion in Crete and the Ju. 88s of II/LG 1 from Eleusis in Greece. It was small wonder that the seas between Crete and the Africa mainland had become known as 'Bomb Alley'. But somehow the convoys had to try to get through. An army cannot advance without constant replenishment of ammunition, stores and especially fuel, and there was no escaping the menace of the desert. Already, in the earlier campaign, General Wavell had appreciated that war in the desert was basically a battle for landing grounds from which aircraft could fly to safeguard precious supply routes. The whole progress of the battles in the Mediterranean hinged on the availability of supplies.

At Suez Road, in the Field Units in the Middle East, and in Malta, we were doing our best to help with these essential reinforcements by monitoring the opposition. The wireless operators were on constant watch, intercepting everything they could. Each message was decoded as quickly as possible, evaluated by the intelligence staff and, if of operational value, passed through to the neighbouring naval and air headquarters. It had to happen that some of the traffic was missed, or it might take too long to decode a message containing a vital reconnaissance report, but, with every month, there was an improvement in the coverage and readability of the traffic.

As I studied each morning the daily signal intelligence summary that had been sent in by Suez Road, and which included enemy claims of attacks on British convoys, or reports of their own losses, I must admit that I tried not to think of them in terms of men lost but rather merely as ships or aircraft, as though they were pawns in a game of 'Kriegsspiel'. When we learned that the Eighth Army ad-

F

vance had been halted at El Agheila, we, in Cairo, were not unduly worried. Both sides were exhausted after the ferocious fighting across the barren wilderness. We assumed that our Army was resting prior to pushing on towards Tripoli. But on 5 January 1942, a convoy from Italy had managed to reach Tripoli unmolested, and this had given Rommel new heart. Soon we were to learn that, despite all the rumours that he was intending to make a further withdrawal, the 'Desert Fox' had counter-attacked, and that he was driving the British forces back again towards Egypt. 'Operation Crusader' had petered out.

But the distance between Tripoli and Benghazi was about the same as that from Benghazi to Cairo, and Rommel was well aware that paucity of fuel and supplies had contributed largely to his recent reverses. Every drop of petrol and oil for his tanks, his aircraft, and his motor vehicles had to be brought from the mainland of Europe. One little island, the island of Malta, lay in the way, like some 'unsinkable aircraft carrier', strategically placed to watch all movements of Axis convoys in the central Mediterranean. The Navy, together with Malta-based aircraft, had already taken a heavy toll of Axis convoys from Italy. In the month of November 1941, alone, over 40 per cent of all shipping en route for Africa had been sunk. With Bletchley reading into more Enigma traffic, the cryptographers were usually able to let Malta know when an enemy convoy was leaving an Italian port, its composition, its destination and probably its cargo.[4]

During the previous summer the enemy commanders had been seriously critical of Hitler's insistence that they should concentrate on conquering the larger island of Crete, instead of first subduing Malta. Now they were aware that the island had taken the opportunity afforded when attention was focused on the Balkans, Greece and Crete and the Russian Front, to bring in much-needed reinforcements of food, equipment, and ammunition, and although these supplies were nothing like enough, they would nevertheless help to prolong Malta's existence as a hostile base. Now, for once, the Fuehrer was in complete agreement with his commanders in the field, and even with Mussolini, who so proudly referred to the Mediterranean as 'Mare Nostrum' ('Our Sea'). Malta was the key to Africa; and unless it could be subdued the Afrika Korps had little chance of permanent success.

But Malta, only seventeen and a half miles long and nine miles wide, had its own supply problem and it was an acute one. In order to sustain this island fortress everything had to be imported. After the fall of Crete and Greece any Allied convoy attempting to get through from the Middle East had to fight its way past two enemy air and naval forces. For the brief period, whilst Cyrenaican airfields were in Allied hands, the RAF had been able to provide some measure of protection to convoys approaching Malta from the eastern end of the Mediterranean; but now that the Allies had again retreated towards the Gazala Line the distance for fighter aircraft was too great and cover could no longer be maintained along the whole route.

The possibility of supplying Malta from the western end of the Mediterranean, through Gibraltar, was equally fraught with danger. The whole of North Africa was under Axis control, and German aircraft based in the South of France, Corsica, and Sardinia were constantly attacking the convoys with disastrous losses of ships. The Mediterranean had become virtually closed to the Allies. It was nevertheless imperative that Malta should hold out and continue to impede supplies to the Axis forces in the Western Desert.

Somehow, despite the lack of equipment and the appalling weather, our airfields on Malta had to be kept serviceable. They were vital for the maintenance of offensive as well as defensive sorties, and for use as a staging post in the Mediterranean for urgently needed reinforcements of aircraft flown out from England to the Middle and Far East. Though by now most of the fighter aircraft were being delivered across Africa from the west coast, many of the longer-range bombers were still routed the quicker way via Gibraltar, refuelling at Malta before flying further east.

Winston Churchill had made it quite clear. Malta must not be lost.

11

The George Cross Island

With the advance of January 1942 the Luftwaffe and the Regio Aeronautica together stepped up their bombing attacks against Malta. Hitler had recalled Feldmarschall Kesselring from the Russian Front to organize the elimination of the threat from the island, and the number of Gruppen available for the offensive against it was considerably increased. Mass raids, giving a foretaste of things to come, were launched from Sicily, with over 500 sorties being flown during the month. But still Malta fought back. Despite the island's deplorably low aircraft strength, and the pouring rain, which turned the airfields into quagmires, Malta-based aircraft kept up a steady harassment of Italian and Sicilian ports and landing-grounds.

Thanks to Ultra, there were now few convoys taking supplies to Rommel's forces in Africa which we did not know about in advance, but we had to be most careful to safeguard the origin of our intelligence. Had there been no clearly apparent sighting by our reconnaissance aircraft prior to an attack the enemy might have become suspicious, and then the precious source of our information would have been in jeopardy. So convoys were assiduously shadowed, and reconnaissance pilots such as Flight Lieutenant Adrian Warburton took great risks, time and time again, to search out and fly over their targets on the high seas and in the ports, bringing back detailed and valuable photographs.

With petrol and aircraft desperately short, the Air Officer Commanding Malta, Air Vice-Marshal (later Air Chief Marshal Sir) Hugh Pughe Lloyd could not afford to keep standing patrols of fighter aircraft airborne over the island ready to pounce on incoming raids. His brief had been to attack and this must be his prime objective. Flying time had to be jealously hoarded. The Axis forces were uncomfortably close, with Sicily only sixty miles away, and the radar cover of the island, though invaluable, had some weak spots, frequently giving too brief a warning of an impending raid to enable fighters from Ta' Qali or Halfar airfields to reach sufficient height to engage in successful combat. Too many Axis aircraft were managing to get through to devastate airfields, gun emplacements, naval installations, and, even more important, destroying precious aircraft on the landing grounds. It was essential that more and earlier information about the enemy's strength, his operational intentions, and the movements of his units be obtained and this was where the Y Service could be of help both from the monitored and decoded Enigma messages and also from the lower-grade material.

We had had one of our Field Units on the island for some time. Placed, as it was, in the heart of the Mediterranean, it was in an optimum position to cover Italian and German traffic in and around the central Mediterranean basin, southern France, Corsica, Sardinia and the Adriatic. Up to the beginning of 1942 the work of the unit had been involved primarily in the monitoring of W/T signals of both German and Italian origin, and a little Italian R/T. In the case of the Luftwaffe traffic, this fell into two main categories. Firstly, there were the Enigma encoded transmissions between ground formations and secondly, there came the operational messages which passed between bomber and reconnaissance aircraft and their bases. Most of these latter were also in code, but, fortunately, the Luftwaffe was nothing if not systematic and most of the operational codes that were used by them pertained to all theatres. With the great quantity of Western Front intercepts that were available, Bletchley had long since broken the back of most of these lower-grade cyphers. Now it took only a few messages before the specific code could be identified, and after that, most of the messages heard during an operation could be read. Furthermore, it was now possible to 'footprint', as we called it, units from their callsigns, and our direction-finding equipment was helping further to pinpoint the source of messages.

Meanwhile the headquarters back at Suez Road kept the Field Unit constantly informed of any changes and developments, thereby enabling the unit to produce intelligence quickly and in a digestible form for the Operations Headquarters in Valetta. The unit's monitoring programme was also steered from Heliopolis, who advised which frequencies to watch and what new traffic to listen for, and supplied details of the enemy airforces operating in the area, all the minutiae that would help them to identify units, and read the messages quickly and accurately. The Field Unit in turn would send back to Suez Road copies of their logs, and keep the parent unit advised by signal of daily activity. All Enigma traffic was signalled straight back to Bletchley for decoding and analysis.

The traffic intercepted, decoded, and handled by the Malta Unit was typical of operational messages transmitted by both sides in the war. Reconnaissance and weather aircraft would report on convoy sightings; bomber aircraft would receive instructions from their bases, and would report the results of offensive sorties; and landing instructions would be given for returning aircraft. Now that Kesselring, who had his Headquarters at Messina, was stepping up operations against the island, the monitors were hard pressed to intercept all the traffic that it was possible to hear – for the opposition by that time included some five Gruppen of Ju. 88s, a Gruppe of Ju. 87s and many Me. 110s, as well as the fighters and also the aircraft of the Italian Air Force.

In addition to the information provided direct from the Field Unit, Bletchley was sending back to Headquarters Malta any relevant high-grade intelligence derived from intercepted Enigma traffic. This was signalled direct to the Special Liaison Unit in Valetta for passing on to the stringently restricted number of senior officers who were allowed to receive this material. The only Enigma traffic handled in its decrypted state by the Field Unit was that which would help them in the decoding and collating of intercepted lower-grade traffic.

From January 1942, there was to be a further increase in the burden of the Unit. Radar operators working at Kaura Point near St Paul's Bay, in the north of the island, were bothered by interference on their radar screens. On examination this proved to be caused by German R/T transmitted on VHF and subsequent monitoring confirmed that it was Luftwaffe traffic, probably emanating from Sicilian-based aircraft. The unit personnel of the Field Unit in Malta had no experience of dealing with German R/T, so they signalled Suez Road for advice. Since I had only just come out from Kingsdown, where we had concentrated on this type of traffic, I was the obvious choice to help them. But women were being evacuated from Malta, not posted to the island. There were Queen Alexandra's Imperial Military Nursing Service officers working in the military hospital at M'tarfa, but there were no WAAF, ATS, or WRNS on the island. The plotters in the Operations Room were mainly airmen aided by the wives and daughters of serving British and Maltese officers and men.

At the time when details of this new traffic were first reported back to Cairo, Rowley Scott-Farnie was away visiting our Y units in the Levant, but I made up my mind that this was something I had to do. Rowley, on his return, did not think much of the idea and suggested that we send someone from Suez Road. I was furious at his decision. Here was the first opportunity since my arrival in the Middle East to put into practice the lessons that I had learned and the experience I had gained at Kingsdown. It hit me forcibly that this was a foretaste of what I would be up against unless I took, there and then, a firm stand. Had I been a man, there would have been no question of my going, but merely because I was a woman I was not eligible for work in which I was much better qualified and experienced than any of the men whom they proposed sending to Malta.

'If this is to be the pattern, why the hell did you send for me from Kingsdown?' I asked. 'I was doing such a worthwhile job there. You said you needed someone competent to cope with the R/T interception, and now at the first opportunity to make real practical use of this traffic in the Med you say "we can't let a woman go there"!'

'I'm sorry but it is out of the question,' Rowley replied in his stubborn way.

I went on arguing but it was to no avail. Finally, choking with rage and frustration, I picked up my heavy German dictionary and hurled it at him. It missed, and that only made me even more angry, so I stormed out of the office. If I did get killed, was that so serious? Was it not better that I, a single girl, died, rather that a married man perhaps with children? The all-important thing was that German R/T was being heard in Malta, and they did not know exactly what to do with the monitored messages, whereas I did, simply because I was used to this type of traffic and knew how to handle it.

I walked down to the YWCA at Dharbanga House and found a quiet corner of the courtyard of the old Arab palace to sit and think about what to do next. The sun was filtering through the fretted 'musharabiya' screens, making patterns of light on the floor. It was so peaceful, my anger subsided, and by the time that Rowley 'phoned some time later, I was feeling very ashamed of my outburst, and I apologized.

'I've been looking for you everywhere,' he said. 'I've been to see

Tedder about the situation.' Rowley explained that the Commander-in-Chief had said that there would probably be opposition from the senior WAAF administrative officer in the Middle East. 'But he says it's up to you,' he added. 'If you're prepared to go, that's fine with him. He gives you his blessing.'

The one thing about Rowley that one could count on was that if he made up his mind to do something he really got on with it. 'I think we may have trouble with the Queen Bee,' he said. 'But Tedder says he'll fix it personally. I've been up to Movements, and they hope to get you off tomorrow night. There's a flying-boat coming through. And Tedder wants to see you tomorrow morning.'

Up to that time I had not met the Air Officer Commander-in-Chief, Air Marshal Sir Arthur Tedder, and being very conscious of my junior rank I was somewhat apprehensive when I reported to him the following day. But I need not have allowed that to bother me.

'I hear from Wing Commander Scott-Farnie you're determined to go to Malta,' he said. 'He has explained to me about the German R/T, and I must agree you would be useful. The radar cover is patchy, and they need any help they can get with early warning of raids. But it's pretty uncomfortable there right now, and I won't pretend it isn't risky. The Hun's throwing everything he's got at the place.'

'Yes, sir, I realize that,' I told him. 'But in the UK we were in a pretty noisy part, and I really do think I could help.'

His response to that was the encouraging comment:

'Fine. Good girl. I'm having a bit of opposition from the Wing Officer but she'll get over it. I've dictated some letters for you to take with you. You can come and collect them later. One is to the AOC – Air Vice-Marshal Lloyd – and one to Miss Mabel Strickland. She's the Editor of the local paper. An unforgettable woman with an indomitable courage. You'll like her and I've asked her to keep an eye on you.'

I thanked him in what I hoped was an appropriate fashion. 'They're having a rough time of it there at present,' Tedder added. 'So we're pulling out as many service wives and children as we can. I hope you realize what you are letting yourself in for?'

This was the beginning of my devotion to Arthur Tedder. There was no quibbling about my being a woman. He appreciated that I could do the job and there it ended. He got up and held out his hand. 'Take care of yourself, Mike. It is "Mike" they call you, isn't it? I'll want a full report when you get back.

'Oh, and by the way,' he called after me as I was leaving, 'take your tin hat – you'll need it.'

Immediately it had been agreed that I should go to Malta I asked Suez Road for copies of the German fighter codes which I had had sent out from Kingsdown, and for every scrap of information that they could let me have about the German and Italian fighter units in Sicily. They also signalled AI4 at the Air Ministry asking them to cable to me at Malta details of any new code-words, and anything further that they knew about the opposing Axis units.

It was arranged that I should leave with the flying-boat 'Clare' departing from Cairo that night but at the last moment, owing to bad weather, the flight was cancelled. The next night, Friday, the 13th, Ken Jowers and Rowley took me down to the landing stage at Rod-el-Farag where I learned that the Duff Coopers were to be amongst my fellow-passengers. They were on their way home from Singapore, where he had been Minister of State advising the Cabinet on Far East affairs. Talking to Lady Diana, who was the only other woman on the flight, I learned that she was quite terrified of flying. Yet, despite this, she showed commendable self-control and appeared to be more concerned with the welfare of her husband than with her own safety.

After we had been flying for a few hours and were somewhere opposite Mersa Matruh, the second pilot came back to announce we were returning to Cairo, as they had received a signal to say that another Sunderland flying-boat was on its way from Gibraltar and Malta was not prepared to have two such tempting targets in Kala-frana Bay at the same time. We landed again on the Nile in the early hours of the morning and made our third attempt to leave the next evening, with Lady Diana becoming increasingly perturbed about the flight. When we did finally reach the island, Malta was in the throes of a many-houred air-raid. The second pilot came back to warn me that 'there might be trouble' and asked me to look after Lady Diana in an emergency. Enemy aircraft were weaving about and a couple of fighters came to escort us in, and then, after circling off the island for half-an-hour or so, we landed on the Marsa Scirocco at Kalafrana and the Duff Coopers were whisked away to Government House. But not before Lady Diana had hugged me warmly. I did not see them again in Malta, but a few weeks later I had a letter from my mother telling me that Lady Diana had very kindly called to give her news of me.

Having been advised by Air Marshal Tedder about my being sent to Malta, the Air Officer Commanding, Air Vice-Marshal Hugh Pughe Lloyd, had arranged for me to eat at the Westminster Hotel at the top of the Strada Reale, as it was not thought proper I should eat in the all-male Headquarters mess. But I was to sleep in the Lascaris Tunnel. This was the underground rabbit warren, which was the nerve centre of Malta operations. I had been assigned the cubicle allocated to the Governor of the Island, Lieutenant-General Sir William Dobbie, who was living at the Palace of St Anton in the centre of the island. I had a quiet chuckle to myself when I saw the 'HE' (His Excellency) that was painted on the door.

On the day of my arrival in Malta more than a hundred enemy aircraft attacked Luqa airfield. Three of the precious Wellingtons were destroyed and a further seven aircraft were damaged, and Valetta and the Grand Harbour were also blitzed. It appeared that the Germans had a habit of coming over in formations of about four or five bombers heavily escorted by a couple of dozen fighters, with a further high cover of Me. 109s. As they approached the island they would screech down from about 18,000 feet or more, unloading their bombs on their chosen target, which was all too frequently the airfields of Halfar, Ta' Qali and Luqa, with a definite preference for Luqa because it was our main RAF bomber airfield. Failing this they would rain bombs on Valetta, the Grand Harbour and the dockyards. Their heavy fighter escort made it increasingly difficult for the RAF fighters to get near them.

My first afternoon in Malta was spent, despite an air-raid alert which continued until dusk, with the Chief Signals Officer, Wing Commander Blomfield, and he drove me out to the Field Unit at Siggiewi. It was some six miles away on the far side of the island, and there I was able to discuss the monitoring and handling of the traffic, and to examine in detail such R/T logs as they had retained. I quickly recognized code-words I associated with units I had monitored earlier on the Western Front. Owing to the acute shortage of linguists, the Unit was only able to allocate one operator, Sergeant Marshall, to listen to the German VHF traffic at Siggiewi, whilst the H/F R/T traffic from both German and Italian units was being monitored at the Royal Naval Station at Dingli by a civilian, Mr De Marier (who was, I believe, Swiss), and who had unfortunately sent all his logs forward to the Admiralty or to the Navy at Alexandria.

There was every indication from the available material, however, that the traffic would be of considerable tactical value. The problem was how to intercept more of it, and how to pass it through to the Operations Rooms in Valetta with the minimum of delay. The existing system was impossible. When Dingli picked up a message it was telephoned through to the Port W/T Officer at Valetta, who wrote it down and then sent it by runner a few hundred yards through the maze of tunnels to the Controller in the Operations Room. This resulted in a thoroughly unacceptable delay. The situation at Siggiewi was not much better.

The Senior Air Staff Officer and the Senior Fighter Operations Officer – Group Captain A. B. Woodhall, OBE, who had commanded the RAF station at Duxford in the Battle of Britain – were as anxious as I to receive the Y material quickly, as they had had experience of its usefulness in England, and they readily agreed that I should sit alongside the Controller in the Valetta Operations Room so that I could handle any traffic that was passed through from the monitors. So keen were they to get the R/T messages that the Chief Signals Officer had even suggested installing monitoring sets with an aerial erected on top of St John's Tower above the cliffs in which the Operations Room was located. His idea was that the signals should be fed through to an interpreter actually sitting in the Operations Room overlooking the plotting table. In this way he could keep the Controller advised as and when any useful information was heard. Conversely, there was a suggestion that a couple of sets should be installed in the Operations Room itself.

But neither of these suggestions was practicable. In view of the frequency allocation system used by the German fighter patrols, the monitor needed to be able to tune the set himself; and I knew from experience that to manipulate a set, write down the logs, pass messages to the Controller, and watch the plotting table all at the same time was incompatible with accuracy or efficiency. Furthermore, the space in the Operations Room was so limited, and the noise level was so high, that monitoring would have been virtually impossible. The operational centre was actually a huge cavern about eighty feet high, near the foot of the 'Rabbit Warren', and it was poorly lit and ill ventilated with a large plotting table and several partitions at one end to form offices.

I was not convinced that we were covering all the VHF traffic possible, and I asked Wing Commander Blomfield if, as a temporary expedient, I might organize a watch at the radar site at Kaura Point, making full use of his 100 foot mast there, which would help in increasing our interception range. I arranged to go there myself for a few days to monitor some of the traffic in order to determine the value of the material. From the logs it appeared to be mainly inter-communication between the enemy bombers and between them and their ground control. We knew by now that elements of K G 54 and K G 77 were stationed in Sicily, supported by J G 53 and J G 3, with the Stuka Wing, III/Z G 26 adding to the onslaught against Malta.

The Germans decided to enliven my second day on the island by conducting a continuous air-raid. We were at 'Red Alert' the whole day. The gun batteries ringing the harbour and the 'Three Cities' – as the districts of Senglea, Vittoriosa and Cospicua are called – kept up a steady barrage. I could even hear them down in my rabbit hole as they accompanied the syncopated throb of the Ju. 88s as they droned across the island. During the day I managed to get transport to visit the Royal Navy unit on the cliffs at Dingli. Driving out through the rubble-filled streets of cream-coloured houses we followed winding, narrow country lanes edged with stone fences.

Looking back towards Valetta, I could see the island laid out like a patchwork quilt of little fields. An air-raid was in progress over the Grand Harbour and Luqa, and aircraft were wheeling about through a veritable snowstorm of anti-aircraft fire. I had not ex-pected Malta to be so cold and wet with a continual biting wind, and I shivered at the thought of yet more Maltese families who that night would be homeless. It seemed that the enemy was dropping high explosives in preference to incendiaries, for they had realized that the simple Maltese homes contained little likely to burn and, in any case, the explosives were causing enough havoc, pitting the airfields with craters and blasting the towns to heaps of rubble.

Out at the well-established naval signals station at Dingli, the monitors were hard at work, and I was very impressed by their enthusiasm, just as I had been the day before at Siggiewi. Despite the privations and discomforts of the island, the morale was excellent at both units, born of a knowledge that they were helping Malta in her struggle for survival. There was obviously a good working relationship between the R A F at Siggiewi and the Navy at Dingli, but I think that Flight Lieutenant R. Davison, who was the signals officer running our set-up, and Flying Officer James Robertson,[1] his hard-working and enthusiastic intelligence officer, were glad to have someone else to help them with their attempts to improve the arrangements for passing Y traffic.

Writing of the bombing attacks during those first months of 1942, Miss Sybil Dobbie, the daughter of the Governor of the Island, Lieutenant-General Sir William Dobbie, has recalled: 'There was a certain horrible regularity and method about them. Up to 100 bombers with fighter escort would come over at a time and go methodically round the various objectives, aiming from a high level or else dive-bombing. They generally came three times a day, with small reconnaissance raids in between to survey the damage. The big raids were usually at about eight-thirty in the morning, the second shortly before lunch, and the third after tea. One could stand on a roof and watch wave after wave of planes attacking first the fighter aerodrome, then other aerodromes, then the harbour and the dockyard and the submarine base, and then finishing up with a few hits at anything else they fancied. One could sometimes see the black crosses on their wings. One could watch each plane following the leader, all diving at the same point and releasing their bombs at the same point with a dreadful care and precision. One could watch each bomb or stick as it fell, and it seemed to fall so slowly.'

Day and night, weekdays and Sundays, the bombers droned across the sky over the island. Sometimes, when I happened to watch, there seemed to be hordes of them, but at other times a single raider would sneak in low from the north, drop his mines or bombs and be away before the fighters could intercept him.

I thought that it was unlikely that the Y Service would be able to help much with these low-level hit-and-run raiders. There would be little reason for them to break W/T or R/T silence, other than to ask, perhaps, for landing instructions at a Sicilian airfield after the raid. But it was different with the larger formations. There would inevitably be a certain amount of chatter between pilots, or between aircraft and their bases, and with their escorts as they collected together prior to and during a raid. In my reading of the R/T logs, I realized that there was considerable information that would augment the radar plots, but it was essential that the monitors at Dingli and Siggiewi should appreciate which messages could be of use, and that the Controllers in the Operations Room should understand how best to dovetail the monitored traffic in with other information on the plotting table.

During the next three days, I sat beside Group Captain Woodhall handling the messages telephoned in from the two monitoring units; but I was beginning to feel like death. It had been freezing cold in the unheated flying boat from Cairo, and my cubicle in the tunnel in Valetta was damp and chilly after the heat of Egypt. I had developed an appalling cold, and I longed for a hot bath, which was quite out of the question with the acute shortage of fuel for heating on the island. I was grateful for the tea and aspirins with which the AOC's kindly batman plied me.

I was not feeling at all chirpy when Air Vice-Marshal Lloyd took me out to the ancient Palace of St Anton at Lija to meet the austere Governor,[2] Lieutenant-General Sir William Dobbie, and Lady Dobbie. I got the impression that the AOC and the Governor were not exactly compatible. The Air Vice-Marshal hinted that the situation was a little delicate since both he and the Naval Commander were primarily responsible to their senior commanders back in the Middle East. Only the Army Commander, it seemed, came directly under the Governor and I gathered that this situation resulted in certain frictions. On the other hand, there was obviously a close co-operation and friendship between the AOC and his naval opposite number, Vice-Admiral Sir Wilbraham Ford.

The day following my visit to the Palace I hitch-hiked, since transport was so scarce, out to Siggiewi. The wind and rain were lashing across the island; but fortunately Sicily was enduring similar weather, and the Luftwaffe was forced to restrict its activity. As a result of this lull in enemy activity there was time to discuss in detail the problems of the unit.

A few days later arrangements were made for me to stay at the Hotel Miramar at St Paul's Bay, which was a short walk of a mile or so across the fields to the radar site at Kaura Point. There the Field Unit had managed to install a receiver manned by two linguists, Bantam and Kelly, keeping watch from dawn until dusk. By using the radar station's high aerial the reception range had greatly increased, and although the two monitors were new to R/T interception they were pulling in a lot of traffic.

It was only to be expected that word should get round the local fighter station at Ta' Qali that there was a WAAF staying at the Miramar and I was besieged by a crowd of boisterous and irrepressible young Hurricane pilots, who whisked me off to their Mess in the ancient capital of M'dina. As there was always the distinct possibility that one of them might be shot down and taken prisoner, the less they knew about what I was doing the better. Fortunately, Group Captain Woodhall was there, and 'Woody', as he was affectionately known to all the pilots, brushed off their curiosity with a nonchalant comment: 'She's working with the RDF (radar) station – on loan from the Middle East.' I embroidered that with the established cover excuse: 'Of course, I haven't a clue how it works. All done by mirrors.' But they were far too wise to ask me any awkward questions.

Whilst I was out at Kaura I was returning one evening to my hotel with an airman from the radar site when we saw a single fighter coming in very low over the water.

'He's low,' I remarked. 'I hope he hasn't been shot up. If he doesn't pull up a bit I doubt if he'll make Ta' Qali.' (The airfield lay beyond the ridge of hills known as the Victoria Lines.)

Suddenly there was the chatter of machine-gun fire.

'Christ!' yelled the airman. 'He's a bloody Hun.' We smartly threw ourselves flat behind one of the stone walls enclosing the field. Having missed us, the Me. 109, for that was what it was, went on its way to beat up the airfield.

'Phew, that was a near one, the f——ing bastard,' the airman exclaimed. 'Are you all right, Ma'am?'

'No, dammit, I'm not,' I replied. 'I've wrecked my stockings, and I've only got one more pair with me.'

The airman roared with laughter. 'You're great!'

The only reply I could make was to comment:

'Well, after all, one must have a sense of proportion. You can't have an improperly dressed WAAF running around.'

Laughing, but feeling a little bit shaken, we went on our way to St Paul's Bay, keeping a wary eye open in case the German took another potshot at us on his way back.

After working for a few days on actual interception, I went back to the Field Unit at Siggiewi. I was convinced that we must have more linguists if we were to cover all the available traffic fully. As an expedient, I interviewed some local RAF personnel but only found one suitable linguist and two 'possibles'. Rowley had already signalled me that two operators were on the way – Sergeant D. Constantinides and Sergeant R. Mantle – but if, as I suspected, some of the R/T being heard at Dingli was of naval origin, probably from E-boats, the Navy would reclaim De Marier for their own work. I had been a bit shaken to realize that De Marier had dismissed some night-fighter traffic as 'some sort of landing instructions' when there were definite indications that it was Little Screw-controlled night-fighter traffic. If this were so, it had to be monitored; any information which could be gleaned about the opposition which Malta-based bombers would encounter was vital. Within a couple of days Bletchley had confirmed the presence of the night-fighter unit, NJG II, at Comiso, in Sicily, and by the time I left Malta, we had identified seven Little Screw patrols.

With the increase of the activity against the island the unit also badly needed more wireless operators. Between eight o'clock at night and eight in the morning the Luftwaffe could transmit in peace without any fear of eavesdropping from the Field Unit. James Robertson was rightly convinced that we were missing a lot of useful W/T material, especially bomber traffic on medium frequencies, but the food situation on the island was so desperate that there was an understandable reluctance to allow reinforcements of personnel. Despite the fact that it called for working fantastically long hours, by the time that I left the island a few weeks later, the unit was monitoring round the clock, with James and another intelligence officer, Flying Officer B. A. C. Yandell, acting as R/T operators, in addition to their other duties.

As soon as direct telephone lines were connected from the Field Unit to the Operations Room, we could justifiably feel that we were really in business. With the advantage of sitting beside the Fighter Controller, I was able to marry up several of the plots on the plotting table with the callsigns of the individual formations and could pass advice on their activities.

Typical of the traffic that we overheard would be a warning from the main control at Comiso to the German formation that they had been spotted, and it was obvious that the information could only have been derived from their own Y Service.

'Look out when returning home,' we would hear. 'British fighters ordered to fly north of Gozo at 6000 metres.'

When he noticed his fighter escort was making vapour trails, the bomber leader would order them urgently to pay attention and to fly more slowly. Then the leading fighter pilot would be heard ordering: 'Close up on the 88s. British aircraft are cutting off the bombers. There is still one 88 on its own.'

Comiso control would butt in with an order: 'Give protection to the bombers. British aircraft have decided to attack.' Then they would follow this with information from their own radar plots: 'British aircraft coming towards you at same altitude.'

All this time our Hurricanes, which were so grossly outnumbered, would be flying towards the enemy, and they would be advised of the stray Ju. 88:

'Red One from Banjo (Halfar control). One Bandit north of Gozo at 16,500 feet.' That would be quickly followed up when the enemy was spotted with the call:

'Red Two to Red One. Tally-ho. Bandit 2 o'clock starboard. Going down to attack.'

Perhaps, on this occasion, the Ju. 88 might not be shot down, and we would hear a crippled German bomber calling:

'Send doctor to airfield immediately. I have one dead on board.' And Comiso would warn the other bombers to 'wait until bomber with dead on board has landed'.

We would know then that at least one bomber was damaged. During the mêlée, we might have heard: 'Me. 109 north of Valetta being attacked.' A little later would come the question: 'Has he gone down?' 'Yes, poor blighter.' In the Operations Room, they would chalk it up as 'confirmed', or as another 'probable' victory.

If, as the result of an attack by Wellingtons on one of the Sicilian airfields, we heard enemy aircraft being diverted to land at another base, we would make good use of this information. Malta Operations would mount a second raid to hit the aircraft on the diversionary airfield.

At all times it was most useful to have advance information of an impending raid. We usually knew immediately a raid left Sicily, and this gave Operations fifteen to twenty minutess in which to get our fighters airborne. Messages such as: 'Go to Cape Acalabri and gain height.' 'Collect together with bombers over lighthouse at 2000 metres,' were of tactical value. We would also be able to warn our own bombers when they had been spotted. This would be especially useful if we learned that the intercepting German fighter formation had been ordered to fly above the clouds until they neared their quarry. But I had to point out to Operations that much of the information passed by the German control to its aircraft could only have been learned by their Y Service, which meant that our own radio security was poor.

Of even greater intelligence value were the encoded W/T messages monitored by the hard-working wireless operators at Siggiewi. These included reconnaissance and weather reports in the western and central basins of the Mediterranean, and in the Adriatic. Weather reports in themselves were helpful, especially when an Allied bombing or mining raid was planned for a target some distance from Malta. Sighting reports of British convoys, giving details of their composition, course and speed enabled the convoys to be identified, even if we had not heard a message giving the convoy's exact position. The Navy could then warn the relevant convoy of the imminent attack which would almost certainly follow a sighting. Every scrap of assistance that could be given to the convoys that were battling their way through the Mediterranean was of utmost importance.

We would also hear enemy bomber aircraft being given instructions from their control base, or their aircraft reporting back the results of offensive action: 'Merchantman ablaze,' we might hear, followed by a reference to its position. From the callsigns it might be possible to determine the size of an attacking bomber force, and by identifying the German or Italian unit involved we would know the type of bomber aircraft taking part in the raid, and the airfields from which they were flying. These W/T messages were of great value to Malta Operations. They also helped complete the over-all picture of the activities and strengths of the Luftwaffe and the Regia Aeronautica that was being compiled back at Suez Road and at Bletchley, and that would be sent back to the Malta Field Unit in collated form.

My bedroom was still the little cubicle in the Tunnel. I would enter the 'Rabbit Warren' by a hole not far from the Opera Square, and then descend some 150 or so steps down a winding tunnel until I came to a short side tunnel. This ended in a rickety little balcony overlooking the Grand Harbour about one hundred feet up the cliffside of what was known as 'The Ditch'. In the neighbouring cubicle was Vice-Admiral Malta, Sir Wilbraham Ford. By now I had learned that the AOC had been using 'HE's' cubicle as his own sitting room, as the Governor was living out at St Anton, and I greatly appreciated his thoughtfulness in lending it to me. His own quarters were, to say the least, cramped, and as an additional kindness he had detailed his own batman to look after me.

When I first arrived the Operations staff had been somewhat dubious about my presence on the island but by now they had accepted me. Instead of taking all my meals, as I had at first, in splendid isolation at the Westminster Hotel, I was now allowed to eat in the combined services Mess at the foot of the Lascaris Tunnel. I was not sure whether this privilege was bestowed because they had come to feel a little guilty about my having to pick my way through the ever-increasing mounds of rubble to the hotel, dodging bombs and ack-ack splinters, or whether they had decided I was a moderately decent type and could be tolerated in an all-male Mess.

One evening I was invited to a dance at the Mess in Sliema, across the water from Valetta. To avoid having to return late through the blacked out streets, I was asked to stay the night. The Hun chose that night to make a direct hit on a neighbouring house. We all rushed out to see if we could be of help. Inside the wrecked building, there was someone screaming in agony – whether man or woman I could not tell – then, as though the sound had been switched off as one switches off a radio, the cry ceased, and there was silence except for the drone of the bombers and the 'crump-crump' of the anti-aircraft fire. A woman nearby started to keen. It was a weird, primeval sound which reached a crescendo of misery, and then, as though the radio had been switched on again, there was noise and bustle once more, with people pulling stones away with their bare hands, yelling and shouting with that anger which so often follows in the footsteps of fear.

I had been on the island about ten days when the AOC sent a message asking if I would come out with him to Luqa and Halfar. This was to be one of his frequent tours round the gun and dispersal sites, and I assumed he had the idea that the presence of a WAAF might be good for the morale of the troops. There had been a terrific onslaught on the Safi strip, which was the improvised dispersal lane joining together the two airfields. Exhaustion, inadequate food, working under difficult conditions in filthy weather, the mounting numbers of casualties, especially amongst the Royal Maltese Regiment, were all beginning to tell.[3]

The enemy was no respecter of persons, and that afternoon they were particularly objectionable. I was glad that Air Marshal Tedder had suggested that I should take my tin hat. But 'Huff-Puff', as the AOC was affectionately nicknamed, had a bull-dog determination, and no wretched Hun was going to upset him. His confidence was such that it did not occur to me to be scared. He was also very impressive in the way that he went from gun-site to reloading bay, talking to the soldiers and airmen, congratulating them on their tireless efforts to fill in the bomb craters between raids, praising the fortitude of the gun crews, and encouraging the airmen in their almost insurmountable task of reloading and refuelling the aircraft whilst under attack.

Another of the inhabitants of the island whose courage impressed me was the Editor of *The Times of Malta*, the indomitable the Hon. Mabel Strickland. Mabel, as she was known to everyone, ran her newspaper from a great bell-shaped cellar carved in the rock below her office, which her father, Lord Strickland, had had the foresight to excavate. The newspaper was published every single morning throughout the war, and through it she conveyed to her fellow-Maltese in those desperate days some of her fearlessness.

In a warning on 27 February, the War Office had informed the Middle East Command that 'our view is that Malta is of such importance, both as an air staging post and as an impediment to the enemy's reinforcements, that the most drastic steps are justifiable to sustain it. Even if the Axis maintain their present scale of attack on Malta thus reducing its value, it will continue to be of the greatest importance to the war as a whole by containing important enemy forces during critical months.' But they had added that 'we are unable to supply Malta from the west. Your chances of doing so from the east depends on our advance in Cyrenaica. The situation will be dangerous by early May if no convoys have got through.'

It was little use the Air Ministry commenting, as they did, that they were 'full of admiration for the way you are standing up to the incessant attacks'.[4] What the island needed – and needed quickly – was more and faster fighter aircraft – especially Spitfires. By this time, particularly during the day, it was beginning to be difficult to determine when one air-raid ceased and the next began. Everywhere homes and churches were being remorselessly reduced to rubble. So continuous were the raids that when the defending fighters needed to refuel and rearm they did so whilst the airfield was under attack. Unless air superiority could be established quickly there could be little hope of holding the fortress. The pilots were taking extraordinary risks in their attempts to penetrate the bomber formations, but it was reaching the point where, as Tedder chided the Air Ministry, it was 'too much to ask of any pilot, however gallant'.[5]

Yet fighter patrols were imperative not only for the defence of the island against offensive raids but also to escort our own bombers, the reconnaissance aircraft, the delivery aircraft refuelling en route to the Middle and Far East, the air-sea rescue launches, and, of course, any convoys attempting to bring in desperately needed supplies of fuel, food and ammunition. Spitfires had been promised but none had yet arrived. The situation was becoming so critical that, on 5 March, Air Vice-Marshal Lloyd signalled Tedder:

Daylight attacks on aerodromes very serious. Little work being done owing continuous alerts. Much minor damage to aircraft sufficient to make them unserviceable for night operations. Deliveries are serious problem, as they are damaged if they stay during the day. The longer they stay, the more damaged. Have 17 Wellingtons in this category including those damaged on landing on arrival here with further damage due enemy action. To avoid this, Wellingtons are being passed through same night as arrival with relief crews. This is difficult with continuous intruder raids but we can take it. Must have more fighters as soon as possible. Delay in Spitfires annoying. Can you hasten despatch.[6]

It had been planned that a squadron of Spitfires should be flown off an aircraft-carrier sailing from Gibraltar and bringing them within flying range of the island, and there were to be further reinforcements of Hurricanes from the Middle East. A few days before I eventually left Malta there arrived, amidst great rejoicing, the first of the long-awaited Spitfires. The first indication we in Y had of their arrival was the incredulous voice of a German pilot yelling: 'Achtung, Spitfeuer!'

A few days after I came back from working at St Paul's Bay and was again working in Valetta, we were given cause for a sudden panic. It seemed that what appeared to be 'Knickebein' type beam transmissions had been heard on the 30-megacycle band. I believe that there had also been evidence, from an Enigma message, of the arrival in Sicily of one of the experts associated with beam transmissions. If the Germans were going to start laying beams on the island, the situation would become even more serious than it was at present. The Chief Signals Officer had signalled his fears back to the Headquarters Middle East, and to the Air Ministry. The latter, knowing that I was on the island, suggested that I be contacted for my opinion and I immediately went out again to Kaura to monitor the signals. But by this time, I was fairly accustomed to the sound of the beams and though I was no signals officer, I was sceptical about the possibility of their being of local origin. The signals were certainly not the normal Knickebein transmissions, and from their fading I thought they could well be 'skip' reception from the Western Front, possibly of blind approach signals. With Sicily so close, I could see no reason why the Luftwaffe should bother with beams on Malta, though it was just possible they might be preparing for eventualities in Africa. I arranged for logs to be kept of the time that they were heard and their frequencies to see if they could be married up with beam or beacon signals that were being monitored in the United Kingdom. We also managed to take some D/F bearings on them. I could find no associated wireless traffic, either W/T or R/T. One of the surest ways to decide the matter would have been for one of the investigational aircraft from No. 162 Squadron, which was based in the Middle East, to measure the width of the beam by flying across it, but this would have meant putting one of their precious aircraft at risk if it had to be based on Malta. I signalled Rowley Scott-Farnie my findings, and eventually it was decided that the signals were not of Mediterranean origin. Meanwhile Kenneth Jowers had signalled asking me to investigate possible enemy radar transmissions on 130 megacycles, adding more to the monitoring load of the Field Unit.

It was not long before Rowley started sending signals asking when I was coming back to Cairo. By now the Eighth Army had been pushed back in the Desert as far as the Gazala line. There was a great deal of R/T traffic being heard over the front line, and I was needed back in Egypt. I asked for a few more days in Malta and he agreed to this. It was then arranged I should fly back to Cairo with one of the delivery Wellingtons.

After a somewhat rowdy farewell party at the Union Club, I was driven out to Luqa, and I embarked around midnight on one of two aircraft that had only just arrived from Gibraltar. Due to the critical situation on the island, women and children were being evacuated by these aircraft when they flew on to the Middle East. Several children had been allocated to one of the Wellingtons, and I, along with, I think, two of the women to the other aircraft. Luqa was pitted with bomb craters, and, as there was the usual raid in progress, the airfield was blacked out. The local No. 37 Squadron bombers were just setting off to bomb Catania airfield and to mine Syracuse harbour, and one of them offered to guide our pilot round the somewhat hazardous perimeter track which led to the runway. The two aircraft were taxi-ing out, one close behind the other so that the delivery 'plane could follow the tail-light of the bomber.

Without any warning there was suddenly the sound of a terrible crash. Another aircraft taking off on the runway had smashed into our guide, and immediately the two aeroplanes were engulfed in flames. Our pilot managed to slew his aircraft round, just grazing the holocaust. Fortunately for us our trap-door had not yet been sealed, and turning to us the pilot yelled:

'For Chrissakes, get to hell out of here. There are mines on board that kite.'

There was no time to put down the ladder, so we dropped out straight to the ground. I was clutching for dear life my precious brief-case which was filled with secret documents. The heat was intense, and for a second I hesitated what to do next. 'Oh God, it's the 'plane with the children,' I thought. To my eternal shame I knew that I could not go into that inferno. But it was one of the other operational aircraft bombed up for the raid, and not the Wellington with the children. Our observer made up my mind for me. Grabbing my arm he yelled 'move', and we started to flounder through the mud. But we did not seem to be able to get far enough away from the ammunition that was whizzing past us. Finding what we thought was shelter, we dived under it to catch our breath. But only a moment later there was another comment from the observer.

'Blimey, we're under a bleeding petrol bowser!' he exclaimed.

Then there was an enormous explosion. The mines on board one of the aircraft had blown up. My companion flung me to the ground, ramming my brief case, which I was still clutching, on to the back of my head. He did it only just in time. A splinter slithered across the case, jamming my face down into the mud, and scarring the leather – and incidentally, breaking my jaw, though I did not realize this at the time.

Guided by the burning aircraft, the Luftwaffe raiders that were already bombing the island must have been delighted to be given the opportunity to indulge in an accurate illuminated night attack on Luqa airfield. The whole situation was getting out of hand, and the noise was appalling. Eventually we found our way back to the underground control room, where, covered in mud from head to toe, I was greeted by the AOC, who happened to be there.

'Thank Heavens you're safe,' he exclaimed. 'Tedder would have taken a poor view if you'd been written off.'

'What a way for a girl to spend her birthday,' I grimaced. 'I really do think someone could have done better than this.' It was 9 March, and I was just 24 years old.

The pilot of our Wellington had stayed at his controls and somehow he managed to taxi his aircraft to safety, but of the crews of the other two aircraft five were killed and eight were injured in the collision. A couple of days later the tail gunner of one of the aircraft told me that he had been trapped in his rear turret, with the door jammed through the impact of the crash. He knew only too well what the aircraft was carrying but when it exploded, the whole tail section was blown off. Although he had escaped that time, he was killed shortly afterwards on another raid.

It was a few days before a passage became available on another aircraft, so I was able to do some more work in the Operations Room in Valetta. At the end of the week, I managed to fly back uneventfully to Shallufa, in the Canal Zone, and then on to Cairo where I reported to Air Marshal Tedder. He himself visited Malta a fortnight later, and on his return he sent for me to congratulate me on the work that I had done there, and to say how impressed he was with the Field Unit. I was later unashamedly pleased to learn that in a signal to the Chief of Air Staff, in which he outlined the precarious position of the island, he had mentioned that the 'recent visit to Malta by a WAAF Y expert has greatly improved the length of warning of an imminent attack.'[7]

An official report reveals that by the end of 1942 – when the siege of Malta was finally lifted – more than 14,000 tons of bombs had fallen on the 143 square miles of Malta and Gozo, which is an average of 99 tons per square mile. The greatest density was round the dockyards and airfields. 1468 civilians – about 1 in every 200 of the population – had been killed or died of injuries, and over 24,000 buildings were destroyed or damaged. The enemy lost 1120 aircraft in this assault, but in the island's defence the RAF lost 568 aircraft. Yet for every one of our aircraft bombed on the ground our anti-aircraft gunners destroyed one enemy machine in the air; and for every civilian killed the Axis paid with approximately one raider.

The month after I returned to Cairo – the cruellest month of the whole bombing – His Majesty King George VI made the statement:

To honour her brave people, I award the George Cross to the Island Fortress of Malta to bear witness to a heroism and devotion that will long be famous in history.

The people of Malta had lived up to the motto of the island, which is 'Virtute et Constantia': Through Courage and Perseverance.

12

Cairo and the Desert

When I arrived back in Cairo I found that Rowley Scott-Farnie was away in the Levant, visiting a Field Unit that had been newly established at Aqir. A mass of work had accumulated, and I had to make further visits to Alexandria to tie up loose ends. Every possible help was needed for the convoys that were battling their way westwards from the Delta in their efforts to bring supplies to the forward troops in the Desert, and to Malta. Despite Malta's gallant attempts to frustrate the arrival of reinforcements and supplies to the Afrika Korps, Rommel's forces continued gradually to gain in strength, and a further attempt to push forward to Egypt could be expected in the not-too-distant future. The RAF bombers were now operating from airfields in the Martuba area and the Delta, and they were constantly raiding the harbours of Derna and Benghazi, and bombing Axis airfields in Cyrenaica as well as on the northern side of the Mediterranean in Greece and Crete in an attempt to reduce the attacks on the convoys. But the loss of the forward landing grounds in Cyrenaica was beginning to tell on our efforts, making fighter protection of our shipping increasingly difficult.

A recent addition to the strength of the Luftwaffe operating in the Desert had come with the arrival there of Me. 109Fs, which the Hurricanes and Kittyhawks of the RAF were finding it difficult to match. With these superior aircraft as fighter escort, coupled with our inadequate anti-aircraft defences, the enemy was managing to get through to bomb our forward airfields and to shoot up aircraft dispersed on the ground. They were also attacking the harbours of Tobruk, Sidi Barrani and Mersa Matruh to hinder the delivery by us of supplies by sea to the Eighth Army. At the same time, their aircraft based in Crete and Greece were making sporadic raids on the airfields in the Canal Zone and the Delta.

To add to our problems there came the fall of Singapore on 15 February, which had meant that the authorities at home began to give preference to the Far East, and even ordered the Middle East to release some of its much-needed aircraft for the defence of India and Burma. On the Russian Front the Germans were again advancing steadily, and were carrying out extensive mine-laying operations in the Black Sea. Already Sevastopol was in serious danger. As it was by now realized that the interception of much of the radio traffic emanating from the Eastern Front was considerably better in the Middle East than in the United Kingdom, our commitments were constantly increasing, especially in the monitoring of Enigma-type messages.[1]

In the German Section at Suez Road the collation of Luftwaffe material was under the guidance of Flight Lieutenant Hugh Waters and Flight Lieutenant Cecil Gould.[2] The senior Y intelligence officer there was Squadron Leader H. H. Laurie, but his main interest was the Italian Air Force, which he had been watching for many months. It was Rowley's considered opinion that Laurie almost resented the instrusion of the Germans into the African theatre, and that he was reluctant to admit that Italian traffic must now, perforce, take second place. However, he was later to be posted home and took over the command of Chicksands, the principal Enigma interception station.

In an effort to help us to cope with the increased Luftwaffe material, the Air Ministry had sent out several additional German-speaking intelligence officers. Amongst these were Section Officers Veronica More and Rosemary Horstmann, both of whom had started their Y career with me in the early days of Hawkinge and Kingsdown. Rosemary was to become an authority on German transport aircraft operating in our theatre, and through her understanding of their activities, several air convoys of Ju. 52s were intercepted and shot down in the following months. Both Rosemary and Veronica were later to be mentioned in despatches.

A Field Unit had now been sent up to Palestine to increase the reception range further north; and as there was then the distinct possibility that the Germans might launch an offensive against Turkey, which would have been a very serious matter, contingency plans had been made for military aid to be given to that country. To cover this, should it happen, Rowley went over to Cyprus for discussions about a possible location for a Y unit on the island. Consideration was also being given to moving a unit over to Iraq. This was to be established later in the year at Maqab, near Habbaniyah, with the object of monitoring traffic from the Russian Front well to the north. It was important that we should extend the coverage of enemy communications to a point where little of usable intelligence value was missed.

Fortunately for us, we had been able, by this time, to recruit sufficient Palestinian airman linguists to provide an R/T monitoring unit covering German and Italian traffic in the Western Desert. The unit, under the command of a signals officer – Flight Lieutenant Lamb – was attached to the Forward Fighter Control at El Adem. Most of the messages that were monitored were from German units engaged on shipping strikes, and in attacks on forward landing grounds, for the Italians seemed to be mainly involved with protecting their own convoys bringing supplies from the mainland.

As had been the case with the Malta unit, the personnel at this unit were inexperienced in the handling of enemy R/T, although 'Larry' Lamb had worked for a few months in the Kingsdown organization. Early in April the Deputy Chief Intelligence Staff Officer at Headquarters Middle East, Wing Commander C. E. J. Baines, visited Desert Air Force, and he was asked if I could be lent to them to sort out, on the lines of my recent work in Malta, some of the problems inherent in this type of Y intelligence. There was immediate and considerable opposition to this from the WAAF administration, who strongly disapproved of WAAF going anywhere that had not first been inspected by them. However, with the Commander-in-Chief now firmly convinced that I could make myself useful, he took it upon himself personally to override their objections. Arrangements were then made for me to fly to the Desert as soon as possible.

As a result of sandstorms that had blown up, I was delayed for a few days in getting away from Cairo. Then, with camp kit borrowed from Ken Jowers, I flew off in a Bombay to the Rear Headquarters of the Western Desert Air Force, which were at Ma'arten Bagush, and from there in a Blenheim, which, after flying low over miles of stony desert, finally deposited me at the forward airfield of Gambut. There I was met by the officer commanding the Field Unit and we set off in a truck along an incredibly bumpy and dusty track to El Adem.

That drive, which was the first of many that I was to make in the desert, was to leave a lasting impression on me. Everywhere beside the road there were the burnt-out wrecks of tanks and trucks – German, Italian and British – and everywhere a litter of empty petrol cans. Here and there, a pile of stones and a rough cross marked a pathetic, lonely grave which was the only evidence that here a man had given his life for his country. As I looked around at the vast nothingness of the desert, I though how futile it all was; and yet, I supposed, if men must fight wars it was better that they should fight them out here rather than devastate towns and villages. But I have never understood why civilians are referred to as 'innocent'. Were not perhaps these dead soldiers also innocent? Did they wish to kill or be killed in this desolate place where only the flies seemed to flourish?

I had become lost in these thoughts, and I scarcely noticed that we were approaching the cross-roads where the road to the right went to Tobruk, the one forward led to the enemy, and the one to the left took us to the 'wadi', or dry river bed, where there were sited the Advanced Fighter Control and No. 4 Field Unit. Here we were stopped by a red-capped military policeman, who warned us not to stray off the main track as there were many unexploded mines about. Suddenly he noticed me sitting beside the driver.

'Christ, a woman!' he exclaimed. He backed away as though he had seen a ghost.

The tent allocated to me on the far side of the camp close to the Field Unit was half-submerged, partly for camouflage and partly in an attempt to keep it cooler, and with the fond hope of reducing the amount of blowing sand which quickly coated everything with a thick layer of dust. I was shown the Mess tent on the far side of the camp, and I was advised that when I used the latrine, which nestled discreetly behind a canvas screen, it would be prudent to sing lustily if I wanted any seclusion. I was also warned that my total allocation of water was one water-bottle a day for both washing and drinking. Larry remarked that as a girl I was rather luckier than the men: I would not have the awful daily problem of deciding whether to shave or to use some of my precious water for a morning cup of tea.

I was still diffident about going into an all-male Mess but I plucked up enough courage to wander over to the main tent where I was promptly asked what I would like to drink. 'A gin and lime with a spot of water, if you can spare it,' I replied. I was given a beer can containing a noxious-looking fluid resembling mud. Having been warned by my aircrew friends that 'they'll probably take the Mickey out of you', I accepted the drink, and then nearly spat it out. It seemed to be saline mixture laced with chlorine and alcohol.

'Aha,' I thought, 'here we go. Now pull the other leg.' And with that I drank it all without comment.

We sat down for dinner, and mugs of tea were handed round. It again tasted like brine, but everyone else seemed to be drinking it quite happily. I was relieved to learn that I was not in fact being teased when one of the pilots casually remarked: 'By the way, the tea here is foul but you'll get used to it. We're too near Tobruk or something, and the water is pretty salty. We did find a fresh water well a few miles away, but there were a couple of dead Germans in it and the doc. condemned it. Pity! It couldn't have been worse than this.'

The next morning brought a clear blue sky, with the Luftwaffe in a most active state. I was able to get a lot of work done both with the Field Unit and in the Fighter Control Room, which was housed in a large dug-out. The radio reception generally was fairly good except for atmospherics, and the Palestinian linguists were logging pages of traffic, most of which was in plain language mixed with code-words. Many of these were the same as those used by the Luftwaffe in Western Europe, so I felt quite at home.

It soon became evident to me that the traffic, which was transmitted on H/F, covered an intricate network involving fighters, fighter-bombers, Stukas, reconnaissance aircraft, observation posts, and forward artillery units. As there are few points of reference in the desert, the positions were usually given in coded grid. We soon decided that this covered an area of 96 grid squares, the code references being given in figure-figure or figure-letter code. We were later able to calculate that the code for each grid changed every fortnight.

Much of the traffic consisted of instructions from ground controlled observation posts to the aircraft, giving the height, the course and the number of any approaching opposition aircraft. Air-to-air instructions were heard, as were aircraft reporting to base on damage to their aircraft, forced landings, and claims of victories. We also listened to Stukas and fighter-bombers contacting their fighter escorts, and their formation leader giving the attack signal. All this was very helpful both to the Forward Fighter Control of No. 211 Group and to Air Headquarters, Western Desert, since it augmented information supplied by the radar stations and the Wireless Units, as the forward observation posts were called.

When I woke up the second day, it was to find that there was a howling sandstorm in progress. This prohibited any hopes of flying operations by either side. The temperature soared well over the 100°F mark, and I finally brought myself to make the effort to go over to the Mess in search of some breakfast. I was convinced that I knew exactly in which direction the Mess tent lay, but groping my way forward from my tent through thick and swirling sand that was very much like a London 'pea-souper' fog, I promptly fell it to a slit trench. 'Orientation poor,' I told myself. 'Obviously you should be a bit more to starboard.' I walked on a little way, hoping to find some point of reference. But this is stupid, I thought, and I decided that it would be better if I went back to my tent and waited until the storm cleared. I retraced my steps, or so I thought I was doing, but in a few moments I realized I was hopelessly lost. I could hear none of the sounds from the camp.

I had been warned that if one should ever become lost in a sand-storm, there was only one thing to do, which was to sit down, cover oneself as best one could so as to reduce fluid loss, and sit it out. Remembering this advice, I followed it, and I crouched down as low as I could whilst the sand whirled and howled around me, filling my nose, my ears and my mouth with grit. I felt terribly alone, and after a couple of hours which seemed to be an eternity, I began to be rather scared. Then, for a brief spell, the sandstorm abated, and, when I looked around I saw the camp, but it was far back in the wadi. I had been walking away in quite the wrong direction. Before the sand closed in again, I hurried back to the safety of my tent, cursing myself for being such a fool. Later that day I mentioned my idiotic behaviour to only one man, swearing him to secrecy. 'Don't mention it to a soul,' I pleaded. 'You know what they'll say . . . "Bloody Waaf"!'

As the weather report the next day indicated that there could be no flying until the evening at the earliest, which was the time when the sandstorms seemed always to cease, the Commanding Officer of the forward control, Wing Commander A. D. 'Ginger' Murray, suggested that we should all go for a swim at Tobruk. We drove along a churned-up road between minefields which were indicated with skull and crossbone notices towards the battered harbour, but after a short time our truck, objecting to the heat, broke down. A dried-up walnut of a South African came to our rescue, and he even managed to spare us a mug of tea to share between the six of us. Our swim at Tobruk was a glorious chance to clean off all the sand.

During the next day I spent some time at the Air Headquarters at Gambut, where I had discussions with the Senior Signals Officer of No. 211 Group, Squadron Leader George Badcock, about communications. On this occasion, as during the many months to follow when he became No. 211 Group's Group Intelligence Officer, he was most helpful. Air Commodore 'Tommy' (later Air Marshal Sir Thomas) Elmhirst, the Air Officer, Administration, Desert Air Force, and Group Captain Guy Carter, the Officer Commanding No. 211 Group, were eager to get everything that the Y Service could provide, and we had valuable discussions on how best to pass messages quickly to fighter control for co-ordinating with other relevant information.

A few days later an accident occurred at El Adem which helped in my acceptance in the desert, especially by the Field Unit men. When we were children we had frequently camped out, and we had been taught then to air our blankets each morning on the guy ropes of the tent. I was shaking mine out one morning when I heard a scream. One of the Field Unit airmen, a lad named 'Ginger', had been burning rubbish in a tip, and he had foolishly thrown on some petrol. The fuel ignited and he was immediately engulfed in flames. While she was a student my mother had been burned in an accident in a science laboratory, and we had been taught that should this ever happen we were to grab anything to hand and to try to smother the flames. I instinctively dashed forward with my blanket, and rolled the poor lad over in it to quench the flames. Sadly the hospital ship in which he was later sent back to Egypt was attacked and sunk, and he was drowned.

I continued with my work between El Adem and Gambut for a few more days, and whenever there was a lull in operations I was whisked around by Wing Commander Fred (now Air Chief Marshal Sir Frederick) Rosier and Wing Commander Clive Mayers, who was the commander of one of the fighter wings, to meet the crews of the squadrons which were dispersed on various landing strips. The Air Officer Commanding Western Desert, Air Vice-Marshal 'Mary' Coningham, had sensibly decreed that all aircrew members of a squadron, regardless of rank, should mess together. He believed that if they could fight and die together, they should also relax together. Visiting one Australian unit,[3] which was using the wing of a wrecked Ju. 52 as a bar, I noticed that all the men wore beards. I was amused when a little later at lunchtime, many of them reappeared with their beards shaved off. It was enough to touch the heart of any woman: they had all been 'out in the blue' for weeks.

On the day that I planned to return to Cairo, I woke up in the morning to find myself almost covered with a layer of sand. Guy Carter had kindly lent me his van at Gambut and was occupying a nearby tent. When he emerged from it he looked like a Red Indian. Sand had crept into everything. I drove over to the landing strip hoping that it would clear sufficiently for me to take off, and whilst I was waiting in the truck the driver informed me that the airmen had held a discussion in their mess the previous evening about whether or not I should be up in the desert.

'And what did you decide?' I asked.

'In principle, Ma'am,' he replied, 'we think it is no place for a woman. But as you are here, even though we know you're an officer, we think it is a bit mean of the aircrews to keep you to themselves.' Since there was no chance of getting off that day, I asked Clive Mayers to take me round that evening to the airmen's mess.

With a welcome change of wind, which veered right round to blow from the opposite direction, the sand settled and we actually had a thunderstorm. I was able to start on my way back from the forward area and my flight back to Ma'arten Bagush was in a Lysander, sitting in the airgunner's position facing backwards. We were flying between Halfaya and Sidi Barrani, keeping low because of the sand clouds, when we suddenly saw aircraft weaving ominously towards us. My Sergeant pilot opened up the throttle and also began to weave. In an obviously forced calm voice he enquired if I 'happened to know how to use a machine-gun?' I had already shown considerable interest in the workings of the thing, but I was glad of his hurried explanation of what to do. But fortunately, the other aircraft veered off out to sea. To relieve our feelings we indulged in 'beating up' Sidi Barrani.

When we landed at Rear Air Headquarters I ran into an embarrassing mob of reporters and press photographers, including Cecil Beaton. They had just been interviewing the King of the Hellenes before he flew off to the front. It was only to be expected, I suppose, that they should be intrigued to see a girl step out of a Lysander having obviously come from the wrong direction, and they were full of curiosity about what I was doing. I naturally had no intention of telling them, and I parried their barrage of questions with inconsequential trivia whilst I waited for the afternoon transport aircraft bound for Cairo. I told them about the problems of getting in and out of aircraft in a skirt and trying to press the pleats in it with an iron heated on a Primus stove. Although the Senior Public Relations Officer and I asked them specifically not to mention that they had seen me, Alexander Clifford of the *Daily Mail* and McMillan of British United Press sent back to England articles along the lines of 'Aileen (and skirt) are in Desert Front Line', and 'First Waaf to serve in Libya runs gauntlet of German fighter 'planes'. When later the WAAF Wing Officer learned of these articles, she smartly hauled me over the coals, and refused unfairly to listen to my protestations that the reporters had broken their promise. Tedder heard of the reprimand, and he sent me a message to let me know that I was to take no notice of 'that petty woman'. He made no bones of the fact that he could not stand her.

It was not surprising that my stomach had been bothering me. When I got back to Cairo, the trouble was diagnosed by the doctor as dysentery, and I had to spend a few days in hospital. This was annoying because there was so much work to do, but fortunately, despite protestations from the staff nurse, Rowley agreed to bring work into the hospital for me to get on with whilst he flew up north to Beirut, where we had now sited a Field Unit. With the better weather on the Russian Front, the Germans were pushing ahead with their spring offensive, and every scrap of information that we could hear from this front was important, especially as our Russian allies were hardly expansive about what was happening in their theatre. The Navy was attempting to ferry supplies to the Eighth Army, and they were planning to run a convoy eastwards to beleagured Malta, which was now desperately short of food. Every move that was made by us was being watched by German reconnaissance aircraft, whose activities Suez Road was meticulously monitoring. It was becoming almost inevitable that within a couple of hours of a sighting, the enemy would despatch bombers to attack the convoy. By keeping a close watch on the movements of enemy bomber units, Y was able to recommend as suitable bombing targets, the bases in Sicily, Italy, Greece, Crete, and the Dodecanese from which enemy attacks would be launched. In the Desert there was increasing evidence that Rommel was preparing to start a new offensive, and if he were to capture our forward landing grounds the situation regarding convoy protection would become even more acute.

While I was up at the front there had been a curious feeling of the

G

lull before the storm. From Y sources, confirmed by reconnaissance, we knew about the build-up of the Axis forces, including considerable reinforcement of aircraft in Cyrenaica – both German and Italian – and to counter this the Desert Air Force were making constant raids, especially against their airfields. About two weeks after I returned to Cairo the storm broke with Rommel opening up the assault. Once again the vast expanse of arid, stony desert became the arena for intense fighting. Stukas and Junkers dive-bombed tanks and gunsites; the fast Me. 109Fs and Italian Macchis ripped through the convoys of motor vehicles and machine-gunned the tented camps. We were worried for the safety of our Field Unit personnel, who reported that on the ground all hell had been let loose – with artillery erupting into an earthquake of shelling. In the front line, duelling tanks were charging against each other, drawing thousands of tracks across the yellow sand and churning up plumes of dust. There were appalling losses of men and machinery on both sides. Nearly all the British positions west of Tobruk had fallen by the middle of June and only El Adem was holding on, with the Desert Air Force refusing to abandon their forward airfields.

Among the stories of the valiant deeds of our soldiers and airmen in the Desert there should be recorded the tenacity of the Palestinian airmen of the Field Unit, who continued to monitor radio traffic from the opposing air forces. As Jews, and escapees from Nazi oppression, with the certain knowledge of what their fate would be if they were captured, their every instinct must have been to run, but they stayed at their wireless sets until finally on 26 May, with the German tanks only a few miles away, the unit was ordered to fall back. From then until the line was again stabilized, they continued monitoring although they were half dead from lack of sleep. They would drive back to a rear airfield setting to work again, and passing vital information to the Fighter Controller. From then on, too, until the end of hostilities in Europe, the Desert Air Force was never without its Field Unit always insatiably monitoring the R/T traffic of the enemy.

As soon as the Gazala Line became untenable, we pulled the forward unit monitoring German W/T traffic – No. 1 Field Unit – out from Sidi Barrani, and after a brief attempt to get under way again at Ma'arten Bagush, they had to retreat to Dekheila, near Alexandria. By this time the whole Middle East situation was causing grave concern, and contingency plans were made for the evacuation from the Delta of as many personnel as possible. In Cairo there was a noticeable feeling of disquiet among the local population. Whilst those with pro-Axis tendencies were already planning their celebration parties for Rommel's triumphal entry into the city, the Jewish and Levantine civilians were very despondent and afraid.

In the midst of all this turmoil, Rowley Scott-Farnie had to return to England for discussions at the Air Ministry, leaving me to hold the fort as the Y staff officer for a couple of months. I was accustomed to handling his work whenever he was away in the Levant or the Desert but now increasingly difficult problems were arising daily. My loyal colleagues at Suez Road and in Signals helped me to cope with the immediate situation, but an event that added considerably to my worries came at the end of June. As part of the evacuation plan, a contingent of Y personnel were sent up to Syria. Unfortunately they were directed to a highly malarial site at Kleate where so many of them fell ill that the unit almost ceased to function, and this just at a time when we needed every message that we could intercept.

Meanwhile, at 'Grey Pillars', all but essential papers were being destroyed in case we had to pack up and leave Egypt in a hurry. On one day, which was later to be referred to as 'Ash Wednesday', a pall of smoke hung over Army and Air Headquarters from the bonfires burning in the compounds, and little gusts of air eddied scraps of half-burnt secret documents across the roof tops until they floated down into the streets of Cairo. And each day, we learned of friends, fiancés, or husbands who were reported missing, overtaken at Tobruk, Sollum, or Sidi Barrani, or killed in the fierce battles at the front. But there was little time for mourning: we had too much work to do.

The flats where we lived became open house for any tired aircrews who managed to snatch a brief rest from the fighting in the desert or over Malta. On their arrival in Cairo or Alexandria, the first thing that they did was to have a long, hot bath, a shave, and a haircut. Then feeling more human, they would appear in the hotels and the Sporting Club at Gezira. But we found that for many of them all that they wanted to do was to sit quietly in someone's home and take stock of what was happening to them. We of the WAAF became 'Universal Aunts', helping to buy presents for their wives or mothers at home, or shopping for their squadrons; but mostly it was just listening, listening to their hopes and fears. A stranger would appear in your office introducing himself as a friend of a friend and explaining that he was 'down in the fleshpots for a couple of days' leave'. He would ask you if you could possibly spare the time to come out to dinner. It became an unwritten law for us that if you were too busy to be able to accept the invitation you telephoned some of your girl-friends. There was always some party or other going on where he would be welcome. Looking back on it this was perhaps our most valuable contribution. I remember there was one boy – 'Swinn' – who looked even younger than my kid brother but he was nevertheless a brave and competent flight commander. His greatest pleasure was to come round to my flat 'to have tea out of a china cup with a tray cloth on the tray, and feel civilized again'. He was an only child and when later, during the Sicilian battles, he was shot down, I received a letter of thanks from his elderly parents which reduced me to tears. Thanking me – for doing what? Perhaps for just being around. I believe that it mattered.

With the enemy almost on our doorstep, Cairo was blacked out and under curfew with frequent air-raid alarms. The temperature was by now up to 115° and in letters to my mother I wrote that I was quite exhausted from the load of the extra work and the oppressive heat. Since the outcome of the fighting was obviously in the balance, I warned her not to worry should she not hear from me for some time.

At the beginning of July a request came through from the Air Headquarters, Western Desert, asking if I would fly up to Burg el Arab to sort out a few problems which had been caused by the retreat and the subsequent reorganization. As a major engagement[4] was expected in the desert, the AOC thought it wiser for me to stay in Alexandria and a Lysander was sent to collect me each day. It was usually piloted by the Flight Sergeant of my previous visits to the desert. On one of these flights the pilot spotted an unhealthy bunch of Me. 109s above us, and he landed hurriedly on a forward strip. I approached an officer who was sitting in splendid isolation near the camp, and I asked the way to my unit. He somewhat peremptorily suggested that I should enquire in the Mess tent. I did not know that the local Medical Officer had ordered the removal of the canvas screens surrounding the latrines, believing that they helped to harbour the swarms of flies. This was an incident that gave the airmen yet another excuse to tease me, for by now I had acquired the additional nickname of 'Sprockette' – the female version of 'Sprog', which was the epithet that was used throughout the RAF to denote all greenhorns.

On my arrival at No. 211 Group I found that the Field Unit was now accepted as an important and integral part of its Operational Intelligence. Unlike the situation in the United Kingdom, where Fighter Command was primarily concerned with defence, the Desert Air Force was deeply involved with the progress of the land battles and the success or failure of the air operations could be measured in terms of the extent to which they influenced an advance or retreat. It was the responsibility of the Air Force to report any ground movements, and to observe the size, type, direction, dispersal or congestion of both enemy and friendly land forces, and also, of course, to estimate the strength and efficiency of the air opposition. Much of this information was being derived from Y sources – from both the Enigma traffic and the lower-grade material – and, since subsequent offensive action meant the closest co-operation with the Army, particularly in view of the increasing task of the Forward Fighter Group in ground strafing and fighter-bombing, there was a need for constant liaison between the Army and the RAF Y Services.

At the time our R/T Field Unit had first been attached to Western Desert, the Group Intelligence section was then located apart from Operations, but now the Intelligence Office had become so integrated with actual Operations that Air Headquarters asked for a suitably trained Y officer, such as Flying Officer Yandell, who had been in Malta, to be on duty at all times in the forward Operations Room. This was achieved by arranging vans around a square with a plotting table in the centre covered by a canvas roof. The Y officer's function was to keep the controller informed of all intercepted information which was of immediate operational use, and to assess, by co-ordinating this information with data from all available sources, the extent of enemy air activity. In this way Operations could be given at any time a complete picture of the opposing airforce, its organization and its methods.

With conditions and locations constantly changing, almost all information regarding the enemy became rather quickly out-of-date, and the Field Unit was hard pressed to keep abreast of the situation. Once the advance of the winter of 1942 began, with No. 211 Group operating in two separate parties leap-frogging each other, there was a need to have a Y officer and a Field Unit with each party, for, in the fluid state of mobile warfare, the value of Y depended essentially on the speed with which the information could be passed to the controller. In view of the difficulty in maintaining land-line communications, and the slowness which would have resulted had messages been encoded for W/T transmission, it was also imperative that the Field Unit itself should be sited in close proximity to the Fighter Control. Once the retreat was halted on the El Alamein line, with enemy operations frequently spilling over from the Desert Air Force's domain into the area controlled by No. 252 Wing, which was responsible for the defence of the Delta, there was also a need for the latter to be supplied constantly with information that was culled from monitored R/T traffic. This was in addition to the material that they had been receiving for some time derived from W/T traffic.

One of the problems of controlled interception of fighters in the desert at that time was the difficulty in getting two radar stations to plot the same formation at the same time, and this was where the R/T Field Unit could help. By monitoring enemy transmissions they could forecast an offensive operation as soon as the first Stuka left the ground seventy or eighty miles away behind the lines. This meant that as soon as the forward radar picked up the enemy fighter escort which was orbiting for rendezvous the plots could be immediately identified. The all-important move that had to be made was to attack the enemy as far forward as possible, thus frustrating his attempts to bomb the front line troops or the naval convoy, and this had to be done by getting our own fighters airborne in time to waylay the opposition.

The personnel of No. 4 Field Unit were now so accustomed to the traffic and to the individual controllers who were handling the enemy squadrons that it was said of them by Major David H. Likes of the 9th USAAF in a report on 'Controlled Interception in the Western Desert' that 'they could almost hear the enemy think'. A great number of scrambles of our fighters were ordered on the strength of monitored German and Italian R/T alone, and No. 211 Group was the first to admit that a great measure of its success during the static pre-Alamein phase could be attributed to the Field Unit.

At that time, the main German and Italian controls were located in the Daba and Fuka areas, and they transmitted on fixed day frequencies. Most of the traffic was a combination of code-words from the regular German day and night-fighter code book and plain language. Positions were given either in grid or in relation to 'Punkstellen' (place-name reference points). The main controller in charge of the whole network was 'Kongo 3' (with 'Kongo 1 and 2' as subsidiaries), and the sighting of RAF and USAAF aircraft was advised by reporting units callsigned 'Kiebitz'. With the aid of information from prisoners-of-war and captured documents, the callsigns of the individual units were soon determined. In this way we knew that when the 'Elbe' aircraft were heard operating, it was I/JG 27. 'Sade' was the callsign of II/JG 27, with 'Donau' and 'Zeisig' used by the third Gruppe, which we had identified as fighter-bombers. The Stukas used the callsigns 'Wespe' and 'Isar', and the Army co-operation unit operated as 'Dragoner'. The numbers after the callsigns indicated to which 'Staffeln' the aircraft belonged and our Palestinian monitors were soon able to identify from their voices many of the individual pilots, as the Kingsdown WAAF were able to do.

With the Italians most of the high frequency R/T traffic was in plain language from the Macchi 202s of the fighter and ground attack units of the 3rd and 4th Regiments. At one time, not to be outdone by the Luftwaffe, the Italian Air Force tried using grid references. But it proved to be too confusing for them, and they reverted to their previous system of compass bearings, using a coded number for a given location. Control 'Aquila' would pass instructions, enquiries and warnings of other aircraft in the area, and the pilots in turn requested orders, or reported combats, damage sustained and other details. Among the ground stations heard there was also a subsidiary control – 'Palo' – which directed standing patrols over coastal areas and convoys, and which was quite informative. Unlike the Luftwaffe, the Italian controls would often call a pilot by name, and since at that time only the aircraft of the formation leader and perhaps one other of the Macchi 200s and CR 42s were equipped with transmitters we would hear control ordering its aircraft to fly over the airfield and dip their wings in acknowledgement of an order. But this was soon to change as all the Italian aircraft became fitted with transmitters.

Just before the Alamein offensive, even though we knew that the Italian Air Force was operating extensively, usually on combined fighter sweeps or as part of an escort for Stukas, we heard little from them when they became airborne as they kept a strict radio silence.

Why this should be so we were not sure but we did hear long periods of ground tuning, and, although we monitored no actual operational traffic, we knew that they were flying. We assumed that for these operations the pilots were given their orders before take-off to rendezvous with the Luftwaffe, and that they then played 'follow-the-leader', taking visual instructions from the Germans. Only in an emergency would radio silence be broken, and there was rarely any mention of actual German aircraft, merely of 'Friends' or 'Comrades'.

The interception of German and Italian R/T traffic was only a small part of our over-all monitoring. Most of the traffic that we heard was between ground formations, or related to operations by reconnaissance, bomber and transport aircraft and was sent in encoded W/T. To handle the monitored W/T, especially the ever-increasing number of channels carrying Enigma-encoded traffic, our organization had been steadily growing. Apart from the headquarters at Suez Road, there were now six Field Units and it was accordingly agreed that we should be upgraded to Wing status. On 1 August 1942, No. 276 Wing came into being. To deal with the increased load of work, Squadron Leader C. F. Pugh-Davies was transferred from Gibraltar to be the Senior Intelligence Officer of the Wing and a new Commanding Officer, Wing Commander M. K. Stephenson, was also posted in. Many more wireless operators and intelligence personnel arrived, and the outposts of the Wing were soon to stretch out from Malta in the west to Habbaniyah in Iraq in the east, with a greatly enhanced range for our listening service.

13

Investigations and Countermeasures

By the summer of 1941 there was evidence, partly from Enigma sources, that the enemy was installing radar equipment near several of the key positions in southern Europe and North Africa. In order to make a preliminary investigation to determine the types of radar and the extent of the coverage, a detachment of No. 109 Squadron, under the leadership of an experienced New Zealand pilot, Flight Lieutenant C. O. V. 'Scruffy' Willis, was sent out in June to the Middle East with orders to work with No. 257 Wing. As the Axis by now controlled most of the seaboard around the Mediterranean, it was imperative for the Navy to have the fullest possible information about any coastal radar along the Mediterranean shores which would be likely to pick up our convoys and submarines, and especially to know which of these stations were used in conjunction with gun-ranging.[1] To help with this they seconded one of their signals experts, Lieutenant P. T. W. Baker RNVR, to fly as a special observer with the investigational aircraft of the special signals unit.

By the end of October Lieutenant Baker had become convinced that the guns and possibly the searchlights guarding the harbours of Benghazi and Derna were radar controlled. During the investigational flights he had persuaded his pilot to cross and recross the target areas, thus deliberately enticing the enemy to open fire on the aircraft. From the monitored strengths of the signals on enemy radar frequencies that were now known to us, and by observing the efficiency with which the guns and the searchlights followed the aircraft, Baker was able to calculate how far away from the target area an aircraft was likely to be picked up at the different heights.

'The Jeep', as Philip Baker was affectionately nicknamed, was to make many flights over Cyrenaica, Tripolitania and the eastern

Mediterranean. In the course of one of these flights over Benghazi, he was to make the first operational, if unofficial, drop of the countermeasure known as 'Window'. This was a means of producing a shower of false echoes on the radar operator's screen by dropping bundles of metal foil strips cut to a calculated length, making it difficult, if not impossible, for the operator to plot approaching aircraft. 'The Jeep' had been involved with the early experiments with this countermeasure, and he persuaded the local maintenance depot at Alexandria to cut strips of metal to his specification. These were then loaded on to the investigational Wellingtons and dropped as they neared Benghazi. There appeared to be little reaction from the enemy, but when the Air Staff at the Air Ministry learned of the operation, they sent urgent orders to the Middle East that no further 'Window' was to be dropped for fear of compromising the countermeasure.

Whether or not this means of jamming should be used against enemy radar at all was the subject of months of controversy at the highest level. The strips had already been successfully tried against British radar, and the Air Staff were all too well aware that 'Window' was so simple to manufacture that the Germans could easily retaliate with a similar jammer, and thereby nullify our own radar. They had already thought of the idea – they called their own version of it 'Dueppel' – but they, too, were inhibited from using these metal strips in case the tables were turned against their early warning systems. In short, both sides were stalemated. Professor Lindemann, who later became Lord Cherwell and who was the Scientific Adviser to the Prime Minister, and Air Chief Marshal Sir Sholto Douglas at Fighter Command were among those who were strongly opposed to the use of this countermeasure, and although it was proposed to drop the foil strips during the famous 1000 bomber raid on Cologne in March 1942, 'Window' was not in fact used on operations until the mass attack on Hamburg on 24 July 1943.

The reports that Philip Baker made on his investigational flights were always understatements of the risks that were taken by him and those who flew the aircraft. Typically, in one of his reports, Baker wrote that 'the (radar) signal became very strong as we neared Benghazi and searchlights came up shortly before the aircraft arrived at the bombing point at height 10,000 feeet (the investigational aircraft usually carried bombs). According to the aircraft's crew, there seemed to be no preliminary searching. The lights came up in a cone of lights on the machine, holding it until out of range, despite vigorous avoiding action consisting of a fast dive, achieved with violent changes of direction. The first flak was violent, and of excellent height, several explosions were heard and one was sufficiently close to lift the aircraft bodily (estimated 50 feet below the bomb doors). At this point, it was observed that an added feeling of security was given by sitting on the bed.* The aircraft sustained no hits but the pilot reported that the flak followed him down as he dived, with the centre of the bursting area slightly ahead of the aircraft. . . .'

By the end of the year, the search for every possible detail about enemy radar was of major importance. The Air Ministry had already asked the War Office to instruct the Army fighting in the desert to obtain any captured radar they could, preferably intact, for technical examination and Air Commodore 'Pedro' Mann, the Chief Signals Officer, had arranged for special RAF search parties to look for equipment.

Meanwhile the investigational aircraft that were making intensive searches of the Mediterranean for evidence of enemy radar installations were meeting with some success and by the New Year of 1942 they had identified at least three further stations on Crete. At the same time the Navy reported signals that were probably from radar sources in the vicinity of Suda Bay. On the two occasions when these had been heard, one of our submarines had been in close proximity to enemy ships. As the investigations continued, it was not long before 'The Jeep' was able to confirm the existence of eight Wuerzburg and thirteen Freya radar stations around the central and eastern Mediterranean.

But Philip Baker was still the only scientific officer working as a special observer with the investigational flights. Rowley Scott-Farnie and I were very concerned about this. 'The Jeep' was far too valuable to risk on operational flights over enemy territory, and we felt that he would be better employed on analysing the results of the flights. We urged the Air Ministry to speed up the training of suitable personnel so that he would be replaced on operations, for there was at that time no suitable RAF Radio Countermeasures Officer available for flying duties. No. 80 Wing was in the throes of a training scheme, and, to add to our problems, there was an acute shortage of VHF

---

*Lieutenant Baker, in true naval style, always slung a hammock in the fuselage of the investigating Wellington.

receivers of a type suitable for airborne monitoring of the signals.

Our worst fears for the safety of this highly experienced scientific officer were confirmed on the night of 7/8 March 1942, when the Wellington in which Philip was flying had to make a forced landing near the island of Rhodes.[2] It was a disastrous loss. Flying with him as a trainee was an Australian airman, Sergeant Robert Tregenza, on his first operational flight as a special operator. Showing great presence of mind before the aircraft crashed, Baker and Tregenza managed to jettison all the accessible scientific gear that they had on board and the pilot, Sergeant Mervyn Knowles, deliberately ditched his aircraft in water deep enough to prevent the possibility of any salvage.

The best way of recording what then happened is to quote from the report that was later made by Philip Baker, who also recommended Tregenza for a decoration. He wrote:[3] 'One of Tregenza's shoulders was completely dislocated by the impact of landing. Upon entering the water, which was found to be at an unpleasantly low temperature, it was observed that the dinghy had failed to release, although the navigator, on landing, had had one thumb nearly torn off by the release toggle, which seemed to be jammed. Wearing full flying clothing, Tregenza then swam ashore, the time being later estimated from rather scanty evidence at about $1\frac{1}{2}$ hours. He was in great pain from his arm, which was quite useless.

'On reaching the beach, which was lined with Italian soldiers, who had been firing their rifles, presumably at random, the aircrew was seized and run up to a nearby guardhouse, each man between two Italian soldiers, with no regard for the physical state of their prisoners. The aircrew was then stripped, given one blanket per man, and a little cognac and taken by lorry to the local artillery HQ at Rodi, a distance of about three miles. Comfort was noticeable by its absence on this journey, the lorry being an old one with solid tyres, and the aircrew, naked except for a blanket, was kept forced into one corner by the guards, and were sitting either on the filthy floor of the lorry or else on bundles of their wet clothing. Opportunity was taken of this situation to remind them of the necessity for security.

'Later the injured were taken to one of the local hospitals where they were very well and competently treated. Until the artillery barracks was reached, I did not realize that Tregenza had been in any way injured, as he gave no sign whatever of being in pain, although the pain must, in fact, have been considerable.' After explaining how each prisoner was kept in a separate room, Baker continued – 'Tregenza's room was opposite mine, and had doors communicating with the rooms on either side. It was therefore possible for him to whisper to the occupants of those rooms through the keyholes and they in turn could communicate with the rooms opposite, either by whispering when the guards, one of whose duties was to ensure we did not talk to each other, were at the end of the passage or, in case of necessity, messages were written on lavatory paper by Tregenza with the end of a lead composition tube of toothpaste and passed by him under the communicating doors and then thrown across the passage to the person concerned. My own room had no communicating doors. It was fortunately possible for me to communicate with Tregenza in the opposite room by the deaf and dumb manual code, and by these means it was possible to ensure that the aircrew was reminded of essential security points. Later, at Bari Transit Camp, in Italy, Tregenza asked me about the possibility of communicating with Middle East. I gave him a suitable address to write to and suggested the type of text required to convey the desired information. The postcard eventually received from him in the Middle East was the result of his own initiative . . . and was the only one known to reach the addressee.'

The cryptic message that we eventually received from Tregenza enabled us in Air Intelligence at Headquarters in Cairo to learn with relief that not only were all the members of the crew of the aircraft alive, but the special equipment had almost certainly not been salvaged, and the Italians had not discovered the aircraft's true mission.

It later transpired that the Italians had been most suspicious about a naval officer being on board the aircraft, and believed at first that he must be involved in some way in sabotage, or espionage, or aiding escape organizations, or some other evil intent, especially as Baker was carrying a Beretta revolver. But he and the crew managed to convince them that he was merely taking an illicit passage back to Egypt with Air Force friends, and that he would almost certainly be court-martialled on his return. He was eventually released in the first exchange of prisoners through Turkey, turning up in my office on 1 April a year after being captured. He was, he assured me, deeply offended that he 'didn't even have to escape; they've handed me back on a plate'.

One of the special tasks that was assigned to the investigational aircraft was operating airborne radio countermeasures. The Army had requested that attempts should be made to jam the VHF tank transmissions through the use of airborne jamming equipment, known as 'Jostle'. The jammer was designed to obliterate all traffic transmitted on a given wave band, and it had been tested in England against the radio sets of captured tanks. During the 'Crusader' campaign, when the battle was raging around the Fort Capuzzo-Sidi Omar area, the aircrews were assigned the unenviable task of patrolling for several hours over the combat zone, frequently in broad daylight, attempting to frustrate any communications between the tanks fighting in the desert below them. The plan of action, which was evolved by the senior RAF Radio Countermeasures Officer, Squadron Leader W. B. S. 'Tim' Simpson and his deputy, Flying Officer Geoffrey Mason, in conjunction with Lieutenant-Colonel R. P. G. Denman, was for the jamming operations to be monitored and controlled from the ground in the battle area. To this end, Wing Commander D. H. S. 'Peter' Rusher, the Officer Commanding the investigational squadron, commandeered a Marmon-Harrington armoured car belonging to No. 2 Tank Corps together with its crew. The scheme was for this car to rush forward to join Headquarters, 7th Armoured Division from where the jamming Wellingtons could be controlled, right in the front line. However, owing to engine trouble, the armoured car only reached as far as LG 25 (Oxford Circus) with its crew of two, together with Geoff Mason and a Sergeant D. Seymour, so perforce it was from there that the jamming had to be controlled.

Flying alone with no fighter escort to guard them, the Wellingtons were sitting targets for the Axis fighters, whose manoeuvrability was far superior to theirs. The skies were frequently cloudless, and there was little chance of concealment. Their jamming transmissions actually made it easy for the enemy to take a D/F fix on their exact position. The strain on the crews scanning the horizon for attacking aircraft during these long flights over the battle-front was an unfair burden, especially as they were well aware that some of their comrades including Colonel Denman[4] had already been shot down or wounded on previous similar sorties. Typical of their courage was an occasion when Flight Lieutenant Willis was attacked by fighters shortly after radiating jamming signals. His crew managed to shoot down one fighter, but his wireless operator was wounded, and his aircraft was damaged. But despite the damage the same aircraft was airborne again the next day and again it was attacked, this time by at least nine enemy fighters, sustaining very serious damage. The communications transmitter was smashed, and the hydraulics tank was holed, and only the initiative of the crew in stuffing the leak in the tank with rags saved the aircraft from having to crash land.

When, as the result of interrogation of captured armoured vehicle crews, it became evident that the success of this form of jamming was questionable, and that it certainly did not justify the enormous risks taken by the aircrews, the 'Jostle' operations were halted. They were not renewed again until the Alamein offensive, when improved jamming equipment was used.

By the end of 1941 the Axis forces had so accelerated their programme of radar installation that there was an increasingly urgent need for considerably more investigational aircraft in the Middle East Command in order to keep pace with the demands for information from all three services. From the nucleus of the No. 109 Squadron detachment, and combining with aircraft used for the calibration of our own radar, a new squadron – No. 162 – was formed under the command of 'Peter' Rusher.[5] This was based at first at Shallufa, but it was soon moved to Bilbeis, in the Canal Zone, refuelling when necessary at a forward desert airfield, or in Palestine, Cyprus, or Malta in order to extend its range over enemy territory.

This was the beginning of a constant surveillance of all Axis radar in the theatre, covering the whole of the coastal chain as well as the installations in the vicinity of the major inland targets. During the flights that were made by this squadron the airborne monitors would keep a careful watch for evidence of any new stations, or any indications that radar apparatus had been moved from one site to another. Sometimes we would learn from Enigma sources that a new Freya or Wuerzburg was to be installed at a certain site, and a watch would then be kept for the signals which would indicate that the station had become operational. In the same way any lack of signals from a known site might confirm the success of a recent bombing attack on a radar station, and Operations could take advantage of the gap in the radar cover when planning the next bombing missions in or over that area.

We knew from British radar that the enemy could make use of inherent weaknesses in the radar cover to avoid early detection. This was equally true for German radar. When an aircraft approached very low, it was nearly always the case, even with a long-range Freya station, that an operationally useful amount of warning could not be given. The exact distance at which an aircraft would first be detected depended on various human as well as technical factors. We were well aware that radar apparatus was rendered virtually blind in the neighbourhood of large land masses, which produced stronger echoes than those from aircraft flying near them, so that approaches planned through mountains might curtail considerably the warning from a particular radar station.

As the months passed, and with the installation of better monitoring and direction-finding equipment in the investigational aircraft, the special airborne operators – or 'Jeeps' as they were all inevitably known in recognition of Philip Baker's pioneering work – became more experienced in locating the radar stations. As soon as an approximate position was determined, photographic reconnaissance aircraft would cover the area to pin-point exactly the position of the apparatus. Sometimes, however, it was the other way round. Photographic interpretation would show up a radar installation not yet detected by No. 162 Squadron, and they would then make an investigational flight to determine the type and efficiency of the station.

Apart from listening to signals on known ground radar frequencies, the operators were always on the look-out for other 'noises'. Although by early 1942 we knew, for instance, that several of the night-fighter units which were defending Western Europe were equipped with the German equivalent of our AI – airborne radar – which they called the 'Lichtensteingeraet' and referred to in their R/T coded traffic as 'Emil, Emil', we had no evidence of its use in the Mediterranean theatre. We knew from Y intercepts when these units were posted south, but it did not necessarily follow that they would bring this new equipment with them. If and when night-fighters fitted with airborne radar did operate in the theatre, the danger to our bombers would be considerably increased. Even whilst I was in Malta, I had been certain that GCI aircraft were already operating from Sicilian airfields and now it was for No. 162 Squadron to keep a watchful ear open for signals associated with airborne radar.

There was also always the possibility that beams might be used, and as a precaution, beam-jamming equipment was already available in the Middle East. It had become a ceaseless radio war on a very large scale: a constant search for improvements on both sides with

5 Me. 110 showing aerials
f the Lichtensteingeraet

Signaltafel für Tag-u. Nachtjagd

Allgemeines

red	Eigene 1-mot.-Flugzeuge	= Radfahrer
mov	Eigene 2-mot.-Flugzeuge	= Möbelwagen
dmw	Eigene 3-u.4.mot.-Flugzeuge	= Dicke Möbelwagen
ind	Feindliche Jäger	= Indianer
aut	Feindl.2-mot.-Flugzeuge	= Autos
dau	Feindl.4-mot.-Flugzeuge	= Dicke Autos
frb	Feindl.Jagdschutz verlässt Kampfverband	= Freie Bahn
fdl	Feindl.Jagdschutz nimmt Kampfverband auf bezw. ist erkannt	= Aufnahme, Starke ... = Aufnahme aus ...
don	Nachtstossen	= Donnerkeil
sta	Sperre fliegen von bis od. über	= Stacheldraht
obj	Befohlenes Schutzobjekt (Stadt, Hafen, Schiff)	= Objekt
mau	Feindberührung	= Mauerblume
spb	Er hat Feindverband erkannt in (mit Ortsangabe)	= Spielbeginn
haL	Luftkampf abbrechen	= Halbzeit
que	Standort	= Quelle
hen	Höhe (in Hm) eigene	= Kirchturm
haL	Feindhöhe	= Hanny
cur	Kurs	= Caruso
sir	Sammeln über	= Zirkus über
gar	Flugplatz	= Gartenzaun
bvm	Benzinmangel	= Ich habe Durst
ana	Peilzeichen	= Tuba
rr	Verstanden	= Viktor
rpt	Nicht verstanden, b.wiederholen	= Ricardus
abs	Abschuss	= Horrido
ang	Angriff	= Pauke-Pauke
kr	Feindmaschine in .....°	= Indianer in ....°
krg	Feindgeschwindigkeit	= Orkan
efn	Entfernung vom Feind	= Ente
bdo	Bodenstelle-Gefechtsstand	= Bodo
rex	Ich habe Ziel gesehen	= Ich berühre
niL	Ziel nicht gesehen (verloren)	= Ich suche
war	Warten Sie	= Gehen Sie ins Vorzimmer
Lfg	Luftgefahr	= Konkurrenz
wmd	Wir machen Dunkelnachtjagd	= Eule
jms	Jagd mit Scheinwerfer	= Weiss
jos	Jagd ohne Scheinwerfer	= Schwarz
nim	Erkennungsscheinwerfer im Raum	= Himmel
sko	Scheinwerfer kommen durch	= Stangen halten
sno	Scheinw. kommen nicht durch	= Stangen brechen ab
sin	Ziel im Scheinwerfer	= Otto, Otto
bs	Bleiben Sie in ...	= Normaluhr
zu	Flakbegrenzung (bis .... hm)	= Feuerschlucker
uq	Flaksperrgebiet	= Hexentanz
rp	Hauptangriffsziel	= Marktplatz
nt	Fehranzriff	= Aussenseiter
akr	Abschuss eigener Scheinkaskaden	= Bauernfang

6 *Opposite: Signaltafel für
Tag-u Nachtjagd*: part of
German day- and night-
fighter code used on operations

7 *Above:* Lieutenant
Philip T. W. Baker, DSC
'The Jeep' – on his return
from captivity, 1943

8 *Above right:* Air Vice-
Marshal (now Air Chief
Marshal) Sir Hugh Pughe
Lloyd, GBE, KCB, MC, DFC

19 *Above:* Me. 323 destroyed off Corsica

20 Officers of Nos 21 and 25 Field Units at La Marsa just prior to Operation 'Husky'. *Back row left to right:* Flying Officers Longinoto and Price, and Flight Lieutenant Hill. *Front row left to right:* Flying Officer Ibbs, Section Officer 'Rusty' Goff, Flying Officer Yates

1 *Above:* Bomb damage in
Malta, 1942 – Main Street,
Senglea

2 Air Chief Marshal Sir
Arthur Tedder discusses
tactics with Air Marshal
Sir Arthur 'Mary'
Coningham and Air Vice-
Marshal Harry Broadhurst,
Italy, 1943

3 *Top left:* With members of No. 162 Squadron on Nicosia Airport, Cyprus, 1943

4 *Bottom left:* Ju. 52s being attacked by Mitchells over Sicilian narrows. Twenty-five out of a formation of thirty-five shot down

5 *Right:* Wing Cdr S. G. Morgan

6 *Below:* Lancasters dropping 'Window' during raid

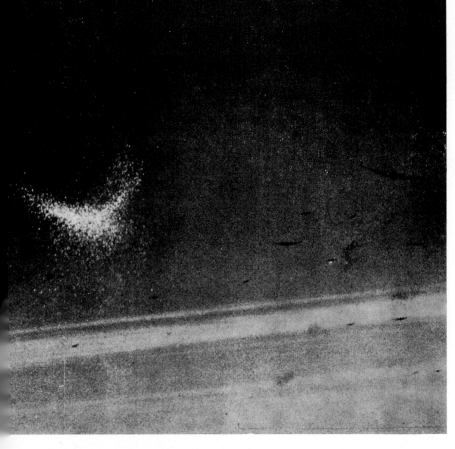

27 The author with her
mother and brother after her
investiture at Buckingham
Palace, 1944

each trying to frustrate the other. The responsibility for co-ordinating the investigation of enemy radar was vested in our office, at the Headquarters, AI4, but the actual search programmes were planned in consultation with the radio countermeasures specialists on the staff of the Chief Signals Officer, 'Tim' Simpson and Geoff Mason who had been involved with the tank jamming. From time to time the Operational Research Section would compile maps showing the extent of the enemy radar coverage at the various heights from information that was derived from the logs of the airborne monitors of No. 162 Squadron.

I was never happier than when I was with No. 162 Squadron at Bilbeis. They would let me fly with them on short air tests around the Delta, and flew me to Palestine, Cyprus and the Desert. I was even allowed occasionally to take over the controls of a 'Wimpey', which was the well-known RAF slang for a Wellington. I greatly admired the Squadron's courage and conscientious effort, and I was constantly battling for more and better equipment for them. In view of the secrecy of their work, they were, unfortunately, the 'Cinderellas' of the bomber force when it came to maintenance and the allocation of new equipment. Yet without No. 162 Squadron's dedicated searches, the planning of bombing raids and convoy routes in the theatre would have been much more difficult. That the Squadron managed to accomplish the demanding programme with Wellingtons that were really well past their prime – or 'clapped out' as we called it – was almost as much to the credit of the hard-working ground crews as to the dedication of the aircrews.

On one occasion the Navy was planning an attempt to sail a convoy through from Alexandria to beleaguered Malta, running the gauntlet of the Axis air and sea forces in the eastern Mediterranean. They particularly needed the latest information on the enemy coast-watcher installations, which were known to the Germans as 'Seetakt'. It was arranged that No. 162 Squadron should make a special check, working from Malta as a forward base. On their return to Egypt one of the pilots cheerfully informed me: 'We went so low, I had to use my windscreen wipers against the spray but we got what you wanted.' It was a 'line-shoot' in the best tradition, perhaps, but it was not so far from the truth.

Aircrews would take the greatest risks in order to get the information that was needed by Operations. It was inevitable that some of them should never return. Some were shot down over the sea, and their bodies were eventually washed ashore. Some were taken prisoner. Others were never heard of again. Should one of the aircraft fail to get back to base on schedule, perhaps because of enemy damage or because of the all too frequent engine-trouble, I would suffer an agony of apprehension until I knew the crew were safe. They had become special friends of mine, and I felt very responsible for them.

So efficient had the crews of No. 162 Squadron become in navigation and searching that they were occasionally assigned some very special task. There was an incident early in May 1942, when a flight of three South African Army Air Force Blenheims under the command of an Air Force major went missing on a reconnaissance training exercise near the Kufra Oasis, which was far out in the desert south of the Delta. The intention had been to show the aircrews the problems of navigating over desert terrain where the innumerable hills were difficult to distinguish as landmarks on the sparse maps available for the area. With sandstorms adding to their confusion, the flight had become completely lost and had been forced to land in the desert. For nearly a week the normal search operations by a Bombay Squadron proved fruitless. Extensive searches by the local Long Range Desert Group Unit also failed to find a trace of the missing aircraft. Finally we were asked if No. 162 Squadron could help in the search. Both Wing Commander Rusher and Flight Lieutenant D. G. 'Bunny' Warren gladly undertook the task. The only clue to the whereabouts of the aircraft was a report, which was by then already a week old, that a wireless operator at Mersa Matruh some 400 miles away had heard a faint signal, possibly from an aircraft in distress, and had obtained a dubious bearing. Making a square search up the bearing, Warren finally found the lost aircraft four days later, and landed in the desert to rescue the survivors. By then, one man had shot himself and all the others had died except for one corporal, who survived the ordeal and was able to make a report. For his tenacity during the search operations Warren was Mentioned in Despatches.

A forced landing in the desert, with no shade, high temperatures, and only emergency food and water, was the dread of all airmen flying across the trackless sandy wastes. When one No. 162 Squadron aircraft came down miles south of Benghazi, at a time when the front line was hundreds of miles farther east, the crew decided to walk south in the hope of meeting one of the Long Range Desert

Group's patrols from the Oasis of Siwa. By good fortune they were rescued, but the pilot told me later that he had become so dehydrated that it was almost a week after his rescue before he needed to urinate.

By June 1942 the Squadron had been considerably enlarged in order to cope with the ever-increasing demands for information about the enemy radar even further afield. The Navy wanted to know if there were radar installations on Sardinia capable of picking up convoys approaching Malta from the west. Where would they be seen by Sicilian stations? Of what types and how efficient were the installations on the island of Pantellaria, which guarded the perilous narrows before reaching Malta? No. 205 Group needed to know where the weak spots in the radar chain were for routing bombers to Balkan and Cyrenaican targets. Special Operations were anxious to find the best places along the enemy coastline for landing parties. Malta knew there was little airborne activity from the island which was not observed by Sicilian radar, but in the planning of attacks on Taranto Harbour, for example, was the best route to fly east and then north? Was there radar guarding Naples harbour, and if so, of what sort? The Eighth Army and the Desert Air Force needed to know exactly where the radar sites were in the desert. No. 276 Wing also wanted help with a watch on enemy M/F beacons. There seemed to be an endless list of demands for information, all of a highly secret nature and all requiring diligent searching.

At long last a Technical Signals Officer was posted out to us as a replacement for the missing Philip Baker. He was Flight Lieutenant Alan Maley and, like his predecessor, he was to make numerous flights over enemy territory, recording and carefully analysing the radar signals and training the special operators who would fly with the No. 162 Wellingtons. Alan was a happy character and very hard-working, and he soon became popular with the Squadron. The excellence of the work he did was recognized and he was later to be awarded the DFC.

Shortly after the first Alamein offensive the Squadron was again employed on airborne countermeasures, and renewed efforts were made to jam enemy tank transmissions using improved 'Jostle' equipment. This time it was with greater success, but, unfortunately, again with loss of aircrews. The Air Officer Commanding Western Desert Air Force, was full of praise for the valuable work of the Squadron, including their bombing efforts, which, though a sideline, were helping in the offensive. Apart from the security cover afforded by appearing to be normal bomber aircraft, it was good for the morale of both air and ground crews to be involved with offensive action, and when direct hits were scored on a ship in Tobruk harbour and a neighbouring oil storage dump there was jubilation at Bilbeis.

With the need to concentrate on frustrating the shipping of supplies from the mainland across the Mediterranean to Rommel's forces in the desert, the emphasis was on identifying the radar cover in the central Mediterranean basin. To help with this a detachment of Wellingtons was again sent to Malta to survey the area Sardinia–Taranto–Tripoli, including flights round the whole of Sicily, which were often made as low as 500 feet. On some of these sorties, as an experiment, we sent along linguists such as Sergeant R. Fresco-Corbu and Sergeant Adler, who were attached from No. 276 Wing in an attempt to monitor night-fighter R/T traffic.

Once the Eighth Army and the Western Desert Air Force started to surge forward after the retreating Rommel, following his defeat at El Alamein in the autumn of 1942, the locations of the enemy's installations were constantly changing. This called for a careful watch to be maintained in order to find any weak spots. By November the Allies had launched the 'Torch' landings in North Africa, and with this there came a rapid increase in the enemy's radar cover in the western Mediterranean. With bombing attacks liable to come from units based as far afield as Rome and Naples, pointing to these areas as targets for our bombers, a detachment of No. 162 Squadron again flew from Malta, this time to investigate the radar cover along the Italian coastlines as far north as Rome on the west and Bari on the east.

This task of keeping the whole Mediterranean under surveillance was now so great that a detachment of No. 192 Squadron was flown out from England to handle the western end of the Mediterranean, leaving No. 162 to deal with the eastern Mediterranean and the Balkans. By the spring of 1943 Peter Rusher had handed over the command of the Squadron to Wing Commander George Scott, and the unit moved forward to fly from Cyrenaican airfields.

Whilst we were trying to find gaps and weaknesses in the Axis radar cover through which to plan routes for offensive sorties, the Luftwaffe and the Regia Aeronautica were ranging over the Mediterranean reporting on Allied land and sea forces preparatory to attacking them. Without beams directed towards their target, the Germans needed to rely more heavily on other forms of radio navigational aid and they rapidly expanded a network of radio beacons and direction-finding stations. By the taking of tail bearings on a selected beacon, the pilot of an enemy aircraft could decide on the course that he would fly towards his target; and by taking bearings on two or more beacons, he could find his exact position. When his mission was completed, he could then use a selected beacon to home on his base. It was essential, therefore, that we should reduce to a minimum the usefulness of the beacons and the obvious answer was, as it had been on the Western Front, to jam or 'meacon' them. Under the guidance of Group Captain Philip Jones, who had gained wide experience of radio countermeasures with No. 80 Wing, jamming units were set up at strategic positions.

The initial headache was to identify the individual beacons, their locations and the frequencies on which they operated. An additional problem was the way that the beacons and direction-finding stations constantly changed their callsigns and frequencies. When one realizes that even by the end of 1942 the Germans were changing these nine times in every twenty-four hours at irregular intervals and using thirty-five or more different frequencies in any one month, it will be appreciated what an enormous task it was to keep track of them. But the German military mind is nothing if not methodical and this very factor alone once again helped the cryptographers to break the rotas of frequencies and their wedded callsigns.

Each month the enemy introduced new sets of callsigns and frequencies, but after a few days of intensive direction-finding we were able to build up the new rota table. Once this had been done it took only a few minutes to identify which rota was in use, and from that to know which callsign and frequency would be used by any particular beacon when it made its next change. Identification of a beacon would help with the decoding of subsequent W/T messages, and also in keeping track of the movements of units, since aircraft were still using their unit markings for landing traffic. Of even more help was the fact that the Germans gave some of their beacons nicknames, and we were soon able to determine, for example, that 'Oskar' was at Pachino, or to decide that if a message were heard ordering an aircraft to home on beacon 'Gustav', it meant the pilot would be landing at Cagliari in Sardinia.

By the beginning of 1942 twenty-six radio beacons had been identified operating in locations as far apart as Italy, Tripolitania, Rhodes, and Albania, and Enigma sources indicated that the erection of beacons in and around the Mediterranean was being accelerated at the expense of the Western Front. This fact in itself confirmed the importance that Hitler was then attaching to the winning of the African campaign. But at the same time as our radio countermeasure experts were devising methods of frustrating the various enemy navigational aids, so in a similar way were the German scientists working at a means of interfering with ours. Both No. 276 Wing and No. 162 Squadron, like their counterparts in the United Kingdom, were constantly on the look-out for enemy jamming transmissions which might interfere not only with RAF transmissions but also with those of the Army and Navy.

There were false alarms enough, which at times caused considerable anxiety, and which involved close research until the troubling signal could be identified. Sometimes these could be quickly dismissed as not of Mediterranean origin, but 'skip' reception of transmissions from the Western Front. Every unusual 'noise' had to be carefully investigated. It might well mean the installation of a new and more efficient type of radar, or perhaps an indication of some completely new equipment. Once again much depended on conscientious listening by the monitors, and there was a ceaseless vigil on every band from medium through to centimetre wave.

14

The Beginning of the Defeat

By the summer of 1942 there can have been little Enigma traffic between the German forces in Africa and their masters back in Berlin and Italy that we did not intercept, and now that the cryptographers at Bletchley were so quickly decoding the messages it was almost like being a member of Rommel's staff. It was not unusual for us to know at almost the same time as his senior officers the details of the planning for the enemy campaign. Enigma was supplying us with details of where and in what strength Rommel would align his forces. We knew of his and Kesselring's constant complaints to the German High Command – the OKW – about shortages of equipment and fuel. We were even to learn well in advance about the details of Rommel's proposed final attempt to reach Cairo and Alexandria by breaking through the Allied forces on the southern flank of the Alamein Line. It was all information that was of priceless value to our Intelligence, and thus to our senior Commanders.

There were now four SLUs assigned to the Middle East Command, working under Colonel Robert Gore-Brown. They distributed Enigma information in its decoded state, as Ultra, to the stringently restricted number of senior officers cleared to receive it. One unit was with Middle East Headquarters, one each with the Army and Air Commanders in the desert and one in Malta. Each day No. 276 Wing received encoded messages containing relevant information from Bletchley derived from Enigma traffic; it was a vast two-way communications system, the Wing sending back the raw, monitored signals, and Bletchley guiding us with collated material.

We were working at top pressure on every aspect of signals intelligence and I was impatient for Rowley Scott-Farnie to return to Cairo. I was desperately tired, and I hoped that when he got back from London in the middle of August he would allow me to go on leave. But the work was piling up, and in any case all leave was cancelled, so I had to be content with a flight to Jerusalem, to sort out some problems with Air Headquarters, Levant, and over to Cyprus with No. 162 Squadron to deal with some outstanding queries there. These brief duty trips were to be the pattern throughout my whole service in the Mediterranean. Somehow I never managed to get any leave other than sick leave, I seemed always to be too busy, but with the Field Units sited in such interesting places, visiting them was compensation enough.

By this time Winston Churchill had taken the drastic step of ordering General Sir Claude Auchinleck to hand over as the Army Commander-in-Chief in the Middle East to General Sir Harold Alexander, with the command of the Eighth Army going to General Sir Bernard Montgomery. There was an air of expectancy in the Command, and even I, as a junior officer, knew that the whole situation was ready for an attempted break-out from the Alamein Line. From Enigma traffic it was evident that Rommel had reached the end of his tether. His lines of communication were now too long, and he was short of everything: equipment, aircraft, and fuel especially.

No. 276 Wing was keeping a meticulous watch on the activities of every Axis air unit based around the Mediterranean. To help us in our work the Air Ministry had sent out Squadron Leader Freddie Maggs, who was an expert on the Luftwaffe Order of Battle. We knew from Enigma that Kesselring had promised to supply Rommel with fuel by air, so particular attention was paid to every message from or relevant to the movements of transport aircraft since, even with a minimum of warning, we hoped to be able to intercept en route any delivery of fuel. Acting on Ultra information, the Navy had tracked down and sunk a ship bringing fuel from Italy for Rommel's thirsty forces in the desert.

Notwithstanding Winston Churchill's visit to Stalin in Moscow and the help that the Allies were giving to the Soviet Forces, the Russians were very reluctant to pass on any information regarding German air activity on their front. We were well aware that, in view of the intensity of the operations on the Russian Front, it was no longer possible to estimate accurately the strength of the Luftwaffe, since about two-thirds of the German Air Force were operating in that theatre and much of the activity was out of our monitoring range. The supply lines to Russia through Persia were being threatened by the German advance on the Caucasus, and there remained the ever-present menace to India. Furthermore, the newly-arrived Liberators, the long-range American heavy bombers, were now flying as far afield as Ploesti, in Rumania, to bomb the oilfields there.[1] All this pointed to the urgency of obtaining the fullest knowledge of the German opposition on the Eastern Front, and the best way to overcome this problem was to extend our coverage. As we already had a large W/T intercept unit at Habbaniya, in Iraq, Flying Officer M. 'Rob' Clapham was sent further north with a test unit to explore the possibility of establishing a Field Unit at Teheran, or even Mosul. However, the increased range did not compensate for the difficulties inherent in maintaining such a distant location, and instead we sited a unit on the airfield at Nerab, near Aleppo, in Syria.

In the desert, there was a noticeable improvement in the liaison between the RAF and the Eighth Army, who were at last appreciating the air support over the front line and the land and sea supply routes, and this co-operation was reflected in the attitude of the two Y Services to each other.

Just before the second battle of El Alamein it was my good luck to be able to go up again to the desert to do some work with No. 211 Group, Advanced Air Headquarters at Burg el Arab, and my beloved Field Units. This time I drove up in a fifteen hundredweight truck, for part of the way reclining in the back on a pile of kitbags and stores. It was not exactly the criterion of comfort, and, as always, we ended our journey coated with sand, which penetrated our eyes, ears, nose, mouth, and hair. We passed convoy after convoy heading towards the front laden with armoured vehicles, stores, and troops. Inevitably, as we overtook each group of soldiers, there were wolf whistles, which I always acknowledged with a wave, for I had that terrible heart-wrenching feeling that, for many of the lads, I would be the last woman they would ever see.

They all looked so fit and so young, too young to die. Some were cheerful in their ignorance of what lay ahead, revelling in the camaraderie of the desert, but others looked pensive, with a hopeless expression on their faces, a mixture of resignation and numb fear. The sheer helplessness of their position dulled their eyes, and I was glad when at last we reached the front, where the fighter pilots were gay and confident in the knowledge of their own ability.

It was good to be working with the R/T Field Units again. They had by now become very competent and the information produced for the Forward Fighter Controllers, combined with the longer-range Y supplied by No. 276 Wing Headquarters, was proving invaluable. But, inevitably, I was fair game for a lot of ragging. It never failed to happen whenever I worked 'in the blue'. Group Captain George Beamish asked me once at Air Headquarters if I still retained my enthusiasm for my work and I replied that it annoyed me that only my sex prevented me from working continuously with the forward Field Units, rather than Staff work, which I regarded as somewhat parasitic. I would much prefer, I declared, to do something productive. There was a rush of offers, and to my acute embarrassment, Air Vice-Marshal 'Mary' Coningham, on hearing the guffaws, asked in his cheerful way for an explanation. He enjoyed it as much as all the others. But, despite the leg-pulling everyone, from the AOC down, was very helpful and now that Wing Commander 'Tim' Simpson, who was formerly in charge of Radio Countermeasures in the Middle East, was Chief Signals Officer at Air Headquarters Western Desert, many of our communications problems were smoothed out. During this visit I stayed in the No. 211 Group camp and was present there when one morning a formation of Stukas made a dive-bombing attack, luckily without doing much damage.

Long afterwards Air Chief Marshal Sir Frederick Rosier, as he was to become, recalled of his own experiences as Wing Commander (Operations) at No. 211 Group at that time that: 'Apart from the advantages of our being alerted in plenty of time, the information from the Field Unit allowed us to make the optimum tactical decisions. For example, it helped us to differentiate between main and diversionary raids; it helped us to decide on the composition and strength of our own intercepting forces; and it gave us time to decide on preliminary tactics designed to provide the Germans with the minimum of warning of our intentions – either through his Y service or by his radar.'[2]

There were two particularly gratifying incidents that occurred just after the Alamein break-through when the Field Units gave warnings of the imminent arrival of a horde of Ju. 87s escorted by Me. 109s. On both occasions our own fighters were up and waiting for them and were able to frustrate the attacks on our forward positions so effectively that the Germans jettisoned their bombs on their own troops.

Until the Cyrenaican airfields could be recaptured, and despite our increasing numerical superiority in the desert both on land and in the air, the speed of the advance of the Eighth Army depended largely on Malta-based air and naval forces stopping any attempts to get fuel to Rommel by sea. But Malta was starving. The Air Ministry had managed to reinforce the island's defence with more Spitfires by flying them off aircraft carriers which made their way eastwards from Gibraltar, but even these long-awaited aircraft could do nothing to alleviate the desperate food shortage. An attempt in June by a convoy[3] to battle its way from Alexandria to Malta had failed as the result of violent attacks by enemy battleships, submarines, aircraft, and E-boats. At the same time, another convoy[4] made an attempt to get to Malta from the west. Out of these two convoys, only two merchantmen[5] managed to reach the starving island at the cost of appalling losses by both the Navy and the Air Forces.

In August, a further five ships managed to get through,[6] and the Navy in Malta was once more in business, forcing the enemy to route his convoys to Tobruk and Benghazi via Greece and Crete. Enigma and the signals monitored from the German long-range reconnaissance units again enabled Y to give Operations the advance information the Malta-based aircraft needed. Now under the command of Air Vice-Marshal Sir Keith Park, who had relieved Air Vice-Marshal Lloyd, they sought out and attacked the Axis convoys.

At the end of September Rowley Scott-Farnie flew over to Malta. His object was partly to boost the morale of the Field Unit, but mainly he wanted to make sure that they were getting every scrap of information from No. 276 Wing and Bletchley that they needed in order to decode traffic quickly, and to provide the maximum of Intelligence for Operations. When he returned Rowley was unstinting in his praise for the Field Unit's fortitude under appalling privations.

In the campaign in the desert the Middle East Air Forces were having considerable success. Aided by the Americans, whose B. 25s, (known as Mitchells) were particularly deadly in their attacks against the enemy tanks, they were attacking enemy camps, landing grounds, dumps, and lines of communication. The harbours of Tobruk and Benghazi were repeatedly bombed, and continuous protective patrols were flow over our own supply lines. By the time that the news came

The approximate ranges of Allied and Axis air forces, July to October 1942 (before Alamein).

R U S S I A

Odessa

CRIMEA

RUMANIA

Ploesti

BLACK SEA

BULGARIA

A V I A

GREECE

T U R K E Y

TRANIA

Athens

Aleppo

KOS

CYPRUS

RHODES

SYRIA

Heraklion

Beirut

CRETE

Haifa

Derna

Jerusalem

Tobruk

Mersa

Alexandria

Port Said

ghazi

El Adem

Matruh

Bilbeis

Sidi

Cairo

PALESTINE

El Alamein

Barrani

E   G   Y   P   T

CYRENAICA

through on 8 November of the Allied landings in North Africa, known as operation 'Torch', Rommel was in full retreat. Now the air forces turned their attention with great determination to attacking the harbours of Tunis, Bizerta, Palermo, and Catania as well as the shipping sailing between these ports. To enable the most favourable routes to be planned to these targets No. 162 Squadron flew patrols during which they carefully assessed the enemy radar cover.

The front line was now altering almost daily, and with the frequent changes in the bases that were being used by the Axis aircraft, No. 211 Group was relying heavily on its R/T monitoring units – Nos 4 and 5 Field Units – to augment its other sources of information. Air Chief Marshal Rosier has recorded one incident when rain had bogged down all our fighters. We had been warned that there was to be a raid against Tobruk, and it occurred to him that he might be able to spoof the enemy by scrambling some imaginary fighters. He got in touch with the commander of the forward control at Gazala, and asked him if, each time that he gave a supposed order to our friendly fighters, he would give the short acknowledgement 'Roger'.

It was not long before information started to come in from the Field Unit giving details of the enemy raid, which was to be by Italian dive-bombers escorted by German Me. 109s. As Rosier scrambled and gave orders to the imaginary fighters, Y advised him that the enemy raiders were being given information by the Germans to look out for these fighters. Just when Fred Rosier was beginning to think that his spoof had been unsuccessful, in that the imaginary fighters had been brought to within ten miles of the raiders, the Field Unit was able to tell him that the Italians had jettisoned their bombs and were scurrying for base, and that the leader of the escorting German fighters was livid with range, calling the Italians all kinds of un-printable names.[7]

We knew very well that the Luftwaffe thought very little of their Italian allies. In his war diary of Fliegerfuehrer Afrika, General Waldau recorded: 'Experience has shown the futility of trying to commit Italian air units close to the front. Their unit commanders seem incapable of grasping a tactical situation as a whole or of visualizing its possible further development. Nor is it practicable to inform them of last minute changes of plan by ground/air radio. Because of these factors, the danger of their bombing their own allies is sufficiently great to warrant deliberately excluding them from front commitments.' Knowing that this was the attitude, it touched a raw spot when a senior Luftwaffe prisoner, asked about their opinion of the Italians, replied 'Much about the same as the Russians think of you.'

Amongst the senior German officers captured during the Alamein battles was General Ritter von Thoma, the Commander of the Afrika Korps, who admitted that he had been greatly impressed by the offensive action of the RAF, which contrasted sharply with the efforts of the Luftwaffe. In his biography of Rommel, Brigadier Desmond Young quotes 'the Desert Fox' as saying 'The strength of the Anglo-American Air Force was, in the battles to come, the deciding factor.'[8]

There has always been a tendency to refer to the victory that was won at El Alamein as being solely an Eighth Army triumph, but it should never be forgotten that it was equally due to the combined efforts of the Western Desert and Middle East Air Forces and the Royal Navy, who so constantly pounded not only the forward positions but also the vital supply routes of the enemy.

During the month of October it was the lot of Malta to be subjected yet again to fierce attacks from Sicilian-based aircraft, but the losses sustained by the enemy in these operations were so high, we learnt from monitored Enigma traffic, that Kesselring had decided to withdraw his Ju. 88s from the battle against the island. By 13 November the Eighth Army had recaptured Tobruk, and a week later the Western Desert Air Force was flying from the Martuba landing grounds, just in time to give effective cover to a convoy which was at long last able to break the siege of Malta. Ahead lay Tripolitania with the prize of Tripoli itself, the star in Mussolini's colonial empire, which had for so long been like the grapes of Tantalus to the Eighth Army.

By this time I was again on my own as A14 at Headquarters. Tragedy had hit Y in the Middle East. At the end of October a new Commanding Officer had been posted to the Wing. He was Wing Commander Michael Stephenson – a charming young man with a delightful sense of humour, tall, good-looking and very interested in his new appointment. On his arrival in the Middle East Michael and Rowley immediately started on a series of visits to the various Field Units, so that Michael might get to know his new 'parish'. During a take-off from Heliopolis on 26 November the engine of his Lysander cut out. In trying to avoid the buildings and houses which surrounded the airfield, Michael apparently attempted to re-land but his wheels hit a slit trench on the edge of the airfield and the aircraft flipped over on to to its back and burst into flames. Michael and Rowley both managed to get out of the wreckage, but not before they were badly burned. Three days later Michael died, and I had the distressing responsibility of attending his funeral as the representative of DDI4 in the Air Ministry, of our own office at Headquarters Middle East, and also of his widow. It was the first funeral I had ever attended, and standing there to attention in the broiling sun, the only woman on the parade, I bit my lip till it bled, determined not to weep, but it was no good. When the buglers sounded 'The Last Post' and the fusillade cracked out over the grave, the tears streamed down my face as I stepped forward to throw a handful of sand on the coffin.

I went back to the hospital where Rowley was bravely enduring his injuries. His face and hands were terribly burned, and I knew that it would be several months, if ever, before he would be able to return to the office in 'Grey Pillars'. As might have been expected, my dear friends at No. 162 Squadron came up trumps. They were determined that I should not become too depressed, and to ensure that I did not lose my nerve for flying, they took me up air-testing a Bisley and insisted that I took over the controls.

With no Commanding Officer out at Suez Road, no Scott-Farnie at Headquarters and all the many problems which were now arising from the rapid advance in the desert, plus the need to co-ordinate our efforts with those of the forces recently landed in North Africa, I realized that I would have a great deal of responsibility on my hands until Air Ministry could find a relief for Rowley. I was fortunate in having many friends in Intelligence and Signals to whom I could turn for help and advice, and to whom I was deeply grateful. These included people like Wing Commander Tom Mapplebeck, a brilliant Intelligence officer working with the SLU, Group Captain Philip Jones, the Deputy Chief Signals Officer, Wing Commander John Tester, the Chief Radar Officer and Squadron Leader Roger Francis who handled prisoner interrogation. And, as always, I found everyone out at Suez Road most generous with their advice. But I was on my own, and I felt it.

Christmas 1942 came and went, spent between visits to Rowley and the other injured Allied airmen in the hospital and the Wing Headquarters, where, even on Christmas Day, I had a lot of work to do. Everywhere there was a feeling of elation. Despite his dire lack of fuel, which we knew from Ultra had almost immobilized the Afrika Korps at Benghazi, Rommel was again in retreat. He had made a stand on the El Agheila Line, but the Allied forces were now swarming into Tripolitania. This time they knew that they would never again withdraw to the Delta.

The news From the North African front was also good if not as happy as we would have wished, for in Tunisia the Luftwaffe still had undoubted superiority in the air. Flying from good airfields, they had the advantage over the Allied air forces who were struggling to operate with inadequate supplies from veritable quagmires of landing grounds in appalling weather. But on the Eastern Front, the Russians, who had broken through the German Sixth Army's defences at Staligrad on 23 November, were holding their line. Morale in the Middle East was high and already some senior prisoners-of-war, whom we had on our hands, were beginning to voice their opinion that Hitler would lose the war.

Early in the New Year of 1943, Air Commodore Colin Cadell at the Air Ministry was able to release one of his most able officers, Wing Commander John W. Davies, and he flew out to hold the fort at Headquarters whilst Rowley was away in hospital. Just before that a Welshman named Wing Commander David Davies had been posted to command No. 276 Wing. It was a great relief to me that 'Long John' Davies was at hand to help the new man, David Davies, win the confidence of the several brilliant, if temperamental, intellectuals who were the backbone of the cryptographic and collation staff at Suez Road. David Davies was completely new to Y, and although I had the highest possible opinion of the cryptographers, I knew that they could be an awkward bunch, particularly with 'outsiders'.

'Long John' must have reported back favourably to DDI4 at the Air Ministry on my competence to hold down the post of AI4 Middle East, because a signal arrived with instructions that I should take over when he returned to the Air Ministry, as Rowley Scott-Farnie was being invalided home. But I knew my No. 276 Wing personnel by now too well, and I was aware that much depended on their relationship with our branch at Headquarters for the smooth running of the overall Y operation in the Middle East. No matter how well I might cope, I was still a woman and there was definite resistance in those days to taking orders from women. Even with the

H

'other ranks', one had to be careful, and diplomatic. With this in mind, I wrote to Colin Cadell, thanking him for his confidence in me. But I had to recommend that a man should be sent out to take over as AI4, Middle East. I knew that I was thereby sacrificing my promotion to Squadron Officer, but the work genuinely mattered more to me than my personal status. In any case, the battle had moved away from our end of the Mediterranean and I wanted to be free to go over to North Africa, where there were now more urgent tasks to do.

Whilst the Eighth Army was pursuing the enemy through Cyrenaica into Tripolitania, the forces under the command of General Eisenhower were fighting their way through the mountains and valleys of Algeria and Tunisia, and moving up with them were, of course, Army and RAF Y Field units. Two RAF Y Units had been formed back in England, and they landed immediately behind the invasion forces. No. 380 Wireless Unit (WU), which would come to be mainly responsible for the interception of W/T traffic in North Africa, including the monitoring of the vital Enigma channels, arrived in Algiers on 12 November and soon found suitable accommodation at the Château Béraud, which was on rising ground at Draria, behind Algiers. The castle was built by Napoleon III for his Algerian mistress, and was in the old French style with two little turrets and an inner courtyard. Surrounded by vineyards, it commanded magnificent views over the Haut Plateau and the snow-capped Atlas range beyond.

By the end of November General Eisenhower had established his headquarters in the Hotel St George overlooking the bay of Algiers and the Y unit was therefore well situated to keep the planners supplied with signals intelligence.

When the second Y unit – No. 381 WU – landed in Bône on 7 December, part of No. 380 WU was already working there, and was shortly to move along the coast to Ain Draham. No. 381 WU was eventually to be responsible for monitoring the shorter range R/T traffic, and for providing tactical information for the locally controlled fighter formations of the North-West African Air Force as they moved up behind the Army's advance. To ensure complete coverage of enemy communications in the theatre, there was constant liaison with both No. 276 Wing and its satellites, and also with No. 351 WU at Gibraltar, whilst the investigation of enemy radar in the western Mediterranean was undertaken by a flight of three Wellingtons of

No. 192 Squadron, augmenting the work of No. 162 Squadron and its Malta detachment.

Once again the Field Units were to come up against the inability of Controllers and the radar Filter Officers to make the fullest use of Y information. It was surprising to find that little or no attempt appeared to have been made to instruct them during their training in England in the value of intercepted intelligence and it was left to the Y Service itself to cultivate their interest, and their trust, in this source of information.

The ideal situation for the forward areas had been evolved in the Western Desert, where the Field Unit was located close to the fighter control with a Y liaison officer working permanently beside the Controller, simultaneously feeding back to the Field Unit information of use to them. Owing to the mountainous nature of the terrain in North Africa, however, reception near the forward airfields was frequently so poor that it was not possible for the monitoring unit to be close at hand. It would be sited anything up to thirty miles away on some suitably high ground with, perhaps, the ancillary direction-finding equipment even farther away. The range and coverage of both enemy air and ground station traffic was dependent on expert siting of the listening unit. By choosing the best possible site, aircraft as far away as 200 miles could be heard.

A further problem was that the Field Unit's strength was, at first, too small to permit the permanent detachment of a Y liaison officer to Forward Fighter Control. Until more personnel could be made available, the only remedy was the establishing of a really efficient communications system. But this, especially in the early days, was sadly lacking, and the situation was hardly improved by the habit of the local Arabs of removing sections of the telephone lines for their own use. But the technical staff of the unit were nothing if not resourceful, and somehow they managed to pass, with the minimum of delay, messages that were of operational value to the Controllers, who were quickly learning to appreciate the vital contribution of both short and longer term Y. It only needed a few instances when Y was able to give information of an imminent enemy attack well in advance of hostile plots being received in Operations for the Controller to be converted. Even so, waterlogged airfields were too far back from the front, and the terrain made the erection of efficient radar and other warning systems most difficult. At times, if the advance happened to be rapid, these facilities were virtually non-existent.

Communications continued to be one of the main headaches throughout the North African campaign. It was most important that there should be twenty-four hour two-way links between Y in North Africa and Y in England. The two WUs, which were later to combine to form No. 329 Wing with ancillary Field Units, on the lines of their counterpart in the Middle East, needed to be in constant touch with Cheadle and Bletchley, exchanging information and receiving help which would enable them to read the encoded operational signals. At the same time Bletchley urgently wanted the monitored traffic which would fill in the gaps in the United Kingdom coverage of the communications sent by the enemy in Enigma cyphers. Similarly, there had to be a continuous exchange of information between the forward monitoring units and the Château in Algiers, where, from January 1943, all W/T interception was coordinated, because the units in the field had neither the time nor the facilities to handle long-term research themselves.

On the R/T monitoring side the Luftwaffe was now adding to our difficulties. In the Western Desert they had transmitted on H/F, but some time after the fall of Ben Gardane, on the Medenine front, new squadrons of Luftflotte II, which had been moved at last from the Russian front in order to try to stem the Allied advance, were arriving in the theatre fitted with VHF radio equipment. By the final phase in North Africa, all aircraft and even the forward Ground Observation Posts with their 'Kiebitz' callsign, had changed over to the new frequency range. In order to pull in this traffic we had to find more receivers and VHF D/F equipment. It was essential to take at least line bearings, not only on signals from enemy formations during operations but also on traffic from the various ground formations so as to be able to keep tabs on them as they moved back. We were fortunately able to borrow Fighter Fixer D/F equipment which was modified to cope with the new frequencies and any possible navigational beams that we might hear. To obtain a good cross-bearing a D/F van needed to be sited several miles away, also on high ground, which meant driving the equipment over appalling roads and tracks. Although the vehicles available might have been strong enough under field conditions in Britain, they were totally unsuited to negotiating the rocky hillsides and the tracks in Tunisia, which were obliterated by deep mud in the drenching rain or, worse, by snow.

Had it been possible for the unit operating in Tunisia to remain in one place even for only a month or so, it would all have been much simpler, but working with the Forward Fighter Controllers meant that the unit, which was under the command of Flight Lieutenant L. F. C. Turner, was constantly on the move: from Souk-el-Arba with a forward section at Tebboursouk on the Medjez-el-Bab front, down to the Kasserine Pass to help the Americans stem Rommel's counter attack on the central front, and then back to the Command Post near Tebessa. Later, it was to move to Ain Draham between Bône and Bizerta, on to La Marsa, and after the capitulation to Cap Bon. Yet, despite these peregrinations, the unit managed to pass between thirty and fifty messages of operational value a day.

Not so!

The tactical enemy R/T traffic fell into seven categories: airfield controls, ground observation posts, day-fighters, fighter-bombers, Stukas, bombers, and night-fighters. We learned a great deal from the airfield controls. They would send long and explicit messages, even obligingly repeating them two or three times. These might indicate an imminent raid by escorted 'Violante' (Stukas) or 'Jabos' (fighter-bombers). In many cases, the rendezvous with the fighters was given, which gave our Fighter Control sufficient time to break the sortie in its initial stage. The GOP reports were mainly helpful to the Allied Filter Rooms as an additional check on hostile plots.

On the whole the bomber units gave little away, keeping good radio discipline and transmitting only when they were over the target, though the W/T monitors back at the Château would normally hear them homing after a raid, enabling us to keep a diary of their activity. The fighters, on the other hand, were at times extremely lax, giving away most useful information in a mixture of Western Front, Desert and Sicilian fighter code-words.

On both sides of the conflict, the 'fighter boys' were much more talkative on the air than their colleagues in bomber and long-range reconnaissance aircraft. Admittedly, the fighters needed to be more closely controlled from the ground, but apart from this, I, personally, believed that it was partly a question of loneliness and fear – though I doubt if either the Luftwaffe or the Allied pilots would have admitted it. In a multi-engined aircraft, the aircrew could chatter between themselves to boost each other's morale but a fighter pilot is very much alone, and the sounds of another voice must be comforting. At times it was apparent that the German fighter pilots must have been reprimanded for their laxity, for there were periods when they would restrict their transmissions to the occasional cough or merely to switching their transmitters on and off, frequently long enough for us to take a bearing on them.

It was when the enemy was reducing his transmissions to the minimum that the alert monitor came into his own. On the W/T side, a good wireless operator soon got to know the 'fist' of the men he was listening to, quickly spotting little idiosyncracies which would inevitably creep into the individual styles of using the key. Perhaps the sender would slur the dots and dashes in a particular letter, or speed up his acknowledgement signal in a certain way, and after listening to only a few messages a good operator could usually identify a frequent sender. Similarly the R/T monitors, who had lived and talked with Germans and Italians for many years or spoke one of these languages as their mother tongue, would notice a slight intonation or a way of speaking which, when heard, might give away vital clues about the movement of a unit, or its participation in an operation. With long watches of six to eight hours of concentrated listening, the linguists needed to be fully engrossed in their task, motivated by the sheer challenge of the work. To get the best out of their effort, the R/T monitors needed to be kept informed of the wider intelligence aspects of any battle that was in progress, so that the traffic they were handling had more meaning. Yet these conscientious and intelligent men, though they had been granted the acting rank of Sergeant, were for many months unpaid in that rank. This was grossly unfair and would often lead to embarrassing situations for them, especially financially, when they visited another Sergeants' Mess. It took me over a year of fighting on their behalf to persuade Middle East Headquarters to give them the pay that was their due as Clerk/Signals/Interpreter. I was later delighted when, in recognition of my efforts, the monitors of No. 4 Field Unit presented me with an illuminated citation of thanks.

In addition to the steady stream of Ultra information that was being passed to the commanders via the S L Us and the short-term tactical intelligence that was derived from R/T intercepts, a vast amount of information culled from lower-grade W/T monitoring was disseminated to our various customers, who were now all clamouring for as much information as we could give them. In November, in order to improve our coverage of W/T traffic in the centre of the theatre, we had moved a Field Unit up to Benghazi.

Careful surveillance of enemy bomber and reconnaissance aircraft returning to Sardinia, Sicily and the mainland helped us in our compiling of the orders of battle of the German and Italian Air Forces, and in recording the movements of units, whilst evidence of increased use of particular airfields helped Operations in the selection of bombing targets. An example of this was when the Ju. 88s of III/KG 77, which were based at Gerbini, were heard using El Djem as a forward landing ground; a heavy raid was quickly mounted to discourage them.

Useful confirmation of successful Allied fighter interceptions could be learnt from enemy distress calls, and messages that were sent by enemy reconnaissance aircraft giving the positions of dinghies in the sea helped our Air Sea Rescue Service to save Allied airmen or, conversely, to capture enemy aircrews. The most useful air-to-ground signals that we heard were probably those from aircraft which were shadowing Allied convoys, since these enemy reconnaissance reports were almost inevitably followed by attacks from their bomber units such as the torpedo specialists, KG 26. But it was not always possible to decipher the messages in time for suitable action to be taken. This might be because interference or atmospherics had prevented the whole of a message from being heard: or the signals might have been too weak or again there might have been too few messages heard in that particular code for the message to be deciphered quickly and confidently. It was also inevitable that the wrong interpretation might occasionally be made of a series of messages but, by and large, there was little that was of major importance or relevance to Luftwaffe or Regia Aeronautica activity in the theatre which was missed by the RAF Y Service.

The German Air Force had always relied heavily on radio aids for navigation, and they had therefore evolved, since before the war, a complex Safety Service Organization, which was divided into 'Bezirke' (districts), each district being responsible for all aircraft airborne within its area of control. It provided the aircrews with assistance in the form of such services as D/F bearings, weather reports, and serviceability of airfields, but it was also responsible for the over-all direction of all air traffic within its area. An aircraft entering a district was always challenged before being given navigational aid and the aircraft itself could challenge the ground station to prove its identity. Although the Air/Ground signals were transmitted in a mixture of letter and figure codes, which changed all too frequently, the cryptographers were rarely at a loss for very long. All these messages provided us with much useful information.

On 23 January 1943 the Eighth Army entered Tripoli. They had advanced 1400 miles since the Battle of El Alamein four months previously, almost the same distance as from London to Moscow. The prize that had eluded them for so many long months of weary desert conflict was now at last theirs.

Cairo that night was in a state of elation. But I was having my own personal problems at that time. I already knew that Cadell wanted me to take over as AI4 when John Davies returned home, until a relief for Rowley could be found. This would inevitably mean more work and responsibility. Then, shortly afterwards, Wing Commander S. G. ('Jimmy') Morgan came over from Algiers to discuss the future of Y in the Mediterranean and indicated that he wanted me to join his staff there. He had been appointed Chief Signals Intelligence Officer with the task of co-ordinating the Y effort in the whole theatre. On top of this I was on the verge of becoming engaged, but I had seen too many of my friends widowed within months of marriage, and I wrote to my mother explaining that 'my job means so much to me, I couldn't have it ruined by constant worry over a mere man. I just cannot let my private life seriously affect my interest in winning the war – that would be too unpatriotic.' To today's reader, for a twenty-four-year-old to make such a dispassionate decision must sound incredibly pompous and jingoistic. But it must be remembered that, young though we were, we had a dedication that is perhaps incomprehensible in the climate of today.

Once they had got beyond Tripoli, the rapid advance by the Eighth Army was slowed down. We knew from Ultra that Rommel had warned his Fuehrer that he would have to retreat to the well-fortified Mareth Line, which the French had constructed to protect Tunisia against attacks from the Italians in Libya. We knew, too, that Hitler had signalled to Kesselring ordering that Rommel should hold the Mareth Line at all costs. But although the Italians, who were far from pleased with Kesselring for having abandoned the pride of their colonial empire, were by now giving only somewhat half-hearted support to their allies, their lack of effort was counter-balanced by the availability of supplies and reinforcements which were being brought into Tunisia by air and sea. Furthermore, the Eighth Army's progress was being hampered by the scarcity of usable airfields near the front line, making it difficult to provide constant air cover for the Army.

During the earlier desert campaigns, many landing grounds had been constructed by both sides to the east of Tripoli, but now the battles were being fought over entirely new territory. The few airfields that there were had been ploughed up and mined by the retreating Axis forces, and, despite the greatest efforts by the engineers, repairing or replacing them during the winter months was no easy task. This meant that the Allied air forces had to operate from landing grounds well behind the front line, with the inevitable reduction in operational time over the forward battle zones. Every minute of advance warning of enemy air activity counted more now than ever, and the R/T Field Units on both fronts were straining their ears to hear information which might be helpful to Operations.

No. 381 WU, which was operating on the central front, was able to provide considerable tactical intelligence during the onslaught on the American troops north of Gafsa, and they covered the subsequent battle at Kasserine. Meanwhile, on the southern front, signals from enemy forward landing grounds near Mareth, Gabes, and El Hamma were being carefully monitored, providing information which helped the Desert Air Force to concentrate its effort on strafing these airfields and the enemy's supplies and transport behind the front line.

Then, though Ultra indicated that Rommel was planning to return to the attack on the Medenine Line, tactical reconnaissance was hampered by poor weather. Once again Montgomery had to rely heavily on Army and RAF signals intelligence to indicate the dispositions of the enemy tanks and guns, and to forecast imminent air attacks. So accurate was the intelligence that Rommel's offensive was doomed to failure. He was recalled to Germany shortly afterwards, sick in heart and in body, handing over his command to the Italian General Messe under the control of General von Arnim, who promptly staged an onslaught on the Medjez-el-Bab front, which necessitated the move of No. 381 WU to cover the traffic there.

During all this time General Leclerc (the cover-name for the distinguished Free French leader, Vicomte Philippe de Hautclocque) was advancing from Lake Chad away to the south in Central Africa. He had crossed the vast tracts of the Saharan desert at the head of a brave column of Fighting French. Their initial objective was to establish themselves at Kasr Rhilane, and thereby to prevent the enemy from discovering the preparations for the Eighth Army to outflank the powerful Mareth defences. But from the signals the Army Y units began to intercept there were indications that a strong enemy force of tanks, armoured cars and artillery were heading towards the French. Tactical reconnaissance failed to show the presence of the enemy column, and the question arose whether perhaps the monitored traffic was 'spoof'.

Urgent calls for help were received from General Leclerc, who was by then being attacked from the ground and the air, but Air Vice-Marshal (later Air Chief Marshal Sir Harry) Broadhurst was prepared. He had recently taken over command of the Desert Air Force from Air Marshal Coningham, and, having been forewarned by Y, his fighters and tank-busters were soon airborne and thrown into a counter-attack. Catching the enemy in the open by flying low so as to avoid early detection, they destroyed or immobilized two-thirds of the enemy's vehicles. The rest were left in a state of panic and were heard calling urgently for reinforcements and doing so in plain language. A follow-up strike by fighter-bombers of No. 239 Wing met the reinforcements and hit them so hard that there were no further attempts to capture Kasr Rhilane.

By one of the happier coincidences of the war, amongst the squadrons that were sent to the aid of General Leclerc's men were those which had helped the French during their gallant stand at Bir Hakeim. In his later official report on operations in the Western Desert Broadhurst stated: 'This action had important political significance, for had General Leclerc's isolated post been overrun through lack of assistance from the Eighth Army (which it was almost impossible for the Army to give at that time), the enemy would have been greatly encouraged and the effect on our relations with the Fighting French and the French population in North Africa would have been most unfortunate.'[9] Harry Broadhurst is emphatic that the success of the operation was largely due to early warning by the Y Service.

15

Sicilian Prelude

Throughout that winter of 1942–43 the Allies had had to fight their way painfully forward through the all-pervading mud and in the miserably cold weather of the Algerian mountains. But now it was spring, and the slopes of the valleys were clothed in a Persian carpet of wild flowers, with bluebells and poppies vying with yellow daisies and lilies to defy the desecration of the land. But another red was staining the earth, for the Germans were desperately trying to stem the advance. Casualties on both sides were heavy, and great feats of bravery were performed by friend and foe alike.

In the south, the advancing Eighth Army was involved in a very different form of fighting from that to which they had been accustomed. No longer were battles being fought across open country. Now there was, instead, a series of skirmishes along narrow roads in efforts to capture valleys and strongpoints, with the enemy heavily mining the territory as they retreated. Stuka attacks were a continuing hazard during the day, but the German heavy bombers were no longer based on the last remaining Tunisian airfields held by the Axis, and even the fighters were finding life increasingly difficult. The Allied air forces had gained superiority in the air and this was reflected in the reduced amount of tactical Luftwaffe traffic that we were monitoring in the field. There was now no need for two R/T Field Units to continue leap-frogging forward with the Desert Air Force which, on the formation of the North African Tactical Air Force, had combined with the 12th Air Support Command and No. 242 Group. These latter were already receiving a considerable amount of Y information from No. 381 WU.

In order to mop up the last of the enemy resistance in North Africa, it was imperative that we should deprive them of fresh supplies, especially fuel, for, despite the outcome that was now inevitable, the German High Command still refused to acknowledge defeat. They continued to pour in troops and weapons for use by General von Arnim. Since the Navy had virtually bottled up the sea route through the Sicilian narrows, reinforcements were ferried in by large formations of Ju. 52s and the ill-fated six-engined Me. 323s.

For several months Section Officer Rosemary Horstmann at No. 276 Wing had made the activities of the transport units of the Luftwaffe around the Mediterranean her special study. By careful scrutiny of the monitored traffic, including Ultra, and with the guidance of Bletchley, she was able to give Operations a fair indication of the departure times of the enemy air convoys. Armed with this knowledge and with the monitored R/T also indicating the times of the rendezvous with the fighter escorts, on 5 April, the North-West African Tactical Air Force, now able to calculate the approximate time and area for an interception of an air convoy, launched 'Operation Flax', designed to frustrate the aerial supply route.

Already several encounters had resulted in the destruction of a number of transport aircraft, but too many were still managing to get through. The heavy enemy aircraft were evidently escaping early radar detection by flying in low. Patrolling Allied fighters often found themselves short of fuel just as they had located an enemy formation, and they would have to break off the engagement in order to get back to base. Air Vice-Marshal Broadhurst's great experience as a fighter pilot enabled him to diagnose that part of the trouble was the inherent reluctance of the fighter pilot to fly low over the sea for long periods. In the event of a dog fight, there would not be enough air space to manoeuvre, and low altitude was an additional hazard should it become necessary to bale out.

So Broadhurst worked out a plan for British and American patrols to cover the approaches to Tunis, stepped up at all levels, but with a formation flying low to try to catch the transports as they neared the African coast. But to ensure the maximum amount of flying time in the possible area of encounter, it was vital to know the departure time of the enemy aircraft. In this Y did not let him down. Rosemary's painstaking study proved invaluable, and Broadhurst's strategy paid off.

On the evening of the 18 April, the fighters[1] of the North West African Tactical Air Force waylaid a convoy of 100 Ju. 52s and before they could reach their destination, the Allied fighters had destroyed 43 aircraft of which 34 were Ju. 52s, four Me. 109s, 2 Me. 210s, one Me. 110 and 2 Ju. 88s.[2] The next day another formation met a similar fate.[3] The immediate reaction from the Axis Command was to set up standing patrols over the Cap Bon peninsula in an effort to protect the air convoys for the last part of their journey. But, again, the Field Units were listening, and the Tactical Air Force Headquarters, duly advised, despatched fighters to deal with the new defence. Then, on the 22nd, a convoy was met in the Gulf of Tunis.[4] It was an armada of the giant Me. 323s, and not one was allowed to escape. From the way that many of them exploded into balls of fire it was obvious that they had been carrying fuel.

Kesselring's air transport fleet had now been decimated, and the demands of the Russian Front were so great that there was little chance that he would receive the urgently needed replacements. He had insufficient aircraft to ferry supplies to the desperate von Arnim, and the German-Italian Army was forced back into the narrow strip of the peninsula. With the Sicilian Straits effectively sealed off by air and by sea, when the end came there was little or no attempt made by the enemy to evacuate their thousands of troops. On 12 May von Arnim himself was captured and the next day the horde of his remaining troops surrendered. In his autobiography Lord Tedder commented: 'This crippling of the Axis air transport effort played a large part in the enemy's sudden and complete collapse in Tunisia.'[5]

The Germans had suffered a defeat comparable with Stalingrad. Thousands of prisoners and huge quantities of arms and supplies were captured and for the Italians their empire in Africa had ceased to exist. At last, after three years of fighting across deserts and mountain ranges, the Allies were victorious in Africa. Now, for those of us in the Y Services – Army, Navy and Air Force – our first task was to plan for the provision of maximum intelligence for the forthcoming invasion of Sicily.

By 7 May, as the British Army was entering Tunis and the Americans were occupying Bizerta, I was again up in the desert. This time I was in Benghazi, where I had been sent by the Chief Intelligence Officer, Middle East, Air Commodore Foster. Plans for Operation 'Husky', the invasion of Sicily, were being completed and No. 276 Wing was already concentrating on the monitoring of traffic from Sicily, Italy, and southern Greece. We had moved a W/T Field Unit (No. 1 FU) up to Benghazi soon after the city was recaptured, but as we were not too happy about the supply of Y information to the local formations in Cyrenaica, Foster had sent me up to investigate.

Known Axis radar cover in the Mediterranean at 6 April 1943, as determi
by airborne investigation.

	2 000'
	6 000'
	10 000'

0   100
   miles

Although the day-to-day control of the Field Units was essentially the responsibility of the Commanding Officer of No. 276 Wing, AI4 at Headquarters was responsible to the Chief Intelligence Officer and to the Air Ministry for the supervision of all matters of Y policy and organization in the Middle East.

Since there were also various matters regarding enemy radar investigation to discuss with Alan Maley, the Technical Signals Officer of No. 162 Squadron, I flew up in one of their Wellingtons to their new base at Benina, outside Benghazi. The pilot of the aircraft was Wing Commander John Irvine, who as senior Radio Counter-measures Officer at Headquarters wished to complete arrangements for the imminent arrival of a 'meaconing' unit that was to be sited in nearby Fort Regina. This would work closely with the Field Unit in the disruption of the enemy's radio navigationals aids. We had no navigator on board, so we flew low over the desert, keeping beneath the haze, and I spent my time lying in the bomb aimer's position in the nose of the aircraft trying to pick up points of reference en route. After a while, my sense of balance began to object to the midday upcurrents, and I was not sorry when we finally touched down at Benina. The crew of the aircraft decently refrained from mentioning my lapse, for which I was grateful, as the new commanding officer of the squadron, Wing Commander George Scott, had not yet become accustomed to the idea of a woman staff officer.

This also startled the Naval Y Officer at Benghazi, when I visited him the next day to find out if the Navy was getting all the Y information that was needed from us. He could not get over a woman being in the desert and he was still flabbergasted by the evening. His colleague in Alexandria, Lieutenant-Commander David Johnson, had long since accepted me, and I had always found his helpfulness and co-operation in marked contrast with the antipathy which patently existed between our two 'masters', the Admiral and the Air Chief Marshal.

When I went over to the American 98th Bombardment Group, which was based at Benina, their G2 Intelligence was equally surprised at the sight of a woman. I had learned that the Americans were worried over the fact that the Germans appeared to know soon after the American bombers had taken off and were on their way to raid Sicily, Italy, or Greece. The G2 even spoke of the possibility of Axis agents in the Benghazi area. Knowing about the poor signals security of the American Air Force in the Middle East at that time,

I asked if I might sit in during a take-off for a raid. The Group knew virtually nothing about signals intelligence, and, as I had surmised, they were far too talkative in the air. The German Y Service must have had an easy time picking up the American bombers as they tuned in over Benghazi whilst collecting and gaining height. Very tactfully, especially since I was both a woman and British, I suggested that it would be wiser, if they wished to reduce the warmth of the Axis reception committee, to be more security conscious.

I had been in Benghazi a few days when a signal arrived ordering me to proceed to Algiers. The newly-designated Chief Signals Intelligence Officer of the Mediterranean Air Command, Wing Commander Morgan, had recently visited Egypt to acquaint himself with No. 276 Wing's resources, and with the demands of our customers. Now, in view of the plans for the invasions that lay ahead, he had called a conference in Algiers to discuss the reorganization of the whole of the Y Service in the Mediterranean. My first problem was how to get from Benghazi to Algiers, and I had only just managed to organize myself a hitch-hike on a flight as far as Tripoli when I learned that David Davies, the Commanding Officer of No. 276 Wing, and his Senior Intelligence Officer, Squadron Leader C. F. Pugh-Davies, were coming through next day with a flight of three D C3s which had been detailed to move one of the Army Y units to North Africa. They would be able to collect me en route.

It was a strange feeling finally to land at Castel Benito, on an airfield which had been in enemy hands for so long, and which we had been watching carefully for many months. The whole place was devastated. It was a mortuary of gutted hangars and derelict aircraft keeling over in grotesque angles around the perimeter. I had difficulty finding somewhere to sleep. The transit facilities were understandably still primitive, but I was rather hurt when the officer-in-charge told me peremptorily that there was no accommodation for women. This was one of the very few occasions when I met with downright hostility towards a woman being in a forward area.

With such a sensitive cargo as a whole Y unit on board the aircraft our unarmed flight was given a fighter escort beyond the Mareth Line until we were out of danger from any prowling enemy fighters. That night, there was a heavy air-raid on the port of Algiers. Smoke generators belched out an asphyxiating screen, and I watched a veritable Brock's firework display of tracer and flak cutting across the sky. As I listened to the drone of the attacking bombers, I thought that it would be just my luck to be bombed in a squalid hotel in one of the seamier districts of the Algiers waterfront.

The next day we drove out through the Algerian countryside to No. 380 WU at the Château at Draria. At the conference that followed our arrival David Davies, 'PD', as we all called Pugh-Davies, and I were representing the Middle East, Squadron Leader G. Cottam and his senior staff the North Africa side, Squadron Leaders R. Staples and Max Buckwell the Air Ministry and Jimmy Morgan co-ordinated as Chief Signals Intelligence Officer. Our object was to decide the future deployment of all available Y resources to ensure a complete coverage of enemy air force signals traffic emanating from southern and eastern Europe, including the vital monitoring of Enigma traffic for Bletchley, and for the provision of Y intelligence to all our customers in all three services. Now, in addition to the RAF element, we would also have the monitoring strength of No. 849 Signals Intelligence Service (SIS), the American unit that had recently arrived in North Africa, and which, although as yet inexperienced, would make a valuable contribution.

During this visit to North Africa Jimmy Morgan and I went out to Blida, the airfield south of Algiers, with the Chief Radar Officer, Wing Commander Johnny Tester, in order to discuss with a detachment of No. 192 Squadron the division of enemy radar investigations between them and No. 162 Squadron. An American Ground Reconnaissance Squadron – the 'Ferret' Squadron – was due to arrive shortly with their B 17s and would relieve the No. 192 Detachment so that they could return to England for the onerous task of investigating the non-Morse transmissions on the Western Front. The new American Squadron would be able to undertake the longer-range flights, but it was agreed that, in the meantime, the detachment would cover the western Mediterranean, whilst No. 162 Squadron would search the whole area from the central Mediterranean basin north to Bari in Italy, over to Gallipoli, Crete, and the Aegean Islands. Seeing the well-equipped No. 192 Squadron aircraft at Blida, I could not help feeling envious when I compared them with the worn-out Wellingtons allocated to 'my' squadron.

The need to reorganize Y facilities in the theatre was a natural consequence of the major changes in command structure that had been agreed in January at the Casablanca Conference in the light of forthcoming operations. Now Air Chief Marshal Sir Arthur Tedder was made Air Commander-in-Chief, responsible to the Supreme

Commander, General Eisenhower, for all the Allied air forces in the Mediterranean. Under him were Air Chief Marshal Sir Sholto Douglas, who was in command in the Middle East, Air Vice-Marshal Sir Keith Park, in Malta, and Major-General Spaatz, the famous 'Tooey' Spaatz, controlling the North-West African Air Forces. This latter Command comprised three subordinate Commands – the North African Coastal Air Force (NACAF), which was responsible for coastal defence, reconnaissance, and anti-shipping strikes and was under Air Vice-Marshal Sir Hugh Pughe Lloyd; the North African Strategic Air Force (NASAF) commanded by Major-General J. H. Doolittle, which was made up of all the bombers not included in the third Command; the North African Tactical Air Force (NATAF), under Air Marshal Sir Arthur Coningham. All of these, together with the Army and Navy, were recipients of RAF Y Intelligence, and called for day-to-day operational information as well as indications of trends and other details issued in the form of periodic reports which would help in the planning of future operations.

Even before the end in Africa, NASAF bombers were attacking deep into Italy. With the invasion of Sicily imminent, it was essential that in addition to destroying or paralysing the Sicilian airfields, we should restrict military supplies to the enemy by destroying ports, communications and industrial targets on the mainland. American Liberators and Fortresses flew daylight sorties, and the Wellingtons of No. 205 Group administered further punishment at night. At the same time, Allied bombers based in the United Kingdom were lending their support by attacking industrial targets in northern Italy.

The German High Command was now in no doubt about the intention of the Allies to attack from the south, though we knew from monitored signals that they were uncertain about where the first blow would be struck. Repeated demands from Luftflotte II for reinforcements could only be met in part, as there was a limit to the number of fighters that could be spared from the hard-pressed Russian Front, and from the western defence of the Reich, which was now being subjected to massive bombing raids from England. Nor could Kesselring expect much support from the Regia Aeronautica. We in Y knew only too well that there had never been any cohesion between the two enemy air forces, and certainly nothing that was comparable with the co-operation which now existed between the USAAF and the RAF. Even their codes continued to differ, making their own ground-controlled interception unnecessarily complicated.

But despite the depletion of the enemy fighter strength, and the added problem for us caused by the changeover to VHF, which had reduced our monitoring range of fighter R/T traffic, there was no diminution of the vast quantity of H/F and M/F W/T being monitored by the Field Units. Through this and information supplied by Y Central in the United Kingdom, the Intelligence staffs at the two Y headquarters were now fully conversant with all the activities of the enemy's early warning system, its extent and efficiency, and the strength and location of any opposition likely to be encountered by raiding aircraft.

To take the Luftwaffe aircraft reporting network in Sicily as an example, we were aware that the main plotting room was at Comiso with subsidiaries at Catania, Gerbini, and other places. Plots were received at this headquarters from radar stations in Sicily, Sardinia, and southern Italy, and from the many ground observer posts as well as monitored intelligence from the German Y station at Noto. The collated information was distributed, as applicable, to all Axis day- and night-fighter units in Sicily, to Fliegerkorps II Flak units, Air Sea Rescue, German Air Force ground organizations and various other units. Comiso recorded messages sent on the radio frequency used by the Luftwaffe reconnaissance aircraft in order to receive the latest details of Allied shipping movements. It further acted as an operational headquarters for all the fighter units in Sicily, controlling by R/T the fighters in the air. Though, inevitably, some of the traffic on this network was passed by land line, enough was transmitted over the air for Y to keep the whole system of the enemy's defence under constant surveillance.

There was a period, prior to the African defeat, when the British Y Service did its best, with malice aforethought, to help their German opposite numbers. When an RAF reconnaissance aircraft sent a signal back to its base in Malta giving details of an Axis convoy that it had spotted, this was usually intercepted by German Y. The message, re-enciphered, was then transmitted verbatim to the enemy convoy. Malta Y, of course, intercepted the German signal, and since they knew exactly the contents of the original reconnaissance message, they were then able to break the code for the day. As even the best of Y operators were not infallible, the German Horchdienst would occasionally miss a message, so, 'pour encourager', Malta would re-transmit the original RAF message at high power, ostensibly to the Navy in Alexandria, thereby presenting the enemy with another opportunity to give us a lead into the current code.

Working on information derived from investigational aircraft, debriefing reports, and photographic reconnaissance, the Operational Research Section was able regularly to produce detailed routing advice for Allied aircraft attacking the various targets. We had by now determined that the major weakness of all enemy radar stations was their inability to provide an adequate search simultaneously on all bearings. Armed with this knowledge and with the pin-pointed locations of the different radar sites, Operational Research was able to recommend, for example, that the most effective strategy for an attack on Naples prior to the Sicily landings would be for a single reconnaissance aircraft to approach close to Ventotene Island from the south-south-east at between 15,000 and 20,000 feet, and to fly on towards Naples. It would obviously be picked up by the Freya on the island, thus providing a good target for tracking by the enemy radar. But, being a single aircraft, it would be unlikely to produce any appreciable reaction from the enemy air defences. Meanwhile, the main formation would be scheduled to arrive simultaneously, flying low over the most westerly of the Pontine Islands and then sweeping in a wide circle to the east to make landfall twenty miles north of Cape Misero. The formation should have split by then into sections of not more than three aircraft, and it should fly line astern at a distance of not less than 300 yards so as to ensure the minimum of detection. Similar approach tactics were worked out for other targets, and the reactions to the raids were carefully monitored from messages heard on the relevant Aircraft Reporting Service (Flugmeldedienst) frequency.

The outcome of our talks in Algiers on the reorganization of Y in the Mediterranean was the redistribution of tasks, and this called for the re-grouping of personnel and equipment, and, indirectly, the renumbering of units so as to meet current requirements as well as to prepare for future operational demands in the theatre.

Now that the Mediterranean was again open to Allied shipping there was no longer a need for a monitoring unit in West Africa and No. 371 WU was brought up from Freetown to join No. 380 WU in Algiers. With the decline in Italian activity in the eastern Mediterranean, the number of channels covering Italian Air Force wireless traffic in Cairo could be reduced and many of the personnel, including Section Officer M. K. ('Rusty') Goff, an ex-Kingsdown WAAF who was experienced in both German and Italian traffic, were transferred to the North African units. In a similar way, with the Russian Front being pushed westwards, the traffic that had been covered by the Habbaniyah Field Unit could now well be handled by a unit which we had established in Aleppo.

Although the American unit, No. 849 SIS, augmented our monitoring strength, it still lacked experience, and its R/T Detachment was not to become fully operational until the Salerno landings. But in addition to airborne investigation of enemy radar, there were now two ground stations, one in Benghazi and one near Algiers, watching non-Morse transmissions and frustrating, as required, the enemy's radio navigational aids. A third station was being erected at Cap Bon, in Tunisia.

The scene was now set for listening in to the reactions of the enemy to the invasion of Europe.

On our return to the Middle East from North Africa, one of our more important tasks was the setting up and equipping of small parties of monitors to work with the Navy on convoy duty, especially on the fighter direction ships which would act as forward sector operations rooms in support of the invasion forces. This had already been successfully tried out during the 'Torch' operations in North Africa.

For several months we had had an unofficial arrangement with my naval opposite number in Alexandria whereby we would lend the Navy monitors to sail with the convoys in the eastern Mediterranean, in HMS *Cleopatra, Orion* and *Euryalus.* A watch was kept mainly on German air activity, especially their reconnaissance aircraft and the eastern Mediterranean Zenit. To help with and to augment the messages being intercepted on board, Flight Lieutenant George Burroughs, the Wing's Senior Signals Officer, arranged a link between the Y party afloat and No. 2 Field Unit at Alexandria for passing on current German and Italian Air Force information. We learned a lot about the technical problems of monitoring on board a ship stiff with electronic equipment, and this was to prove helpful for later operations. The team was also able to train the less experienced naval operators.

The whole scheme worked well, and on a number of occasions, the small team on board ship had been able to pass invaluable information to the Fleet. For example, during a raid on Benghazi they had intercepted R/T messages which gave warning of a low flying attack by torpedo bombers ten minutes before the ship's radar had picked up a hostile plot. The Admiral, understandably, wanted the arrangement to be made a permanent one and he asked for a small party to be kept ready for service with the Fleet.

But not all the combined operations staff were yet equally convinced of the value of Y intercepts. For Operation 'Corkscrew', which culminated in the capture of the island of Pantellaria on 10/11 June 1943, Flight Lieutenant Rob Clapham and his team were assigned to HMS *Largs*, which was the fighter direction ship acting as a forward control for the Sousse–Le Sebala sector. He soon learnt that R/T intercepts were treated with reserve, and he later recalled: 'We picked up a raid of fighter-bombers several minutes before they attacked *Largs* and we also heard the actual attack signal but the Chief of Staff to whom I reported said he could not see any hostile aircraft and so took no action. As a result, not a shot was fired at the Focke-Wulf fighter-bombers, which escaped back into the clouds after the attack. The ship had sustained four near misses and limped back to Malta damaged and listing badly. It was repaired in time for "Husky" but the Chief of Staff had learnt his lesson and from then on hung on my words. It was to be quite a different story at Sicily. . . .'[6]

'Corkscrew' had served as a useful dress rehearsal for 'Husky' and by then, as soon as a Y intercept indicated the presence of enemy aircraft, a Red Warning was issued to the Fleet.

Once again the success of the RAF Y party had reflected the team spirit of No. 276 Wing. Flight Lieutenant Lawrie Turner, who was then in command of No. 10 Field Unit in Malta, arranged with Rob Clapham to send half-hourly signals giving him information about the movements of aircraft to new bases, reinforcements brought into the battle area, sightings of Allied shipping, forecasts of targets likely to be attacked, patrol areas, enemy airfield serviceability reports, and air–sea rescue messages. Experience had shown that it was not important for the fighter direction ship to know which actual Luftwaffe units were engaged in an attack. But it was essential that the R/T monitors should be so highly experienced in local traffic that they could identify with reasonable reliability from the first enemy R/T messages heard whether the aircraft were bombers, fighter-bombers, Stukas, fighters, or reconnaissance aircraft and, in view of the lack of D/F equipment then available to the

Y party, that they should be able to calculate from the signal strength the proximity of the aircraft.

For the Sicily landings HMS *Largs* was assigned the responsibility of controlling the day-fighters off Pachino in the 'Bark' sector and during the subsequent voyage from Cap Passero to Augusta Harbour, and round to Syracuse, the Y party were once again constantly in touch with Turner in Malta, who was able to give considerable assistance by filtering W/T intercepts, and by broadcasting essential information to *Largs*. The result was that Rob Clapham was able to keep the Chief of Staff advised when night raids would take place, what the targets would be, and when there would be no raid or merely a light one. From the R/T intercepts, he could warn when flares or bombs would be dropped, and equally important, when an attack was over and the raiders were returning to base. He also kept Operations posted with enemy reconnaissance reports, those from the dusk flights being especially useful as they indicated what the target would be for the night. Since the bombers involved came from airfields in southern Italy, and as the Luftwaffe always preferred to land before the moon was down, it was not difficult to calculate the time of the intended attack.

The monitoring of R/T, especially by Sergeant R. L. Arje, who was Czechoslovakian, was so successful that practically no fighter, fighter-bomber, or Stuka raid took place without warning of its approach being given to Operations. In the vast majority of cases the raiders were heard long before they reached their target, or before they were picked up on radar, and the Y party was usually able to give positions, heights, and the numbers and types of aircraft involved. As the teams on HMS *Bulolo* and *Hilary* were less efficient, Y warnings of approaching raids were broadcast by HMS *Largs*. At the same time, the Malta Field Unit was advising Operational Headquarters when there was considerable fighter activity, so that the appropriate Sicilian airfields could be bombed. It is an indication of the amount of traffic heard on HMS *Largs* alone that fifty pages of monitored R/T log were recorded in a single day.

Vital Y experience was gained from 'Husky' which would be of great value for the later landings in the Mediterranean, and for 'Overlord'. We appreciated that the success of the Y party afloat lay primarily with the personnel, who had to have the highest standard of proficiency, and to be accustomed to working together as a team. This had been amply demonstrated by the fact that the

Y parties on HMS *Bulolo* and *Hilary* produced little effective intelligence. They had sailed out from England with the invasion force, completely ignorant of their destination, and so had arrived in the assault zone with the wrong equipment, and with personnel who were untrained in the idiosyncracies of the Luftwaffe in the immediate theatre. On the other hand, Clapham and Arje on HMS *Largs* knew their opposition well and they were in constant touch with their back-up in Malta. As a result they were able to produce a great deal of intelligence which was of tactical value.

The need for experienced teams had become vividly demonstrated, as had the realization that monitoring on board should be restricted to R/T traffic, leaving the wider field of W/T interception to be covered by the larger monitoring units ashore where there were better facilities for decoding and collating intercepted material.

16
Advance into Europe

Shortly after my return from North Africa, the Deputy Director of our branch at the Air Ministry, now Group Captain I. J. Fitch, signalled the welcome news that Squadron Leader G. R. Betton-Foster was flying out to Cairo as the long-awaited replacement for Rowley Scott-Farnie. Now that future action would be focused on Sicily and Italy, I was anxious to rejoin Tedder's staff and work in North Africa with Jimmy Morgan. But the Deputy Chief Intelligence Officer at the Headquarters, Middle East, Group Captain C. E. J. Baines, was adamant that any move would depend on how soon Betton-Foster could become conversant with enemy activities in the Middle East, and how soon we could put into effect the planned reorganization.

There had been a marked reluctance on the part of the Queen Bees to allow WAAF to work in North Africa, and to save arguments, I had made no attempt to let them know from Benghazi that I was flying over to Algiers. But we had recently learned that a batch of photographic interpretation girls was being sent out from England. This was good news for Intelligence and Operational Research, for experienced girls from the Middle East were badly needed over in Mediterranean Air Command. No. 276 Wing could now send over Section Officer 'Rusty' Goff to work with the Field Unit sited at Ain Draham and later on the Cap Bon peninsula in Tunisia, where she would be the only woman in the team.

I was badly in need of a rest when Betton-Foster arrived but as he was comparatively new to Y, I contented myself with a short visit up to the Levant to sort out some problems with the fighter defence Group there – No. 209 Group – at Mount Carmel, whose particular interest was countering offensive reconnaissance activities by the German and Italian units, which were operating from bases in Crete and the Aegean. From Palestine I made a quick trip to Beirut

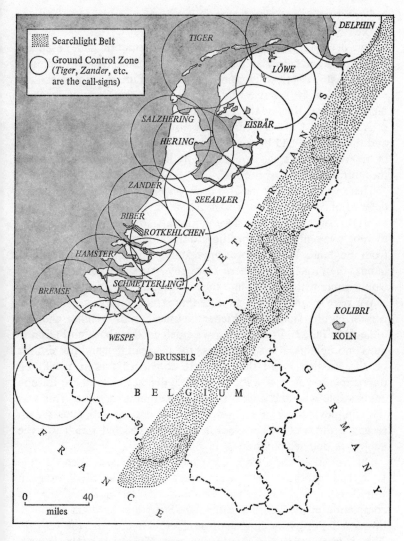

German coastal night-fighter defence, showing some of the callsigns of the closely integrated zones in which the night-fighters were guided to the incoming bombers by ground controllers. It is interesting to note the weakness of the German's love of order, which helped us to sort out which zones were operating: the callsign for Hamstede was 'Hamster', 'Zander' was the callsign for Zandvoort, and Terschelling (the most successful of the controllers) was 'Tiger'.

before returning to Cairo, where we were soon watching the reactions of the Axis air forces to the invasion of Sicily.

The decision to invade Europe from the south had not been welcomed by our Russian allies, who were anxious that there should be an Anglo-American invasion of Western Europe with an assault of such strength that it would greatly reduce the German pressure on their front. But, at the Casablanca Conference in January, the pros and cons had been carefully considered by the Allied leaders, and the decision had been reached that an operation against France in the west at this stage would be more hazardous than an attack on the 'soft underbelly of Europe'.

There was an urgent need to draw off German air units from the defence of Western Europe. An attack on Italy would almost certainly encourage the transfer of aircraft to the Southern Front, thereby weakening the opposition to the mounting bomber offensive from England. Furthermore, once Italian airfields were in Allied hands, the targets in southern Germany, Austria, and the Balkans, would come within bombing range of aircraft based in the south.

We were aware from Y sources that strategic targets such as the Messerschmitt factory at Wiener Neustadt, near Vienna, and the oilfields at Ploesti, in Rumania, were defended by both anti-aircraft guns and fighters. But so great was the German demand for aircraft on the Russian Front that we were convinced that it would be impossible for the Luftwaffe to set up a defence in southern Europe comparable with the now formidable Kammhuber Line. This was the complex system of night-fighters and anti-aircraft guns set up to guard the western approaches to the Reich, and which was the subject of detailed study by Y in England.

Our initial briefing from the Chief Intelligence Officer, Middle East, had indicated that future operations in the Mediterranean would be in three phases to be mounted consecutively. Firstly, on completion of the Tunisian campaign, Sicily and Sardinia would be invaded, followed by an assault on Crete, Greece, and the Aegean. This, it was anticipated, would encourage Turkey to enter the war. Y would then be required to provide a unit for the new front there. Tentative plans had been drawn up to cover these future operational requirements, even to the extent of purchasing civilian clothes for an advance party to proceed to Eskeshir in Turkey, though, as these were purchased in bulk, they were so similar as to be almost uniform. But now our policy had crystallized into an initial invasion of Sicily, following the capture of Pantellaria and Lampedusa. But the Chief Intelligence Officer told us that it had not yet been finally decided whether the next place to be invaded would be Italy or Sardinia, and we had accordingly to modify our plans.

One of our constant problems was that Y in the Middle East had so many masters, reflecting the complicated division of responsibilities between the various headquarters spread across North Africa from Oran to Cairo. No. 276 Wing was technically controlled by DDI4 in the Directorate of Intelligence at the Air Ministry through the office of AI4, in the Intelligence Branch at Headquarters Middle East, which was responsible for interpreting Air Ministry policy in Y matters, and for combining this policy with that of the local operational requirements as determined by the Chief Intelligence Officer, Middle East. Now that there was a Chief Signals Intelligence Officer with Mediterranean Air Command in Algiers, AI4 Middle East, had further to interpret his requirements in the light of the over-all strategy in the Mediterranean.

But overriding all these authorities was Station X at Bletchley, whose paramount demands regarding coverage of the vital Enigma traffic were made known to the Wing either direct or through the inter-services Combined Bureau Middle East (CBME) – the Middle East satellite of Bletchley. In addition, although the operational control of the Field Units was exercised by No. 276 Wing, they were administered locally by the Air or Group Headquarters in whose area they were physically operating. On top of all this it was not unusual for senior officers at the Operational Headquarters served by these units to behave like thwarted prima donnas should the over-all demands of Y require the withdrawal of what they had begun to regard as 'their' Field Unit.

My sympathies were with Wing Commander David Davies. His was not an easy task, especially since he had no knowledge whatsoever of the Y Service when he took over command of No. 276 Wing. The whole Y structure in the Middle East had expanded in a somewhat haphazard fashion, and was an inheritance from a mainly civilian peacetime organization largely composed of a heterogeneous collection of linguists, cryptographers, and specialist signals officers handling the traffic monitored by several hundred wireless operators. Many of them, people like Hugh Waters, Cecil Gould, and George Burroughs, were exceptional in their field. The country owes them a great debt. But some of their colleagues resented the constraints of a uniformed service. Though David Davies, a first-class Signals Officer, may have been, from time to time, at loggerheads with his Intelligence staff, he succeeded in regularizing the activities of the Wing so that they conformed, more or less, within the framework of the RAF: and yet he was ready to make allowances for the inevitable irregularities.

It was in short a complicated jigsaw puzzle that Squadron Leader Betton-Foster was to inherit from me. It was not an easy task for a newcomer.

As soon as Sicily had been finally approved as the initial invasion area we had set about the re-allocation of tasks between North Africa and the Middle East. Two of the Field Units of No. 276 Wing, one of which was handling Italian traffic, had already been absorbed by Y in North Africa, where the organization was shortly to be re-named No. 329 Wing. In addition to the unit in Malta, No. 276 Wing controlled Field Units monitoring W/T traffic in Alexandria, Benghazi, Derna, and Aleppo. The Aqir and Habbani-yah units had by now been withdrawn, and the personnel re-assigned to other Y units. The strength of each W/T Field Unit was between 150 and 250 men, but the two further highly mobile R/T Field Units were much more compact, each with only about two dozen person-nel. RAF Y in the western Mediterranean was a smaller set-up than No. 276 Wing and the division of the responsibilities between the two organizations was roughly that the North African element covered traffic relating to activities in the western Mediterranean basin, including the southern France, Sardinia, Corsica, western Italy, and Sicily, while No. 276 Wing based on Cairo monitored traffic emanating from the eastern Mediterranean, including eastern Italy, and from the Balkans and the Russian Front. The Malta Field Unit overlapped the tasks of both organizations. The division of responsibilities was not rigid but depended partly on operational requirements and partly on traffic loads.

Although we enlarged the Malta unit to handle the requirements of the invasion headquarters, which were established at Valetta, it needed the backing of the units in Africa, especially for taking bearings on signals, and was constantly in touch with the Field Unit at Alexandria. By now the latter had established an efficient D/F network with three D/F stations along the Egyptian coastline from Burg el Arab in the west to Baltim in the Delta, so that, despite constant changes in coded callsigns and frequencies, the operators were able quickly to pinpoint and identify enemy ground stations and beacons. As in North Africa, we had the added problem that the local Arabs were always acquiring the telephone lines. The Malta unit, on the other hand, was handicapped by its inability to erect D/F equipment sufficiently far apart to give a good base line for cross-bearings, and it was for this reason that there had to be constant liaison with the mainland units. An essential element of the whole Y organization was a routine for requesting and obtaining bearings quickly from other units, and we greatly envied our opposite numbers in the United Kingdom with their more sophisticated equipment.

To help the Field Units in interpreting and collating traffic, they continued to be advised by signal daily from the headquarters in Algiers and Cairo of important details about callsigns, frequencies, codes, movements of units and such like, as well as which channels to watch. In addition, there were the important links with Y in England for the exchange of essential information. The original 'LM' codes which were used by the German Air Force for the passing of signals from bomber, dive-bomber, heavy fighter and reconnaissance aircraft operating over land and sea to their control and for co-operation between aircraft and naval forces had now been superseded by the 'AuKa' codes (Aufklaerungs – und Kampf-fliegertafel) which were harder to 'crack' as they had a daily changing sheet and so speedy help from Bletchley was invaluable. There were now many different codes in use, to which we gave the names of musical instruments for brevity and security. The 'Notfunksignal-tafel' was used exclusively by stations, vessels and aircraft concerned with air-sea rescue work; another code was used for the ground-to-ground traffic of the Army liaison troops. There was a special aircraft reporting code, one for weather stations, a special Flak code, another for transport and courier aircraft and so on. In the end, our 'orchestra' of code-names would have been worthy of any Philharmonic orchestra playing 'The Enigma Variations'.

From early in 1943 there had been a slow but steady decline in the over-all activities of the Axis air forces in the Mediterranean, but during the six weeks following the fall of Tunis we were aware that the Luftwaffe in our theatre was drastically reorganizing, and that it had increased its strength from 820 aircraft to about 1250. Most of these reinforcements had been sent to the South Eastern Command, which covered Greece and the Balkans, mainly because of the brilliant plot that became known as 'the man who never was',[1] which encouraged the Germans to believe that the eastern Mediterranean was the most likely area for future Allied operations.

Kesselring knew that one of the pre-requisites for a successful amphibious operation was superiority in the air, and, as an airman, he envisaged that an invasion could not be mounted outside the range of possible fighter cover. He ensured, therefore, that the Axis air forces maintained their systematic reconnaissance and shadowing of Allied shipping throughout the whole Mediterranean. For signals intelligence this meant that there was even greater emphasis on the task of monitoring and quickly decoding reconnaissance reports since, as before, these reports were almost invariably followed by attacks by bombers, usually at dusk, for the enemy was finding attacks during daylight too hazardous.

As a prelude to the invasion there was a massive build-up of Allied air assaults on Sicily, with constant harassing by day and by night of enemy airfields. This forced the long-range bombers to withdraw to southern Italy and Sardinia. By the end of June there was a further withdrawal from the heel of Italy, and Y carefully recorded every movement as the bombers pulled back to Grottaglie, Viterbo, Ciampino, and the Foggia airfields. We noted, too, that our old friend, KG 26, which was now the principal torpedo bomber unit in the Mediterranean, was transferring its He. 111s from Sardinia to the rather safer area of southern France, where the specialist wing of KG 100 had rather ominously arrived. As always, Y was in constant touch with the photographic interpreters, who confirmed the build-up of arrivals on the enemy's rear airfields.

Apart from the relentless attacks on the Sicilian airfields of Comiso, Gerbini, Castelvetrano, and Trapani, and the harbours of Messina, and Reggio di Calabria, Allied bombers were raiding the more northerly targets of La Spezia, Leghorn, and the Foggia air-fields. Particular attention was being given to severing lines of com-munication in accordance with the so-called 'Zuckerman Plan'. The marshalling yards outside Rome, Naples, and Foggia were repeatedly bombed, thereby exacerbating the effects of the bottle-necks on the Italian railway system, and in order to deprive the Axis forces still further of supplies, long-range bombers using new techniques were flying from England and delivering attacks on the heavy industrial installations in northern Italy.

A constant watch was maintained on the ever-changing radar

cover. From information culled from various sources – photographic reconnaissance, investigational flights by Nos 162 and 192 Squadrons and the American 'Ferret' Squadron, traffic monitored from the enemy's aircraft reporting network and other German ground organizations – details of the positions of the enemy radar stations were carefully recorded, as were their types and their efficiency. From this data the Operational Research Section compiled charts and maps indicating the best approach routes to follow, with the ranges of the various radar stations. To help with this task we were fortunate in having in North Africa as a scientific adviser on enemy non-Morse transmissions one of the most capable colleagues of Dr R. V. Jones. He was the enthusiastic and courageous young Eric Ackermann, who had already made many flights over the Western Front investigating enemy radar signals.

We had noted that the Germans were already installing at strategic points the superior long-range radar – the 'Wassermann' apparatus – which could pick up an aircraft farther away than the Freya apparatus. The scientists at TRE had already nicknamed it 'Chimney' because of the shape of its aerials. We were also able to warn the bomber units when twin-engined night-fighters, fitted with the 'Lichtensteingeraet' or airborne radar, arrived in the theatre, since their arrival was an added hazard for the No. 205 Group bombers.

For several weeks prior to the invasion of Sicily every effort was made by Allied fighter-bombers to destroy the radar installations in the areas of the proposed landings. After these raids, checks were made by investigational aircraft to find out which sites had been put out of action, and from some of these hazardous searches some of the aircraft failed to return. As we knew from Enigma traffic that the Axis were still uncertain where the landings would be made, to keep them guessing, radar sites on the northern coast of Sicily were also attacked. And for good measure, the USAAF bombed the San Domenico Hotel at Taormina, where the Germans had their headquarters.

As this softening-up onslaught progressed the R/T Field Units at La Marsa and Malta listened to the frustration of the German fighter squadrons as they failed to deter the large formations of our bombers droning their way towards the Straits of Messina and the Sicilian airfields. The Me. 109s and the Fw. 190s were finding it increasingly difficult to penetrate the Allied fighter escorts and to attack the American B 17s and even the use of aerial bombs did

I

Dispositions of monitoring units pre-'Husky', July 1943.

RUSSIA

Odessa

CRIMEA

RUMANIA

Ploesti

BLACK SEA

GREECE

TURKEY

Athens

RHODES

Aleppo

SYRIA

CRETE

Heraklion

No.6 F.U.
Aleppo

CYPRUS

Beirut

No.3 F.U.
ex Habbaniyah

Haifa

No.2 F.U.
Amriyah

(M) - Fort Regina
Benghazi

Jerusalem

Alexandria

Port Said

Derna

Mersa
Matruh

Bilbeis

Tobruk

Cairo

El Adem

Sidi
Barrani

El Alamein

H.Q.276 Wing,
Cairo and No.4 F.U.
(awaiting re-assignment
det. to go to Kos)

CYRENAICA

No.162 Squadron
Benina

E G Y P T

little to stem the flow. They were outnumbered and outclassed, and they knew it. The appalling losses in North Africa of men and equipment were beginning to tell. Lack of spares was reducing the serviceability of aircraft, and many of the new Luftwaffe aircrew arrivals in the theatre were not of the same calibre as those who had fought in the desert. We could always tell when pilots lacked combat experience (and this applied equally to the Allies). The monitors would hear a squadron commander calmly acknowledging orders from Control at Comiso, Gerbini or Trapani as, perhaps, they gave him the grid reference position of the attacking formation and vectored him towards the raid:

'"Moebelwagen" (furniture vans, i.e. enemy bombers) flying north – very high. Fly zero-two-five. Watch out for Spitfires.'

'Viktor' (message received).

The Allied formation would have been picked up by the Freya radar chain and the radio chatter from the fighters would have been monitored by the German Y stations at Noto and Erice.

As soon as our intruders were spotted by the enemy utter chaos would reign on their R/T. It became a babel of orders and encouraging yells, often reaching a point of near hysteria. We would listen, as the enemy did, to all that was being said:

'Look out, Spitfire on your tail!'

'You are making a vapour trail. Pay attention. Fly a little slower.'

'Look out – bombers below us, lots of them.'

'Get into the clouds quickly.'

'For God's sake, fly slower.'

'I've been hit – am baling out.'

'Heinz, watch out. Spits behind you at two thousand.'

The ground control stations would interject from time to time with instructions to the fighters and always using the fighter code.

'Watch out when returning home. Enemy fighters are south of coast at 6500 feet.'

'Collect together over lighthouse at 7000 feet.'

'Enemy fighters twenty miles north of St Paul's heading towards you.'

'Spits are being turned away from you. Return and land.'

Sometimes, even before an encounter, a pilot would be heard saying he was returning to base owing to 'engine trouble'. And just as a mêlée was really developing, there always seemed to be some pilot announcing: 'Ich habe Durst' (I am thirsty), or it might be that his 'red light' was 'showing', both of which meant that he was running short of fuel and that he would have to break off the engagement and return home. I am sure the squadron commanders knew as well as we did if there was genuine trouble, or if it was just a case of a young pilot becoming too scared to face up to combat.

It was not surprising that enemy morale was low. We knew from 'Ultra' that 'Der dicke Hermann' – Field-Marshal Goering – had ordered that 'one pilot from each of the fighter wings taking part (in the defence of Sicily) should be tried by court-martial for cowardice in the face of the enemy'.

As they listened in, the monitors knew that many of the pilots were at the end of their tether. They had escaped by the skin of their teeth from Tunisia, sometimes carrying an extra passenger crouched in the tail of their single-seater aircraft. Their losses both in the air and on the ground were ever greater. The weather was unbearably hot with hardly a breath of wind to disturb the humid Sicilian air whilst they rested between sorties. There was not even any peace at night, for the Wellingtons of No. 205 Group flew over to bomb their airfields and many a night was spent in the air-raid shelters.

Despite the fact that I/ and II/JG 77 had as their commander one of the most experienced of all the German fighter pilots, Johannes Steinhoff, who was to survive the war to become the Chief of German Air Staff, not even he could dispel the gloom which pervaded his unit, and the fighter-bombers of J G 51 and J G 54 were equally unhappy. To add to their misery, Goering followed up his earlier signal with a reprimand to Luftflotte II. 'Together with the fighter pilots in France, Norway and Russia, I can only regard you with contempt,' he stated. 'I want an immediate improvement in fighting spirit. If this improvement is not forthcoming, flying personnel from the commander down must expect to be reduced to the ranks and transferred to the eastern front to serve on the ground.' Those were words that were hardly conducive to inspiring even the most patriotic Nazi.

Our interrogators of prisoners-of-war also sensed an air of defeatism. Sicily was about to be added to the German reversals of Stalingrad and Tunisia, and their Italian allies seemed to be doing little to help. Their morale had been seriously weakened by the apparent ease with which Allied bombing had brought about the surrender of their fortress island of Pantellaria.

From the earliest days in the desert, relations between the Luftwaffe and the Regia Aeronautica had not been good. There had
always been resistance to any suggestion of a unified air command,
and this had resulted in completely different control systems. As far
as we could calculate, the Italians did not have access to German
radar information, so they rarely knew what was going on. It was
not unusual for Italian fighters to be scrambled only to be told as
soon as they were airborne that the unidentified aircraft that they
were chasing was, in fact, a German. As far as the Luftwaffe was
concerned, it seemed to operate as though the Italian Air Force did
not exist, except, perhaps, in Sardinia, where the Italian fighters
still outnumbered the German. By the end of June we knew that the
six squadrons of the Italian 4th Regiment active in the Catania area
had been reduced to two, but that there were still six squadrons
operational in Sardinia.

On the night of 9/10 July, Operation 'Husky', the invasion of
Sicily, was under way, but there was an unexpected storm which
seriously hampered the fleet of gliders bringing the Allied airborne
troops from Africa. The weather, coupled with the inexperience of
the pilots towing the gliders, resulted in only a few reaching their
pre-arranged landing places. It was a tragedy that several of the
gliders landed well out to sea, and others were strewn across southern
Sicily. Some were even fired on by Allied ships. Only about a dozen
actually landed on target, and they had been towed by the Royal
Air Force. A ripple of disgust at the poor navigation of the American
aircrews swept through the British forces throughout the Mediterranean. Fortunately the fiasco was soon lived down in the hard-
fought battles in the hills and plains of Sicily.

While these airborne operations were taking place, the main
forces were landing on the beaches after a miserable voyage through
heavy seas. The US Seventh Army assailed the area between Licata
and Scoglitti, and the British Eighth Army penetrated the coast
from the Pachino peninsula to Syracuse. General Eisenhower later
wrote about this, commenting: 'Up to that moment, no amphibious
attack in history had approached this one in size. Along miles of
coastline, there were hundreds of vessels and small boats afloat and
ant-like files of advancing troops ashore.'[2] But the incessant bombardment of the airfields and the landing grounds had so seriously
disrupted both the German and Italian fighters that by now they
did not have a single airfield in Sicily which was fully operational,

and our monitors listened whilst they were constantly re-routed to other landing strips. Not surprisingly, there was little fighter opposition during the initial stages of the invasion. Sporadic attacks were made by Axis bombers and fighter-bombers, but they again had difficulty in getting through the continuous protective patrols of our fighters which were flown from bases in Tunisia and from the 'unsinkable aircraft carriers' of Malta, Gozo, and now Pantellaria. The enemy air efforts did little to interfere with the progress of the landings. Indeed, the combination of the bad weather and the element of chaos inevitable during this, one of the first joint Allied operations, was probably more of a hazard than the enemy.

In the early planning for 'Husky', the intention had been to allocate one R/T Field Unit to the Desert Air Force, another to work alongside the air support for the US Seventh Army and a third to be attached to a Mobile Operations Room Unit – No. 1 MORU – which had been sent out direct from England for the invasion. But we could not provide sufficient linguist-monitors to man three R/T Field Units for Sicily in addition to our other commitments, and Air Vice-Marshal Broadhurst, the Air Officer Commanding Desert Air Force, was reluctant to release No. 211 Group's Field Unit. He was well aware that the initial success of an assault might well depend on an efficient fighter cover, which in turn relied on early warning. In the first days of an advance, when communications were poor, radar cover thin, and identification difficult, the Y unit could well be invaluable to forward operations. As the personnel of No. 1 MORU were new to the theatre, it was decided that, until they could become more accustomed to the enemy that they were having to face, No. 25 FU should continue to work with the forward controllers of No. 211 Group, sailing with them from Malta on D-plus 3. It was not until later in the campaign that they were handed over to No. 1 MORU.

We had not planned for the R/T Field Unit to move in with the initial landing force on D-Day because it was felt that the larger Field Unit in Malta could cope adequately with both R/T and W/T monitored traffic from Sicily during the early stages of the assault. But this was to prove unwise, as the forward controllers operating in the 'Bark' landing area, who were now so accustomed to the availability of tactical Y, found the delays in getting information from Malta unacceptable. They tried their best to appropriate the Y party from the Headquarters ship, HMS *Largs*.

Further west, in 'Dime' landing area, the Americans had similarly made no provision for the early arrival of a Field Unit, and they had had no facilities for monitoring German Air Force traffic on the US Headquarters ship during the assault phase. No. 23 Field Unit was not to move over from Cap Bon to join the US 12th Air Support Command until later in the Sicilian operations, and by then the withdrawal of the enemy's fighter and fighter-bomber units to the mainland limited the amount of useful intercepted R/T. Unlike the Desert Air Force, the Americans had not yet fully appreciated the tactical use of monitored R/T, though they were avid recipients of longer term Y information.

To handle the Allied night raids on Italy and Sicily, the Luftwaffe increased the strength of twin-engined night-fighter units, especially in the Naples area, and we listened as they defended Palermo and Messina as long as they dared. But by now we were not getting so much useful information from monitored night-fighter traffic, other than the knowledge of approximately when and where they were operating. This was partly compensated for by the return from Crete of a unit of Stukas, which, though fairly security-conscious, were more talkative, and therefore more useful. This applied equally to a reinforcement of thirty Me. 109s ordered over from Greece to help hold back the Allied tide.

But if there was less bomber and fighter activity to monitor, the same could not be said of the transport units. Constant battering of marshalling yards, ports, bridges, and the Messina ferries, by day and by night, had forced the Germans to resort to massive airlifts for the movement of personnel and supplies to Sicily and later their evacuation to the mainland. The movements of Ju. 52s, Me. 323s, Ju. 290s and SM. 87s throughout the whole theatre were carefully monitored, and these were to reach a crescendo of activity immediately prior to the invasion, only to be repeated again at the end of the campaign in so far as the availability of transport aircraft would then allow. During the final stages of the Sicilian campaign, Y was able to give warning of the movements of these aircraft, and there were many successful encounters. On 24 July our Spitfires had a field day, destroying twenty-one of an armada of Ju. 52s en route to Milazzo, in Sicily. During this time we were listening to large-scale troop-carrying glider activity and parachute training in southern France, and photographic reconnaissance was able to show the presence of about 100 gliders there, but the Luftwaffe was to find it operationally inadvisable to use them during the Sicilian campaign.

In the planning of the invasion of Sicily there had been a serious under-estimation of the vast quantity of signals intelligence traffic which would have to be transmitted over the radio links. The Special Liaison Units found themselves handling a great deal of Ultra traffic and there was a constant exchange of information between the Y units within the theatre and with Y in England. In addition, Nos 276 and 329 Wings broadcast collated Y information each day to their customers. This miscalculation of the volume of traffic was, however, to serve as a useful lesson for the planning of later landings. It should be remembered that the RAF Y Service normally monitored only Axis air force signals – ground and airborne. The Army and the Navy had their own networks for monitoring the signals which originated from their opposite numbers, but the SLUs on the other hand were essentially inter-service.

It was inevitable that, from time to time, there would be hold-ups in passing signals intelligence to interested parties, if only because of our inability to read part or all of an enemy message, but during 'Husky', the culprit was more often poor communications. When we were unable to decode a sighting report quickly the Navy had a tendency to be intolerant, even though this might be due to insufficient traffic having been heard in a particular code. But an indication of the frustrations that were caused by poor communications was given in a rueful report by No. 1 MORU which read:

We had a bit of bad luck before 08.00. Y Service picked up R/T chatter from some Hun Jabos (fighter-bombers) and learned they were to attack Augusta. One pilot asked if the target was Catania and was told – 'No, we'll go to Augusta first and go over Catania on our way home.' The message was picked up 5 minutes before the raid was first plotted 25 miles out to sea but 25 FU could not get a reply from here because the buzzer on the telephone decided at that moment not to function. As a result, no interception was made and 4 Me. 109s with possibly 2 Fw. 190s attacked unmolested.[3]

Speed in dealing with monitored traffic – either in its raw state or collated – was always of the utmost importance and never more so than during an assault.

In the early days of the North African campaign the Americans had had some doubts about the tactical value of Y, but these had come to be well and truly dispelled. To show his appreciation, Lieutenant-General 'Tooey' Spaatz, who was in command of the North-West African Air Forces, sent a letter of commendation to Wing Commander G. V. Cottam of No. 329 Wing which read:

The organization and operational efficiency of 329 Wing, RAF has contributed materially to the successes of the NWAAF in all phases of the North African, Tunisian, Pantellarian and Sicilian campaigns. You and your personnel have displayed an unusually high degree of efficiency. This has been confirmed repeatedly by the high order of your work as well as by my personal visits to elements of your command. The high order of your work has contributed most definitely to the air operational successes in the various campaigns and has reflected great credit on 329 Wing of the Royal Air Force.[4]

It was perhaps a little unfortunate that reference was made only to No. 329 Wing, since probably the greater credit should have gone to the personnel of No. 276 Wing, who had worked in the desert and on Malta since the beginning, and who had manned the Y parties afloat.

Although even before the landings it was obvious that the Allies had gained undoubted superiority in the air, this did little to mitigate the bitterness of the struggle for Sicily. Both sides tried desperately to hamper reinforcements. Veteran Eighth Army officers were heard to say that they had never known the Germans fight more fiercely than they did on the Catanian front, and it was not until 4 August that Catania fell. But when the Sicilian operations officially ended on 18 August the Allies were forced to admit that the Axis had managed to evacuate successfully to the mainland more than half of its forces. Constant naval and air attacks in the Straits of Messina had failed to prevent this, due largely to the sheer concentration of enemy anti-aircraft defences, and to the tenacity of the gun crews, who had secured the safe passage of all too many enemy ships and ferries across that narrow stretch of water.

The campaign had left both sides exhausted. Now the Germans needed to regroup their land forces, and to transfer their forward air units to less vulnerable airfields in central Italy. Meanwhile the Allies were speeding up their preparations for 'Operation Avalanche', the invasion of mainland Italy which was to be made on the beaches of Salerno. Ahead for them lay the pursuit of the Germany Army into 'Fortress Europe'.

17

From Sicily to Salerno

Even before the fall of Sicily the enemy reconnaissance units were engaged in a feverish search for Allied convoys throughout the whole of the Mediterranean, mainly because the German High Command was still in doubt about where the next blow would fall. A Calabrian landing was obviously imminent, but would the next major amphibious assault be against the Naples area, Sardinia or in the eastern Mediterranean? Kesselring was still rightly convinced that the Bay of Salerno offered the most promising area for the Allies to make a landing. The beaches had good gradients, and the area was within range for the all-important fighter cover. Repeated attacks by Allied aircraft on airfields and lines of communication in the region surrounding Salerno were further confirmation of this. Nevertheless, the Germans were taking steps to cover any eventualities which might arise further east.

Every day during the week following the end of the Sicilian campaign the Field Unit monitors recorded the activities of an average of six enemy aircraft on daylight reconnaissance. These were backed up by a further two or more sorties each night so that the Axis could keep a constant watch on activities in the harbours and the sea approaches to Sicily. They were also mounting at least four long-range patrols each week to scan the north-west African coast, whilst the eastern Mediterranean was searched in an equally systematic fashion. To augment sorties by the normal reconnaissance units such as I/F.123, II/F.122, III/F.33, and the meteorological unit Westa 26, all of which were by now based at Frosinone, fast fighter-bombers stationed in Sardinia were pressed into reconnaissance duties. It was for them vital to determine the size and direction of the next onslaught. These fighter-bombers could be ill-spared from defence tasks for, despite the arrival of replacements, the enemy's available strength of fighters in the Mediterranean was diminishing seriously. To add to Kesselring's problems some of his night-fighters were withdrawn from Italy to help the hard-pressed night defences of the Reich.

As soon as a message that was believed to be a sighting report was intercepted by the Y wireless operators every nerve was strained to decode it as quickly as possible and the whole network was alerted to listen for probable dusk attacks. At the same time, Allied naval and air Operations received from us the appropriate warnings. By 1 August there had been a serious raid on shipping in Palermo harbour when, for the first time in the Mediterranean, the Luftwaffe used their new anti-shipping weapon, the radio-controlled bomb. Although, earlier that day, Y had heard a sighting report which gave details of the ships seen around the harbour, it had not been possible to give sufficient warning of the actual attack, which involved some twenty-four aircraft of the crack units, KG 100 and KG 26.

The scientists had known for some time about the German's development of radio-controlled glider bombs, of which there were two types: the Fx 1400 and the Hs 293. The first mention that had been heard of experiments with these bombs was as early as July 1941. Knowing the propensity of our old 'bêtes noires', KG 100, for being involved in operations using special radio equipment and techniques, we had been watching every move on their part since the arrival a few weeks earlier of the IInd and IIIrd Gruppen at Istres, in southern France. This was the unit, by now enlarged to a full Geschwader, that had acted as pathfinders for the ill-fated Coventry raid, and they were the early users of the X-Geraet beams. And as we had feared might happen, it was from the Do. 217s of KG 100 that the first glider bombs were launched.

A fortnight after the Palermo raid, one of the patrolling German aircraft sighted an Allied convoy off the North African coast, and the enemy reacted immediately by staging an attack with some sixty aircraft. First came the special torpedo units, I/ and III/KG 26, flying from their bases at Salon and Montpelier and led by their Geschwaderkommodore, Major Klumper. This force was backed up by a second wave of the Italy-based KG 54, aided by their colleagues of II/LG 1. On this occasion, our North-West African Coastal Air Force Headquarters and the Navy were given prior warning, and radar picked up the approaching attack as soon as it materialized. Although two merchant vessels were hit, Allied aircraft and guns accounted for the destruction of eighteen enemy bombers.

By this time part of the fleet of ships for 'Avalanche' – the Salerno invasion – was beginning to assemble in the harbour of Bizerta. It was inevitable they would be carefully observed and later attacked. On 17 and 18 August came the first major raids and the wireless operators of the Field Units in North Africa and Malta recorded some one hundred aircraft of III/KG 30, II/KG 54, I/ and II/KG 26 and II/LG 1 operating against the harbour and shipping in the worst raid that was experienced by Bizerta. Considering the number of aircraft involved, the damage that was caused to our shipping might have been much worse. Three weeks later the harbour was attacked again, whilst shipping collecting at Algiers was bombed at the end of August, with KG 100 acting as target indicators with flare markers.

According to one prisoner-of-war who was shot down later at Salerno, it was whilst raiding Bizerta that KG 30* used 'Dueppel' for the first time in the Mediterranean. 'Dueppel' was the German equivalent of the British 'Window', the metal strips which were dropped in bundles from aircraft to jam, in our case, the enemy's short-range 'Wuerzburg' radar equipment. By producing a snow-storm of echoes on the radar screens it made accurate plotting of a raid almost impossible.†

The pattern of enemy day reconnaissance followed by dusk attacks was to be repeated time and time again. Y was frequently helpful to Operations, but sometimes our Intelligence staff were unable to

---

KG 30 We were amused to learn that this Geschwader, commanded by an Oberstleutnant Bloodern, sang as a unit song to the tune of an old German student song 'Ich hatt' einen Kamaraden . . .', a similar ditty which began – 'Ich hatt' einen Kommodore, einen bloodern gibt es nicht' (I had a commodore, a dumber one doesn't exist . . .').

†'Window' had been dropped by Bomber Command for the first time operation-ally during the saturation raid on Hamburg of 24 July. Up until that time, as we have seen, both sides had been reluctant to use this comparatively simple radar jammer for fear of retaliation by their enemy. So effective was 'Window' initially against the German night-fighter ground control that the complex organization of night defence on the Western Front – the so called Kammhuber Line – had been thrown into disarray. The resulting chaos had been listened to with glee by the monitors of the Kingsdown Y teams. Indeed the success of 'Window' forced the Luftwaffe to alter its whole system of night defence in Western Europe. During the months that followed this activity the Luftwaffe was to use 'Dueppel' during many raids in our theatre, as well as against Great Britain, but with varying degrees of success. Allied radar, on the whole, was not seriously affected.

decode a message until too late to be operationally useful, usually because insufficient material in the relevant code had been intercepted that day. The German bomber crews generally kept good radio security on their way out, but we were able to check them in like pigeons coming home to roost as they requested homing instructions. There were, nevertheless, occasions when we were lucky enough to get wind of an imminent bomber attack in sufficient detail for an intruder raid to be despatched to the bases of the units involved.

There were even occasions when messages were heard by us which indicated that the operation for the night had been cancelled because the presence of intruders had grounded the bombers. No. 23 Squadron, which was equipped with Mosquitoes, specialized in this type of intruding, and if we could give them adequate warning, they could be relied upon to intercept the bombers as they approached their home bases. If nothing else, the presence of intruders over their airfields must have seriously affected the enemy's peace of mind. So successful was No. 23 Squadron, who were based first in Malta and later in Sardinia, and so willing were they to act on Y information, that they became one of our favourite customers.

One indication of the direction from which a raid would come was gleaned from listening in to the enemy's M/F radio beacons. By observing which of the beacons were transmitting, Y had a fair indication of when and from which area a raid would materialize. The German pilots still relied heavily on their radio aids to help them navigate to and from a target and during convoy shadowing. During 1943 there had been a rapid expansion of their M/F beacon system throughout the whole of the occupied territories, and by June of that year nearly thirty beacons had already been located around the Mediterranean. In addition to this the enemy had introduced a new beam system, the Elektra-Sonne, which was virtually a fan of beams 5° apart, and was used mainly by long-range aircraft on shipping reconnaissance patrol, or when raiding Allied convoys. This beam system was found to be useful as an additional navigational aid for RAF crews, especially those of Coastal Command which operated out in the Atlantic.

When a German pilot needed verification of his position he would normally either take a bearing on suitable M/F beacons or ask his D/F control to take a bearing on his transmissions and thereby fix his position. In either case, the obvious answer for us was to prevent him from getting this information. In view of the very considerable success that No. 80 Wing was having on the Western Front in masking or 'meaconing' M/F beacons and generally interfering with the enemy's radio navigational aids, arrangements had been made for three mobile 'meaconing' units to be sent out to North Africa and the Middle East. They were to operate there until they were disbanded in November 1943, when their monitoring tasks were taken over by No. 276 Wing.

The function of these special units, known as Type 'M' W/T Units, was to select suitable enemy signals and to re-radiate them with the object of destroying the enemy's direction-finding activities. Through the use of special apparatus the monitored signal operated a transmitter which reproduced the original signal exactly as it had been received, and on the same frequency. This 'meaconing' was more subtle than jamming because it re-radiated the same signal, with the same modulation, as well as on the same frequency. The only difference was that the locations of the aircraft and the 'meacon' transmitter were miles apart, and, as there was no method by which the ground station could differentiate between the two signals, it was quite impossible to take a bearing on the aircraft.

The places at which the 'M' stations were sited were: No. 21 at Bordj Menaïel, thirty-eight miles east of Algiers, responsible for beacons in Sardinia, the west coast of Italy and southern France; No. 20 outside Benghazi, handling the Crete, Aegean and Greece area (including the broadcasting station at Athens, which the German aircraft used for D/F purposes); and No. 22 which was a new arrival in the Cap Bon peninsula, and was used to back up No. 21, from which it would take over in due course. Both No. 20 and No. 21 had covered the beacons in Sicily before and during the 'Husky' operations.[1]

The main problem for the 'M' stations was the selection of the channels to be 'meaconed', since the availability of transmitters restricted the number of channels that they could handle at any one time. This was normally three M/F channels, and one H/F, which meant that they had to be in constant touch with the Field Units monitoring the traffic. The enemy M/F beacons that were working in the Mediterranean at this time fell into two categories: those which transmitted a full twenty-four hours and the others which transmitted at selected times. They operated on a rota system, changing their callsigns and frequencies several times a day at irregular intervals that varied from day to day. New sets of wedded callsigns and frequencies were introduced each month and with so many beacons operating, this necessitated extensive direction-finding, sometimes for several days, before the new rota system could be worked out. As the 'M' stations had no D/F facilities of their own, they relied on the Y Service to identify the various beacons. Each month Y Headquarters issued a table of location rotas, as soon as it could be determined, together with a list of callsigns and frequencies, giving the co-ordinates and code-names of the various beacons.

In the same way the 'M' stations needed guidance when 'meaconing' homing signals from aircraft. It was arranged that whenever a convoy was passing within the area covered by a particular 'M' station, the unit would be advised, and they would keep a special watch on one channel and a transmitter ready solely for 'meaconing' requests by enemy aircraft for homing instructions. It was Y's responsibility to keep the unit informed of the current frequency and the callsigns used by the aircraft and their ground station callsigns and any other useful information. There were times, as with the Elektra-Sonne beams, when it was helpful for Allied aircraft on a distant raid to make use of the enemy's beacons as an extra navigational aid, in which case the appropriate beacons were left unmolested.

We were left in no doubt that 'meaconing' was a constant source of confusion to the enemy. In the first week in August, for example, No. 21 'M' Unit had successfully 'meaconed' ninety-four aircraft transmissions working on M/F, and another three on H/F. Messages were constantly heard from both aircraft and ground stations complaining that the bearings were useless.

All the 'M' units, being mobile versions of those operated by No. 80 Wing in the United Kingdom, were controlled by the Communications Officer at Mediterranean Air Command, Colonel Draper F. Henry, whose deputy, Group Captain A. M. Rodgers, was an experienced radio countermeasures officer. The Field Units, on the other hand, were responsible to the Chief Intelligence Officer, through Wing Commander Morgan as the Chief Signals Intelligence Officer. Whether or not this division of responsibilities between the two organizations was the reason for the failure to make a study in depth of the successes or otherwise of the radio countermeasures used for 'Husky', or whether it was merely because planning for 'Avalanche' overtook events, that failure was a pity. It was always Jimmy

Morgan's belief that a great deal could have been learnt from such a study which would have been helpful in the later planning for 'Overlord'.

Such was the necessary, albeit callous determination of war that even distress signals sent by damaged aircraft were 'meaconed' so as to ensure that the enemy's Air Sea Rescue Service would be uncertain where to search should the aircraft come down in the sea. I recall one particular incident when a signal from an enemy aircraft indicated that the crew were baling out west of the Bosa lighthouse. It appeared they had an emergency wireless set in their dinghy and although the signal was weak, it was nevertheless 'meaconed'. Some time later, the crew was heard telling Cagliari that they were still waiting to be picked up. Whether or not they were eventually recovered I never heard, but I always tried not to think in terms of the men involved. I knew that our attitude had to be that every airman saved by the enemy lived to be an enemy able to fight another day.

About this time, there came an extra urgency for me to end the war. I had learned that my young brother, Geoffrey, had received his pilot's wings after training in Canada, and now, at the age of 19, he was a fully-fledged pilot and about to be assigned to Coastal Command. Again I had a premonition, and I wrote to my mother sharing with her a blending of pride and fear. In my letter I told her I knew how she must be feeling – terribly proud but very sad and afraid, begging her not to think of all the things that might happen to him when he started on operations and stressing my feelings that:

'If someone has been as good and as sweet as you have been, they think many times before hurting them. But if they should so decide that otherwise is for the best, it is because they think so highly of the person concerned that they deem them fit for dying a hero's death. Have you noticed that it is nearly always the best people who join the land of heroes? For myself, I could think of nothing finer than to die for my country. So much more satisfactory than dying of old age in one's bed.'

As women, we always had the extra worry of what might befall our menfolk, and this applied equally to friend and foe. On my way back from North Africa a few months earlier, I had acted as interpreter for the escort of two young German airmen when the escort had been unable to make his prisoners understand what he wanted them to do.

I had learned that they were survivors of a bomber shot down over the Mediterranean, and that they had been adrift in a dinghy in the blazing sun for four days. They looked so very young – mere children – which reminded me of my brother, and they were obviously very scared and bewildered. I wanted so much to put my arm around them, and to say – 'Don't be afraid. No one will harm you. For you now the war is over.' But I knew that I must not show any sympathy, or chatter with them to reassure them because they had not yet been 'processed' by the prisoner-of-war interrogation centre and I might compromise its work.

At the end of July I was again holding the fort for a few weeks at Headquarters in Cairo, as Betton-Foster was sick. In view of the possible imminence of 'Accolade', the proposed offensive in the Aegean, there were certain queries which had been raised by our customers in the Levant, and various problems to sort out regarding future commitments for the Field Unit at Aleppo. As these had to be dealt with urgently, David Davies asked me to accompany him on a tour up north. We were just about to make a start on our trip by car to Palestine and Syria when a signal arrived authorizing my transfer to Algiers to join Jimmy Morgan at Allied Headquarters and also suggesting that David should go home for discussions with the Air Ministry. As there was no firm date yet for either of these movements, we hurried off on what was to become a journey of exceptional interest, across the Sinai Desert, and via Jerusalem, Haifa and the Lebanon.

Our main reason for visiting Aleppo was to check that the unit there was working smoothly. As was often the case with the smaller, ostensibly mobile Field Units listening in to W/T traffic, the signals that they heard were to prove only marginally more useful during the events that followed than those that were heard at the large, static units, and they were soon to be withdrawn to Lydda, in Palestine, and then back to the Delta.

For our return trip through Damascus, Tiberias and the Sea of Galilee, David Davies and I were joined by Flight Lieutenant T. D. 'Tommy' Martin, who was one of the Wing's most able signals officers. He had been supervising the erection of direction-finding equipment at the Aleppo Field Unit.

Arriving back in Egypt, I learned with mixed feelings there was now a definite posting for me and that I was to move over to Algiers in a couple of weeks. Betton-Foster wisely decided to take the opportunity before I left Egypt to fly over to North Africa for talks with Jimmy Morgan, and to visit No. 25 FU in Sicily, but by the time that he reached there the unit had already crossed over to Italy with the Desert Air Force in the wake of the Eighth Army's landings in Calabria.

Even before the end of the Sicilian campaign, the air war against mainland Italy had been accelerating. The greater part of Italy's supplies of oil and coal and many other products was brought across her northern frontiers, with half the imports filtering in through the Brenner Pass, and another third via the Swiss Simplon and St Gothard Passes, whilst two thirds of her vital oil supplies came from Balkan sources through Trieste. Once inside Italy there were virtually only three routes to the south, and it was these, the arteries and veins down the leg of Italy, which received persistent attention from the Allied bomber forces.

There could now be no element of tactical surprise at Salerno. The Germans had been awaiting an attack on the beaches for a couple of weeks, and had even carried out a dress rehearsal of a repulse of such an attack. During the build-up immediately prior to 'Avalanche' the Allied air forces stepped up their onslaught, concentrating on strategic targets. Particular emphasis was placed on neutralizing airfields so as to reduce air opposition to the landings, and on disabling road and rail communications. There was ample evidence that this bombing programme was proving successful, and we learned from feedbacks through Enigma traffic that the disruption of the Italian railroad system, for example, was causing major hold-ups in the delivery of the fuel that was so badly needed by the Axis air forces which were operating from the Foggia airfields.

We now knew that the toe of Italy was almost denuded of fighter units. They had been pulled back to defend the Naples and Foggia areas, and as a result of that the fighter R/T heard in the forward Field Units was considerably reduced. It was, of course, especially important for us in Y to keep a careful watch on the movements of fighter defence units and anti-aircraft gun concentrations in order to provide intelligence for the briefing of aircrews flying on interdiction raids.

As with the previous amphibious assaults, for the landing at Salerno efforts were made to destroy in advance those radar installations which would be most likely to pick up the approaching naval and air formations. The Freya at Ventotene Island was singled out for special attention because of its position *vis-à-vis* the invasion beaches. And in order to check on the serviceability of the other radar sites, as well as to watch for the erection of new equipment, investigational aircraft flew regularly along the enemy-held coastlines. We had already gained both audible and visual evidence of the existence of a 'Wassermann' on the Île de Porquerolles, near Toulon. This apparatus, with its range of 200–250 km, was considered by experts to have been the best early warning radar put into service by either side during the course of the war. We realized that the new station would be an added hazard for any aircraft approaching targets in southern France, which included the airfields of Istres, Montpelier, and Salon, where the more dangerous of the anti-shipping squadrons were based.

By this time the US 16th Reconnaissance Squadron, the 'Ferrets', had taken over from No. 192 Squadron the surveillance of enemy radar in Sardinia, Corsica, and the Italian peninsula. Sometimes they would carry a British scientific officer, Mr A. Potts, as a special observer and it was during one of these flights that they noted the absence of signals from installations in Sardinia. This was confirmation of traffic that we had monitored ordering the removal of radar apparatus from the island, and it was a helpful indication of a weakening of the screen that was facing the south and which was capable of picking up the invasion convoys as they sailed north.

Later, after the Salerno landings, the 'Ferrets' were to record the reinforcement of the radar cover in Corsica, before that island was evacuated by the Germans; and they also quickly spotted the erection of further equipment in northern Italy. The enemy were finding it increasingly difficult to cope with penetration by both Allied long-range bombers into southern Germany and Austria from the south, and, at the same time, by Bomber Command aircraft from the United Kingdom attacking heavy industrial and communications targets in the Po Valley. For some weeks Bomber Command aircraft had also been shuttling between their bases and North African air-fields, attacking selected targets en route. RAF Pathfinders were using their new techniques, and were leading the bombers to the targets. It was essential that we should provide as comprehensive a picture as possible of the radar, anti-aircraft, and fighter defences in the areas over and near which the raiders would fly.

With the knowledge that we had gained about the locations, the types, and the ranges of the various installations that would be likely to give early warning of the approaching 'Avalanche' forces, a radar jamming programme was evolved, as it had been for 'Husky'. Specially equipped B 17s were assigned to fly in advance of the troop-carriers immediately prior to the actual assault. Their task was to operate 'Mandrel' and 'Carpet' jammers* to confuse the ground radar, and, although there was no conclusive proof that these countermeasures were successful, the loss of troop-carriers was certainly low during 'Avalanche'.

Before any jamming programme was undertaken, the effects of the proposed jamming had first to be considered carefully by the Inter-services Radio Countermeasures Board in the theatre concerned. We were well aware that the jamming of communications channels might reduce, if not kill, the value of intercepted signals intelligence on certain bands from which, perhaps, extremely valuable information was obtained. It might be that jamming of selected frequencies, though helpful to the Allied air forces, might swamp fruitful channels monitored by the Army or the Navy. It was for the Board to consider whether the value of a particular countermeasure would outweigh the loss of any such intelligence material.

There was also the very real risk that the German scientists might develop apparatus that was capable of reading through our jamming, in the way that they were later able to read through 'Window' by means of equipment they called 'Wurzlaus'. Or they might even turn the tables on the Allies by producing equipment that could 'home' on the airborne jammer carried by an attacking aircraft, as they did with 'Freya Halbe', which they evolved to home on our 'Mandrel' transmissions. It was an unrelenting battle of wits between the scientists.

From traffic that was monitored from the German aircraft reporting network we were usually aware when jamming operations were successful, if only by the inability of the reporting stations to plot incoming Allied formations. The vast quantity of intercepted R/T traffic from the night-fighter defence network on the Western Front provided useful additional information on this subject. But in the

---

*'Mandrel': the code-name for British jammer to counter long-range radar (Freya, Chimney, etc.).
'Carpet': the code-name for British jammer to counter short-range radar. Both of these were noise barrage jammers.

Mediterranean there was now little controlled night-fighter traffic within our monitoring range, because most of the twin-engined night-fighter units had been withdrawn from Italy for the defence of the Reich.

As well as a marked decrease in the amount of monitored German night- and day-fighter traffic, the signals that we were intercepting from the Italian Air Force were clearly becoming less valuable. Even before the capitulation, there was little point in keeping many sets in the Middle East engaged on Italian monitoring, and this, coupled with the need to concentrate our resources in the central Mediterranean, resulted in various changes in the organization of both No. 329 and 276 Wings. Most of the Italian-speaking Intelligence personnel were released to the Allied Military Government (AMGOT), where their talents could be put to better use, whilst the Signals personnel and the equipment were reassigned to augment our coverage of German Air Force traffic. With the probability of an amphibious assault against the Axis-held Aegean, and the continued importance of monitoring the Russian and Balkan Fronts, we still had, however, to keep a considerable Y contingent in the Middle East.

As the various campaigns in the theatre developed, so the locations of the different Field Units changed in order to meet operational requirements. The actual numbers allocated to the individual Field Units similarly altered from time to time, and to such an extent that it was my fond hope that in the monitoring of our traffic, which they undoubtedly tried to do, the 'Horchdienst' would be kept in a state of constant confusion as to which unit was where. By 'Avalanche', both the German and Italian Air Force communications were thoroughly covered by us throughout the Mediterranean, the Balkans, and the South Russian Front. Apart from No. 351 WU at Gibraltar, which was largely engaged on tasks allocated direct from England, Nos 329 and 276 Wings between them had 113 receivers listening in to Luftwaffe W/T channels and a further thirty sets monitoring their R/T.[2] RAF Y stations now spread across the theatre all the way from Algiers to the Tunisian peninsula, Malta, Sicily, and Calabria, and from Benghazi to Alexandria, and Aleppo. But up to the time of 'Avalanche', the Signal Intelligence Service of the US Army had not played an active part in monitoring enemy air – as opposed to military – traffic.

In view of the success of the ship-borne Y parties during the

'Husky' operation, two small parties were hastily organized for HMS *Hilary* and HMS *Ulster Queen* and a further party was assigned to the American Headquarters ship USS *Ancon*, the flagship of Vice-Admiral Henry Kent Hewitt, with General Mark Clark, Commander of the United States Fifth Army, on board. The monitoring parties on the British ships were entirely RAF; but for the first time, the American No. 849th SIS was able to provide a Y party for USS *Ancon* comprising three linguist/monitors and an Intelligence officer. They were to work closely with our now very experienced Flight Lieutenant Clapham and his Czech colleague, Sergeant Arje, who had joined the Americans at Algiers to give them the benefit of their Y experience.

The organization of the Y units that were monitoring both naval and air traffic aboard British ships was technically in the hands of the senior naval officers in charge of Y, known as the SO 'Y', who for this operation had made a somewhat hazy arrangement for the RAF party to receive longer-term intelligence – as opposed to the tactical R/T which they would monitor on board ship – through the SO 'Y' in Malta. But we knew from past experience that naval handling of Y traffic was often too slow for air operations, when minutes might make all the difference between information being useful or useless. So, once again, and with the blessing of Jimmy Morgan and Cottam of No. 329 Wing, Clapham made his own somewhat illicit arrangements to be fed with essential information by means of what we called 'Clatter' broadcasts. These broadcasts supplied the Field Units with information on enemy activity such as movements of units to new bases, reinforcements brought into the battle area, warnings when enemy ground stations were sending 'spoof' traffic, enemy sightings of Allied shipping, forecasts of targets likely to be attacked, areas to be patrolled by Axis reconnaissance aircraft, bases unserviceable, and also technical Y data on callsigns, codes, and frequencies. The broadcasts were made at half-hourly intervals with the messages suitably encoded, and, just in case the German Y Service was listening, dummy transmissions were sent during periods of inactivity.

Through experience Rob Clapham realized that whereas for the Pantellaria and Sicily operations the low-powered transmitter at the Malta Field Unit had been adequate, this would not be the case during the forthcoming operation off the west coast of Italy. So before embarking, he arranged with Flight Lieutenant John Simmonds, the Senior Intelligence Officer at No. 329 Wing, to pick up the 'Clatter' broadcasts on the much stronger link between No. 329 Wing Headquarters at Draria and the Field Unit near Tunis. But as the invasion convoys neared Salerno even the Algiers signals faded, and Clapham made an arrangement with Simmonds for the Tunis Field Unit, which was nearer, to act as a repeater station, re-transmitting the information that he needed. This was later to prove to be of invaluable help.

It was surprising that General Mark Clark should have made such a grave mistake in deciding not to carry out a preliminary bombardment of the defences covering the Salerno beaches, preferring, as he did, to rely on an element of surprise and the assistance of the Italians rather than on any softening up by naval and air action. For by 8 September, the Panzer troops had already been brought to the highest state of readiness, and they had received a warning that Operation 'Achse' – their code-name for the landings – was imminent. The Germans had been anticipating the defection of the Italians, and they were duly ordered to 'bring in the harvest' (Ernte einbringen), which called for the immediate disarming of all Italian troops.

It was nevertheless not until D – 1 that the 'Avalanche' convoys were first attacked in the Tyrrhenian Sea. The fuel shortage was reducing the enemy's reconnaissance patrols, and the weakening of the radar cover in Sardinia may also have contributed to the failure to identify the invasion convoys earlier. When the attack did come, our fighters were able to ward off most of the enemy aircraft; but unfortunately, as the convoys neared the mainland, the range of hills behind the beaches caused considerable hindrance to the seaborne radar and hence to the control of our fighters, especially when attacking aircraft approached from that direction. This had been a problem in the earlier Sicily landings and once again, Y monitoring was able to fill the gap by providing useful advance warnings. Even by the end of the first day it was realized by the Allied commanders that 'Avalanche' was going to be a desperate fight. The Italians were now unable to give them any support, and the whole might of the German Tenth Army was aligned against General Clark's Fifth Army. With observation posts strategically placed in the hills overlooking the beaches, and with the enemy artillery blasting the vessels unloading troops and equipment, the Germans were in a commanding position. Later, General Mark Clark was to write: '. . . it was difficult even after the battle . . . for anyone except the men engaged to know how gravely disaster threatened the first Allied assault on European soil. And even in the course of battle, we did not fully realize how great was the advantage of the Germans in holding all the high hills surrounding the beachhead.'[3] It was only after he flew over the German positions at Salerno that Clark realized how well the enemy had been able to observe every movement of the Allied troops and how they had been able to shift their strength and artillery to oppose any thrusts by the Fifth Army.

Two days after the initial landings the Germans made a determined effort against the assembled convoys. Amongst the attacking aircraft, which numbered over 120, were elements of KG 100 who flew from their base in southern France and were armed with their new radio-controlled bombs. As the attack developed, the US cruiser *Philadelphia* was lying on one side of the US Headquarters ship *Ancon*, which had General Clark still on board. On her other side there was the USS *Savannah*. Suddenly, there came a shattering noise as a glider bomb screeched down on the ships, just missing *Ancon* but penetrating through *Savannah*'s deck and exploding below, causing many casualties. Tugs rushed to her aid, and she was able eventually to struggle back to Malta for repairs. The next bomb was a near miss on *Philadelphia*.

This was to be the first of many attacks against the Salerno convoys in which radio-controlled bombs were used, and some bright spark on one of the American ships thought up the idea of a Do-it-Yourself radio countermeasure. All electrical appliances, including even electric razors, were to be switched on during an attack in the hope of jamming the radio-controlled bombs and/or the Luftwaffe aircraft frequency. Apart from possibly helping the morale of the troops, it was, of course, a useless innovation.

The morale of many of the troops needed a boost. They had learned of the capitulation of the Italian government as they sailed northwards towards the invasion beaches. Many had optimistically believed that now that Italy was out of the war, there would be nobody to fight. In a conversation later with one of our Army officers we discussed the deplorable mutiny by a batch of mainly Scottish troops a few days after the initial assault. It was his opinion that part of the trouble might well have stemmed from a resentment over being attached to the American Fifth Army instead of to the British Eighth Army. But he was convinced that the trouble was chiefly caused by reaction when the men realized that the war was far from won. He felt that they had been reluctant to grasp the fact that they would still have to face a German Army even more determined than ever to resist. Perhaps, too, the calmness of the sea and the beaut of the night as they sailed towards Salerno, which contrasted so vividly with the stormy passage that had been experienced before the Sicilian landings, had lulled them into a state of complacency.

The first counter-offensive by the Germans was launched two days after the initial landings and it was on the same day that the first of the radio-controlled bomb attacks was inflicted on the support ships. Allied fighters were putting up a magnificent effort patrolling the convoys and striking at any identified strongpoint on shore. There was now no question that we had superiority in the air, but nevertheless, too many enemy bombers were still managing to get through and causing damage. The problem was partly the lack of airfields in the battle area. There was insufficient carrier-borne aircraft, and, until forward landing grounds could be established, most of the fighters were still based in Sicily, which severely restricted the amount of time that they could spend on patrol over the invasion forces.

For this reason alone it was vital that we should identify and be able to confront the enemy formations quickly, and once again, Y was to prove helpful, with Rob Clapham's unofficial link with Algiers paying off. From the traffic that we were intercepting, John Simmonds and his intelligence team at No. 329 Wing had determined that the KG 100 aircraft were dropping their Fx bombs from Do. 217s from over 20,000 feet. Armed with this valuable information, Clapham managed to get ashore and to find his way to the US fighter control, which was by this time established on the beachhead. A fighter patrol was then laid on specifically to fly over the anchorage at 25,000 feet, armed with the knowledge that it was the Do. 217s which caused the most damage. The plan was almost immediately successful, with one Dornier shot down, and another damaged. There was subsequently a marked disinclination by the Luftwaffe to repeat the attack.

The situation at Salerno by 13 September was so critical that there seemed a possibility that the Allies would be pushed back into the sea. The now strongly reinforced German Army was jabbing through the Allied lines. But there was to be no repetition of Dunkirk. Despite constant attacks from the Luftwaffe, our ships kept up a steady barrage of shelling against selected targets, making it increasingly difficult for the enemy to reform.

Appreciating the devastating accuracy of the naval gunfire, the German Air Force was ordered to concentrate its attacks on the supporting ships. On 13 September HMS *Uganda* was badly hit and only managed to limp back to Malta under tow. On the same day USS *Philadelphia* was again lucky, narrowly escaping near misses. But two days later, a flight of Fw. 190s carried out a successful raid using glider bombs, and scored a direct hit on HMS *Warspite*. She survived, but she was extensively damaged.

In order to hamper the German air offensive against the ships and the ground forces as much as possible every effort was being made to reduce the air strength of the enemy by mounting raids against their airfields, with the group of landing grounds around Foggia becoming favourite targets. On 14 September waves of Fortresses, Bostons, and Mitchells flew 700 sorties, attacking selected targets around the battle area and those airfields in the hinterland on which photographic reconnaissance and Y indicated a build-up of aircraft.

Four days later, Y was to be incidental in a highly successful operation. The Wing had intercepted messages during the late after-noon which indicated that, owing to bad weather, a great many aircraft were grounded on the Foggias. The intelligence team at Draria had been able to 'footprint' – as we called it – the units in-volved and had advised Clapham. In describing the incident long afterwards he commented: 'This was the chance of a lifetime. I tackled the Americans on *Ancon* asking them whether they would like to destroy all the front line GAF bombers.'[4]

At the Americans' request, Clapham calculated how many of the various types of bombers were probably on the airfields. He ad-mitted later that 'there may have been a little poetic licence in my calculations'. Immediately *Ancon* command sent a signal to the North Africa Strategic Air Force in Tunisia giving them details of the number of Ju. 52s, Do. 217s, Ju. 88s, and fighter-bombers on Foggia and satellite airfields. A request was made for their immediate destruction. As a result of this a force of ninety-one Lightnings was despatched to reach Foggia by first light, and this was backed up by eight heavy bombers of the RAF. The resultant destruction of forty-five enemy aircraft with a further seventeen seriously damaged curtailed considerably the Luftwaffe's efforts over the battle area during what was one of the most crucial periods of the Salerno operations.

For nine desperate days the Allies fought across the heavily mined terrain at Salerno under ceaseless fire from German strongpoints in the encircling hills. It was a fearful struggle for the Allies to keep a foothold on the beaches. During that time three regiments of US airborne troops were dropped at strategic points on either side of the front line in an effort to provide greatly needed reinforcement to the hard-pressed Fifth Army. It was not until ten days after the initial landing that General Clark was certain that the Salerno bridgehead was firmly in Allied hands, and that the Germans were in retreat.

By 16 September, Colonel-General von Vietinghoff, the Commander of the German Tenth Army, was forced to concede that there was now no likelihood of being able to evict the Allies from the beachhead. Already the leading patrols of the Eighth Army had joined up with the Americans in the south, having worked their way from Calabria, and they were now pressing the rear of the German lines. To avoid further losses to von Vietinghoff's troops, and to enable them to withdraw and be redeployed before the Eighth Army attacked their rear, Kesselring authorized 'a disengagement on the coastal front with the express proviso that the Volturno line, to which the Tenth Army intended to fall back, must not be abandoned before 15 October'.[5]

The Battle of Salerno was over, and the Allies were now established in Fortress Europe. But ahead there was to be a hard slog through mountains and across rivers, through towns and villages, and across marshy plains. The campaign for the conquest of Italy had hardly started.

18

A Question of Strategy

When I finally arrived at my new posting in Algiers, I found that Jimmy Morgan was away at the front in Italy. I was met at the airfield at Maison Blanche by another officer on our staff. My flight over in a DC4 had been comfortable, unlike the previous journey to North Africa when we had travelled in what was rudely nicknamed 'a flying bedpan', the famous American DC3, known to us as the Dakota. It had a row of metal bucket seats down each side of the fuselage, designed in such a way that there always seemed to be a projecting piece of metal jabbing you in the neck or in the back. I was to fly many hundreds of miles in Dakotas, sometimes managing to find a more comfortable seat in the form of mailbags, or a huge aircraft tyre. I admit to having been from time to time ingloriously airsick but I learned to weather any rude cracks about 'disgracing the Waaf'. My airsickness never detracted from my love of flying.

My first task on arrival was to find a billet, since I would not be living in the WAAF Hostel at El Biar. There was a considerable discrepancy between the billeting allowance given by the Americans, and that provided by the British. We gave a mere nineteen francs, whereas the Americans paid thirty. It was understandable that all the best billets should go to the Americans, and that the canny Frenchwomen were reluctant to accommodate the British. Eventually, by paying at the American rates, I found a room near the Headquarters in the home of a French General and his family. They were quite kind to me personally, but they were too obviously resentful of the turn of events in North Africa, and I had to regard them as security suspects.

The lack of hot baths – or the means of getting one – became almost an obsession with many of us, yet by one of those ironies of fate, my little office at Headquarters was in fact a windowless bathroom, sadly without hot water, in what must have been, in peacetime, a pleasant ground-floor suite. My desk was a wooden cover over the bath and the lavatory was discreetly hidden behind a filing cabinet. It was a far cry from my airy office in Cairo.

As soon as I set foot in the office at Headquarters I was presented with a list of matters which Jimmy Morgan hoped that I 'could deal with before he returned from Italy'. There was obviously a great deal of work to do, and the whole Headquarters had an air of urgency about it which had been sadly lacking lately in the Middle East. As far as the work was concerned there was, amongst other things, my appointment as Secretary of the Y North Africa Committee. That was inevitable, as I had held the similar post in Cairo. It meant that I would be involved with both Navy and Army Y as well as RAF but I knew that there would be no difficulty, as several of the Committee had also moved over from the east, and they had already accepted me.

Jimmy Morgan was prepared immediately to give me responsibility, and he assigned various specific signals intelligence tasks to me. He was also quite willing to send me off to sort out problems in Tunisia, Malta, Italy, and later, Corsica and Sardinia. In many ways he was very like Rowley Scott-Farnie – tall and heavily built, and with a boyish sense of fun, and from the start he treated me rather as if I were a younger sister. 'I don't have to worry about you, Mike,' he would say, 'I know you'll be able to cope whatever turns up.' I appreciated his confidence in me. During the whole of the war it was my good fortune always to work for men who were prepared to accept that I could do a man's job. In North Africa and Italy my strongest advocate was Air Commodore Frank Woolley, the Chief Intelligence Staff Officer, to whose staff we were assigned. With the advantage of hindsight I am sure that the realization of women's capabilities during the war was the turning point for the women's movement.

During my first weeks in north-west Africa I was desperately worried about a small group of Y personnel in the Aegean far away to the east. Just after I had left Cairo the ill-fated Operation 'Accolade' got under way. At the outset the operation that had been envisaged was the capture of the island of Rhodes, from which an assault would then be made on the smaller neighbouring Dodecanese Islands to the north. The objects were firstly, to open up a shorter route for supplies through the Dardanelles to Russia; secondly, to provide closer bases from which to attack the oil installations in Rumania and, perhaps, thereby encourage defection by the Balkan countries; and thirdly, to influence Turkey to enter the war on our side. Since early in the year I had been working with those responsible for ensuring that there should be adequate coverage and analysis of the enemy signals traffic and radar both before and during the operations, and especially for keeping a watch on any developments and movements of Axis air units in the Balkans and the Aegean. We had also had to plan, together with Signals and Operations, for the neutralizing of the enemy's early warning screen and ground-based radio navigational aids. Already the staff at Suez Road had a very clear picture of the strength and disposition of the enemy air forces in the eastern Mediterranean. There was little that escaped the scrutiny of Hugh Waters and Cecil Gould and their team. Most of the relevant W/T traffic from the German and Italian Air Forces was adequately covered by Field Units in the Delta and Cyrenaica but, to fill any possible gaps in our coverage, another unit, which was previously sited in the hills behind Beirut, had been moved up to Nerab, close to the airfield at Aleppo, in Syria.

Winston Churchill had pressed strongly for the opening of this new front against stiff opposition. Tempted by the recent success in North Africa and Sicily and knowing that the Germans would be heavily involved in Italy, he had encouraged the Commanders in the Middle East to finalize plans for the immediate occupation of Rhodes. But Hitler and his Generals were also appreciative of the importance of the Aegean in protecting their vital oil supplies from the Balkans and had taken the precaution of reinforcing the garrison on Rhodes and of increasing the German air strength in Crete, Greece, and the Balkans. We knew from Y sources that more than 300 aircraft had recently been moved to the area, having watched their arrival from other theatres. The Chiefs of Staff were warned about this build-up, but Churchill was still very much in favour of mounting the operation, despite the now depleted state of the Allied armed forces in the eastern Mediterranean, and the obvious reluctance to participate on the part of the Americans. 'This is the time to play high,' Churchill had signalled to the Middle East Commanders, 'Improvise and dare.'

And dare they did, but with considerably less reinforcements available than was wise, reinforcements which the Middle East Commanders – General Sir Henry Maitland Wilson, Air Chief

Marshal Sir Sholto Douglas and Admiral Sir Andrew Cunningham –
requested from the controlling Supreme Headquarters in Algiers.
Had the Allies struck hard at Rhodes the very day that the Italians
capitulated the story might well have been different, but they hesitated, still hopeful of receiving the naval and air assistance for which
they had asked. But the Italian Commander in Rhodes had thrown
in his lot with the Germans, who were now preparing to resist any
assault. Over in Salerno, the situation was still critical, and Eisenhower was unwilling to release to the eastern Mediterranean the
reinforcements so desperately needed if the operation there were to
be a success.

A direct attack on Rhodes had to be abandoned and instead there
was the initial capture of the smaller islands, further into the Aegean,
of Kos, Leros and Samos. The securing of Kos was vital for it contained the only sizeable landing grounds in the area other than on
Rhodes. With the Allied air bases in Cyprus and Cyrenaica over
300 miles away, until airfields in the Dodecanese could be established
the flying time for fighter aircraft operating over the islands would
be dangerously short.

The invasion plans included the transfer of aircraft of No. 243
(Fighter) Wing to Antimachia, in Kos, under the command of Wing
Commander R. ('Bubbles') Love, and Y was asked to supply an R/T
monitoring unit to work with the forward fighter control. As available air transport for the assault was seriously restricted, No. 276
Wing was ordered to keep the personnel and equipment of the Y
team down to a bare minimum.

On 26 September a small Field Unit detachment left Palestine by
air for Kos. The unit, consisting of Flying Officer George Curtis,
five Sergeant linguists, some of whom were Palestinian airmen –
Sergeants R. Coltman, H. S. Bowman, I. Jacobsen, S. W. G. Isaac,
G. J. Kochmann – and a Wireless Mechanic, Corporal Whittle, was
formed from personnel from the successful Field Unit withdrawn
from the desert at the end of the African campaign. We had been
assured that transport would be made available for them on their
arrival, but, owing to a shortage of vehicles, it was to be almost two
days before they were able to move to Antimachia. And even then,
after hurriedly erecting their equipment, there were problems
establishing a telephone link with the Fighter Control. However,
once established, the Field Unit began to intercept valuable Luftwaffe
traffic.

Early on their second day they were able to warn Operations that German fighters were airborne and, half an hour later, that three Staffeln of Ju. 88s, escorted by at least one Staffel of Me. 109s, were approaching Kos. Fighter Control was given details of the attacking formation, which comprised eighteen Ju. 88s and their Me. 109 escort, and as the enemy drew nearer, the Field Unit was able to give their course and height. No. 243 Wing immediately scrambled four Spitfires to intercept the raid. This was half the available strength of our defending fighters, and although outnumbered they claimed as destroyed four Me. 109s and one Ju. 88. But the weight of the raiders was too great. Most of them got through, and they damaged the landing ground so seriously that it was never again serviceable. Of the remaining four Spitfires, which might have been better employed in the air against the attackers, only two survived.

From the R/T traffic, most of which was in plain language with grid positions given in double-letter code, the monitors learned that the German fighters were based on Rhodes and were flying out to rendezvous with the bombers coming from Greece, and that after the raid, they would escort them part of the way back. As the enemy approached Kos and Leros they obligingly gave their position and height, and could be easily plotted. It was the same with the bombers, who were heard a good hour before a raid materialized. Each bomber raid consisted of three waves of approximately five to eight Ju. 88s. The monitors heard such details as the formation's intentions and the amount of fuel the fighters had left, all of which was invaluable information for the fighter control. On only one raid, when He. 111s attacked the main harbour at Leros and bombed Kos on their way back, did the bombers keep radio silence.

But there was little that No. 243 Wing could do about the warnings, other than to send emergency signals back to ADEM (Air Defence of Eastern Mediterranean) Headquarters in Egypt. Had they been able to get sufficient fighters airborne, they might have been able to hold off the attackers; and it was particularly frustrating for the monitors because the traffic that they were hearing would have counteracted the weakness of the radar early warning system. Of the two mobile radar stations sent to Kos with the invasion, one was never to be put into operation at all. The other had difficulty in finding a suitable site, and for a large part of the time passed no plots, and then only at a range of twenty to twenty-five miles and when the enemy aircraft were flying at a favourable height, whereas

K

the range of the VHF monitoring by Y was around 150–170 miles. By listening in to early indications of a raid, warnings of up to one and a half hours could be given by the Field Unit of an imminent attack. This was confirmation, yet again, of the value of intercepted R/T during the early days of an assault.

But the unit's stay on Kos was to be all too short-lived. Within a week, during which they were subjected to constant bombing, the operators were forced to close watch. They had lived and slept in the open, and their 'Set Room', where they listened to the attacking aircraft, was merely a hollow in the rocks on the side of a hill covered with a sheet of canvas to keep off the sun.

The Chiefs of Staff in Washington had decided that they could not allow Eisenhower to release any further reinforcements from the Italian theatre. In this they were adamant because of their fear that the Aegean operations might escalate into a full-scale Balkan campaign, and they were unwilling to jeopardize forces that they had already earmarked for the major offensive in north-western Europe.

Again, on 3 October, enemy bombers raided Kos and crippled the Antimachia landing ground still further; and just as the monitors were preparing to open their morning watch Wing Operations telephoned to warn them that the Germans had landed an invasion force on the salt flats eight miles away. Only a few minutes later, Curtis and his men watched a drop of 150 paratroopers descending about a mile and a half north-west of them. They informed Operations, who an hour later ordered them to close down and report to No. 243 Wing. The enemy attack appeared to be an overwhelmingly large one, with armoured cars and field guns.

All the unit's papers were immediately burned, and the radio receivers and the power engine were smashed; and taking with them a few rations and their small arms they then made their way to Operations, keeping hidden as best they could. Wing Commander Love then told Curtis to try in any way possible to get his men away from the island. As the paratroopers were now too close to be healthy, and in view of the secrecy of their work and the fact that the Palestinian Sergeants were escapees from Nazi oppression, Curtis decided that it would be wise to destroy his NCOs' pay books.

Slinking along the beds of the 'wadis', they set off south towards the coast at Cardemena. Small arms fire was cracking all around them, and overhead Stukas and Me. 109s were wheeling about looking for likely targets, so they thought it best to lie low until dusk in a deep, narrow 'wadi' before continuing towards the coast. They reached it just as darkness fell.

Curtis realized that if they could not get away that night, they must hide up in the mountains during the day and attempt to escape the following night. There were a number of troops on the beach, all searching for boats, but the few craft that they found had all apparently been sabotaged. The members of the local Italian garrison were of no help, and they simply disappeared after throwing away their arms.

George Curtis was later able to report: 'We started to build a raft using everything possible, stockings, belts, torn up battledress trousers etc. to tie together wood which we took from the small pier. Here mention must be made of Sergeant Jacobsen, who showed extreme energy and persistency in the building of the raft, and later in the salvaging of the boat.

'At 2030 hours aircraft flew overhead and dropped flares. Expecting bombs to be dropped, we launched the raft, which proved incapable of supporting more than two persons, so we returned to the beach, everyone now being thoroughly wet. Previous to embarking on the raft, we had thrown our small arms into the sea.

'We had heard that a sailing-boat which had left for Turkey at six o'clock might return at midnight, so we decided to move further along the beach to be away from the village and possible bombing and wait there until midnight, keeping a lookout for the returning boat (which took 20 hours for the trip).

'About half-past eleven Sergeant Jacobsen remembered seeing a small boat completely submerged near the pier and he and I returned to examine it. We could find no holes in it, but luckily did not pursue our investigations further as a number of Italians appeared on the scene and wanted to lend unwelcome help. We left our boat and returned to our holes in the sand along the beach. Just before midnight we returned to the pier as there was no sign of the sailing boat returning. Sergeant Jacobsen again went into the sea and examined the submerged boat which appeared to be undamaged. We started to salvage it, dragging it to the beach and baling it out with our tin hats. We had baled it nearly dry when three Italians appeared and showed me where I could find two oars and a rudder. For this service, we took them with us.

'As we were almost ready, a large number of Italians appeared and demanded to be taken but as we were already fully loaded this was

not possible. Expecting trouble, we pushed off hurriedly, unfortunately leaving our water bottles behind. By now it was 0200 hours on
4 October, and wishing to be as far from the island as possible by
dawn, we rowed hard and unceasingly in relays. The three Italians,
proving useless as oarsmen, kept the boat fairly dry by constant
baling.

'We steered for a beacon on the mainland which we knew was the
nearest point but the currents were strong and sometimes we made
little progress. When dawn broke, we were roughly half-way over
and the island still looked uncomfortably near. We saw a motor-
boat to the east, which I at first feared was an 'E' boat – knowing that
there were two with the invading forces – but it kept on its course
and did not trouble us.

'Formations of Stukas and Me. 109s started passing overhead and
we could see them bombing and strafing the unfortunates still left on
the beach but none came down to us.

'We landed on the mainland at 1100 hours after rowing continuously for 9 hours. At the point at which we landed there was a small
coast-guard and gendarme station and, luckily, we were able to get
water. There was a small 'caique' there commanded by a British
officer who gave us some rations but was unable to take us away.'[1]

Here they joined seven more airmen who had been brought over
from Kos by Greek civilians. The gendarmes told them that they
would have to walk to the next village, and then on to Marmaris,
which was the administrative centre of that part of Turkey. When
they landed neither George Curtis nor Sergeant Jacobsen had shoes,
but they managed to persuade the Greek refugees to part with a
couple of pairs. None of the unit had stockings. After walking three
miles to the next village, where they encountered members of No. 7
South African Air Force Squadron who had sailed over early the
previous day, they spent the night on the floor of the village school-
room, and the next morning they all continued their journey on foot
a further thirty kilometres to the next village. By then the valiant
Sergeant Jacobsen was too exhausted to be able to walk any further,
but they managed to find a donkey for him to continue the journey.
It was midnight when, twelve hours later, they reached the next
village, and there they were given a meal of boiled rice. They rested
there for a day before pressing on again, but they had to leave
Jacobsen and three others behind. They could go no further, and the
Turks promised to send them on as soon as they were fit. With only

two small loaves of bread per man as sustenance, they trekked on the following day from five in the morning until eight at night, trying to get a night's sleep in the open near a small gendarme station. Continuing on again at five the next day, they reached Marmaris at six o'clock in the evening, where they were given a meal and beds.

They rested at Marmaris for a day before being put aboard an over-crowded caique. Their only rations were a little bread and some German spinach. On the afternoon of 13 October they finally reached Famagusta, in Cyprus, where Sergeant Coltman and Corporal Whittle were admitted to hospital, whilst George Curtis and the other three Sergeants were flown back to Cairo. Curtis ended his report with the comment: 'All personnel of the unit showed great coolness, fortitude and endurance at all times.'[2] For the part that he had played he was awarded the Military Cross. Sergeant H. S. Bowman was Mentioned in Despatches.

Squadron Leader Pugh-Davis, the Senior Intelligence Officer of No. 276 Wing, who met the men on their return to Egypt, reported: 'In spite of their gruelling experiences, their morale was of the highest. Their conversation showed that long desert experience and their team work under the sympathetic and shrewd guidance of Flying Officer C. G. Curtis contributed largely to their successful getaway.'[3]

I have purposely given this long account of what happened to the Field Unit in this particular operation because, to me, it typifies the integrity, the conscientiousness, and the comradeship which prevailed amongst the personnel of the Y Service with whom it was my privilege to work.

The occupation of Kos lasted less than three weeks; Leros fell a fortnight later, and then, by 2 November, Samos was overrun. Further efforts were made by Mediterranean Air Command to hinder the German bombers by attacking airfields in Crete and Greece and by harassing the Axis shipping in the area. A few Beaufighters were transferred to help the beleaguered forces in the Aegean towards the end of the campaign but it was an offer which was too limited and too late.

In terms of the whole war, 'Accolade' was a very minor invasion, but I shall forever wonder whether Winston Churchill, the great strategist, was not in fact right. Had he perhaps already his fears about the imperialist ambitions of the Soviet leaders? Had the Americans shared Winston Churchill's enthusiasm for the operation and had they agreed to more support, the outcome might well have been successful. With the Aegean in our hands, Turkey would surely have entered the war on our side and her airfields would then have been at our disposal. The resultant pressure on the Germans in the Balkans, which their every move had shown they greatly feared, might have curtailed the subsequent hard slog by the Fifth and Eighth Armies up the leg of Italy. And perhaps even more important, would Rumania and Bulgaria today be under Russian domination?

In his diary for 1 November 1943, Field Marshal Viscount Alanbrooke, who was then the Chief of the Imperial General Staff, recorded: 'If only I had had sufficient force of character to swing those American Chiefs of Staff and make them see daylight, how different the war might be. We should have had the whole Balkans ablaze by now, and the war might have been finished in 1943.'[4] Fifteen years later he was to add: 'Success in Crete and Rhodes might have had the happiest repercussions in Turkey and the Balkans without committing a single man in the Balkans.'[5]

More recently, Mr Harold Macmillan, who was Minister Resident at Allied Headquarters in north-west Africa at the time of the Dodecanese operation, was interviewed on the BBC on the occasion of his 85th birthday. Regarding the strategy for the Mediterranean area, he was asked whether he thought 'we got it right or could it have been played differently, in a way that might have produced a better post-war world?' In reply he said: 'It seems to me, looking back, and perhaps seemed even at the time, that the Americans made a fatal mistake of broad strategy. Churchill was the most extraordinary man because he was always thinking forward; he was always thinking about the future – brooding . . .'

'And what Churchill was interested in was what happened next. Now our American friends were at that moment rather obsessed with their new ally, Russia; they thought the Russians marvellous, perhaps better than effete Europeans, like the British. At any rate, they stuck absolutely to their own plans.

'Churchill, of course, would have had us invade through the Balkans, gone through the Ljublijana gap. Field Marshal Alexander's armies had a complete plan and we would have been 250 miles east of where the Iron Curtain now is drawn. But it was all turned down. The Americans insisted upon the landing in Western Europe, in France, when the problem, if the Germans were now beaten, was how far the Soviet imperialism would stretch, and how to keep it as far away as possible to the east.'[6]

19

Reconnaissance and Reorganization

By October 1943 the success of Allied operations against the enemy airfields in the central Mediterranean, southern France, and in Greece, had seriously depleted the Luftwaffe's available long-range bomber strength. The Eighth Army had advanced rapidly along the Adriatic coast of Italy, and had captured the nine important landing grounds at Foggia. This was a bitter blow to the Germans as this complex of airfields had for months provided them with their main bomber bases in Italy. Our monitoring of the traffic was giving evidence of the resultant disorganization, and we carefully recorded the withdrawal of their bomber units back to more northerly locations.

During September the bombers had admittedly scored a measure of success, especially II/ and III/KG 100, whose use of the new radio-controlled bomb had been the cause of too many Allied shipping losses. They had even succeeded in sinking the flagship of their erstwhile ally, the Italian battleship *Roma*, as it sailed south to surrender at Malta. But their success had been short-lived. Poor serviceability had added to the problems caused by the destruction of or damage to scores of aircraft on the ground. Now, except for offensive operations, in which elements of KG 100 took part, against our intrusion into the Dodecanese islands, the enemy's long-range bombing missions in the Mediterranean were largely restricted to infrequent attacks on eastbound convoys.

Their fighter-bombers were nevertheless busy enough as they had returned to their normal task of close support of the Army, especially over the bridgehead, and were no longer concentrating on shipping attacks. Our forward Field Unit, which was up with the Eighth Army and the Desert Air Force, and listening carefully to the traffic from these squadrons, was able to keep No. 1 MORU and No. 211 Group constantly informed of their activities. Up to thirty sorties a day were heard as they operated against Allied troop concentrations and vehicle convoys, and several successful combats resulted from the early warnings given by the Field Unit.

In addition to operations over the Italian Front, some of these enemy fighter-bomber units had moved east to handle operations in the Aegean and others were operating over Corsica. When the Germans made their hasty evacuation from Sardinia, following the capitulation of the Italians, they had met with only negligible opposition, but in Corsica the French were not so co-operative. Aided by the Italians who were stationed there they had forced the German Army to retreat to the Bastia area from whence an armada of ships, Siebel ferries, and transport aircraft evacuated the troops to the mainland. But, forewarned by monitored Enigma traffic and photographic reconnaissance, Allied submarines and aircraft moved in to intercept the evacuation fleet. Although several ships and ferries were sunk, and some Ju. 52s were shot down, the enemy, unfortunately, managed to rescue the greater part of their forces and equipment from the island, just as they had done earlier in Sicily.

So far as the fighter units were concerned, the German Air Force in the Mediterranean was hard-pressed to spread a little butter over a wide slice of bread. The mounting onslaught against the Reich from the United Kingdom necessitated the withdrawal of fighter units from the Italian theatre to augment the Western European defences. The Allies were now attacking further and further into Germany with ever-larger formations, and the successful attack on the experimental station on the island of Peenemuende on the Baltic coast on August 17/18,[1] had caused, along with the heavy raids on Berlin, consternation in the German High Command. Furthermore, now that the capture of the Foggia airfields had increased the depth of the penetration by Allied bombers flying from the south, the defence of the industrial areas in the north of Italy, in southern Germany, in Austria, and in Hungary was becoming an increasing headache for the enemy fighters. Although they moved a larger force of protective fighters to these areas, they lacked sufficient aircraft to meet all the attacking Allied bomber formations and were obliged to select specific formations as targets. Over in the eastern Mediterranean, the Aegean operations were occupying further units, whilst escort duty over the evacuation fleet from Corsica had further added to their commitments.

The announcement of the Italian armistice and the subsequent Allied offensives had imposed increasing demands on the German long-range reconnaissance units, especially those based in Italy and southern France. By October their situation had so deteriorated that No. 329 Wing recorded the unusually low total of only 160 reconnaissance flights during the month, which was a third less than in September, and about half the effort that had been made in August. We noted with particular interest that they were flying less night reconnaissance. This reduction in effort was partly due, we knew, to poor replacement of losses, but we listened with considerable satisfaction to the disorganization which resulted from the successful Allied raid on Frosinone, where many of the reconnaissance units were based. They moved back first to Guidonia, but they soon decided that this airfield was too vulnerable and they retreated a further 100 miles to Perugia. But by the time they arrived there, the weather had turned so bad that we would constantly hear aircraft returning from patrols being re-routed to Forli and Viterbo.

Now that the Eighth Army had captured the ports of Brindisi, Bari, and Termoli, the reconnaissance units stepped up their watch on Allied shipping in the Adriatic and along the Dalmatian coast, whilst reports were heard from at least one Ju. 88 each day as it patrolled the Tyrrhenian Sea, and the harbours of Corsica and northern Sardinia. With the Germans still apprehensive about a possible Allied move against southern France, the Me. 410s of the unit 2/F.122 made regular photographic surveys of west coast ports, including the areas around Naples and Salerno, and they were backed up by aircraft of 1/F.33. This latter unit, we gathered, was by the end of September more or less permanently committed to security patrols in the western and north-western Mediterranean. They were now on their own for their colleagues, 1/F.122, had been transferred to the eastern Mediterranean.

Back in North Africa, John Simmonds and his staff at No. 329 Wing had developed an excellent relationship with both the Coastal Air Force and the Navy; and at Headquarters level, I was more than happy that Air Vice-Marshal Sir Hugh Pughe Lloyd had become AOC of the Mediterranean Allied Coastal Air Force. From the time of my early encounters with him in Malta, he had shown a real appreciation of the value of Y. This was reflected in the response from the members of his staff with whom I was on friendly terms; in any case, I had worked closely with his Senior Intelligence Officer,

Wing Commander H. L. Tudor, when he was in Alexandria.

The passing of information that was gleaned from reconnaissance patrols became one of No. 329 Wing's more useful tasks, as we knew only too well that these patrols more often than not foreshadowed an attack on a convoy. The torpedo-carrying He. 111s of I/ and III/KG 26 had made little contribution to any intimidation of the Salerno convoys, and the Luftwaffe was obviously anxious to use them against Allied shipping sailing along the North African coast, and also to give the Do. 217s of KG 100 a further chance to use their new radio-controlled bomb.

But with the deterioration of the weather we would hear the reconnaissance aircraft being forced to break off patrol and subsequently having difficulty in re-establishing contact with the convoy. Monitored reports from these aircraft were immediately passed to MACAF and to the Navy, who, being forewarned, were ready for the possible arrival at dusk of the Do. 217s and torpedo-bombers. The Luftwaffe always preferred to attack the convoys at dusk because although it was light enough for bombing and torpedo-aiming, it was unfavourable for the defending fighters.

One example of an operation of this kind occurred on 20 October. A large Allied eastbound convoy was spotted by reconnaissance aircraft west of Oran, and we heard it being reported again the next morning. We duly recorded the aircraft's message back to base and advised MACAF and the Navy. The subsequent planned attack was to miscarry because as a result of No. 329 Wing's warning, the Ju. 88 torpedo-bomber sent out during the afternoon to act as a spotter met a reception committee before it could reach its target and was shot down. With no pathfinder to help them, the main bomber formation comprising some twenty-five He. 111s and Do. 217s attacked the wrong ships – an empty westbound convoy.

The bomber aircraft of the units KG 30, KG 54, and KG 76 had been moved back from their landing grounds in central Italy to more northerly airfields such as Ghedi, Villafranca, Bergamo and Villa-orba, whilst part of KG 76 had moved over to La Jasse in southern France. On 12 October we heard II/KG 76 during an attack on Ajaccio harbour, aided and abetted by KG 30 and a few Do. 217s. A week later, we monitored KG 76 and KG 54 as they raided Naples, during which raid they used the radar-countermeasure 'Dueppel'. Two days later the same port was again attacked, the bombers dropping such massive quantities of 'Dueppel' that the fighter defence was seriously handicapped. However, of the ninety enemy bombers that participated only about a quarter succeeded in reaching their target, and the bomb-aiming of these appeared to be inaccurate, indicating the use of inexperienced crews. And, to add to our delight, thick fog in the Po Valley caused chaos with the returning raiders, and we listened as they were diverted to various landing grounds from Viterbo to Grossetto – some even being sent as far afield as Munich.

After every anti-shipping operation a careful study was made of the involvement of the Luftwaffe, not only for the information of MACAF and the Navy but also for the Air Ministry, in view of any bearing that it might have on 'Overlord', which was the code-name for the forthcoming invasion of north-western France that was scheduled to take place the following summer.

By November 1943 the euphoria that had been engendered by the German defeat in Africa and the success of the Sicilian campaign began to wane. Since the Salerno landings the Allied progress on mainland Italy had been disappointingly slow, and, to say the least, we had been surprised by the speed with which the Germans had called up reinforcements from Western Europe and the Eastern Front. From a strength of only eleven Divisions in Italy prior to the landings, the opposition had increased to twenty-six Divisions; and over in the Balkans, an indication of Hitler's determination to hold the territory from which so much of his oil, copper, chrome and bauxite came, could be seen in the fact that the Wehrmacht there now totalled twenty Divisions.

So far as the air was concerned, the Adriatic and Dalmatian coasts were now receiving more attention from enemy reconnaissance aircraft, and we heard the long-range patrols of II/F.22, I/F.123 and Westa 26, operating on most days, with the shorter range photographic missions being left mainly to the Me. 410s of II/F.122. All of these units were based in Italy. Each night we listened to a veritable milk-run, which was neglected only if the weather closed in, with an aircraft flying down the west coast as far as Naples and Salerno, and then across to the Adriatic side. On occasions, this route might be reversed, and if two aircraft could be mustered, one would take the Adriatic side, and the other the Tyrrhenian Sea, with almost all the sorties being concluded by midnight, or by one o'clock in the morning at the latest.

In the case of 1/F.33, the reconnaissance missions that were flown by them could be related to the activities and intentions of the anti-shipping long-range bombers based in southern France, but the association between the reconnaissance Staffeln and the bomber units that were based in Italy was less obvious. We realized this was partly due to the fact that when a reconnaissance aircraft was detailed to photograph a specific ground target, it had no cause to refer to the target on W/T. The most that could be hoped for was an intercepted message that might indicate that the aircraft had completed its unspecified task, or a request for landing instructions. It was the same with those aircraft that were engaged on routine defensive patrols. But just occasionally, if the mission was altered after an aircraft was airborne, we would hear a pilot break the traditional silence of these units. Such messages were almost always of tactical value.

We were more fortunate with the German convoy-shadowing aircraft because they were dealing with a moving target, and if and when an aircraft located a convoy it had to send back to base frequent reports on changes in position, course and speed, thus providing us with a warning of subsequent attacks. These sighting messages not only helped us to identify the unit involved but by direction-finding we could determine the aircraft's position, which was helpful when it was out of radar range. But, of course, if the patrol was unable to make contact with the convoy, or was flying a short-range security patrol, there was no cause for it to break W/T silence.

By November, there was a marked increase in enemy bomber and reconnaissance activity, especially in the western Mediterranean. The Ju. 88 units, which were now established on their new airfields in northern Italy, were making every effort to hamper the provisioning of the Allied armies in Italy and Corsica, and we had ample evidence that the strength and serviceability of these units was sufficiently improved for each of KG 30, KG 54, and KG 76 to provide two Gruppen for raids on the harbours of Naples, Bastia, and Maddalena. During these raids their W/T security was impeccable, but by listening to their homing signals, we calculated that at least five or six aircraft from each Gruppe had been despatched on each operation. By tying this up with radar plots it looked as though a considerable number of aircraft had failed to reach their target. In any case, the results of their bombing hardly justified the effort expended.

The anti-shipping units based in southern France were, however,

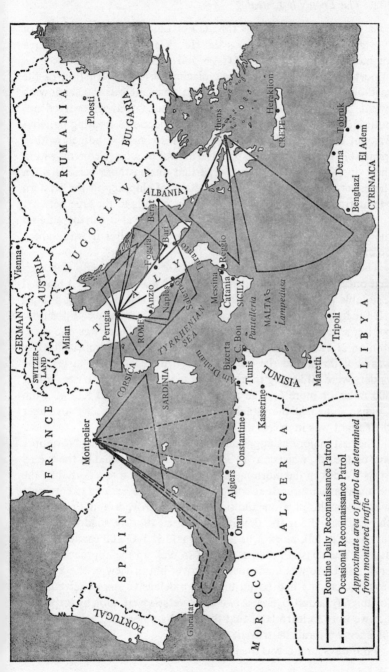

German Air Force reconnaissance in the Western and Central Mediterranean, December 1943.

constituting a more serious threat. For the first time at the end of November, we heard Fw. 200s and He. 177s from the Bordeaux area augmenting the efforts of KG 26 and KG 100. This stressed the importance that the enemy was placing on the destruction of the eastbound convoys. So regular and so constant was the shadowing by Ju. 88s of 1/F.33 that very few eastbound convoys escaped unnoticed, but it was our belief that their success in locating convoys was not exclusively the result of their own vigilance. Somehow they invariably knew when to expect the arrival of a large convoy within their operational area. We noticed that during those periods when there were no important concentrations of shipping in the western Mediterranean the enemy confined their patrols to the area between southern France and the Balearics, but whenever a convoy entered the Mediterranean through the Straits of Gibraltar it was sighted before it had even reached Oran.

The patrol routine that was followed by the Luftwaffe was such that once the convoy was identified, it was shadowed until it reached a suitable position for a dusk attack. As the last shadowing aircraft left for home it would broadcast to the bombers the exact position, course, speed and composition of our convoy. There was one occasion on 21 October when the final reconnaissance aircraft of the day was shot down and the bombers failed to locate their target. The raiders were all having to make long flights from their bases – often 800 miles or more for the round trip – and when III/KG 40 from Cognac joined in the attack on convoy 'Annex' on 26 November their flight was in excess of 1500 miles.

The first major onslaught on one of our convoys during November was on the 6th, when convoy 'Peacock' was first sighted by the enemy at six o'clock in the morning off Cap Matifou. It was reported by the reconnaissance aircraft as comprising five destroyers and twenty-nine motor vessels, plus an additional two destroyers and three other ships. Throughout the day it was conscientiously shadowed until, just as dusk fell, aircraft of I/KG 26 and II/KG 100 carried out an attack. The coastal radar had failed to pick up the approaching aircraft and there was inadequate air cover but in view of the Y warnings, the convoy had begun to make a defensive smoke screen. Unfortunately, a destroyer and two other vessels were sunk by torpedoes but we were to learn later that the ships' gunners had accounted for six enemy aircraft destroyed.

Four days later it was the turn of convoy 'Untrue' to be spotted by the enemy. Shortly after noon the next day, the 11th, the Y monitors intercepted a message from 1/F.33 control stating that the reconnaissance aircraft was to make all further sighting reports on the frequency to be used by the bombers that evening. At dusk the He. 111 and Ju. 88 torpedo-bombers of III/KG 26 and the Do. 217s of II/KG 100 made their attack. Once again, ground radar and fighter defence were ineffective but as the convoy had received our Y warning, it had laid on a smoke screen which proved effective against direct bombardment and against the radio-controlled bombs launched from the Do. 217s. But the torpedo-carrying He. 111s of KG 26 dropped flares and were able to inflict serious losses on the convoy. On their way home two Do. 217s were destroyed by Allied aircraft and the ships' gunners accounted for at least one Ju. 88.

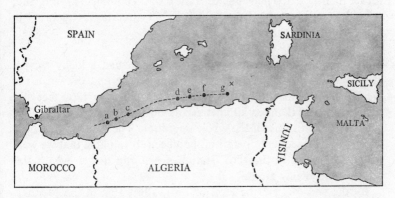

German Air Force sightings and attack on convoy 'Annex', 25–6 November 1943. Monitored traffic from the unit I/F. 33 indicated seven sightings of the Allied convoy code-named 'Annex'. It was stated to comprise thirty merchant ships, screened by eight destroyers and covered by one bomber and four fighters (later given as covered by four twin-engined fighters), and to be proceeding eastwards at a speed of 15 knots. The sightings were transmitted at: a – 1204, b – 1240, c – 1635 on 25 November; d – 0650, e – 0750, f – 1120, g – 1520 on 26 November.

At 1615 on 26 November, at the point marked X, the convoy was attacked, but it had been well warned by the Y Service. (As the convoy was picked up before Oran, it is probable that the unit was advised as soon as it passed the Straits of Gilbraltar.)

Spurred on by their success, the next operation that the Luftwaffe planned was against convoy 'Dimmock' the next day. All went according to routine, with the aircraft of 1/F.33 reporting the appropriate details about the convoy and the weather. But someone had to go and make a mistake. At seven o'clock in the evening, when the bomber force was well on its way, the enemy control erroneously gave the position of our convoy – in code, of course – as being overland, placing it at ten miles south-west of Cap Tenez. This mistake was repeated by the German controller a quarter of an hour later and it was not finally corrected until twenty-eight minutes past seven when the position of the convoy was given as it had been transmitted by the reconnaissance aircraft at four in the afternoon. But by then the convoy was miles away, and the bombers failed altogether to locate their target. The whole operation was a complete failure, and, to add to their troubles, one of I/KG 26's aircraft was reported in distress on the return flight.

And then, on 22 November, convoy 'Creeper' had a lucky escape. It was shadowed by the enemy all day, at the end of which the weather closed in with a reported 10/10th cloud at 1200 feet and visibility of less than ten kilometres and obviously deteriorating. The Germans had to call off the whole operation. The contribution of Y in this and subsequent operations had been so valuable that we were asked to erect a further D/F station near Oran to get even better fixes on the enemy aircraft.

By the end of 1943 the level of Luftwaffe traffic in the Mediterranean had so declined that there was no longer justification for keeping one Y headquarters in Cairo and another in Algiers. Furthermore, looking ahead to 'Overlord', we knew that experienced personnel from our theatre would be needed back in Britain, not only because such a vast amount of German Air Force traffic was being intercepted in England but also because a considerable proportion of the actual monitoring and collating staff in the United Kingdom were women, who would almost certainly not be permitted to advance with an invasion force into north-western Europe. There might also be a need to re-train personnel for work in the Pacific theatre.

As Chief Signals Intelligence Officer for the Mediterranean, Jimmy Morgan submitted recommendations for the amalgamation of the two Wings with the object of reducing the total Y personnel in the theatre to about the same number as there was in the existing No. 276 Wing. Allowance had to be made, however, to cover requirements in areas not in the actual combat zone, such as Egypt. In addition, until American monitoring units that were working under the Commanding General, 12th Air Force, were more experienced, we had to allow for the probability that Field Unit personnel would have to be loaned to them from the RAF Y Wing. There was also a need for an 'Intelligence School' to cover long-term research and co-ordinating intelligence derived from Y with information from other sources: but the intention was that this section should form a part of the Intelligence Branch at Command Headquarters, rather than of the actual interception organization.

There then arose the delicate question of which of the Wings should survive. Both had acquitted themselves magnificently: No. 276 Wing before, during, and after the Western Desert battles, and No. 329 Wing during the Tunisian and Sicilian campaigns. It was understandable that the personnel had a keen pride in their respective Wings, and that the losers would be somewhat hurt. Eventually the AOC in C, Middle East, Air Chief Marshal Sir Sholto Douglas, agreed, somewhat reluctantly, that there should be centralization of the organization, and that the bulk of Middle East Y should be transferred to Mediterranean Air Command, but only on the condition that the continued supply of Y intelligence to all sub-Commands would be assured. His reluctance to cede personnel to Mediterranean Air Command was almost inevitable in view of the rather strained relationship between the two commanders, which made itself felt even at our level. It was finally agreed by all concerned that No. 276 Wing would be the surviving Wing under the command of David Davies, and would move to Italy as soon as suitable accommodation could be found. No. 329 Wing was to be disbanded, and plans were made for a Mediterranean Air Y Bureau to be set up at Mediterranean Air Command Headquarters.[2]

The proposal for the coverage of German Air Force traffic was that we should now allocate sixteen sets for the monitoring of W/T in Algiers, twenty-four at the Wing Headquarters, which it was then thought might possibly be set up in Naples, sixteen sets in Malta and a further sixteen in Alexandria, with the suggestion that the latter might later move to Cyprus. At that juncture we were still hopeful of a successful outcome to the Aegean operations. R/T traffic would be well covered in the forward battle areas of the western and eastern

Italian Fronts, and operations in the eastern Mediterranean would be monitored at both western Cyprus and Benghazi; and, shortly, watches would be opened in northern Corsica as near as possible to mainland Italy and France. The number of watches on Enigma-type ground-to-ground station traffic would depend, as always, on directions from England. Subsequent developments in the theatre necessitated certain amendments to these outline plans, but they were more in terms of location of units than of the extent of the monitoring.

The next problem that we had to face was where to site the headquarters of the new No. 276 Wing. We knew from Ultra that Hitler feared that the Allies might cross over from southern Italy to Albania and Yugoslavia. It was important, therefore, for Y to keep a watchful ear on the Luftwaffe's South-Eastern Command. There was also the need to complete the over-all picture of the German Air Force by recording as much as possible of all movements and activities on the Eastern Front. The Allies were doing all that they could to supply Russia with equipment, in spite of terrible losses at sea, and were keeping them informed of operations on the Southern and Western Fronts. The Russians, on the other hand, were giving little back in the way of information. Almost everything that the Allies knew about the Luftwaffe in the Russian theatre had been derived from intelligence collected by themselves.

In view of the eventual debacle of the Dodecanese, there was little point in setting up a unit in Cyprus. Taking into consideration this and all other factors, it seemed preferable to site the new No. 276 Wing Headquarters on the Adriatic coast of Italy, where reception of Balkan and Eastern Front traffic would be better than on the western side of the Apennine range. Any signals from Fliegerkorps II, which had taken over from Luftflotte II on 15 October, and its units operating in Italy, could easily be monitored by east coast units, whilst units located in North Africa and, later, in Corsica, could monitor activity originating from southern France.

The Headquarters of the Allied Supreme Commander was scheduled to be established in the Royal Palace at Caserta, just north of Naples, but the value of the better reception on the Adriatic side outweighed the desirability of siting the Y Headquarters near to the Command Headquarters at Caserta. The place to be selected was partly dependent on its acceptability by the WAAF administrative hierarchy. It had to be a location that would be suitable for the twenty-one WAAF Code and Cypher officers who were responsible for the essential encoding and decoding of the mass of high-grade signals that were sent between the Wing and the United Kingdom, and distributed to other bodies.

The place chosen eventually was Conversano, a comparatively clean, if cramped, small country town situated on a hill some twenty miles south of Bari. Here an empty Fascist school, an elementary school, and various other buildings round a large square served as Wing Headquarters, with a pleasant house about a mile outside the town as the RAF Officers' Mess. One of the Field Units was sited in the nearby town of Castellana, where they were later joined by the American monitoring unit, 'F' Detachment of No. 849 SIS.

Although special consideration had been given to the WAAF's welfare when siting the new Headquarters, they were not, in fact, to stay long at Conversano. By the following April, some had returned to England, others had moved to a new location at Bitonto, west of Bari, whilst one contingent was assigned to handle the very considerable cypher traffic to and from the Field Unit in Malta.

One of the first WAAF to arrive in North Africa had been Section Officer M. K. 'Rusty' Goff, who had been posted over to join the Field Units operating in the Cap Bon area. But to her chagrin, when the unit moved over to Sicily for 'Husky', she was not allowed to go with them. However, when the Italian naval vessels surrendered after the armistice, the energetic and irrepressible 'Rusty' flew over, first to Taranto, and then to Gibraltar, with our scientific officer, Eric Ackermann, to act as his interpreter when he examined the radar equipment on board the Italian warships.

I doubt if the WAAF 'G' ever knew about either of these visits and we conveniently forgot to tell them. The WAAF administration's view was that they should always make a prior visit to whereever WAAF were to work but there was still the ruling that had been laid down by the Air Ministry as early as 1940 that Y WAAF could serve wherever required by operational commitments. And, furthermore, both Eisenhower and Tedder were convinced that women could safely and efficiently undertake work, which had previously been looked on as being strictly a male province.

20

The Luftwaffe Retaliates

I met General Eisenhower for the first time soon after I started to work at Supreme Headquarters in Algiers. His suite of offices was on the same corridor as those of our own Branch. 'Ike', as he was affectionately known to everybody, fascinated me by his almost computer-like memory. He seemed never to forget a fact or a face. I would take him a report on some subject, which he would read with incredible rapidity, and then he might say 'I read something recently which ties up with that. Let me see, it is in a file on . . . about page 57, second paragraph from the bottom . . .' I would go back to my office, call for the file, and, sure enough, he would be right. It was a gift that I envied.

Through the visits during the course of my work to his office, I got to know his personal staff, and his Army aide, Major Ernest (Tex) Lee, became one of my best friends. This tall, bespectacled Texan was one of the kindest of all the men whom I was to meet during the war. He was Eisenhower's administrative aide, and he dealt efficiently with the smooth running of the Supreme Commander's office and chasing up papers, people, and problems. He was particularly helpful to me whenever I had to fly to Tunis or to some other part of the Command, as he usually knew of some senior officer with whom I could hitch-hike a lift. Although there was a well-organized Communications Flight, the demand for seats as a result of the split headquarters was high and a lift often saved waiting for a couple of days.

There can have been few military commanders during the war who had a more loyal and hard-working 'family' than General Eisenhower. His senior aide was Harry C. Butcher, then a Lieutenant-Commander in the US Navy. He had been a vice-president of Columbia Broadcasting Corporation, and if 'Butch' had a fault, it was his over-enthusiastic public relations drive for his chief. Then there was the blue-eyed little Irishman, Sergeant Mickey McKeogh, the best orderly a man could hope for, and the attractive Kay Summersby, who was Eisenhower's faithful driver, hostess, and confidante. She was untiring in her devotion to him, and she drove him on long and frequently hazardous journeys.

Mediterranean Air Command provided my first experience of working with the Americans in an integrated headquarters. It was generally the case throughout the Headquarters that wherever the senior officer of a branch was an American his deputy was British, or vice versa. In the case of Air Intelligence, the Chief Intelligence Staff Officer was Air Commodore Frank Woolley, while his deputy was Lieutenant-Colonel Palmer Dixon of the United States Army Air Force. The main part of our branch was still in Algiers, while up at La Marsa in Tunisia, Group Captain James Luard, who was the Assistant Chief Intelligence Officer, led a hard-working group at Air Command Post, which would shortly move over to Caserta with Advanced Air Headquarters.

There were surprisingly few WAAF in the north-west African theatre of war in 1943, and they were all officers. The first batch were photographic interpreters along with the inevitable administrative WAAF 'G'. They were followed by the 'cypherines', a few intelligence personnel assigned to various tasks, including the SLU, a couple of women working with the Operational Research Section, and an occasional Personal Assistant to a senior officer.

The US forces were paid considerably more than the British and their service women were paid, rank for rank, the same as their men, whereas we had to put up with an iniquitous five-eighths of the men's pay. The Americans, who were enviably well catered for seemed to be embarrassed that there should be such a difference in our pay and allowances.

An amusing incident relating to that tiresome situation occurred shortly after I had been promoted Squadron Officer. Our American office messenger, the extent of whose responsibility was to tote files around the Headquarters and to fetch tea for us from the canteen, was one named Smuljan. He was a spotty lad with an adoring mother and several aunts back in the United States, who showered him with parcels of cookies and candies by every mail. One day he staggered into my bathroom-office in Algiers laden with boxes of goodies. Dumping them on my desk, he said: 'Here y'are, Ma'am – for you.'

I protested, thanking him for his kind thought, but insisting that his family had sent them out for him. 'Go on, Ma'am,' he persisted, 'I got plenty. Anyways, I earn more'n you do.' And he was right. There was no secret about pay and he had discovered the difference. At that time, Smuljan was a mere Private, First Class, while I was the equivalent, in his army, of a Major.

The rear party of our branch was responsible in principle for the longer term intelligence, for the organization and the direction of Intelligence policy throughout the Mediterranean, for the collection of data from the Air Ministry and other sources such as Y, CSDIC, photographic reconnaissance, and SOE (Special Operations Executive) and for distributing the collated information as applicable to the Commands, the Planning Staff, and the subordinate formations in the Middle East, Malta and in North Africa. The forward Command Post, on the other hand, collected, analysed and collated the shorter-term operational Intelligence, which included target intelligence, enemy tactics, the initial interrogation of prisoners, and the inspection of captured equipment in the forward areas. It was inevitable that the division of the branch necessitated a great deal of travelling between Algiers and La Marsa, and later, between Algiers and Caserta.

The team that worked under Air Commodore Woolley was fortunate in the friendly spirit of liaison which existed between the various sections. I do not recall any major differences between us. In our dealings with the other intelligence sections Jimmy Morgan, Major Dick Tandler, our American colleague, and I, found everyone most co-operative. We might need information on a certain point about, say, KG 26. We would ask CSDIC at Bir Quadem to question prisoners on the subject. Or the 'Ferret' Squadron, flying from Tunis, might have been puzzled by a new enemy signal. I would go round to Flight Lieutenant Jim Thoday's office to see if he had any photographic evidence of a new installation in the area in which the signal had been heard. Conversely, Wing Commander Joe Hurst of Operational Intelligence might ask us for the latest Y information about fighter units in Austria; or we might have to discuss with Major Thornton Wilder certain requirements for the planning committee. All this was, of course, normal Intelligence work but the friendliness that existed between us was such that we were an exceptionally happy branch. Thornton Wilder was with us at that time in the American Air Force, and he brought a breath of sanity into our otherwise somewhat unnatural military existence. It is interesting that he was so intrigued by the timelessness of the name of one of our prisoner-of-war interrogators – Antrobus – that he used it for the central character of the play *The Skin of Our Teeth* that he wrote after the war.

There was one major restriction within the branch, and it was that straight Ultra information could only be divulged to those who had been 'indoctrinated' and then only if they needed to know. Any papers containing information derived from Ultra sources had to be carried from one place to another by hand of officer.

If the number of people who were permitted to handle Ultra material at the Headquarters was strictly limited, the need for security was even greater in the field, and this inevitably resulted in, as one historian has recorded: 'Ultra's inescapable limitations'; the same historian added: 'It was impossible to risk disclosing its intelligence to those in actual contact with the enemy or liable to capture for other reasons, even though the knowledge might improve their chances of success or survival.'[1] It was only by adhering meticulously to these strict security rules that the Ultra secret was preserved throughout the war.

It was not so much the Luftwaffe in itself which kept us busy during December but more the production of various statistics and reports that were needed by the Joint Planning Staff, and for the many top-level conferences and meetings that were being held throughout the Mediterranean and the Middle East. The list of visitors to the theatre from November through to January read like an international 'Who's Who'. The Prime Minister, the President of the United States, Stalin, and General Chiang Kai-Shek of China – not to mention General Marshal and Lord Louis Mountbatten on his way to the Far East – every conceivable high-powered politician and military leader appeared at some time somewhere in the theatre. Officially their arrivals and departures under different code-names were shrouded in secrecy, but the inevitable flaps, caused by such things as bad weather delaying flights, the fear of attacks by German aircraft, the steady stream of requests for special information, and, later, Winston Churchill's illness, ensured that we were usually well aware within hours of just who had arrived. If we had not known we would have been pretty hopeless intelligence officers.

When the President of the United States was due to arrive in

Oran we had the usual cryptic request that our small D/F unit which had recently been installed there should keep a special watch for signals from enemy aircraft reconnoitring or attacking eastbound convoys. Such specific requests always indicated the arrival of 'someone special', or an important convoy. And during the whole time senior officers were dashing between Algiers, Malta, Tunis, and over to Cairo, and with some going on to Teheran. Knowing how much we in Y could detect or deduce from monitored lists of passengers or requests for air bookings on the enemy's transport routes, I prayed to Allah that the 'Horchdienst' was not equally skilled in being able to read the Allied messages.[2]

We were aware from Ultra information that the Germans had known in advance about the Cairo Conference. It was hardly surprising, and I frequently wondered whether the excessive zeal of the American secret service in guarding their charges was not self-defeating.

Tex Lee was by now a Lieutenant-Colonel and although he was discretion itself I knew from his comings and goings more or less where his 'Master' was visiting or conferring. And even Tex could not keep from me his secret that he had met his President. He knew that it would go no further, that I would not even tell Jimmy Morgan, but, understandably, he wanted to share his pride with someone, as I would have done had I met the King. I also learned that Tex would shortly be returning to England with General Eisenhower, who had been appointed the Supreme Commander for 'Overlord'.

The Eighth Army on the Adriatic side of Italy had at last managed to battle its way across the River Sangro, and it was to capture Ortona before the end of the month. But in the American sector on the west coast, the Fifth Army was almost stalemated. Progress was now painfully slow for the terrain on that front was even more favourable to the defenders. Throughout Italy the winter rains had swollen the rivers into torrents, adding to the misery of the men who were fighting their way forward against an enemy which left everywhere a trail of destruction. Whenever the Germans pulled back they first made certain that every bridge was blown up, and where an escarpment road clung to the side of a mountain it, too, would be destroyed. Much of the railroad system was already ruined by Allied bombing, and it seemed to the weary troops of the

Fifth and Eighth Armies that there was a river or stream to cross every few miles. So winding were the valleys that in many cases a river had to be crossed several times, for example the Volturno. Field Marshal Kesselring was fighting hard to hold his Winter Line, and as Tedder later recorded: 'The bright hopes of a prompt seizure of Rome and an advance to the north had long since disappeared . . . and the prospect now seemed to be a slogging match in winter conditions.'[3] Yet the possession of Rome was of major psychological importance for both sides.

Plans had already been made for mounting a small amphibious operation, code-named 'Shingle', in which the object was to land a battalion at Anzio, south of Rome. The plan thereafter was to seize the Alban hills in an operation that would coincide with the Fifth Army's capture of Frosinone as it pressed northwards towards the Holy City. But by mid-December General Clark's army had not advanced far beyond the Volturno River, and was held up still fighting in the Mignano Gap.

General Alexander was, therefore, compelled to modify his plans for the Anzio landings so that a sufficiently strong force could be sent in 'to hold its ground by itself for a longer time than we had previously considered'. This meant for us that, in addition to supplying Y parties afloat to sail with the invasion fleet, we would be required to detail a small Field Unit or detachment to go ashore and work with the Forward Fighter Control on the beachhead.

The provision of R A F Y parties on board vessels escorting major convoys had now become a regular feature of our work. Sometimes, they were assigned specifically to monitoring non-Morse transmissions but usually for straight Y monitoring. We had had a small group on HMS *Warspite* earlier on and since October a team had been on board HMS *Palomares*, which would take part in the Anzio assault. But providing an additional Field Unit ashore was stretching our resources, as we had recently sent a small unit to work with the American 63rd Fighter Wing in Sardinia and two further units were already operating in Corsica. After consultation it was decided that a small American unit, a part of 'D' Detachment of No. 849th SIS, under the command of 1st Lieutenant Pierre de St Phalle, should be sent to Anzio with the invasion forces. It would be their first real operational commitment on their own.

During the month of December there was an appreciable reduction in the number of W/T messages that we intercepted from Luftwaffe bomber units. The revival of the enemy long-range bombing operations in the western and central Mediterranean which were promised by the November raids on Naples and the Corsican ports, and by the persistent attacks on eastbound convoys in the western Mediterranean, came to a halt soon after the beginning of December. But not, however, before the units which were based in northern Italy, and which for some months had been conspicuous by their lack of success, had suddenly justified their existence by combining with other units to launch a devastating raid on the port of Bari.

Most of the supplies for the Eighth Army, the Desert Air Force, and General Doolittle's US 15th Army Air Force were arriving through Bari. The harbour was constantly crowded with ships, and we knew from monitored traffic that almost every day since 26 November German reconnaissance aircraft had systematically photographed the port.

The enemy decided that here was the opportunity that they had been seeking to bring to a halt the advance of the Eighth Army in the eastern sector, and to disrupt supplies for the Allied bomber force for long enough to enable the German Army to establish a defence line across the narrowest part of the Italian peninsula. Kesselring was aware that most of his bomber units would shortly be recalled from Italy to reinforce the renewed offensive against England: the period between January and March, 1944, which was later to be called 'The Little Blitz'.

Reconnaissance reports informed Kesselring that a large convoy was approaching Bari. If a major strike was to be made against the port, this was the time. All available German bomber units were alerted. On the afternoon of Thursday, 2 December, the pilot of an enemy photographic reconnaissance aircraft confirmed the presence of many ships moored alongside, with many more at anchor within the harbour. The bomber squadrons were sent in to the attack. A total of 105 aircraft were involved, comprising elements of KG 26 and KG 100 brought over from their southern France bases, and others from KG 30, KG 54, KG 76 and KG 77.

Although Bari was dangerously close to the German airfields which were located across the other side of the Adriatic, the Allied radar cover looking eastwards was not yet adequate. Apparently aware of this weakness, von Richthofen routed his bomber force east from their northern Italian bases, and then down the Adriatic nearer the Dalmatian side, where they were joined by aircraft of

LG1 from Greek airfields. The bomber force then headed towards Bari using 'Dueppel' to confuse Allied radar, and flying low to escape early detection. It happened that, on that day, our main radar installation in Bari was unserviceable.

Ironically, only that very afternoon, Air Marshal Sir Arthur Coningham had held a press conference at which he had stressed that we had air superiority over the German Air Force in Italy. He had stated flatly that 'I would regard it as a personal affront and insult if the Luftwaffe should attempt any significant action in this area'.

The raid that followed just after dark was to result in our greatest single loss of shipping during the entire Allied campaign in the Mediterranean and Europe. It was the worst shipping disaster since Pearl Harbour. In all seventeen vessels were destroyed, and eight more were badly damaged. Some of them were loaded with the most valuable cargoes. Perhaps more by good luck than by good judgment one of the first bombs that was dropped hit a fuel ship which spewed burning oil over the neighbouring ships, setting them alight. A ship carrying ammunition was also one of the early victims. The toll of both military and civilian casualties was about 1000 killed, and a further 800 badly injured, but the tragedy might have been much worse. The cargo of one of the ships that was hit, the American SS *John Harvey*, included canisters of mustard gas, which the Allies were forced to have available as a precaution, in case the Germans resorted to gas warfare. The wind that night was off-shore, but nevertheless deadly clouds of smoke drifted across the harbour, adding to the heavy casualties. Evidence of these casualties was stringently suppressed, but, inevitably, the secret leaked out.[4]

The raid on Bari coincided not only with the defective radar but also with a state of flux in the Y organization in the Mediterranean. No. 329 Wing was about to be disbanded, with its personnel becoming absorbed into the new No. 276 Wing, which was preparing to move over from Cairo to Italy. The advance party was already in the throes of assembling, packing documents and equipment, and arranging for a rear party to be left behind to function at Suez Road until the new Headquarters could be established. A Field Unit was admittedly already operating at Conversano, with a link back to Cairo, but it was too newly arrived to have been able to establish that personal liaison with its neighbouring operational formations which was so essential for the full exploitation of Y intelligence.

On that same day, No. 276 Wing recorded, amongst other messages, traffic from Ju. 88s of the armed anti-naval reconnaissance unit, II/ZG 26 as they homed on Athens, and that morning they intercepted traffic which proved later to refer to a large move of Ju. 88s to the Milan area, including eight aircraft of I/KG 54 and forty-one aircraft of an unidentified unit. These were obviously some of the raiders on Bari gathering together for their assault. The traffic must have taken some time to decode because the records show that No. 276 Wing did not advise No. 329 Wing or AI3 in Intelligence at Command Headquarters of the movements until the next day. After all the time that has passed since then it is not possible to determine whether, had there been more Y intelligence staff available, the decoding could have been accelerated.

If ever confirmation was needed of the value of strict radio security by an attacking force, the Luftwaffe's raid on Bari surely provided it. There is no record available of messages being monitored from the bombers as they approached the target. When we did hear them, the damage had already been done. But the raid did show up the weaknesses in the defence system, and the outcome was the establishment of much better co-operation between naval, ground, and air forces in the area, and we were immediately given direct links to the defending air formations. The Bari raid was to be the swan song of the bomber Geschwader that were based in northern Italy. No further activity was heard from them during the remainder of the month, and there was ample evidence to show that by 31 December most of them had left the Mediterranean theatre. However, elements of the remaining Geschwader – LG1 – inflicted raids on Bari, Augusta and Catania during the month.

If there was a decrease in the number of missions that were flown by the enemy bombers based in Italy, the same could not be said for the recently formed American 15th Air Force, which operated mainly from the Foggias. The US Chiefs of Staff had agreed that the primary strategic objective – known as 'Pointblank' – should be the destruction of the German aircraft industry so as to reduce the opposition in the short time available before 'Overlord'. Despite constant Allied attacks on enemy airfields, so prodigious was their production of fighter aircraft that the Germans were managing to keep fairly constant the number available for defence, though there was a definite decline in the production of bombers.

Although the weather in Italy and over the Alps had deteriorated during the last weeks of the year, the flying conditions were perhaps erroneously believed to be marginally better than those being endured by the large formations that were flying day and night raids from airfields in the United Kingdom. The 15th Air Force was therefore given the task of destroying industrial installations in southern France, northern Italy, and Austria, including the ball-bearing factory at Annecy in Haute Savoie and the aircraft factories of Wiener-Neustadt and Schweinfurt, as well as targets in Hungary and the Balkans.

There had been a marked reduction in Allied losses over Western Europe during the so-called 'Gomorrah' raids on Hamburg and the subsequent attacks on the Ruhr. This was a direct result of the introduction of the radar countermeasure 'Window', which had caused the whole of the enemy's night-fighter defence to be thrown into a state of confusion. I received an ecstatic letter from Rowley Scott-Farnie, who was now back on duty in DDI4, in Intelligence in the Air Ministry, telling me how he and 'RV' – Dr Jones – had gone down to Kingsdown to watch the reactions of the Luftwaffe to this radar jammer. The monitors at Kingsdown and its outstations had gleefully recorded the initial response on the part of the Germans, which was little short of chaos.[5] Finding it impossible to read through the 'chaff' of echoes presented on the radar screen, the night-fighter controllers had become exasperated. One was heard bitterly complaining: 'I cannot follow any of the hostiles. They are very cunning.' During a raid on Essen, one of the ground controllers 'lost' his aircraft for a good eighteen minutes, whilst another in disgust ordered his aircraft to 'break-off; the bombers are multiplying themselves'. The night-fighter pilots became equally confused.

By August 1943 the Germans were employing a new defence technique, which came to be known as 'Wilde Sau' (Wild Boar). This involved the use of running commentaries which were based on the existing Observer Corps routine, giving the height and direction of the Allied bomber stream and the area in Germany or occupied Europe over which it was flying. As soon as this information was known, the night-fighters would be directed to the area to search for and find and then to attack the bombers. By using searchlights in large numbers, and sometimes by illuminating the cloud base or by using flares, the fighters were helped to track down their quarry.

As they listened in to the night-fighter traffic, those at Kingsdown were aware that there was a limit to the number of our bombers that

Allied strategic air control of Europe by bombers based on the air
of Lincolnshire and Foggia.

the German controllers could follow at any one time. The answer was, therefore, to saturate the route, and the target area, with as many aircraft as possible, and with the minimum time lag between aircraft. Furthermore, in view of the ever-deeper penetration into enemy territory, more care had to be taken in routing the strike force so as to confuse the ground defences. If our bombers were to fly on a zig-zag course, the German controllers would be uncertain until too late which was to be the main target and they would delay sending up their fighters. This was especially important following the introduction in the winter of 1943 of a further variation on this new night-fighting technique called 'Zahme Sau' (Tame Boar), whereby the German ground controllers would direct twin-engined fighter units into the bomber stream as it was en route to the target, with the night-fighter often tracking the bombers over long distances. Amongst the most successful Luftwaffe pilots using this technique was the young Major Prinz Heinrich zu Sayn-Wittgenstein, who was to claim 83 victories during his night-fighting career. By an ironic coincidence, I had skied with him and his brother in the Harz Mountains the winter before the war, and when he was finally shot down on 22 January 1944 I grieved for the death of a brave young man.

In order to plan the most effective route for the bombers to follow and thereby to reduce losses, the operations staff of Bomber Command Headquarters and its equivalent in the Mediterranean needed to have as much information as could be gathered about the location and efficiency of the enemy radar stations, the anti-aircraft and searchlight belts, and the area of operation of the different day- and night-fighter units. In the Mediterranean, we and Operational Research Section compiled a series of charts which revealed this information, not only for the briefing of the Mediterranean Allied Strategic Air Force but also for the bombers based in the United Kingdom which were shuttling between England and our theatre. This was a task after my own heart as the German fighter organization was my special interest.

One of the problems with these long-distance raids was that we lacked monitored R/T traffic from fighters defending distant targets, as these were out of reception range of the Field Units. In the autumn of 1943 a suggestion was made that it might prove helpful if the bombers of MASAF were to carry R/T monitors on board some of the American aircraft during their daylight raids on such targets as were beyond the monitoring range of the Field Units. The tactical value of intercepted R/T to the forward fighter controllers was now well established; No. 162 Squadron had already used R/T monitors successfully during their investigational flights, and airborne interception of R/T was by now a regular feature on raids by UK based formations.

With the permission of the Air Ministry, arrangements were made for the training of selected American personnel under the guidance of Flight Lieutenant J. S. Prior at No. 329 Wing (later disbanded). Fifty airmen volunteered for the task, but of these only four were initially selected. Sergeant J. Rosenthal, one of our most experienced Palestinian R/T monitors, who had worked with the forward Field Unit that had been attached to the Western Desert Air Force, was appointed to undertake test flights with an American bomber formation. By 3 October the four American NCOs, all of whom showed aptitude and promise, completed their monitoring course and they were then posted to various bomber groups. One of them was Sergeant Kurt Hauschildt, who was to fly fifteen combat missions with the 97th Bomber Group, USAAF.

The value of R/T interception in the air made an immediate impression on MASAF. During a raid the airborne monitor was able to inform the leader of the bomber formation when enemy fighters were airborne, and, although there were no direction-finding facilities on board, he could warn when increased signal strength indicated the approach of the defending fighters. The formation leader could then, on the basis of this information, give the bombers ample warning that they should close up and prepare for action. This warning rendered surprise attacks unlikely, and it gave confidence to the bomber pilots. The traffic intercepted by the R/T monitors of the 15th Air Force USAAF had already confirmed that the enemy had a predilection for attacking bombers which became detached from the main bomber stream and the Americans had taken immediate steps to give their aircrews a salutory warning. Intercepted messages occasionally made it possible for the airborne monitor to give more detailed information, such as the direction and the height of the approaching fighters. The main problem faced by the monitors was the difficulty of trying to read enemy R/T through the electrical interference caused by the bomber's engines.

Apart from any tactical advantages that might accrue from the German traffic heard during the actual raids, it was obvious that

L

much information of strategic value could be obtained from a detailed study of the logs. But MASAF did not at first appreciate the longer-term value of this material. It was understandable that the staff of the 15th Air Force were inexperienced in reading R/T logs, and there was every indication that they were not making the fullest use of what was being heard. About six months later a conference was convened by Colonel Young, the A-2 of the 15th Air Force, to discuss this matter, and as a result Flight Lieutenant J. D. Simmonds of No. 276 Wing made arrangements for copies of the logs that were kept by the airborne monitors to be sent to the Wing for further scrutiny.

From the logs it often became possible to identify the German units that were attacking the Allied bombers over central Europe, and to determine where these units were based. As the ground-stations and the aircraft callsigns used by the units in the hinterland were fixed, 'footprinting' of the units did not present the same problem as those that were presented by the constantly changing callsigns which were used by the units in the battle area. From this we realized that, providing that there were no far-reaching changes in the enemy's organization, the task of collating information about the central European-based fighter defence would become progressively easier, and our knowledge of the scale and form of the enemy's probable reaction to Allied raids over any given target could be usefully supplemented.

So valuable was the intelligence derived from the airborne monitoring that the 15th Air Force made ambitious plans for four R/T monitors to be assigned to each American bomber group, with two of them accompanying each mission carried out by the group. MASAF became so enthusiastic about the scheme that we had to warn them about the need for careful selection of personnel. They began talking in terms of 100 German-speaking personnel being made available in the United States for this work in the Mediterranean theatre. We advised that only those airmen who were thoroughly fit – and this included having exceptional hearing, and being quick on the uptake and yet reasonably phlegmatic – should be chosen. We stressed, moreover, that it was important that they should be briefed on a plausible cover story that they could tell in the event of their being shot down and interrogated. We also warned the 15th Air Force that it was imperative that any R/T communication between bombers during a raid should in no way disclose to the enemy that their traffic was being intercepted by the bomber formation.

Airborne monitors were later to be used extensively by the USAAF during their flights over enemy-occupied Western Europe,* and it is an interesting sidelight that as early as during the Sicilian campaign we had evidence from German prisoners-of-war that the Luftwaffe themselves were occasionally using airborne monitors on their raids.

Shortly before Christmas, Air Commodore Woolley, the Chief Intelligence Staff Officer, suggested that I should return home for a liaison visit to bring myself up-to-date with the developments in the Y Service in England, as it was two years since I had left Kingsdown. But as Jimmy Morgan was constantly away, in Italy or at La Marsa, and with the Anzio landings imminent, we agreed that I could not be spared.

Despite my disappointment at not returning home Christmas 1943 in Algiers was fun. The weather was glorious, and we at Headquarters were a happy crowd. General Eisenhower was convinced that we would win the European war in 1944, and his optimism was infectious.

But even on Christmas Day, there was work to do in the office, and before the festivities were ended we were already very busy with the final preparations for 'Shingle'. Churchill, Eisenhower, Alexander and Wilson had met in Tunis, and they had agreed that a larger force than had originally been envisaged should land at Anzio on 22 January, which was less than a month away.

It was during the days that followed this decision that it was forcibly brought home to me that I, as with so many others, had mislaid my youth. One morning at a planning meeting I had seen a list of the units which were to take part in the Anzio landings. In the evening I attended a party given by one of the Army Messes, and while I was dancing quite happily with a young British officer, I casually asked him to which unit he belonged. When he told me, I recognized it as one that had been on the list I had seen that morning, and I thought: 'Oh, God, you're destined for Anzio. In a fortnight you may be dead. I know this, but I cannot tell you. There is nothing I can do to warn you, to suggest, perhaps, you might write a letter

---

*The task of training the American airborne monitors fell to Section Officer 'Rusty' Goff after her return to England. When she had occasion to criticize the paucity of their logs during operational flights, she was challenged to do better herself. She took up the challenge, flying on a raid over Wilhelmshaven. The logs that day were so good that they were praised by the Kingsdown control, who had, of course, no idea that they had been taken down by Rusty.

to your parents which they could treasure if you should die.' I suddenly felt cold and very alone, and almost old. It was an intolerable responsibility for a young woman of twenty-five. Even after all the years that have passed since then, I can still remember my feeling of desperation. I was to learn later that he had been killed a few days after landing.

21

Stalemate at Anzio

Despite conscientious enemy reconnaissance over the whole sweep of the eastern Mediterranean from Cyprus and the Nile Delta to Malta and the heel of Italy, and including the Aegean and the Dodecanese, there were only three major attacks during January of 1944 on shipping in that area. We knew that the only heavy bomber units left to undertake commitments in the central and eastern Mediterranean were those based in Greece and Crete. From intercepted traffic we deduced that better convoy protection could be achieved if, in addition to fighter escort patrols, a concentrated effort were made to bomb simultaneously the airfields of Eleusis, Heraklion and Kastelli. And to help with these intruder operations, the Field Unit at Alexandria was in constant touch with their neighbouring No. 219 Group, advising them as quickly as possible to which airfields they believed the enemy would be returning. We then began to realize that the enemy reconnaissance patrols were avoiding confrontation with our fighters because their Y Service was monitoring W/T transmissions which were broadcast in RAF self-evident code between the radar stations along the coast and the fighter control. The enemy were thus able to advise their own aircraft immediately they had been picked up by our radar. It was a case of our listening to German messages about them listening to us. Such was the nature of the electronic war.

The task of decoding the traffic from the enemy patrols shadowing the Allied convoys would have been made much easier for us had we known exactly where the convoys would be sailing, but the Navy were, unfortunately, reluctant to give us this information. On one occasion early in January, we decoded a message from a German aircraft reporting two of our convoys off Derna. At first the Navy denied that there were convoys in that area, but later they had to admit that the enemy reporting was correct. However, on this occasion we were able to put the Navy's mind at rest about the possibility of a torpedo-bomber or glider-bomb attack because we knew that there were no enemy units in the eastern Mediterranean at that time that were capable of such an operation. As we had heard both the relevant enemy beacons and the German Safety Service transmitting, we were fairly certain that some form of an attack was imminent, but whether German submarines would also participate only the Navy could determine from their own Y intercepts. The convoys were, in fact, attacked that night by moonlight, and we recorded the subsequent enemy air traffic.

At the western end of the Mediterranean K G 26 staged an attack on a convoy off Oran on 10 January, and from later messages we knew that they lost several aircraft during the operation. We heard their reconnaissance colleagues, 1/F.33, searching for rubber dinghies, one of which they found later that evening between the Balearics and Spain. The next day K G 26 joined in the search for their missing friends, and between the two units they managed to locate further dinghies, and also arranged for a Do. 24 seaplane to be despatched from southern France to effect a rescue. During this torpedo attack No. 276 Wing had had no evidence that the Do. 217s of II/K G 100 had taken part but by the end of the month we knew that they were again back at Istres, and operating against Allied shipping off Anzio. We noted with some satisfaction that the casualties inflicted on the Luftwaffe units based in southern France were sufficiently heavy to preclude any further attempts to cover the North African convoy route until 22 January. On that day an enemy reconnaissance aircraft reported spotting some of our shipping north of Oran.

The Anzio landings on that same day apparently took the Germans by surprise. We were aware from Ultra that they had not expected the invasion to be launched so soon. At the beginning of the month the reconnaissance Staffeln based at Perugia – 2/F.122, 1/F.123 and Westa 26 – were regularly heard flying up to six sorties a day. This was obviously to be discouraged, and, as a precaution, an Allied raid was mounted on 7 January against their base in an effort to reduce their surveillance of the gathering invasion fleet. The raid had the desired effect, and Y was able to inform Operations that so great was the damage to the airfield that aircraft which were still airborne during the raid were forced to divert to Forli.

For a few days there was a noticeable decrease in enemy patrols.

Then, once again, the scale of effort increased in a belated attempt to frustrate the obvious Allied objective, 'to tie down the German troops as far away from the Channel as possible'. With 'Shingle' now imminent such reconnaissance was particularly undesirable, so a further sharp raid was inflicted on Perugia on 19 January. Heavy raids were also mounted against other central Italian airfields – Ciampino, Centocelli, Guidonia, Rieti, and Viterbo. So successful were these attacks that, during the next four days, all further reconnaissance patrols were brought to a halt. There can be little doubt that the inactivity that was forced on these units immediately prior to our landings greatly helped the invasion fleet of nearly 250 vessels to approach Anzio undetected and unopposed.

One of the first indications that Kesselring and his staff received that the Allies had landed at Nettuno, near Anzio, sixty miles behind the German right flank, was a startled message from an Me. 109 reconnaissance pilot yelling: 'My god! It looked like another Salerno.' This message, which was intercepted by the R/T Field Unit working with No. 1 MORU and the Desert Air Force on the eastern side of Italy, was heard at twenty minutes past eight on the morning of 22 January, six hours after the landings had started. Subsequent intercepted messages between ground formations confirmed the enemy's consternation.

The most interesting development now in the watch we were maintaining on the Luftwaffe was their hurried transfer of bomber units to bases in northern Italy, which was a reflection of the enemy's apprehension over the Anzio assault. The first arrivals that we heard were twenty-one Ju. 88s of I/ and II/L G 1 from Crete and Greece on the afternoon of the 22nd, several hours after the initial landings. By that evening they were already operating over the bridgehead, as were the He. 177s of KG 40, which had made the long flight from Bordeaux to join with the torpedo-bombers of K G 26 in an attack on the invasion convoys. Fortunately we were able to give Operations warning of the imminent attack, having heard K G 26 just before four o'clock on their way from Istres to Rome, when they were instructed to fly overland because of unfavourable weather. It was obvious that they were on their way for a dusk raid, and Operations arranged in time for a reception committee of fighters to be there to greet them. In true KG 26 style, they kept strict W/T silence during the operation, but we monitored the survivors as they asked their base for homing instructions.

Two days later K G 26 were again attacking shipping off Anzio, flying over in two waves, and they were probably assisted on this raid by the glider-bombers of KG 100. We were able to identify twenty-eight aircraft during the raid, and were also able to confirm that the units of II/K G 40 and both Gruppen of L G 1 had been involved. During the attack several bombers were damaged by Allied fighters, though we heard one of them just managing to reach Pisa. We alerted Operations as to which airfields we calculated the various attackers would be returning and fighters were despatched to lie in wait over the Ligurian Sea. At least two aircraft were soon known to be in difficulties, and to be transmitting S O S messages. On the 29th, however, the raiders had rather more success. A Do. 217 of K G 100 succeeded in sinking with a glider-bomb the British cruiser H M S *Spartan*. In checking the enemy bombers back to their bases we realized that the Ju. 88s of L G 1 were now using Aviano as a forward base. Photographic reconnaissance confirmed this, and the next day Allied bombers were sent to attack the airfield.

The Luftwaffe in the Mediterranean was by now desperately short of aircraft, especially for reconnaissance duties, and No. 276 Wing were aware of the eroding of the strength of the enemy units that were based in Italy, which had reached such a pitch that the efficiency of their daylight patrols was suffering. No longer could the Luftwaffe keep a daily watch on the happenings in the Adriatic, and around Corsica. The unit 1/F.33, which was normally responsible for patrolling the western basin, had had its operational area extended to include the Tyrrhenian Sea, where, incidentally, we heard them complaining about the presence of Allied fighters. The weather squadron, Westa 26, still continued its nightly routine mission, and succeeded in identifying Allied naval units operating off Ancona. But, it was an indication of the damage that had been done to Perugia airfield that the Westa 26 aircraft did not dare risk a night landing there, preferring to land instead at Forli.

As on the previous amphibious operations, R A F Y parties afloat were assigned to sail with the Anzio invasion fleet – this time on board H M S *Bulolo,* in addition to the existing team on H M S *Palomares*. However, due to the enemy's failure to oppose the initial assault, the ship-borne Y parties monitored considerably less traffic than during the Sicily and Salerno landings. But this happy situation was not to last long, and the operators were soon listening to enemy air attacks against ground forces and the supply convoys. Nevertheless, in the first month after the landings the Luftwaffe could rarely mount more than 100 sorties a day, of which more than half were by fighters. Apart from the problem of the acute shortage of aircraft, the enemy fighters were also having to contend with fog at their home airfields.

In addition to the ship-borne parties and the small American detachment on the beachhead, an R/T Field Unit was installed in the Benedictine monastery at Camaldoli, on a hill overlooking the Bay of Naples and the wide sweep of the Bay of Gaeta. It was well positioned to listen to traffic from aircraft that were operating over the Anzio beachhead and the nearer Liri Valley front. The unit had moved up from Sicily under the command of Flight Lieutenant Bill Turner,[1] and it was fully conversant with the activities of J G 77 and J G 53, which were the fighter units that had borne the brunt of the air war in Tunisia, Sicily and Salerno. The primary task of the Camaldoli Field Unit was to keep the 62nd and the 64th Fighter Wings, the 12th Air Support Command and the Navy in Naples supplied with tactical Y intelligence, including any information that could be gleaned from monitored traffic about Allied aircraft casualties.

The unit soon earned the reputation of filling in many of the blanks left by radar and photographic reconnaissance. Once again one of the urgent problems that had to be faced by the Allied fighters which were defending the assault ships and the invasion troops was the distance that they had to fly from their bases before they reached the battle area. Until usable airfields could be established at or near Anzio, combat time against the German aircraft which were attacking the invasion forces was seriously limited. For this reason alone, any information that could be passed to the fighters in flight was of particular help.

There was no doubt about the enemy's close air support effort having diminished. The increased intrusion of Allied bombers against targets in southern Germany and Austria and against communications in the north of Italy was tying down fighter units badly needed over the battle fronts, and we had evidence from Ultra that this apparent neglect of the front line troops was damaging relations between the Luftwaffe and the Wehrmacht. The responsibility for supporting the German ground forces on the Italian battle fronts lay with Fliegerkorps II, under the command of General der Flieger von Richthofen. But there were now less than seventy-five Me. 109 fighters and twenty-five Fw. 190 fighter-bombers in the front line, with a further fifty fighters retained in the Po Valley for defence. There was an Army Co-operation unit – 2(H) 14 – also operating in the forward areas and we listened to the messages from these aircraft as they flew over the battle zone observing and directing artillery fire, and indicating suitable targets. And from the traffic from the enemy Ground Observation Posts, we were able to warn the Allied artillery-spotting aircraft when they had been observed.

Amongst the many helpful messages which No. 276 Wing and its Field Units were recording were the meteorological reports from enemy aircraft and ground stations. The atrocious weather was definitely working in Kesselring's favour, and was proving to be more serious an obstacle to an Allied advance than the opposition of the Luftwaffe. So quickly did weather conditions change on the Italian peninsula that 'squadrons were experiencing every variation of climate at very short notice and flying conditions which at the beginning of a sortie were good, often became in the twinkling of an eye so bad that a close-knit system of diverting and recalling aircraft became urgently necessary'.[2]

Information from decoded intercepts could frequently fill in gaps, and help to confirm the charts which were compiled by our own meteorologists. Information about weather conditions as far away as the Russian front were of considerable value, and this we would glean from the messages from the many German bomber and reconnaissance aircraft operating in that area. We would listen to what we called the Black Sea Zenit, the patrol which covered the area from Odessa to Turkey, and to the Crimean Coastal Staffel as it made day and night reconnaissance over the Crimean coast and eastern Black Sea, shadowing Russian motor vessels. The weather in that area was now so bad that it appeared to be hampering operations, particularly from the seaplane bases.

The reports of conditions in the Po Valley were of special interest to MASAF in view of the rapid changes in weather there. We were also listening to the Yugoslav Zenit, which was constantly active over the Dalmatian coast and inland towards the Balkans, and we recorded the weather reports from patrols in the western Mediterranean. And from enemy ground formations in Rumania, Bulgaria and Hungary we learned of the climatic conditions in those areas.

By the end of January 1944 No. 276 Wing had finally chosen its site at Conversano. The advance party was in operation and the rear

party was due shortly from Egypt. When the two Y Wings had amalgamated, the surplus No. 329 Wing personnel from Algiers and La
Marsa were flown home. By the end of January the exodus had included several of the old No. 276 Wing's most able Intelligence
officers, including Flight Lieutenants Hugh Waters and Cecil Gould
and we had had to release thirty of our German-speaking monitors.
It was inevitable; we knew that the invasion of north-western Europe
must take priority. As soon as the American Signal Intelligence teams
arrived in Italy even more R A F Y personnel were sent home.

The Americans now had two fully operational units monitoring
Luftwaffe traffic in the Mediterranean. The larger unit, 'F' Detachment of No. 849th SIS, which covered W/T transmissions, moved
over from North Africa to Castellana, just south of Conversano, to a
site adjacent to one of the main Field Units. Since the days when they
were at Hammam Melouâne behind Algiers, the American signal
intelligence officers had worked in the closest liaison with their R A F
opposite numbers. The smaller unit, 'D' Detachment, moved over
from La Marsa to the monastery site at Camaldoli and worked together with the Field Unit there covering operations over the Anzio
beachhead and the Fifth Army front. Four of its monitors under
their Commanding Officer, First Lieutenant Pierre de St Phalle, were
already working under difficult conditions with a small unit at Anzio.

In view of the decrease in available personnel, No. 276 Wing had
by now reduced the number of Field Units under its control. Those
monitoring W/T traffic were sited at Alexandria, Malta, Algiers,
Corsica and nearby Castellana, though this unit would later move to
Bitonto, west of Bari, to work alongside the main Army Y unit. Of
the R/T Field Units, three remained; two would move forward on
either side of the Apennines as the Eighth and Fifth Armies advanced
and a third was sited on the northern tip of Corsica. A further two
small units were keeping a close watch on non-Morse transmissions.

Yet for all our reduction in personnel and the decline in the
strength of the opposing enemy air force, the list of our customers
was constantly increasing. So many formations, both American and
British, were now pressing to be included in the list of recipients of
Y information that Jimmy Morgan, as Chief Signals Intelligence
Officer, had to make a ruling, for the sake of security, that any such
requests should be channelled through him. It had to be proved
that there was an operational need: mere interest or curiosity was
not enough. We also had a problem with what I would call 'posses-

siveness' on the part of those formations which had become accustomed to having what they regarded as their own Field Unit. It was important that the Wing should retain full operational control of all its units, as it was essential that they should be able to implement quickly the requirements of Y in the Mediterranean, as determined by the Air Ministry and the Headquarters of the Mediterranean Allied Air Force.

Even allowing for the considerable help which we were now getting from the Americans, there were insufficient Y intelligence officers available to permit of a liaison officer being attached to every interested air and naval formation. The next best thing was for us to organize an efficient broadcast system, whereby we could not only keep our own Field Units up-to-date but also ensure that our customers were informed of the latest developments. Operational items would be sent out immediately as and when they occurred and these might include first indications of reconnaissance flights, convoy sightings, warnings of attacks on shipping or other targets, movements of units or elements of units giving indications of new bases or moves to advance landing grounds and any other deductions from collated Y sources which appeared to be of immediate importance. Twice a day the Wing broadcast a summary and amplifications of the intelligence distributed in the earlier broadcasts. These were augmented by daily, monthly and periodic reports compiled at Wing Headquarters and by our signals intelligence section at Headquarters, Mediterranean Allied Air Forces, which was the new name for the Mediterranean Air Command. A third type of broadcast covered purely technical and cryptographic matters specifically for the use of the Field Units. Apart from these 'SigInt' broadcasts, the Field Units, their D/F stations and the Wing Headquarters were constantly in touch for the purpose of obtaining fixes on enemy transmissions.

As so much depended on the efficient working of radio equipment the officer-in-charge of a Field Unit was almost always an experienced Signals officer, ably supported by his team of wireless mechanics, who worked wonders frequently with inadequate equipment. In the same way, the organization would not have been able to function without its hard-working code and cypher personnel, which included the twenty-one WAAF officers. Owing to the secrecy of the work it was always difficult to write a citation for an award and compared with other RAF formations – including Y in the United

Kingdom – the staff of No. 276 Wing fared ill where recognition of their efforts was concerned. But about this time the Senior Intelligence Officer, Squadron Leader Pugh-Davies, and the Senior Signals Officer, Squadron Leader George Burroughs, were Mentioned in Despatches, along with Pilot Officer Hoskins, Sergeants Constantinides, Herman, Kon, Rewcastle, and Ryder and Corporal Rogers and Aircraftman Bedford. Flight Officer Rosemary Horstmann, whose research on Luftwaffe transport aircraft had proved so valuable, and Section Officer Cathie Sutton, who had worked as a cypher officer with the Wing since 1941, were also commended. And I was delighted to learn that the two who had done such excellent work on board ship during three invasions, Flight Lieutenant Rob Clapham and Sergeant R. Arje, were also 'Mentioned', but Clapham was shortly to leave us to return to England where he would be needed for 'Overlord'.

While the US General John F. Lucas had been landing his 50,000 US and British troops at Anzio, the Fifth Army under General Mark Clark had been painfully battling its way northwards towards Cassino and Frosinone. The casualties on both sides were heavy, particularly during the fighting to the east of the Rapido River, and the campaign on this front was proceeding altogether too slowly. In the over-all plan for the advance towards Rome it had been intended that the Fifth Army should be much farther forward when 'Shingle' took place. But the difficult mountainous terrain was more suited to defence than to attack, and the Wehrmacht was showing great bravery and tenacity. But, above all, the appalling weather was making Allied progress doubly difficult. The troops on all fronts were sloshing around in a sea of mud, or freezing with cold in the snow and ice on the higher slopes of the rugged mountains.

At the time of the Anzio landings the opposing Allied and German armies were about equal numerically in strength, yet, despite constant urging and the Allies' undoubted superiority in the air, General Lucas allowed himself to become stalled and he began methodically to build up his beachhead. This even though the initial opposition to the landings had been so slight that a scout patrol had managed to get through as far as Rome.

The high hopes that the leap-frog assault of Anzio would bring about the speedy fall of Rome were to be frustrated. There had been an immediate reaction to the landings by Kesselring, and within twenty-four hours he had thrown a defensive perimeter around the invasion forces. By 18 February the situation there was critical and it was not until 20 February, after three days of determined effort by Allied aircraft in close support of the ground forces that General Alexander was confident that the beachhead could be held. When, finally, the Allies did push inland from Anzio, they had lost the element of surprise, and they had to fight a considerably stronger opposition on the ground.

Meanwhile, the Allied air forces were concentrating on attacking Kesselring's lines of communication and thereby impeding the delivery of supplies to the forward areas. The medium and fighter-bombers of the Tactical Air Force were keeping up a steady pressure against roads and railways, while the heavy bombers of the Strategic Air Force were bombing the big rail centres and attempting to cut off the vital route through the Brenner Pass. Particular attention was being given to the destruction of bridges, as this was proving to be of maximum hindrance to the enemy. At the same time, the Coastal Air Force was harassing the barges and small craft that were bringing in essential supplies at night through the many little ports along the Italian coastline. Unfortunately, the atrocious weather was constantly restricting Allied air missions and whenever the opportunity was afforded by a lull in the Allied air effort, the enemy were able to build up their stocks of fuel, ammunition and rations.

The Desert Air Force which was doing all it could to prevent the movement of German troops from the Adriatic front over to the western battle area, had by now evolved new tactics, which came to be known as 'Rover David' – after the Christian name of Wing Commander David Haysom, one of the instigators of the scheme. The new system was for a squadron or squadrons of fighter and fighter-bombers to patrol over the battle front in an area decided upon the previous evening. A Mobile Operations Post situated with the forward troops at Brigade Headquarters was in constant touch with the aircraft flying overhead. As soon as the Army had identified a specific target, one or more of the aircraft from the patrolling formation, inevitably nicknamed the 'Cab Rank', would be called up to bomb or to shoot up the chosen target. At first, the Mobile control was effected from armoured vehicles but these proved to be too cramped and later, it was found to be more efficient to use a lorry and a trailer with a Jeep for mobility. The 'Rover David' controller would be kept constantly fed with current intelligence from various sources, including photographic reconnaissance and Y, and the scheme was soon to prove highly effective, both tactically and as a morale booster for the troops fighting on the ground. The 'Rover David' was virtually a forward control of the Mobile Operations Room Unit which was the main control of the Desert Air Force.

Since the beginning of December No. 1 MORU had been working at Penna Point, between Ortona and Vasto, where it had been joined by its faithful R/T Field Unit which had moved up from a site on the mountainous promontory of the Gargano peninsula. For control and radio reception the site at Penna Point was a magnificent vantage point, surrounded as it was by sea on three sides. To the west there rose the snow-capped range of the Gran' Sasso d'Italia; to the north there was the coastal plain beyond the flooded River Sangro, where the Eighth Army was battling its way forward; to the south lay the airfields of the Foggia plain from which heavy bombers were flying on the long-distance raids; and over to the east there was an uninterrupted view across the Adriatic towards Yugoslavia. From this ideal position No. 1 MORU was also able to control aircraft which were engaged in attacks on enemy convoys as they made their way along the Dalmatian coast, and the Thunderbolts which were escorting the Dakotas of the Balkan Air Force towing gliders with supplies for Tito's partisans. But, as the diarist of No. 1 MORU has recorded with pained restraint 'as a summer site, it would be difficult to imagine anything more superb but in winter it had its drawbacks'.[3] To add to the misery of the rain and the mud, a hurricane, known locally as the 'Bora', ripped the tents to pieces and reduced the camp site of both No. 1 MORU and our Field Unit to 'a scene of indescribable desolation'.

The date for the forthcoming invasion of north-western Europe was now less than six months away and it was becoming increasingly obvious that the original plan that an invasion of southern France – Operation 'Anvil' – should coincide with 'Overlord' was no longer practicable. The forces on the Anzio bridgehead were stalemated and General Clark's troops of the Fifth Army were still fighting their way into the Liri Valley. Lowering over them was the great Benedictine Abbey of Monte Cassino – or The Monastery as it was known to us all – which the Army commanders had convinced themselves, on somewhat tenuous evidence, was occupied by the Germans. Later it was to be proved that there was no substance in this. However, on

15 February, much to the reluctance of Lieutenant-General Ira C. Eaker, who had taken over from Air Chief Marshal Tedder as Allied Air Commander-in-Chief of the Mediterranean Allied Air Forces, and his deputy, Air Marshal Sir John Slessor, the Allied air forces were ordered to bomb the beautiful and ancient building. Only after this attack and the concurrent shelling did the Germans occupy what was by then the ruins of the Abbey and, yet, despite a further massive bombardment a month later, it was not until 18 May that the Abbey was finally captured by the Allies. By then the Abbey had taken on an almost psychological importance for the troops on the ground.

Whenever we were over at the Advanced Headquarters now established in the Palace at Caserta, if the wind blew from the north, we would hear at night the distant rumbling of the heavy artillery on the Cassino front. The now divided MAAF Headquarters entailed constant flights between Algiers and Caserta – with further travel over to the new No. 276 Wing Headquarters at Conversano on the Adriatic side of Italy. It was essential, therefore, for our section to be increased and so, in mid-January, Flight Officer Toni Beckett was posted over from Cairo. She was a delightful girl, whose strawberry blonde hair caused quite a stir in the Headquarters and ensured a marked increase for a few days of visitors to our office.[4]

As soon as she was settled in Air Commodore Woolley decided, in agreement with Jimmy Morgan, that it would be an ideal time for me to fly home on my postponed visit. The invasion of southern France would now almost certainly be delayed, although the Americans, especially, were anxious that the operation should start as soon as possible. Meanwhile we, in Mediterranean Y, wanted urgently to know how best we could dovetail in with the over-all requirements for the invasion of Europe.

Epilogue

It was arranged that I should fly home on 25 February. Just before leaving I received a note from Rowley Scott-Farnie telling me that he was arranging a comprehensive tour for me around the various Y establishments in the United Kingdom – Kingsdown, Cheadle, Chicksands and, of course, Station X. There had been many exciting developments in signals intelligence in England during the recent months and it was important that I should be conversant with any aspect of these which might affect the activities in our theatre.

Two days after leaving Algiers, having been held up in Gibraltar owing to bad weather in the Atlantic, I arrived back in England as I had left it over two years before – to a country blacked out by dense fog. I was astonished by the growth and complexity of the Y Service network in England as the Allies prepared for 'Overlord' and the subsequent advance into Europe. Any trace of amateurism had long since vanished and as I made my visits to the various Y establishments and to Bletchley, I could not but be envious of the sophisticated facilities that were now at their disposal.

After a few weeks in England, during which I went to Buckingham Palace to collect my medal from the King, I returned to Algiers inspired anew and duly briefed by the Air Ministry on the part that we, in the Mediterranean, were expected to play in the forthcoming invasions of France.

The story I have told so far covers only a small part of the work undertaken by the Y Service. I have made little mention of the vast and invaluable contribution by the Army and the Navy – or of the American SIS. Lack of space and an ingrained sense of security preclude my covering every facet of our work but I hope that I have been able to convey to the reader the team spirit which prevailed throughout the Y Service.

It was by the conscientious and sustained effort made by the ordinary airmen and airwomen, as well as by their officers, that we were able to achieve our many successes.

Glossary of Code names and Abbreviations

'Accolade'	Allied operations in the Aegeans – September/November 1943
AHQ	Air Headquarters
AI	Airborne interception radar carried by fighters
ADEM	Air Defences, Eastern Mediterranean
ADI(Sci)	Assistant Director of Intelligence (Science) later D of I (R)
AI4	Department of Air Intelligence responsible for Y Service
AMES	Air Ministry Experimental Station – cover name for radar station
'Anvil'	Allied landings in southern France – August 1944 (see 'Dragoon')
'Aspirin'	Jammer to counter German Knickebein beams
ASV	Anti-Surface Vessel radar
'Avalanche'	Allied invasion of Italy (Salerno) – September 1943
'Benito'	British code-name for Y-Geraet beams
'Benjamin'	Jammer to counter Y-Geraet beams
'Bromide'	Jammer to counter X-Geraet beams
'Cab-rank'	Small formations of patrolling fighters and fighter-bombers
CBME	Combined Bureau Middle East
CH	Chain Home radar
CHL	Chain Home low-level radar
'Chimney'	British code-name for Wassermann long-range early-warning radar
'Corona'	System of broadcasting false warnings and instructions to mislead German night-fighters

'Crusader'	British offensive in Cyrenaica – November 1941
CSDIC	Combined Services Detailed Interrotation Centre
DAF	Desert Air Force
DDI4	Deputy Director of Intelligence (4) – Head of RAF Y Service
DDS(Y)	Deputy Director of Signals (Y) – later DDI4
D/F	Radio direction-finding
'Domino'	Counter measures to the ranging system of Y-Geraet
'Dragoon'	Final name for 'Anvil' – Allied invasion of southern France – August 1944
'Dueppel'	German name for metal foil dropped to confuse radar
E-boats	Fast German torpedo and mine-laying boats
'Elektra'	German radio-navigational system transmitting a 'fan' of beams for long-range navigation
'Enigma'	Machine used by Germans for enciphering high-grade messages
Flak	Fliegerabwehrkanonen – anti-aircraft fire
'Freya'	German early warning radar
FSU ⎱ FU ⎰	Field (Signals) Unit of No. 276 Wing engaged in radio interception in the Mediterranean/ Middle East
GAF	German Air Force
GC and CS	Government Code and Cypher School, Bletchley Park – syn. 'Station X'. The British code-breaking organization, responsible through MI6 to the Foreign Office
GCI	Ground Control Interception radar
GL	Gun-laying radar
HDU	Home Defence Unit – cover name for Y units of Kingsdown network
'Headache'	General term for German beams, alleviated by 'Aspirin' and 'Bromide'
H/F	High Frequency
'Himmelbett'	German close-controlled night-fighting
Horchdienst	German Y Service
'Husky'	Allied invasion of Sicily – 10/17 July 1943

IAF	Italian Air Force
IFF	Identification – Friend or Foe radar
'Intruder'	Offensive night patrols over enemy territory intended to destroy hostile aircraft and to disrupt enemy flying control
JG	Jagdgeschwader – a fighter unit of 3 Gruppen
JIC	Joint Intelligence Committee – a tri-service committee which evaluated intelligence for the British Chiefs of Staff
JPC	British Joint Planning Committee
'Kammhuber Line'	Belt of night-fighter patrols across Western Europe – named by British after General Kammhuber
KG	Kampfgeschwader – a bomber unit of 3 Gruppen
KGr	Kampfgruppe – a unit of 27 aircraft in 3 Staffeln plus staff flight of 3
'Kleine Schraube'	Little Screw – German radio beacon for night fighting
'Knickebein'	The original German beam bombing system
Luftwaffe	German Air Force
LRDG	Long Range Desert Group
'Lichtenstein'	German airborne radar used for night fighting
MAAF	Mediterranean Allied Air Forces
MAC	Mediterranean Air Command
MACAF	Mediterranean Allied Coastal Air Force
MASAF	Mediterranean Allied Strategic Air Force
MATAF	Mediterranean Allied Tactical Air Force
M/F	Medium Frequency
'Meacon'	Device to mask German radio beacons
MI9	Military Intelligence 9 – section responsible for creating escape routes through Europe
MI8	Military Intelligence (Signals)
NACAF	North African Coastal Air Force
NASAF	North African Strategic Air Force
NATAF	North African Tactical Air Force
NID9	Naval Intelligence (Signals)
NJG	Nachtjagdgeschwader – a night-fighting unit of 3 Gruppen
NWAAF	Northwest African Air Forces

OKL	Oberkommando der Luftwaffe – High Command of German Air Force
OKW	Oberkommando der Wehrmacht – High Command of German Army
'Overlord'	Allied re-entry into north-western Europe – June 1944
'Pointblank'	The attack on German fighter forces and the industry upon which they depended – 1943/44
PRU	Photographic Reconnaissance Unit
RAAF	Royal Australian Air Force
Radar	Radio direction and range – a term used by US Navy and subsequently adopted generally
RCM	Radio countermeasures
RDF	Radio direction-finding – the original British name for radar
'Rivers'	Early code-name for X-Geraet beams, later called 'Ruffians'
RNZAF	Royal New Zealand Air Force
'Rover David'	Attacks on tactical targets in forward areas by 'Cab-rank' fighters and fighter-bombers
R/T	Radio-telephony
'Ruffians'	Code-name for X-Geraet beams
SAAF	South African Air Force
'Station X'	GC and CS – code-breaking centre at Bletchley Park
'Seeburg'	Plotting table used by German fighter control
'Seeloewe'	Sealion – code-name for German plan to invade England in 1940
'Shingle'	Allied amphibious operations to facilitate ultimate capture of Rome – Anzio – January 1944
SLU	Special Liaison Unit – the section responsible for handling, distributing and ensuring the security of Ultra signals transmitted by Bletchley
'Starfish'	Decoy fires lighted to mislead German bombers
SOE	Special Operations Executive
'Torch'	Anglo-American invasion of French North Africa – November 1942

TRE	Telecommunications Research Establishment
Ultra	Code-name for intelligence derived from German high-grade Enigma traffic
USAAF	United States Army Air Force – the over-all American Air Command
VHF	Very High Frequency
WAAF	Women's Auxiliary Air Force
'Wassermann'	German long-range early warning radar with height-finding facilities (British code-name 'Chimney')
WIDU	Wireless Intelligence and Development Unit – the airborne signals investigation unit
'Wilde Sau'	Wild Boar – German free-lance night fighting
'Window'	(American 'Chaff') – Aluminium foil strips dropped in packets to give radar echoes simulating a bomber
'Wotan'	General term for X- and Y-Geraet beam bombing systems
WRNS	Women's Royal Naval Service – the 'Wrens'
W/T	Wireless Telegraphy
WU	Wireless Unit – cover name for RAF Y units
'Wuerzburg'	Standard German radar used to direct AA guns, searchlights, and, in the early days, night-fighters
'Wuerzlaus'	Modification of 'Wuerzburg' radar to counteract 'Window' jamming
'Wuerzburg Riese'	Giant Wuerzburg – (British code-name 'Basket')
X-Geraet	Receiver for the X-beam system of precision bombing, also known as Wotan I
Y-Geraet	Receiver for Y-system of precision bombing, also known as Wotan II (British code-name 'Benito')
Y Service	The British organization for intercepting hostile radio communications
'Zahme Sau'	Tame Boar – Night-fighter system introduced 1943 in which formations of night-fighters were directed into the bomber stream
'Zenit'	Code-name given by Y Service to German long-range weather and reconnaissance patrols

Notes and Sources

1 Prelude to a War

1 *The Women's Auxiliary Air Force* (HMSO, 1953), p. vii.
2 Even signposts at road junctions were taken down and the names of railway stations obliterated with the intention of confusing possible enemy agents parachuted into the country.

2 'Hellfire Corner'

1 By July 1940 Air Intelligence were able to give a revised estimate of the GAF's first-line bomber strength, but it was not until 5 August that GCCS were able to compile a detailed Order of Battle. (Professor F. H. Hinsley and others, *British Intelligence in the Second World War* (HMSO, 1979), p. 177.)

3 The Battle for Britain

1 Professor F. H. Hinsley and others, *British Intelligence in the Second World War* (HMSO, 1979), p. 182.
2 PRO File Air 40/2243.
3 PRO File Air 40/2243 – signal from DD Signals 'Y' to OC, Kingsdown of 2 October 1940.

4 Bombers and Beams

1 PRO File Air 24/602.
2 PRO File Air 26/580.
3 Ibid.
4 Ibid.
5 Winston S. Churchill, *The Second World War*, Vol. III, *Their Finest Hour* (Cassell, 1949), p. 342.

5 X-Geraet and the Coventry Tragedy

1 Sir John Slessor's Foreword to F. W. Winterbotham's *The Ultra Secret* (Weidenfeld and Nicholson, 1974).
2 PRO File Air 20/2419.
3 Personal to author from Wing Commander R. K. Budge, OBE.
4 PRO File Air 20/2419 – Notes on German operation 'Moonlight Sonata', and counter-plan 'Cold Water' dated 17 November 1940.

6 'Little Screw'

1 PRO File Air 20/1442.
2 For full details of this operation see PRO File Air 20/1564.
3 PRO File Air 20/1442.
4 In December 1943 W/T traffic was intercepted from the 15th Air Signals Experimental Regiment indicating that they were 'challenging' and hence able to plot British bombers which had left their IFF sets switched on whilst flying over enemy territory.
5 See Plate 16.
6 PRO File Air 20/1442.

7 Luftwaffe Pressure

1 R. V. Jones, *Most Secret War* (Hamish Hamilton, 1978), p. 180.
2 PRO File Air 40/2242.
3 The Y-ranging system was later (autumn 1943) to be fitted to German night-fighters operating the 'Zahme Sau' method of bomber interception.
4 By March 1941 the six AI squadrons of Fighter Command were all equipped with the new Mark IV apparatus and five had changed their Blenheims for the faster Beaufighters, and by April eleven GCI stations were in operation.
5 The *Prinz Eugen* had been bombed and put out of action whilst in Brest harbour in July 1941. With repairs completed, she left dry dock on 16 December but was immediately subjected to heavy bombing by the RAF.

8 The Sphere of Listening Widens

1 *The Women's Auxiliary Air Force* (HMSO, 1953), p. 28.
2 Ibid. p. 22.
3 PRO File Air 20/1673.
4 Mr A. C. Dilloway and Mr D. C. Peacock.

9   The War Moves East

1 From Enigma traffic, we knew by 6 February that Hitler had given the command of the Afrika Korps to Rommel.
2 AI4(b).
3 The ill-feeling between the Army and the RAF reached such a pitch after the hurried retreat from the Desert in 1942 that Tedder warned that he would court-martial any RAF personnel who referred to the Army as 'pongos' or 'The Retreatists'.
4 Marshal of the RAF Lord Tedder, *With Prejudice* (Cassell, 1966).
5 DDI4.
6 The first WAAF Code and Cypher Officers arrived in the Middle East in September 1941. A large number were subsequently to be employed at TME (Telecommunications, Middle East) working in appalling heat in an underground building at Helmieh in the desert outside Cairo. The noise from the high-speed and teleprinter rooms was deafening and the air-conditioning plant was more often out of order than serviceable, reducing the WAAF to a state of exhaustion after a six-hour shift.
7 There had been an unsuccessful Anglo-French attempt to capture Dakar from the Vichy French in September 1940.

10   Y in the Middle East

1 Later, while serving as the Commanding Officer of No. 84 Squadron, Wing Commander Jeudwine was to organize an epic escape with ten others in an open boat from Tjilitjap to Australia at the time when the Japanese overran Java. The story of their heroic voyage, which was to last for forty-seven days, is one of the legends of the Second World War.
2 When I arrived in the Middle East, some of the CBME personnel were still civilians.
3 Ronald Lewin, *Ultra Goes to War* (Hutchinson, 1978) p. 112.
4 The Italian Navy was using a machine known as the Hagelin machine for enciphering its high-grade traffic, the decoding of which was the responsibility of a team at GCCS under Professor E. R. Vincent.

11   The George Cross Island

1 After the war James Robertson was to become Director of the London Opera Centre after a distinguished career as a conductor.
2 Sir William Dobbie was a member of the Plymouth Brethren.
3 The Army were indefatigable in filling in bomb craters and making aircraft bays on the airfields.
4 PRO File Air 2/2703.
5 Ibid.

6 PRO File Air 24/1082.
7 PRO File Air 2/2703.

12 Cairo and the Desert

1 The traffic from this area was well within monitoring range.
2 Cecil Gould was to become Keeper of the National Gallery after the war.
3 No. 3 Royal Australian Air Force.
4 Alam-el-Halfar.

13 Investigations and Countermeasures

1 'Seetakt' – German naval gunlaying radar.
2 PRO File Air 27/1004 – No. 162 Squadron Operations Record Book gives the crew as Sergeants Knowles (Capt.), Murrel, Tregenza, West-brook, Levy, Drever, Rawlins and Lieutenant Baker.
3 PRO File Air 23/1214.
4 Lieutenant-Colonel R. P. G. Denman of the Royal Corps of Signals was shot down on 20 November 1941 and is buried in the Halfaya/ Sollum War Cemetery.
5 Wing Commander D. H. S. Rusher was awarded the DSO for his exceptional work in command of No. 162 Squadron.

14 The Beginning of the Defeat

1 The first raid on Ploesti was on 12 June 1942 when a combined force of the American 'Halpro' unit commanded by Colonel H. A. Halvesen, together with bombers of No. 160 Squadron bombed the Rumanian oilfields.
2 Personal to author.
3 Operation 'Vigorous'.
4 Operation 'Harpoon'.
5 The battered *Troilus* and the *Orari* struggled into the Grand Harbour at Valetta late in the afternoon of 15 June – see Air Marshal Sir Hugh Lloyd, *Briefed to Attack* (Hodder and Stoughton, 1949).
6 Operation 'Pedestal'.
7 Personal to author.
8 Brigadier Desmond Young, *Rommel, the Desert Fox* (Putnam, 1957).
9 'Report on Operations of the Western Desert Air Force from the Capture of Tripoli on 23rd January, 1943 until the final surrender of the Axis Forces in North Africa on 13th May, 1943' – p. 6, para. 51.

15 Sicilian Prelude

1 Four Squadrons of Warhawks of the 57th US Fighter Group with a top cover of Spitfires from No. 92 Squadron.
2 RAF Narrative, *The Middle East Campaign* Vol. IV (HMSO).
3 At the hands of Kittyhawks of No. 7 (SAAF) Wing.
4 By a patrol of Kittyhawks of No. 7 (SAAF) Wing and Spitfires of No. 1 (SAAF) Squadron.
5 Marshal of the Royal Air Force Lord Tedder, *With Prejudice* (Cassell, 1966).
6 Personal to author.

16 Advance into Europe

1 A body dressed in the uniform of a Royal Marines officer with an official letter in his pocket suggesting that future operations were to be directed against Greece, was dropped by submarine off the Portuguese coast. The body was washed ashore and the contents of the letter were duly relayed to the OKW by an agent in Portugal. The whole story is told in the book entitled *The Man Who Never Was* by Ewen Montagu.
2 General Dwight D. Eisenhower, *Crusade in Europe* (Heinemann, 1948).
3 PRO File Air 29/21a.
4 PRO File Air 26/436.

17 From Sicily to Salerno

1 PRO Files Air 29/152 and Air 23/1013.
2 PRO File Air 40/225b.
3 General Mark Clark, *Calculated Risk* (Harper, 1950).
4 Personal to author.
5 *The Memoirs of Field Marshal Kesselring* (William Kimber, 1953).

18 A Question of Strategy

1 PRO File Air 23/1266.
2 Ibid.
3 PRO File Air 29/166.
  Viscount Alanbrooke, *Diaries* (Edited by Sir Arthur Bryant) (Collins, 1957/59).
  Ibid.
  The Listener 8 February 1979 (BBC).

19 Reconnaissance and Reorganization

1 R. V. Jones, *Most Secret War*.
2 PRO File Air 40/2256.

20 The Luftwaffe Retaliates

1 Ronald Lewin, *Ultra Goes to War* (Hutchinson, 1978).
2 Lists of everyone mentioned on either military or civil air transport throughout occupied Europe were meticulously kept, showing when and where they were flying.
3 Lord Tedder, *With Prejudice* (Cassell, 1966).
4 Glenn B. Infield, *Disaster at Bari* (Robert Hale, 1974).
5 R. V. Jones, *Most Secret War*.

21 Stalemate at Anzio

1 Flight Lieutenant W. H. Turner commanded a forward R/T monitoring unit for two years and was awarded the MBE for his work. He died in an accident in November 1944.
2 Denis Richards and Hilary St G. Saunders, *Royal Air Force 1939–45*, Vol. II, *The Fight Avails* (HMSO, 1975).
3 Roderic Owen, *The Desert Air Force* (Hutchinson, 1948) and PRO File Air 29/21a.

Bibliography

ARDIZZONE, EDWARD, *Diary of a War Artist* (Bodley Head, 1974).

ASTLEY, JOAN BRIGHT, *The Inner Circle* (Methuen, 1971).

BABINGTON-SMITH, CONSTANCE, *Evidence in Camera* (Chatto and Windus, 1958).

BEAUMAN, K. B., *Wings on Her Shoulder* (Hutchinson, 1943).

BEESLY, PATRICK, *Very Special Intelligence* (Hamish Hamilton, 1977).

BEKKER, CAJUS, *The Luftwaffe War Diaries* (MacDonald, 1967).

BENNETT, RALPH, *Ultra in the West* (Hutchinson, 1979).

BRYANT, SIR ARTHUR, *The Turn of the Tide* (Collins, 1957). *Triumph in the West* (Collins, 1959).

BUTCHER, HARRY C., *Three Years with Eisenhower* (Heinemann, 1946).

CAVE BROWN, ANTHONY, *Bodyguard of Lies* (Harper and Rowe, 1976).

CHURCHILL, SIR WINSTON, *The Second World War* (Cassell, 1948–54).

CLARK, GENERAL MARK, *Calculated Risk* (Harper, 1950).

COLLIER, BASIL, *A History of Air Power* (Weidenfeld and Nicolson, 1974).

COOPER, LADY DIANA, *The Rainbow Comes and Goes* (Hart Davies, 1958).

CUNNINGHAM OF HYNDHOPE, ADMIRAL THE VISCOUNT, *A Sailor's Odyssey* (Hutchinson, 1951).

DE GUINGAND, MAJOR-GENERAL SIR FRANCIS, *Operation Victory* (Hodder and Stoughton, 1947).

DEIGHTON, LEN, *Fighter: The True Story of the Battle of Britain* (Jonathan Cape, 1977).

DOBBIE, SYBIL, *Grace under Malta* (Lindsay-Drummond, 1943).

DOUGLAS, MARSHAL OF THE RAF LORD (with Robert Wright), *Years of Command* (Collins, 1966).

EISENHOWER, DWIGHT D., *Crusade in Europe* (Heinemann, 1948).

GALLAND, ADOLF, *The First and the Last* (Methuen, 1970).

GUEDELLA, PHILIP, *Middle East* 1940–42 – *a Study in Air Power* (Hodder and Stoughton, 1944).

HART, B. H. LIDDELL, *The Rommel Papers* (Collins, 1953).

HAY, IAN, *The Unconquered Isle* (Hodder and Stoughton, 1942).

HINSLEY, F. H. (with E. E. THOMAS, C. F. G. RANSOM and R. C. KNIGHT), *British Intelligence in the Second World War*, Vol. I. (HMSO, 1979).

HOUGHTON, G. W., *They Flew Through Sand* (E. R. Schindler, 1942).

HOWARD, MICHAEL, *The Mediterranean Strategy in the Second World War* (Weidenfeld and Nicolson, 1968).

INFIELD, GLENN B., *Disaster at Bari* (Robert Hale, 1971).

IRVING, DAVID, *The Rise and Fall of the Luftwaffe* (Weidenfeld and Nicolson, 1973).

JACKSON, W. G. F., *The Battle for Italy* (Batsford, 1967).

JOHNSON, BRIAN, *The Secret War* (BBC, 1978).

JONES, R. V., *Most Secret War* (Hamish Hamilton, 1978).

KAHN, DAVID, *The Codebreakers* (Weidenfeld and Nicolson, 1974).

KENT, JOHN, *One of the Few* (William Kimber, 1971).

LEWIN, RONALD, *Ultra Goes to War* (Hutchinson, 1978).

LINKLATER, ERIC, *The Campaign in Italy* (HMSO, 1951).

LLOYD, AIR CHIEF MARSHAL SIR HUGH PUGHE, *Briefed to Attack* (Hodder and Stoughton, 1949).

MACMILLAN, HAROLD, *The Blast of War, 1939–1945* (Harper and Row, 1967).

MAJDALANY, F., *The Fall of Fortress Europe* (Hodder and Stoughton, 1969).

MONTAGU, EWEN, *Beyond Top Secret U.* (Peter Davies, 1979). *The Man Who Never Was* (Evans, 1966).

MONTGOMERY OF ALAMEIN, FIELD MARSHAL THE VISCOUNT, *Alamein to the River Sangro* (Hutchinson, 1948).

MOOREHEAD, ALAN, *The Mediterranean Front* (Hamish Hamilton, 1941). *The End in Africa* (Hamish Hamilton, 1943). *The Desert War* (Hamish Hamilton, 1966).

OGILVIE, E. G. O., *Libyan Log* (Al-Magraf, Cairo, 1942).

OWEN, RODERIC, *The Desert Air Force* (Hutchinson, 1948).

PEROWNE, STEWART, *The Siege Within the Walls* (Hodder and Stoughton, 1970).

PLAYFAIR, MAJOR-GENERAL I. S. O. (with others), *The Mediterranean and the Middle East* – Volumes III and IV (HMSO, 1960).

POND, HUGO, *Salerno* (White Lion, 1961).

PRICE, ALFRED, *Instruments of Darkness* (William Kimber, 1967). *Pictorial History of the Luftwaffe* (Ian Allen, 1969).

RAWNSLEY, C. F. and WRIGHT, ROBERT, *Night Fighter* (William Collins, 1957).

RICHARDS, DENIS and SAUNDERS, HILARY ST GEORGE, *The Royal Air Force 1939–1945* (HMSO, 1953–4).

ROMMEL, ERWIN, *The Rommel Papers* (Ed. B. H. Liddell Hart) (Collins, 1953).

SCHIEPHAKE, HANFRIED, *The Birth of the Luftwaffe* (Ian Allen, 1971).

SHORES, CHRISTOPHER F., *Pictorial History of the Mediterranean Air War*, Vol. I. RAF 1940–43 (Ian Allen, 1972).

SHULMAN, MILTON, *Defeat in the West* (Secker and Warburg, 1947).

SLESSOR, MARSHAL OF THE RAF SIR JOHN, *The Central Blue* (Collins, 1956).

STEINHOFF, GENERAL JOHANNES, *The Straits of Messina* (André Deutsch, 1971).

STEVENSON, WILLIAM, *A Man Called Intrepid* (Macmillan, 1976).

STRONG, SIR KENNETH, *Intelligence at the Top* (Cassell, 1968).

TAYLOR, TELFORD, *The Breaking Wave* (Weidenfeld and Nicolson, 1967).

TEDDER, MARSHAL OF THE RAF LORD, *With Prejudice* (Cassell, 1966).

TOWNSEND, PETER, *Duel of Eagles* (Weidenfeld and Nicolson, 1970).

WATSON-WATT, SIR ROBERT, *Three Steps to Victory* (Odhams, 1957).

WINTERBOTHAM, F. W., *The Ultra Secret* (Weidenfeld and Nicolson, 1974). *Secret and Personal* (Kimber, 1969).

WOOD, DEREK and DEMPSTER, DEREK, *The Narrow Margin* (Hutchinson, 1969).

WRIGHT, ROBERT, *Dowding and the Battle of Britain* (MacDonald, 1969). *Night Fighter* (with Derek Rawnsley) (Collins, 1957). *Years of Command* (with Lord Douglas of Kirtleside) (Collins, 1966).

ZUCKERMAN, SOLLY, *From Apes to Warlords* (Hamish Hamilton, 1978).

Appendix

Dispositions of 'Y' Units in the Mediterranean monitoring German and Italian Air Force signals June 1943 – Pre Operation 'Husky'

ROYAL AIR FORCE

No. 276 Wing	Headquarters:	Type of traffic covered
	Heliopolis, Cairo	W/T
Field Units:	Benghazi area	W/T
	Alexandria area	W/T and R/T
	Nerab, Aleppo, Syria	W/T
	Habbaniyah, Iraq (being withdrawn to HQ)	W/T
	Malta	W/T and R/T
	Tunisia (attached to Western Desert Air Force)	R/T
	Egypt (ex Western Desert and awaiting re-deployment. Detachment to go to Kos with Operation 'Accolade')	R/T
No. 380 WU	Headquarters:	
	Draria, near Algiers	W/T
Detachment:	La Marsa, Tunisia	W/T
No. 381 WU	2 Units at La Marsa/Cap Bon (one covering German and the other Italian traffic)	R/T

M

ROYAL AIR FORCE continued		*Type of traffic covered*
No. 351 WU	Gibraltar (unit under control UK 'Y'. Liaison with other Mediterranean units only)	W/T
No. 371 WU	ex-Freetown, West Africa (personnel moving up to augment No. 380 WU)	W/T
'*Y' Parties Afloat*	on HMS *Largs* ex No. 276 Wing	W/T and R/T
	on HMS *Warspite* – ex No. 380 WU	W/T and non-Morse transmission
	on HMS *Bulolo* and *Hilary* – ex UK en route for Operation 'Husky' (incl. Naval personnel)	W/T and R/T

Airborne Investigation

No. 192 Squadron Detachment	Maison Blanche, Algiers (Home base in UK)	
No. 162 Squadron	Benina, Benghazi (with aircraft detached to Malta as required)	

'Meaconing' Units

No. 20 Type 'M' Unit	Fort Regina, Benghazi	'Meaconing' and monitoring non-Morse transmission
No. 21 Type 'M' Unit	Bordj Menaïel, Mènerville, Algeria	
No. 22 Type 'M' Unit	en route Cap Bon, Tunisia (not yet operating)	

UNITED STATES FORCES

Type of traffic covered

	Headquarters:	
No. 849th SIS	Hammam Melouâne, Rovigo, Algeria	W/T
'F' Detachment:	La Marsa, Tunisia	W/T
'D' Detachment:	Cap Bon, Tunisia	R/T

Airborne Investigation

No. 16th Reconnaissance Squadron	El Aouina, Tunis

Notes

1 Locations, strengths, number of wireless sets employed, etc., constantly under review and subject to operational requirements.

2 All units had their ancillary D/F stations located at a distance from the main monitoring site.

3 W/T monitoring units were assigned to cover Enigma-enciphered and lower-grade traffic, as required.

4 Nos 380 and 381 WUs amalgamated to form No. 329 Wing on 29 June 1943.

5 The 'M' Type Units were controlled by the Chief Signals Officer but with constant liaison with 'Y' units.

Index